GHALIB

A CRITICAL BIOGRAPHY

GHALIB

A Wilderness at My Doorstep

MEHR AFSHAN FAROOQI

PENGUIN ALLEN LANE

An imprint of Penguin Random House

ALLEN LANE

USA | Canada | UK | Ireland | Australia
New Zealand | India | South Africa | China

Allen Lane is part of the Penguin Random House group of companies
whose addresses can be found at global.penguinrandomhouse.com

Published by Penguin Random House India Pvt. Ltd
7th Floor, Infinity Tower C, DLF Cyber City,
Gurgaon 122 002, Haryana, India

Penguin
Random House
India

First published in Allen Lane by Penguin Random House India 2021

10 9 8 7 6 5 4 3 2 1

ISBN 9780670094295

Typeset in RequiemText by Manipal Technologies Limited, Manipal
Printed at Thomson Press India Ltd, New Delhi

www.penguin.co.in

MIX
Paper
FSC FSC™ C010615

To Fran Pritchett,
The first woman commentator on Ghalib.
With love and admiration.

Contents

Timeline for Ghalib

1750s: Ghalib's grandfather, Mirza Quqan Beg Khan, comes to India from Samarqand, settles in Lahore

Mid-1754: Mirza Quqan Beg Khan moves to Delhi

Mid-1756: He takes up service with Prince Shah Alam

1763 (approx.): Mirza Quqan Beg Khan marries

1765: Ghalib's father, Abdullah Beg Khan, is born in Delhi

1767–80: Five more children are born to Mirza Quqan Beg Khan, including Ghalib's uncle, Nasrullah Beg Khan

Mid-1771: Mirza Quqan Beg Khan takes up service with Zulfiqar ud-Daulah

1782 (approx.): Mirza Quqan Beg Khan takes up service with the Maharaja of Jaipur and settles in Agra

Mid-1778: Mirza Quqan Beg Khan dies

1793 (approx.): Ghalib's father, Abdullah Beg Khan, marries Izzatun Nisa Begam. Getting married at the age of twenty-eight seems unusual for the men at the time. Perhaps they were married earlier

1795 or earlier: Abdullah Beg Khan's first child, Chhoti Khanam, Ghalib's sister, is born

Before 21 September 1797: Abdullah Beg Khan takes up service with Navab Asif ud-Daulah in Lucknow

21 September 1797: Navab Asif ud-Daulah dies

27 December 1797: Asadullah Khan is born in Agra (or maybe a couple of years earlier). The first instance of his date of birth is recorded in the 1837 manuscript of *Divan-e Farsi*. The *divan* (collection of poetry) of 1837 includes a *qasidah-e manqibat* (an ode in praise of the Prophet's companions and descendants) in honour of Hazrat Imam Husain. The manqibat has a section in which Ghalib eloquently describes the conjugation of stars that have dealt him misfortunes. A subsequent version of this divan, prepared in 1848, has Ghalib's horoscope, in his own hand, attached with the manqibat. The horoscope mentions that Ghalib was born four hours before sunrise on Sunday evening (*yak shambah*), 8th of Rajab, 1212 hijri. But 8th of Rajab, 1212 hijri was *not* a Sunday; it was a Wednesday (*chahar shambah*)

Late 1799: Ghalib's younger brother, Yusuf Ali Khan (also known as Mirza Yusuf), is born

Before 1802: Abdullah Beg Khan takes up service with the maharajah of Alwar

1801/2: Abdullah Beg Khan dies, buried at Rajgarh in Alwar; his younger brother, Nasrullah Beg Khan, takes guardianship of his children. Nasrullah Beg Khan was married to the sister of Ahmad Bakhsh Khan, the Navab of Firozpur-Jhirka and Loharu (the date of the marriage is unknown)

1803: Nasrullah Beg Khan is the commander of Agra Fort, under the Marathas

1803: Nasrullah Beg Khan changes sides, joins Lord Lake; is appointed the commander of 400 cavalry at a salary of Rs 1700 per month

April 1806: Nasrullah Beg Khan dies after falling off an elephant

4 May 1806: His family, i.e. Nasrullah Beg Khan's mother and three sisters, and Ghalib and his sister and brother, are granted a pension of Rs 10,000 annually, to be paid from the revenues of Ahmad Bakhsh Khan's estate (who was probably granted some of Nasrullah Beg Khan's property)

7 June 1806: The grant is reduced by Ahmad Bakhsh Khan to Rs 5000; half of this is granted to Khwaja Haji, a dependent of Nasrullah Beg Khan. Khwaja Haji was married to the daughter of Nasrullah Beg Khan's paternal aunt (Ghalib's father's *phuphi*). Khwaja Haji is entrusted with the command of fifty horsemen

1807–08 (approx.): Nazir Akbarabadi is alleged (probably not accurately) to have been Ghalib's tutor for some time during this period; Ghalib begins writing poetry, using Asad as his pen name. His famous short *masnavi* (a long poem written in rhyming couplets) about kite-flying has been attributed by Hali to this period

1810: Ghalib is said to attend the *maktab* (elementary school) of Maulvi Muhammad Mu'azzam, Agra

18/19 August 1810: Ghalib is married in Delhi to Umrao Begam (age eleven), daughter of Navab Ilahi Bakhsh Khan Ma'ruf, the younger brother of Navab Ahmad Bakhsh Khan of Firozpur-Jhirka and Loharu; none of the seven children they have live beyond infancy

1811: Hurmuzd (Abdus Samad) allegedly (though perhaps not in reality) arrives from Iran, stays for two years as Ghalib's Persian tutor and teaches him the Persian of a native speaker

1812/3: Ghalib moves to Delhi permanently; he lives for a while with his father-in-law, then moves to a rented house in Gali Qasim Jan

c. 1816: Ghalib compiles his first Urdu divan, its only extant copy is in his own handwriting. The original manuscript surfaced in Bhopal in 1969; printed facsimile editions of it were produced—one by

Akbar Ali Khan Arshizadah (Rampur, 1969) and another by Nisar Ahmad Faruqi (Lahore, 1969). The manuscript disappeared under mysterious circumstances in 1970 and resurfaced under equally mysterious circumstances in 2016. It has now been digitized by the Ghalib Institute, New Delhi

1816: Ghalib adopts 'Ghalib' as his *takhallus* (pen name), in addition to Asad

1821 (approx.): Ghalib compiles the second version of his Urdu divan, which is commonly known as *Nuskhah-e Hamidiyyah*. This manuscript was found in Bhopal in 1917. First printed in 1921, it was edited by Mufti Anvar ul-Haq of Bhopal with the famous unfinished preface by Abdur Rahman Bijnori; and again, much later, it was unearthed from Lahore in 1969, edited by Hamid Ahmad Khan. The original, reported to have disappeared from the State Library in Bhopal in 1947, resurfaced for sale with an art dealer in London in 2015. *Nuskhah-e Hamidiyyah*, bought by Shahab Sattar, was digitized and published in 2016.

1822: Navab Ahmad Bakhsh Khan appoints his eldest son, Navab Shamsuddin Ahmad Khan, as his heir and the manager of his *jagir* (land grant). Ghalib's relations with the latter were strained both for political and personal reasons

1825/26: Ghalib compiles the third version of his Urdu divan, which is now known as *Nuskhah-e Sherani*; this manuscript, discovered by Hafiz Mahmud Sherani, is now in Punjab University, Lahore. It was published by the university in a facsimile edition (1969). This version contains most (though not all) of the ghazals from 1821, and many new ones.

1825: Khwaja Haji dies; Ghalib begins seeking restoration of the full pension; he goes to Firozpur-Jhirka to talk with Navab Ahmad Bakhsh Khan and General Ochterlony

November 1825: Ghalib makes a second fruitless visit to Firozpur-Jhirka, hoping in vain to meet Ochterlony's successor, Charles Metcalf, the newly appointed Resident of Delhi, through Ahmad Bakhsh Khan and improve his pension situation; he goes to Bharatpur with Khan, is unsuccessful in meeting Metcalf, returns with Khan to Firozpur-Jhirka in December and stays till September 1826

August/December 1826: Ghalib's father-in-law, Navab Ilahi Bakhsh Khan Ma'ruf, dies; Ghalib's younger brother, Mirza Yusuf, becomes insane around this time

Early October 1826: Ghalib leaves Firozpur-Jhirka for Kanpur, where Metcalf is reported to be encamped, but is unable to meet him; he impulsively decides to go to Calcutta to petition the Governor General. It is not clear if he secretly went to Delhi to arrange for funds, but in his petition dated 28 April 1828, he mentions that he sold off all the valuables in his possession to partially appease his creditors. In Kanpur, he falls ill, and upon his recovery, proceeds to Lucknow

1826: Ghalib spends five months in Lucknow in the company of friends, recuperating. At the time, Navab Ghaziuddin Haider was the ruler of Avadh. In preparation for meeting the navab, Ghalib composed a *qasidah* (a classical Arabic or Persian monorhyme poem in uniform metre) of 110 verses and a petition in Persian crafted in the *san'at-e ta'til* (the device of composing without the use of dotted letters). The meeting did not happen because Ghalib set some conditions that were declined

June 1827: Ghalib leaves for Calcutta

August 1827: Ghalib travels to Banda, where he stays for about six months

1827 (later in the year): Mirza Afzal Beg is appointed as a vakil, or agent, of Emperor Akbar Shah II, and arrives in Calcutta much before Ghalib. Afzal Beg's sister was married to Khwaja Haji. Beg makes it a point to defame Ghalib in order to weaken his pension claims

October 1827: Navab Ahmad Bakhsh Khan dies

1828 (very early in the year): Ghalib travels to Banaras, where he stays for about a month. He composes the famous masnavi in Persian *Chiragh-e Dair* (Lamp of the Temple), in which he envisions Banaras as a beautiful bride

20 February 1828: Ghalib reaches Calcutta, petitions the East India Company government for redressal of his pension grievances

June 1828: Ghalib participates in Persian and Urdu *mushairahs* (a social gathering at which Urdu poetry is read, typically taking the form of a contest); some linguistic objections are raised against his Persian usages by the pupils of Mirza Muhammad Hasan Qatil. He replies to them in his masnavi *Bad-e Mukhalif*, written in a conciliatory tone, but insisting on his view that Indian Persian writers were not authoritative when it came to usage and idiom

June 1828: Company government directs Ghalib to submit his pension petition in Delhi

September 1828: Ghalib compiles *Gul-e Ra'na*, a selection of his Urdu and Persian poetry, for his friend Maulvi Sirajuddin Ahmad; the manuscript was missing for almost a century but then one version was found in 1957 by Saiyyid Naqi Bilgrami, who gifted it to noted Ghalib scholar Malik Ram, who in turn published it in 1970. At least five codices of *Gul-e Ra'na* surfaced since the first one, including one beautifully calligraphed by Ghalib himself. There are three editions of *Gul-e Ra'na*—the first by Vazirul Hasan Abidi in 1969, the second by Malik Ram in 1970 and the third by Qudrat Naqvi in 1975.

February 1829: Ghalib receives a place and honours in the Governor General's durbar

August 1829: Ghalib is present at the Governor General's second durbar; he leaves Calcutta for Banda

October 1829: Ghalib reaches Banda and stays for a week, then leaves for Delhi

29 November 1829: Ghalib reaches Delhi

January 1831: Ghalib's pension claim case is dismissed

1832 (approx.): Ghalib becomes friends with Mustafa Khan Sheftah

April 1833: Ghalib compiles the Urdu divan and writes a *dibachah* (foreword) to go with it in highly literary Persian; it is not published till 1841. Before publication, Ghalib adds a paragraph that is a prototype of copyright attestation

1835: The manuscript of *Panj Ahang*, Ghalib's first collection of Persian prose is ready; it is put together by Mirza Ali Bakhsh Khan, who also wrote an introduction. It is not published until 1849.

1835: Ghalib proposes the name *Mai Khanah-e Arzu Sar Anjam* for his first Persian divan. This *nuskhah* has not been found yet. The oldest nuskhah we have is at the Khudabaksh Oriental library, Patna. It dates back to 1837. Ghalib's friend Chajja Mal Khattri is the calligrapher

June 1837: Ghalib is sued for debt by an English wine merchant, has to stay in his house to avoid creditors, and is briefly arrested, too. Amin ud-din Khan of Loharu pays off the debt

September 1837: Bahadur Shah Zafar ascends the throne

1840: Ghalib's mother dies

1840: Ghalib refuses the interview for an appointment as professor of Persian in Delhi College

1841 (first half): Ghalib is arrested for running a gaming house in his own home; he is fined Rs 100, which is paid then and there

October 1841: *Divan-e Ghalib* in Urdu is published by Saiyyid ul-Akhbar Press, Delhi; it runs to 108 pages. It has a Persian introduction by Ghalib and an endnote by Navab Ziyauddin Ahmad Khan, dated 1838, saying that the total *she'r*s (couplets) are 1070 (though it's actually 1095, Ghalib might have added the extra ones in the interim period)

1845: Ghalib's Persian divan (compiled 1834–35) is first printed. No copy of this first edition seems to be known

May 1847: *Divan-e Ghalib* in Urdu, second edition, Matba Dar ul-Salam, Delhi, runs to 98 pages. It has 1159 she'rs.

June 1847: Ghalib is arrested for gambling and sentenced to six months' imprisonment and a fine (which is paid by his friends); he is treated leniently and released after three months; only Sheftah is loyal. Ghalib stays as a tenant in a house owned by Miyan Kale Sahib (Maulana Nasir ud-din)

1847–48: Ghalib's first surviving Urdu letters are written at this time

1849: *Panj Ahang* (Persian work in five sections), comprising the rules of address, the rules of Persian grammar, his Persian verses, miscellaneous quotes and references and some of his Persian letters, is published by Matba Sultani, Delhi (Red Fort), and runs to 493 pages.

4 July 1850: Ghalib is engaged by Bahadur Shah to write the history of the Timurid dynasty. He is given an honorary title and an annual pension of Rs 600, besides the titles of Najm ud-daulah and Dabir ul-mulk.

2 April 1852: Ghalib writes a *sehra* (wedding ode), at the request of Begam Zeenat Mahal on the occasion of royal prince Javan Bakht's wedding. In this poem, he makes a sneering remark in the closing she'r about his contemporary Ibrahim Zauq, who was the ustad of Bahadur Shah Zafar:

> *Hum sukhan fahm hain, Ghalib ke tarafdar nahin*
> *Dekhen keh de koi is sehre se barh kar sehra*
> [I don't favour Ghalib, I am simply a connoisseur of poetry
> I challenge someone to write a better sehra than this]

The emperor took offence and asked Zauq to write another sehra, in which Zauq delivered a rejoinder:

Jin ko da'va ho sukhan ka yeh suna do unko
Dekh is tarah se kehte hain sukhanwar sehra
[Those who claim to be poets, recite this to them
See, this is how poets write wedding odes]

Ghalib later apologized.

1852: Ghalib's wife's nephew, Zain ul bidin Khan Arif, whom Ghalib truly loved, dies of an illness; Arif's wife, Zainab, had died just a few months prior to this. Ghalib and his wife end up bringing up both their young sons, Baqir Ali Khan and Husain Ali Khan

1853 (or earlier): The heir apparent, Mirza Ghulam Fakhr ud-Din (Mirza Fakhru), starts paying Ghalib Rs 400 a year; another prince, Mirza Khizr Sultan, also patronizes him

April 1853: *Panj Ahang*, a second edition, is brought out by Dar us-Salam, and runs to 444 pages

November 1854: Ustad Ibrahim Zauq dies

Late November 1854: Ghalib becomes the royal ustad

1854/55: *Mehr-e Nim-roz*, the first part of the Timurid history (the creation of the world up to Humayun), is published by Matba Fakhr ul-Matabi, Delhi, and runs to 116 pages. It is reprinted twice more in the same year, but all the printings are called the 'first edition'

1854/55: Ghalib is asked by Saiyyid Ahmad Khan to write a preface to his new edition of *A'in-e Akbari*. Instead, Ghalib writes a Persian poem deprecating the project and urging Sir Saiyyid to move with the times

1855: Ghalib is awarded cash and a pension by Vajid Ali Shah, the Navab of Avadh

7 February 1856: Vajid Ali Shah is dethroned and Avadh is annexed

July 1856: The heir apparent, Mirza Ghulam Fakhr ud-din, dies of cholera

1856 (second half): *Qadir-namah*, mnemonic rhymes for children, is published by Matba-e Sultani, Red Fort, and runs to 8 pages

1856: Ghalib composes a qasidah for Queen Victoria

5 February 1857: Ghalib becomes the ustad of Navab Yusuf Ali Khan 'Nazim', of Rampur

10 May–October 1857: The Revolt of 1857 occurs; Ghalib is protected by the Maharaja of Patiala; all his valuables are lost when his wife secretly sends them to Miyan Kale Sahib's house for safekeeping; Prince Khizr Sultan is shot dead by Hudson; Bahadur Shah is exiled

18 October 1857: Ghalib's younger, mentally unstable brother, Yusuf, dies, shot by British soldiers who entered his house

1858: Ghalib sends various qasidahs for the Queen and the officialdom, but they are returned as gifts of mere flattery

November 1858: *Dastanbuy*, Ghalib's 'old Persian' (with Arabic words avoided) account of 1857, is published by Matba Mufid-e Khala'iq, Agra, and runs to 80 pages

1858: Munshi Naval Kishor launches *Avadh Akhbar* from Lucknow. The paper's role in the development of a modern Urdu prose style was facilitated by a number of eminent editors from the literary world. Ghalib was an avid reader of newspapers and began perusing *Avadh Akhbar* almost as soon as it started publication

July 1859: Ghalib begins to receive a pension of Rs 100 a month from the Navab of Rampur

1859: Munshi Naval Kishor writes his first letter to Ghalib. The extensive correspondence between the two, and some other publishers, is one of the best sources on author–publisher dynamics in nineteenth-century Urdu literature

19–27 January 1860: Ghalib travels to Rampur

17–24 March 1860: Ghalib travels back to Delhi at the insistence of his two adopted children; he stops at a sarai in Moradabad after his boat overturns, but Sir Saiyyid offers him hospitality

24 March 1860: Ghalib's British pension is reinstated through Sir Saiyyid and/or the Navab of Rampur's help. He receives Rs 2250 as arrears

29 July 1861: *Divan-e Ghalib*, Urdu, third edition, is brought out by Matba Ahmadi, Shahdara, Delhi. It is full of misprints and inaccuracies. It is rejected by Ghalib but is published without his permission, against his will

22 March 1862: *Qati-e Burhan* (Cutter of the Argument), his Persian polemic attacking the reputed seventeenth-century Persian dictionary of Muhammad Husain Tabrizi, *Burhan-e Qati* (The Cutting Argument), is brought out by Naval Kishor, Lucknow, and runs to 98 pages. Ghalib's harsh criticism of Tabrizi landed him in a long-drawn exchange of invectives

June 1862: *Divan-e Ghalib*, Urdu, revised fourth edition, is published by Nizami Press, Kanpur, and runs to 104 pages

3 March 1863: Ghalib's official durbar honours are restored

June 1863: *Kulliyat-e Nazm-e Farsi* is published by Munshi Naval Kishor, Lucknow, and runs to 562 pages. It has 10,424 she'rs

Later half of 1863: *Divan-e Ghalib*, Urdu, fifth edition, is published by Matba Mufid-e Khala'iq, Agra, and runs to 146 pages

December 1863: Ghalib's first and only meeting with Munshi Naval Kishor takes place. The latter travelled to Delhi by the mail coach to meet Ghalib. It appears that Ghalib granted exclusive copyright to Munshi Naval Kishor for many of his works. The press continued to publish Ghalib's writings long after his death

1864: Controversies about *Qati-e Burhan* begin. The dispute ends on 23 March 1868, when Ghalib files a petition withdrawing the case against one of his attackers

1864: Ghalib's Persian masnavi, *Abr-e Gohar-Bar*, is separately printed by Akmal ul-Mataba', Delhi, even though it was already in his Persian *kulliyat* (a collection of the poetry of any one poet)

1864: The second edition of *Qadir-namah* is published by Mahbas Press, Delhi

2 October 1864: The title page of *Lata'if-e Ghaibi*, an Urdu pamphlet part of the *Burhan-e Qati* controversy, claims authorship by Ghalib's *shagird* (pupil) Miyandad Khan Saiyyid

November 1864: *Savalat-e Abd ul-karim*, another Urdu pamphlet continuing the *Burhan-e Qati* controversy, is published under the alias of 'Abdul Karim'

21 April 1865: Navab Yusuf Ali Khan of Rampur dies, succeeded by Kalb-e Ali Khan

August 1865: *Namah-e Ghalib*, another Urdu pamphlet part of the *Burhan-e Qati* controversy, is published by Matba-e Muhammadi, Delhi, and runs to 16 pages. It is now included in *Ud-e Hindi*

7 October 1865: Ghalib travels to Rampur to attend the coronation, and falls sick in Moradabad during the return journey. He reaches Delhi on 8 January 1866

1865: *Dastanbuy*, second edition, is published by Rohilkhand Literary Society Press, Bareilly

December 1865: *Darafsh-e Kaviyani*, a revised edition of *Qati-e Burhan*, is brought out by Akmal ul-Mataba, Delhi, and runs to 154 pages

May 1866: Ghalib's health begins to decline, his sight and hearing begin to fail

September 1866: Ghalib makes another *intikhab* (art of selection) of his Persian and Urdu poetry for the Navab of Rampur. The navab wanted to prepare a *bayaz* (a poet's notebook of his favourite verses) consisting of his Persian and Urdu poetry. He asked Ghalib to nominate his own verses for this project. Ghalib was invited to make the selection on 25 August 1866. He had the Urdu section ready by 18 September and the Persian on 27 September. While the Persian one was carefully preserved in the navab's library, the Urdu manuscript languished among heaps of papers at the Raza Library in Rampur. Maulana Imtiaz Ali Khan Arshi, the distinguished editor of Ghalib's Urdu divan, recovered the manuscript and published it with a scholarly introduction in 1942

1866: Volume 2 of *Insha-e Urdu*, edited by Maulvi Ziya ud-din Khan of Delhi College, is published by Matba Faiz-e Ahmadi, Delhi, with selections of Ghalib's Urdu prose

1866–67: *Dua-e Sabah*, a Shi'ite masnavi that Ghalib translates from Arabic into Persian, is published

1867: *Tegh-e Tez*, another Urdu pamphlet part of the *Burhan-e Qati* controversy, is published by Akmal ul-Mataba', Delhi, and runs to 32 pages

18 February 1867: *Nikat-e Ghalib Va Ruq'at-e Ghalib*, model Persian letters selected for schoolboys, and a small text on Persian grammar, is published by Siraji Press, Delhi, and runs to 16 pages, composed on the request of Master Rai Bahadur Pyare Lal

11 April 1867: *Hangamah-e Dil-Ashob,* Part 1, is published, containing verse texts from Ghalib and others (in Urdu), connected with the *Burhan-e Qati* controversy

August 1867: *Sabad-e Chin*, a Persian masnavi that Ghalib wrote in jail, is published separately by Matba Muhammadi, Delhi

24 September 1867: *Hangamah-e Dil-Ashob*, Part 2, is published

2 December 1867: Ghalib lodges a complaint of defamation against Maulvi Aminuddin Dihlavi, the author of one of the most scurrilous of the polemical tracts that resulted from the *Burhan-e Qati* controversy

January 1868: *Kulliyat-e Nasr-e Farsi*, Persian prose (*Panj Ahang, Mehr-e Nim-Roz* and *Dastanbuy*), is published by Naval Kishor Press, Lucknow, and runs to 212 pages

23 March 1868: A compromise is arranged and Ghalib's legal complaint is dropped; since only Hali and Sheftah supported his linguistic claims

27 October 1868: *Ud-e Hindi*, a collection of Ghalib's Urdu letters, put together by Munshi Mumtaz Ali and others, initially against his opposition, is published by Matba Mujtaba'i, Meerut, and runs to 188 pages. Ghalib objected to the many errors and worked on a new edition

15 February 1869: Ghalib dies after slipping into a coma on 14 February. He is buried in Nizamuddin, near his father-in-law's grave. His wife, who died the following year, is also buried there

5 March 1869: *Urdu-e Mu'alla*, Part 1, a second collection of his Urdu letters, is published by Akmal ul-Mataba', Delhi, and runs to 464 pages

4 February 1870: Ghalib's wife, Umrao Begam, dies

1897: Hali publishes his path-breaking critical biography, *Yadgar-e Ghalib* (Memorial to Ghalib), in which he highlights aspects of Ghalib's Persian and Urdu poetry (Nami Press, Kanpur)

1899: *Urdu-e Mu'alla*, parts 1 and 2, is published by Matba Mujtaba'i, Delhi

1900: Ali Haider Nazm Tabataba'i publishes the first commentary on the Urdu *Divan-e Ghalib*—*Sharḥ-e Divan-e Urdu-e Ghalib* (Hyderabad: Matba Mufid ul-Islam, n.d. [1900]). Many commentaries follow Tabataba'i's

1921: *Divan-e Ghalib Jadid*, edited by Maulvi Anvarul Haq, is published. Haq included Abdur Rahman Bijnori's definitive essay, 'Mahasin-e Kalam-e Ghalib'. The *Divan-e Jadid* includes verses omitted by Ghalib in his published divans

1955: The present marble tomb is built after the success of Sohrab Modi's film *Mirza Ghalib*, which starred Bharat Bhushan as Ghalib

Introduction

If a taste for poetry was the law of the land,
My poems would have fame like the Pleiades;
And Ghalib, if this art of poetry was a religion—
This book of poems would be its Revealed Book.

—Ghalib, afterword (*khatimah*) to the Persian *divan*[1]

Mirza Asadullah Khan Ghalib was born in Agra in the closing years of the eighteenth century. A precocious child, he began composing verses at the age of nine (or maybe even earlier) and had a divan (a collection of poems organized alphabetically) of Urdu poetry before he was twenty. At that time, he wrote mostly in Urdu and a little in Persian. Later, he devoted more attention to Persian. Ghalib's deliberate switch to composing in Persian during a long and important period in his life (from about 1825 to 1860) might suggest that he wanted his work to go beyond political boundaries and linguistic barriers.

He was a great letter writer, too. In the early years, his letters were written in Persian; later in life he switched to Urdu and became known as a major stylist of Urdu prose. Ghalib was a careful, even strict, editor of his work. He realized the advantages of print technology and published his poetry long before his peers.

Maybe because of his reputation for being a 'difficult' poet, and given his predilection for writing ambiguous, even obscure, poetry, especially in Urdu—peppered with complex, abstract metaphors and finely crafted imagery—his Urdu poetry produced a unique commentarial tradition that didn't extend to other 'difficult' poets, such as his immediate predecessor, Imam Bakhsh Nasikh (1776–1838), and his close contemporary Momin Khan Momin (1800–52). Commentaries on his current or 'authorized' (some scholars prefer 'published') Urdu divan have produced a field of critical writing that eventually lead to the crafting of a somewhat new critical lens with which to view the classical ghazal.

The nineteenth century saw the height of European colonialism. British colonialism in India produced definitive and drastic changes in the way literature was produced, circulated and consumed. Ghalib responded to the cultural challenge with a far-sightedness that doesn't seem to have been evinced by his contemporaries. He foresaw the effects of change in India's sociopolitical and economic conditions, which were wrought by colonialism, and his imagination sought engagement with the new world, a world that created and sought a new kind of reader, a new atmosphere for literary production, a wider community of readers.

Ghalib died in 1869 and was buried in a modest grave in the neighbourhood of Hazrat Nizamuddin in Delhi, not far from the *khanqah* (hospice) complex of the great Chishti Sufi saint. The graves of his father-in-law, Navab Ilahi Bakhsh Ma'ruf, who was a recognized poet, and his wife, Umrao Begam, are in the same compound. In his seventy-three-year life, he achieved great fame, though somewhat less than what he thought he deserved. Yet it was a fame that continued to grow after his death, with posterity finally placing him on a pedestal as the greatest Urdu poet of all time. Many reasons can be proposed for this, the changed literary culture not the least important among them.

Ghalib's reputation as Urdu's greatest poet—and not just one of the greatest—was further elevated by Abdur Rahman Bijnori (1885–1918), a young scholar well versed in the European literary tradition and with a knowledge of many European languages. He presented Ghalib as a poet of superior intellectual powers, whose peers and equals could only be found in, say, Heinrich Heine, Arthur Rimbaud and other European poets. Bijnori's stimulating book-length essay, *Mahasin-e Kalam-e Ghalib* (Merits of Ghalib's Poetry, 1921), begins with a resounding rhetorical claim, which in one bold stroke puts Ghalib on the same plane as the Vedas. He said: 'India has just two scriptures or divine gospels, the holy Vedas and the Divan-e Ghalib.'[2]

Bijnori's essay was added as the introduction to the rediscovered manuscript of Ghalib's early poetry when it was published in 1921. The manuscript is dated 1821 and contains mostly Urdu poetry. The manuscript divan recorded numerous Urdu verses that Ghalib didn't include in his published, 'authorized' edition. In fact, his authorized divan went through five editions in his lifetime. The manuscript Divan of 1821 showed that Ghalib had composed nearly twice as many verses than what he published as *Divan-e Ghalib* (1841). The recovery, or rediscovery, of the so-called rejected verses (*mustarad kalam*) in 1917 became a landmark in Ghalib studies. For one thing, it kindled some interest in the 'rejected' verses that had not received searching, scholarly attention so far.

Even so, the so-called rejected verses didn't find full-length studies and interpretative commentaries for many years. One commentary, dated 1934, wasn't published until much later. Another one from around the same year (1931) became so rare that not many people are even aware of it. Many summers ago, I began to study, translate and annotate Ghalib's rejected verses in an attempt to understand the poems in depth and also investigate why Ghalib had omitted them when he made the selection for his Urdu divan. I noticed that often entire ghazals were left out. Sometimes, only certain verses were taken out. Occasionally, new verses were added. What was left in and left out helped me understand the process of selection somewhat, and also Ghalib's own poetics or poetic perceptions. Clearly, there was much about the selection that needed analysis.

The general opinion of scholars has been that Ghalib rejected verses that were too complex and mostly belonged to the early phase of his career. His early poetry was perceived to be loaded with far-fetched, abstract and sometimes meaningless metaphors, or too full of wordiness, or simply imperfect, especially when compared to his later compositions. Therefore, it was assumed that most of the excisions have been from the early period, which abounded in difficult verses and high-sounding Persianate constructions that didn't repay the mental labour needed to decipher them. To be sure, some percipient scholars, Malik Ram being the foremost among them, did say that some of Ghalib's best and most illustrious verses dated from precisely that early period. But a systematic study of all the issues involved was not attempted. I found that Ghalib composed both difficult and deceptively easy verses throughout his poetic career. That is not to say that he made a somewhat unwilling transition to 'simple' poetry from his early 'difficult' poetry.

Ghalib's poetic trajectory begins from Urdu, moves to composing almost entirely in Persian and then swings back to Urdu. It is nearly as intricate as his poetry. If tracing this trajectory were merely a question of understanding the challenges of being equally creative in two languages—although that in itself is complicated enough—one could provide reasons. In fact, when Ghalib took to Persian, he became more prolific and less abstruse. When his Persian divan was published in 1845, it had 6000 verses. Why did he not edit the Persian divan as strictly as the Urdu one? Finding answers to questions like these became the catalyst for the larger problem of how to understand the kaleidoscopic, asymmetrical corpus of Ghalib. Although Persian poetry was slowly dying in India after a glorious phase, and Urdu was in what could be called its golden age, Ghalib gave more importance to his Persian compositions than Urdu:

> Look into the Persian so that you may see paintings of myriad shades and hues;
> Pass by the collection in Urdu for it is nothing but drawings and sketches.[3]

Posterity has not, however, agreed with this judgement, or followed this advice. Ghalib's great admirer and pupil Altaf Husain Hali (1837–1914) published *Yadgar-e Ghalib* (Memorial to Ghalib, 1897), the first biographical and critical book on Ghalib. Hali's unorthodox biography described Ghalib as a witty, handsome man whose creative genius was incomparable. It is not possible to write about Ghalib without a reference to Hali's indispensable work. Hali knew Ghalib personally and had spent many evenings at the poet's home during the first two years he was in Delhi.[4]

> In the days when I lived in Delhi, I would often go to Mirza Asadullah Khan Ghalib's house to pay my respects. I would bring with me verses from his Urdu, and/or Persian divan, that I did not understand well and ask his help in getting the meaning. I even read some of his Persian *qasidah*s under his guidance. In those days, he discouraged people from writing poetry, but when I showed him a couple of my ghazals, he said that while he did not encourage the writing of poetry, for me it would be a punishment [*zulm*] on my disposition [*tabi'at*] not to write.

The idea of writing a book on Ghalib had been on Hali's mind for many years. Finally, when he returned to Delhi as a lecturer at the Anglo-Arabic College (1888–89), Hali collected remembrances from friends who had known Ghalib to add to his own notes. But numerous other commitments didn't allow him to start the work.

He was finally able to begin in 1892 and completed the book in 1896. Writing a biography or 'life' (as Hali calls it) was an idea that had been imported from the West.[5] Hali gives the following justification for writing about Mirza Ghalib's life:[6]

> Although one can't see any major accomplishment except poetry and literary prose [*insha pardazi*] throughout Ghalib's life, yet this work alone has made his life a remarkable event in the last phase of the Mughal capital [*Darul khilafat*]. I think that in this country, Mirza is the last word in Persian prose and poetry. Urdu poetry and prose are no less indebted to him. That is why I often thought that I should collect from reliable sources whatever information I could about Mirza's life. And whatever I could write about his poetry and prose essays, I must record in a manner that should be intelligible to the people.

Hali asked a critical question about Ghalib's Persian writings:[7]

> What is worth pondering about Mirza's Persian poetry and Persian prose is: What were the reasons that kept Mirza intensely occupied for fifty years in the pursuit of perfecting an art which had no one to really appreciate his value [*qadr dan*]. His patrons were mostly English Government officials who were strangers to the Persian language, especially its poetry; and kings, nobles and wealthy men who did not have the time, or need, to read or understand Mirza's Persian qasidahs.[8]

Hali was worried that Persian literature was disappearing from India, and that there was no hope for its revival. He felt that 'it was foolish to expect that Mirza's Persian poetry and prose would be popular now or in the coming years'. But he also hoped that in his book he could reveal the finer points of Mirza's poetry that were not appreciated in his lifetime.[9]

There are two points to note here. First, that Hali was puzzled by Ghalib giving so much importance to Persian, and second, that he felt there was an urgent need to immortalize Ghalib's accomplishments in Persian (more so than in Urdu), because the world was likely to forget Ghalib's Persian soon enough. The greater part of Hali's *Yadgar-e Ghalib* is devoted to selections from Ghalib's Persian works. The poetry selection is notable for Hali comparing Ghalib with the Persian master poets Naziri and Zuhuri, with a view to highlight Ghalib's extraordinary imaginative and creative genius.[10] According to Altaf Husain Hali, Persian had become a stranger in his country. Only a few in India could understand Ghalib's power of imagination and poetic skills. He quoted the following verse from Ghalib's Persian poetry to illustrate the poignancy of the situation:[11]

If there is a knower of tongues here, fetch him;
There's a stranger in the city and he has many things to say.[12]

Hali's view of the decline of Persian scholarship is exaggerated. There were many among Ghalib's peers, his own pupils, who admired his Persian poetry. But as we shall see, Urdu had a wider readership beyond the elite circle of literati.

What caused Ghalib to begin, and then sustain, a passionate pursuit of Persian? This question led to more questions as I dived deeper into Ghalib's textual history. It seems to me that his pursuit of Persian was with the view to open a wider, transregional dialogue with the Persianate. His goal and purpose as an Indian Persian poet was to prove his mastery in a classical language and thus connect himself with the long-standing tradition of composing in Persian. Once he started composing poetry in Persian, Ghalib felt that it was crucial for him to separate from the less prestigious 'Indianized Persian' of his peers and predecessors.

Ghalib became seriously prejudiced against Indian Persian writers after a couple of his Persian usages were criticized in

Calcutta at a mushairah, a social gathering at which Urdu poetry is read, typically taking the form of a contest (1829). His opponents quoted Mirza Muhammad Hasan Qatil (1757/58–1818) as their authority. Ghalib, however, refused to acknowledge the authority of an Indian in matters concerning Persian. In the literary battles that followed, ugly epithets inscribed in pamphlets were exchanged. Ghalib (maybe a little exaggeratedly) even feared for his life and was advised to conciliate the hostile group. He wrote a long poem (masnavi), *Ashtinamah* (a document of peace and reconciliation), in which he defended his Persian usages, citing the authority of Persian masters such as Shaikh Sa'di.[13] The unfortunate incident left deep scars on his tortured psyche. From this point, Ghalib began to distance himself from Indian Persian writers, even Mirza Bedil, to whom he had paid an adoring homage as an epigraph to his Urdu divan (1816).

Ghalib removed most of the adulatory references to Bedil (1644–1721) from his Urdu divan. He declared that his admiration for Bedil and other poets of the *tazah-goi*, or 'fresh style', was youthful waywardness which he now claimed to correct. The fact is that Ghalib continued to write in the Bedilian mode, both in Urdu as well as Persian. Although Ghalib admired and claimed to be no less than Hazin, Urfi, Naziri, Zuhuri and Sa'ib, all poets of the early modern style or the so-called Indian style, he also declared allegiance to the 'pure' Iranian idiom, which is somewhat conflicting.

Ghalib nursed his hurt ego, the humiliations he perceived to have been heaped on him, at the Calcutta mushairah, until he became established as the leading Persianist of the age. He shared his painful experience in the mushairah in letters to his friends. I use these historical–biographical details to explain how these events were important for Ghalib—how his life as an Urdu poet changed after Calcutta. From being a chiefly Urdu poet, he became a Persian poet. A string of illustrious publications in Persian, including

Divan-e Farsi (1845), *Panj Ahang* (Five Melodies, a collection of Persian writing first published in 1849, with a second edition in 1853), *Mehr-e Nim Roz* (Midday Sun, the first volume of a history of Mughal rulers, first published in 1854/55) and *Dastanbuy* (1858),[14] left no doubts about his mastery of Persian.

Ghalib was not a lexicographer or a scholar of Persian and Arabic. Nonetheless, in order to prove his untutored superiority, he claimed, for the first time in 1857, to have had a special tutor from Iran, one he called Abdus Samad Hurmuzd. According to Ghalib, Abdus Samad happened to arrive in Agra in 1811.[15] He was Ghalib's tutor in Persian and imparted to him all that he knew about classical Persian and also standard Persian.

Ghalib also invoked mythic characters from *Shahnameh* in his Persian poetry, as his forebears and from whom he claimed some vague biological–cultural heritage. Before the modern modes of conceptualizing belonging came into being, it was not uncommon to have transregional sensibilities of identity. The distinction between the native and the foreign was a creation of the colonial state that wanted to pin down the former as a category to be dominated. The Indian subcontinent, with its history of Muslim rule and transregional cultural complexities, defied the binaries of the native and the foreign until the British rule categorized Muslims as foreigners, as opposed to the Hindus who were deemed natives. In the realm of literary culture, or *adab,* the sharing of language, the transmission of knowledge and service to patrons all accounted for ties as strong as kinship. Ghalib's claimed affiliations with Persian were multiple. He emphasized his ancestral origins (Samarqand), his place of birth (Agra) and his residence (Delhi). He carried the weight of two languages on his shoulders: Urdu and Persian. The two languages were related through a common script, a mass of shared vocabulary and an overlapping literary tradition. The literary spaces were inclusive. The Persianate was the larger of the two worlds, with a deep literary tradition and a wider circulation of its adab. But we must not forget that Persian in India, even at the end of the nineteenth century, and in spite of the colonial emphasis on modern, Western education and vernaculars, was very much a part of the literary–cultural fabric in most of the subcontinent. Perhaps it wasn't so much transregionality as deep historical–cultural roots for himself that Ghalib sought to establish. Persian was a classical language by this time.[16]

We must also remember that the beginnings of Urdu as a literary language have much to do with regional culture.[17] The earliest literary compositions in Urdu date back to fifteenth-sixteenth century Gujarat, where the local language, Gujarati, was also developing side by side. Early Urdu in Gujarat was called Hindi/Hindvi, and then Gujri. A little later, Urdu reached the Deccan, where the independent kingdoms became a salubrious milieu for its growth. Though never a court language, Hindi/Hindvi/Gujri/Dakani enjoyed prestige as a favoured language patronized by the kings and nobility.[18]

In the north, by the end of the seventeenth century, Urdu, then called Hindi and Rekhtah, marched ahead as a Persian-influenced literary language for poetry and prose.[19] The earliest version of Rekhtah inclined towards a macaronic form, from which it took off to become mainline Urdu, still called Rekhtah or Hindi. This points to the multilingual literary choices that were available to poets at that time.[20] Literary networks in precolonial India nourished multilingual cultures where poets could choose from several registers of expression, or even languages, aimed at diverse audiences. By the time Delhi entered the second quarter of the eighteenth century, the macaronic mode had entirely given way to a distinct, native literary language. After Vali Dakani's divan arrived in Delhi around 1720, the trend to write in Rekhtah, albeit in a Persianized register, became popular.[21]

Ghalib's bilingualism is a subject that needs closer scrutiny than what it has received so far. Obviously, literacy in Persian was a given for the educated class. However, the vernacularization of education, which began after Macaulay's 'Minute on Education' (1835), eventually led to a noticeable shift from the classical learning imparted at traditional schools to instruction in the modern languages, such as Urdu. There was now a pressing demand for printed literature in Urdu. Ghalib, in spite of his valorization of Persian, moved back to Urdu in his later years. His Urdu divan went through five editions (1841, 1847, 1852, 1862 and 1863) in his lifetime, while the Persian divan was printed only twice in the same period (1845 and 1863). Ghalib's intricate Persian prose was considered exemplary, but it was his letters in Urdu that became the hallmark of literary Urdu prose.

Around 1862, the idea of publishing his Urdu letters was mooted by some admirers.[22] Initially, Ghalib demurred, saying that they were casual writings not to be treated as high literature. In fact, his letters in Urdu were informal, witty and filled with his views on poetry and advice for his pupils.[23] Two of his dear pupils—Munshi Shiv Narain Aram and Munshi Hargopal Taftah—first thought of publishing the letters but were not able to carry out the plan. Munshi Mumtaz Ali Khan rose to the occasion and, by 1862, a sizeable number of letters had been collected.

My point in bringing up the subject of Urdu letters is to underscore the fact that Ghalib's Urdu divan comprised a fraction of what he had composed in Persian. If the Urdu letters had not been published when they were published, they would most likely have languished with their addressees, unknown and not accessible to a wider audience. Their vital influence on the Urdu prose of that time might not have happened either. More importantly, all that we would have of Ghalib's Urdu compositions would have been his slender divan. As I mentioned earlier, there was a demand for printed literature in Urdu, spurred on by colonial educational policies to include modern vernaculars in the curriculum. Ghalib astutely bought into this opportunity. As the project of collecting letters gained momentum, Ghalib took an active interest, sending copies of letters to Munshi Mumtaz Ali Khan. He became impatient when the process dragged on:

> Dear Sir,
> What is this Munshi Mumtaz Ali Khan doing? Collected the letters but did not publish.[24]

Ghalib was not satisfied with Mumtaz Ali Khan's efforts and had the manuscript sent to another friend, Ghulam Ghaus Bekhabar. He personally wrote to Bekhabar, asking him to speed up the publication of his letters:[25]

> Janab Kempson Sahib Bahadur, Director of the schools in the north and west, wrote to me. He inquired about the development of Urdu (prose) and I responded. He asked for Urdu poetry and prose, I sent him a collection of my Urdu poems. About the prose, I didn't mention your name, but wrote that the prose collection is currently in press in Allahabad.

By August 1866, the manuscript was ready for publication. It was eventually published from Meerut in 1868 as *Ud-e Hindi* (The Indian Aloe or, alternatively, the Indian 'Ud', a musical instrument). Its importance is evidenced by the multiple forewords and afterwords that accompanied it. The book was dedicated to Sir William Muir, the governor of the United Provinces. Although the book was riddled with proofreading errors, it was well-received and sold out immediately. The collection of letters in *Ud-e Hindi* is special because it contains much literary discussion, issues of Persian language; some letters even contain commentaries on verses, both Ghalib's own and of other (mostly Persian) poets; there are also scattered remarks on the poetics of the ghazal. One reason behind the urgency to get the letters published was to get excerpts included in the Urdu textbooks prescribed for high school and universities. Compilers of textbooks, such as *Insha-e Urdu* (Urdu Literary Prose), were looking out for exemplary writings, and Ghalib's letters were much sought after. Indeed, Ghalib's popularity and the sale of his Urdu writings received a considerable boost from the pragmatics of curricular design.

The print industry, in the early stages, did not produce new books as readily as it did old books. Grammars, dictionaries, and so on, were published, but almost all had been transmitted in manuscript form before print. The main effect was the easy availability of the classical texts of poetry and prose. Yet, print changed attitudes towards contemporary language and literature, too. New literary practices accompanied it, such as calls for script reform and developing a system of punctuation (closely based on the English system), and more discursive as well as historical prose. Print enabled change by allowing certain texts to spread more quickly and widely than was previously possible. Print increased literacy. It allowed easy and cheap access to literature and its distribution. One reason why Ghalib dominates over his contemporaries, as well as famous poets of the eighteenth century, could be the power of publishing.

The large number of commentaries on Ghalib's Urdu divan filled a niche in the new curriculum: the need to explicate poetry to young people.[26] Ghalib's Urdu ghazals were an important part of the syllabi, and they were difficult compared to those of other classical poets, such as Mir Taqi Mir (1723–1810), Mirza Rafi Sauda (1706/13–81) and Momin Khan Momin (1800–52). Ghalib's Persian work was included in the syllabi for Persian literature, but there was a much smaller market for it now. Print played a role in conferring status on one linguistic register over another, and in establishing a literary canon. Ghalib is the only Urdu poet to have inspired an entire commentarial tradition, even though most of the commentaries are not as helpful as one might wish. Some of them are distracting, many are selective, but on the whole, the commentaries did much to help readers and students with insightful interpretations—or at least 'solutions' of complex, ambiguous verses.[27]

Despite having the reputation of being a 'difficult' poet, Ghalib became a household name because his work was published regularly. One can also reverse the argument and say he was published because he was a household name. Nonetheless, we cannot deny that authorial–editorial choices and print publication played an important role in making Ghalib the most recognized name in the Urdu canon.

The Persian canon presented a different situation. Ghalib had gone to great lengths to prove his mastery of the language. He practically invented a Zoroastrian tutor for himself, took a deep interest in pre-Islamic Persian, such as the dubious Dasatiri language,[28] critiqued non-Iranian usages, and even denigrated, on occasion, Iranian-Persian writers who lived in India. Ghalib was undoubtedly a great Persian poet, but achieving transregional acceptance of his creative genius in Persian wasn't easy. Part of the reason may be traced to the somewhat fraught relationship between the Indian writers of Persian vis-à-vis the Iranians. By the beginning of the eighteenth century, a feeling began to gain ground among Iranian circles that since Persian was not the native language of Indians, they could not have natural and intuitive command over it. On the contrary, the great Delhi linguist, lexicographer, critic and poet, Sirajuddin Ali Khan Arzu (1689–1756), popularly known as Khan-e Arzu, strenuously held that the Indians' command of Persian was as solid and reliable as the Iranians'. He believed that literary language could be learned by concentrated effort, which meant a studious and diligent study of the works of the master users of the language.

In the end, Ghalib, echoing the Iranians like Ali Hazin (1691–1766) and Valih Daghistani (1712–56), was inevitably grouped by the academic world as just another Indian, and not as authoritative as the Iranians, whose diction was un-Iranian and whose themes were riddled with unfamiliar metaphorical compounds. Unfortunately, university-level Persian studies in India marginalized Indian Persian writers, even Ghalib. Ghalib wasn't a favoured subject of study among the academics who applied his own formulation upon him and refused to accept his tall, vague claims that the subtleties of Persian were so embedded in his psyche that he could never go wrong. Hali's lament proved to be quite accurate. By the time my generation came around, we read Ghalib only in Urdu. Perhaps his exceptional richness in Urdu so satiated my thirst that I did not consider reading the Persian verses. Even *Yadgar-e Ghalib* did not push me to think about the Persian until I began working on Ghalib's textual history.

Ghalib's voice presents us with a double bind, a linguistic paradox. He felt his control of Persian to be as 'native' as his control of Urdu. His literary imagination is ineffable because it has many dimensions; some are extreme, some edifyingly trivial. I am mapping Ghalib's textual history in order to get a better understanding of the ever-fraught, complicated relationship between circumstance and choice—can biographical history help us interpret his decision to lean more towards Persian when Urdu was in its golden age?

Perhaps Ghalib was thinking in Persian and writing in Urdu. Was he trying to experiment with a new style, or did he find Urdu inadequate when it came to expressing his thoughts? In Urdu, Ghalib often leaves the meaning of the verse suspended. He suggests a meaning but leaves the reader striving in order to arrive at his meaning. This can often leave the reader—or especially the listener—puzzled or lost. Often, Ghalib deploys a vocabulary that has multiple layers of meaning, one can't always know which one the poet intended. Sometimes there is an obvious meaning that veils a deeper one. Ghalib explores unfamiliar emotional states or reveals new responses to familiar emotional states. In fact, Ghalib often laments at the inadequacy of language to express his thoughts, or that language is an inadequate medium of expression:

Hujum-e fikr se dil misl-e mauj larze hai,
Kih shishah nazuk-o sahba-e abginah gudaz
[My heart trembles like a wave with the surges of thought,
The wine glass is delicate and the wine fiery hot]

The greatest challenge for anyone writing about Ghalib in English is that of translation. Translatability is an assumption. In rendering Ghalib into English, one constantly faces the wall of untranslatability, or the need to sacrifice the intellectual–cultural nuance to reach an anglophone readership. The second challenge is sifting through the vast body of work on Ghalib in Urdu, piecing it together to get answers to questions that are vital in putting together his fragmented textual history. Chapter 1 begins with an examination of Ghalib's early life. There are discrepancies in the dates ascribed by Ghalib. He was orphaned at the age of five; he lost his paternal uncle, Nasrullah Beg Khan, who was his guardian, at the age of nine. A stipend or pension was determined for the dependents of Nasrullah Beg Khan by British governor Lord Lake on the basis of a recommendation from Navab Ahmad Bakhsh Khan. Ghalib felt that the pension was unfairly proportioned between the dependents, but he did not challenge the allocation at the time, presumably because he was too young. It seems unfair to allege that Ghalib deliberately deducted some years from his actual birthdate in order to strengthen and justify his litigating it when he was worldly-wise.

Chapters 2 and 3 narrate the background stories of the discovery of several significant manuscript divans (nuskhah) of Ghalib's Urdu verses. It seems hard to believe that the Urdu literary world may have been entirely deprived of Mirza Ghalib's early poetry and/or unselected verses, and perhaps even forgotten about it, had some rare manuscripts not surfaced nearly half a century after the poet's death. The earliest one dates to 1816 and is largely believed to be in Ghalib's own handwriting. The importance of these divans is not only that they contain the verses that Ghalib did not select when he published the Urdu divan in 1841, they also reveal, in many cases, Ghalib's choices and emendations to verses from time to time. The stories are fascinating from many perspectives on Ghalib's reception history, of which the fickleness of public memory and the pervasiveness of print are primary. The first manuscript of the divan, dated 1821, was found in 1918 in Bhopal, by which time the general public had already forgotten that Ghalib had composed a lot more than what was available in the authorized, published divan. This, despite Hali's *Yadgar-e Ghalib*, which mentions the unselected verses. The 1821 divan, which included the unselected verses, was published, albeit not without controversy. It was later incorporated into a comprehensive edition of Ghalib's all-known Urdu poetry in a volume published by Maulana Imtiaz Ali Khan Arshi in 1958. In spite of this, the unselected verses have not gained much recognition.[29]

Chapter 4 details the tribulations of Ghalib's journey to Calcutta (now Kolkata), the seat of the English government. On the way, he made several important stops, but the city of Banaras (now Varanasi) on the River Ganga truly captivated him. He composed a dazzling masnavi in Persian, *Chiragh-e Dair* (Lamp of the Temple), in which he spoke of the exquisite delights of Banaras. When we think of the challenges of a nearly 3000-kilometre journey that was interrupted by long episodes of illness (five months spent recovering in Lucknow, six in Banda and one in Banaras), we have to admire Ghalib's tenacity of purpose. It seems like a miracle that he even reached his destination. Ghalib, meanwhile, kept pouring his heart out in letters. He wrote Persian in an elaborate but emotional style, creating a wonderful archive of the sojourn in his ornate yet elegant prose.

Chapter 5 tracks Ghalib's transition from Urdu to Persian. He made a selection of his Urdu and Persian verses for Maulvi Sirajuddin Ahmad, the editor of the weekly *Ainah-e Sikandar*. The manuscript, titled *Gul-e Ra'na* (The Two-Coloured Rose, 1828), was never published in his lifetime, and probably wasn't meant for publication either. Although several copies were made, they were buried in private collections, the owners perhaps not aware of their importance. The first of these was recovered in 1951.

Gul-e Ra'na provides a valuable opportunity to sample Ghalib's early Urdu and Persian in one volume, as an anthology. Perhaps the idea of making a selection of his Urdu verses for a divan occurred to Ghalib at the time he was preparing *Gul-e Ra'na*. What caught my attention was the insightful foreword, or the dibachah. It is here that Ghalib addresses the demanding task of writing in two languages. It brings up his own issues with the reception of his poetry:

> They say that the blood of two languages is on my head, and the corpses of the two I have killed are on my shoulders[30] . . . Where is that silence that would remove me from the vengeance being sought for these languages from me, and also free me from the ups and downs of acceptance and rejection of listeners?[31]

Throughout this book, I have provided critical readings of Ghalib's many forewords with a view to tease out his poetics.

Chapter 6 examines the reasons for the popularity of the Urdu divan and compares the Urdu with the Persian divan. The two divans have forewords, but the Persian divan's dibachah is a classic in its own right. It has never been translated, not even into Urdu. I compare the dibachahs in the two divans to find answers to issues that have not been examined by Ghalibians thus far. The dibachah to the Urdu divan has a controversial passage:

> I hope that literati, and also those who appreciate my work would not declare those scattered pages, which are not included in this Divan, to be the result of the ink from my quill and would not oblige the collection of my writings with praise of those verses, nor would they lay blame on me for their adaptations.

What exactly did Ghalib mean by the reference to the scattered pages not being from his pen? Some scholars think it means that Ghalib was brushing off his early work, maybe the unselected verses. This argument was used to resist the publication of the Divan of 1821. But I think that this passage is one of the earliest expressions of authorial intent, perhaps even a semblance of copyright. As we shall see, it wasn't uncommon to attribute, or rather misattribute, verses. An early commentator on Ghalib even went to the extent of inserting his own ghazals into the corpus of the unselected verses. (Perhaps that should be attributed to playful mischief, not deliberate fraud.)

Chapter 7 analyses Ghalib's forewords and afterwords (khatimahs) with a view to understanding these somewhat neglected but critical genres of Indian Persian literature. When we look at Ghalib's dibachahs, we encounter a rhetorical mode of discourse that uses tropes to organize modes of perception. Their literary make-up is so complicated and challenging that it often defies translation. The language is loaded with cultural allusions, multiple meanings, puns, plus an inherent ambiguity that produces a textual structure that is not easy to comprehend. It is also not conclusive. Perhaps this is why Ghalib's Persian dibachahs haven't attracted much scholarly attention. I found that in spite of the challenges of translation and interpretation, Ghalib's dibachahs are filled with critical perceptions that are not simply figurative but can also be interpreted to derive an understanding of his poetic self. Ghalib's dramatic self-presentation in these texts that form the bookends to his divans emphasize the newness of his compositions while also reiterating his links with the poetic tradition of his forebears.

Chapter 8 presents a reassessment of Ghalib's passionate engagement with Persian by re-examining his sense of belonging to a larger literary world. His fascination with the *Dasatir*, the Arabic–Persian linguistic rivalries and restyling of the Persian language are wrapped up in his claim of literary lineage with what he thought was pristine Persian. Ghalib, in his keenness to claim native competence in Persian, rejected all lexicographers who didn't actually write their dictionaries in Iran, or were not actual, practising Iranian poets. More interesting is his effort to write a so-called diary of the events of the Revolt of 1857 to present to Queen Victoria. We have several leads to the nagging question as to why he wrote the *Dastanbuy* in 'pure' Persian, or what was to him the Dasatiri mode. Ghalib believed the *Dasatír* to be an authentic account, instead of a fabricated one in a made-up language, which claimed to be 'pure' Persian. It is ironic that Ghalib's position as a nineteenth-century Persian poet, in what became colonial India, is wrought with issues of his engagement with the preceding literary canons. It is entwined with his efforts to be recognized as the leading poet in a classical language.

The last two chapters of this book are an effort to understand Ghalib's literary methods, the reach of his imagination and his engagement with literatures beyond political and geographic boundaries. Ghalib follows the tradition of intertextual dialogue (*javab-goí*) with his precursors in Persian. I have scrutinized his creative engagement with the poets of the classical past and those that are described to stylistically represent tazah-goi. Tazah-goi in itself means newness or freshness, perhaps as much as every innovative creative urge could be. The element of Indianness that supposedly made the poetry obscure seems to have had more to do with temporality than geography. Iranian émigrés at the Mughal court were bound to have a subjective engagement with the cultural aesthetics that coloured their metaphorical use of language.

In the end, Ghalib received everlasting fame in the modern language: Urdu. The book wraps up with Ghalib's return to writing in this language. His last years were bittersweet. Bedridden with many ailments, he continued to respond to his large body of admirers, dictating letters and receiving visitors. He was unconscious in the last couple of days before he passed away in 1869. His death was commemorated in an extraordinary outpouring of poetry and chronograms.

While writing on Ghalib, I was faced with the monumental contributions of all the Ghalibians before me. However, my approach has been different. An invaluable and large portion of Ghalib studies focuses on interpreting the Urdu divan. The unique commentarial tradition began with Maulvi Ali Haider

Nazm Tabataba'i (1854–1933), who published *Sharh-e Divan-e Ghalib* (Commentary on Ghalib's Divan) in 1900, continued with Shamsur Rahman Faruqi's *Tafhim-e Ghalib* and was carried forward by Frances W. Pritchett's *A Desertful of Roses*, all exemplifying the range of possibilities of reading Ghalib. Faruqi and Pritchett opened new vistas for the appreciation and translation of the classical ghazal, particularly Ghalib's, for Western readers.[32]

The discovery and publication of Ghalib's earliest divan opened new doors to a more holistic study of his Urdu poetry. It facilitated a more rigorous dating of his compositions and new editions such as Kalidas Gupta Raza's *Divan-e Ghalib Kamil* (Mumbai, 1988 and 1995). Raza's edition integrates and arranges Ghalib's corpus date-wise.[33] However, the verses that Ghalib unselected were still not given the kind of analytical scrutiny and commentary that the published divan has produced. Gyan Chand Jain's commendable effort, *Tafsir-e Ghalib* (1971), has been, so far, the only complete commentary on the unselected verses.[34] Jain's volume contains annotations on a total of 1956 verses, including those from qasidahs and rubais (verse containing four lines). Recently, a full (*mukammal*) commentary by Saiyyid Muhammad Zamin Kantoori, edited by Professor Ashraf Rafi of Hyderabad, was published (Delhi, 2012).[35]

A remarkable body of work resurrects Ghalib's life. Most notable in this field are Malik Ram, S.M. Ikram, Ralph Russell and Khurshidul Islam. Qazi Abdul Vadud's erudite musings on many recondite issues are always very helpful—did Ghalib actually have a Zoroastrian tutor named Abdus Samad who piqued his interest in pre-Islamic Persian? Qazi Sahib says no. My position on this subject is ambivalent. In verifying the truth about Abdus Samad, I was led to explore the discourse around pre-Islamic Persian, the relationship of Persian with Arabic loan words and the Dasatiri movement.[36] Ghalib's fascination with the *Dasatir* was unusual. I did not find similar inclinations among his peers. There was a complexity here that most Ghalibians have not considered important enough to pursue, perhaps because Abdus Samad (if he did exist) was not Ghalib's preceptor (ustad) in poetry. Ghalib did not have an ustad in poetry in the traditional sense. In the Urdu literary culture, an ustad is a mentor who corrects his pupil's verses and offers advice on numerous points on usage and poetics. But the presence, shadowy or real, of Abdus Samad in Ghalib's life does facilitate an understanding of our poet's absorption with language register and diction, and his claims of native fluency and total command over Persian. Ghalib's abiding interest in the capacity of language and its use in poetry and prose can be understood on its own terms.

Ghalib writes in two languages. In fact, he often laments the inadequacy of language to express his thoughts. He is, in his own words, the bulbul of a garden that is yet to be created:

Hun garmi-e nishat-e tasavvur se naghamah sanj
Main andalib-e gulshan-e na afridah hun
[I sing from the heat of the joy and excitation of my own imaginings
I am the bulbul of a garden that is yet to be created]

The ineffability of Ghalib's literary imagination has many dimensions—some in fact extreme and pathetic. Language in its authentic reality is born and lives in a perpetual combat and compromise between the desire to speak and the necessity of silence. The stupendous reality that is language cannot be understood unless we begin by observing that speech consists, above all, silences—each language represents a different equation between manifestations and silences. Each people leave some things unsaid *in order to* be able to say others. Because *everything* would be unsayable. Hence the immense difficulty of translation: translation is a matter of expressing in a language precisely what that language tends to pass over in silence.[37] Therefore, the challenge to translate Ghalib lies in transcending the silences of the receiving language, which, in this case, is English.

This book essentially approaches the relationship between writing literary history and how this relates to interpreting Ghalib's Persian and Urdu oeuvres. I wanted to know why Ghalib unselected so many of his Urdu verses. The art of selection (intikhab), especially when creating a divan, was very particular. What distinguishes a divan from a collection (*majmu'ah*) is that it presents an arrangement of poems in alphabetic order. Divans are arranged by order of refrains (*radifs*) that include nearly every letter of the alphabet. Thus, the divan is a display of poetic craft. Ghalib's authorized divan has a specific arrangement of ghazals within each section. He culled verses from his earlier divans to make this unique selection. In constructing Ghalib's textual history, I make the argument that each divan is an entity and possesses a sanctity that is violated when they are merged by editors. Each divan reflects Ghalib's own arrangement of ghazals and the other poetic genres contained in it. Divans provide a specific temporal snapshot of the time in which the poet was writing. They are specific to a poet's life. Nearly half of the unselected verses are from Ghalib's early career, but the act of selection was performed at a mature age (1828–33), which tells us something unique about the poet's rapport with his poetic crafting.

Ghalib's selection of verses is unique because it goes hand in hand with a publication trajectory, which means that there is also a reception history of his work that is somewhat unusual. I am referring to the resistance in publishing his earlier divans, as well as the lack of interest among readers for those verses. Of course, there is also the unequal reception of his Persian and Urdu corpus.

The importance of print culture also intersects with Ghalib's poetry. Print demands a new reader, new sensitivities, not quite the same as the aural reception of poetry. I have examined at length the evolution of Ghalib's affinity with print and the extent to which it might have influenced his selection for the Urdu divan. The example of Ghalib's Urdu letters being printed and circulated widely has a bearing on what one can glean about his personality. Once again, there is a contrast between the formal and impersonal style of letters in Persian and the witty, chatty style in Urdu.[38] Urdu readership was Ghalib's immediate domain. Persian was a testament to his connection with the deep, classical tradition of poetry. Ghalib's textual history is remarkable in so many respects that I can only hope this present study opens up new paths to approaching his life.

1

The Kite Rises into the Air

One day, my heart like a paper kite,
Took off on freedom's string,
And began to shy away from me,
Became so wayward, it pestered me.[1]

—Ghalib, from an early composition

To tell the truth—for to hide the truth is not the way of a man free in spirit—I am no more than half a Muslim, for I am free from the bonds of convention and religion and have liberated my soul from the fear of men's tongues.[2]

—Ghalib, in *Dastanbuy*

'Mirza Asadullah Khan Ghalib, known as Mirza Naushah, titled Najmuddaulah Dabir ul-Mulk Asadullah Khan Bahadur Nizam Jang, with the nom de plume Ghalib for Persian, and Asad for Rekhtah (Urdu), was born on the eve of 8th of Rajab 1212 *hijri* (27 December 1797) in the city of Agra.' Thus begins Maulana Altaf Husain Hali's important biographical account, *Yadgar-e Ghalib*.[3]

Indeed, Hali's critical, path-breaking memoir of his great ustad reconstructs the poet's life story in a thrilling narrative woven with anecdotes, letters, personal trivia, first-hand observations and, most importantly, a penetrating analysis of Ghalib's poetry and prose. Ghalib's colourful personality shines in Hali's lucid prose. It is hard to imagine how much or how little we would have known of Ghalib without Hali's seminal work.[4] There were Ghalib's letters—volumes of them, a vital source of information—but the inspiration and direction that Hali's work provided to generations of scholars remains undeniable.

In his youth, Ghalib was counted among the most handsome men in the city, be it Agra or Delhi. He was tall, with broad shoulders; his hands and feet were noticeably strong. Even in old age, when Hali first saw him, the signs of beauty were apparent on his face and demeanour. He was married on the 7th of Rajab, 1225 hijri (1810 ce) to Umrao Begam, the daughter of Navab Mirza Ilahi Bakhsh Khan Ma'ruf.[5] Ghalib was thirteen years old at the time, and his bride eleven.[6] Some years after his marriage, Ghalib moved to Delhi. It appears that he lived in Delhi for the next fifty years, till the end of his life. According to Altaf Husain Hali, in this long period, he never bought a house. He chose to live in rented houses; when he got tired of one house, he moved to another, but always remained in the same neighbourhood: Gali Qasim Jan, or Habsh Khan ka Phatak, or a place nearby.[7]

Ghalib became an orphan at the impressionable age of five, when his father, Mirza Abdullah Beg Khan, was killed by a stray bullet in Rajgarh, Rajasthan, where he had gone with a force from Alwar to quell a rebellion. He was buried in Rajgarh.[8] Raja Bakhtawar Singh of Alwar fixed a generous allowance for Ghalib and his siblings—his older sister, known as Chhoti Begam, and his younger brother, Mirza Yusuf. The children and their mother had always lived at the maternal home in Agra. In fact, Ghalib was born in the grand mansion of his maternal grandfather,

Khwaja Ghulam Husain Khan Kamidan. Khwaja Ghulam Husain, a military commander (*kamidan* in colloquial speech) in the province of Meerut, was among the leading elite of Agra. His estate included numerous villages, and he owned many properties in the town itself. Ghalib's mother, Izzatun Nisa Begam, was literate. Because Ghalib's father lived with his in-laws, he was fondly known as Mirza Dulha, or Mister Bridegroom. Ghalib himself was known as Mirza Naushah, which, too, means Mister Bridegroom. Such nicknames were terms of affection used for males living with their in-laws. Presumably, Ghalib's father died in 1801 (although Ghulam Rasul Mehr gives 1803 as the date), because we know that his paternal uncle, Mirza Nasrullah Beg Khan, died some five years later, in 1806, because of the injuries he suffered after accidentally falling off his elephant. Although Ghalib recorded his uncle's death as an important event in his life, there is no evidence that he was close to his uncle; however, he and his siblings did become entitled to a pension because they were among Mirza Nasrullah Beg's dependents.[9]

Ghalib's Tutors and the Controversial Abdus Samad Hurmuzd

Maulvi Muhammad Mu'azzam, a well-known Persian scholar and teacher in Agra, was Ghalib's first tutor. His next tutor was allegedly a traveller from Iran, Hurmuzd, who was known by his Islamic name of Mulla Abdus Samad. Abdus Samad came to Agra in 1811. Ghalib, according to his own account, invited Abdus Samad to stay with him in order to improve his Persian. Abdus Samad then spent two years with Ghalib, first in Agra, then presumably in Delhi. Mirza was fourteen years old at the time and had already begun writing poetry in Urdu.[10] It is speculated that Abdus Samad was not a real person but an imaginary figure created by Ghalib to authenticate his claim to unique fluency in idiomatic Persian.[11] Abdus Samad's presence is corroborated vaguely by some sources, notably Navab Alauddin Ahmad Khan Alai,[12] who refer to him as a merchant who came to Agra. Hali mentions that Navab Mustafa Khan Sheftah[13] referred to a letter that Abdus Samad wrote to Ghalib from some distant land.[14] The fact that Ghalib did not mention Abdus Samad until much later in his life, till the point when he was writing a feisty critique of the Persian dictionary *Burhan-e Qati*, has prompted scholars to doubt the existence of Abdus Samad.

Hali's account of Abdus Samad, too, is quite contradictory. It appears that he could not make up his mind whether Abdus Samad was an important influence in Ghalib's life or not. He writes:

> Mirza was fourteen years old when Abdus Samad landed [*varid hua*] at his house and stayed there for two years. Thus, when we consider Mirza's age at the time he had the benefit of his company, and the short period spent with him, then Abdus Samad, and the significance of his tutoring, become moot. Therefore, Mirza is quite right when he says that he had no ustad except the generous originator [God].[15]

On the very next page, Hali presents the benefits Ghalib received from Abdus Samad in a different light:

> As Mirza has mentioned, Mulla Abdus Samad, in addition to knowing Persian, which was his mother tongue and the language of his religious community, was also learned in Arabic. Although Mirza had very little time with him, yet for an erudite jewel like Mirza to have such a tutor who was affectionate, ideal and knower of many languages was an uncommon coincidence that happens seldom. Even though Mirza did not have the opportunity to learn much from him, the beneficence of his companionship must have produced that disposition for poetry in Mirza about which it is said: 'If you have [the disposition], learning or unlearning is the same; if you don't have it, learning and unlearning is the same too' [a Persian proverb].[16]

Apparently, Hali wanted so much to defend Ghalib that he lost his own sense of judgement. Indeed, the disposition to write poetry is God-given. Ghalib, according to Hali, says so himself. Yet, in his eagerness to corroborate Ghalib's claim of having Abdus Samad as a tutor, Hali trips on his own statements regarding the benefit Ghalib would have received from Abdus Samad. Hali then goes on to describe the impression that Ghalib had made on Abdus Samad, who remembered him years later and spoke of him affectionately in a letter mentioned by Navab Mustafa Khan Sheftah.[17] We really need to read Hali carefully and critically in reconstructing Ghalib's early life because he does not pay attention to matching dates with events or, in this instance, to providing concrete evidence. Hali borrowed quite liberally, even indiscriminately, from Muhammad Husain Azad's section on Ghalib in *Ab-e Hayat*. Khalilur Rahman Daudi's critical edition of *Yadgar-e Ghalib* helps us identify some of Hali's inaccuracies, discrepancies and borrowings.

*Tazkirah*s, or anthologies, often compiled by poets themselves, were traditional sources of information about the literary scene. They seldom recorded dates and were often uncritical in their approach because their purpose was to provide a survey of poets and samples of their poetry. However, under the influence of English literary practices, tazkirah writing evolved into a hybrid form of literary history. Muhammad Husain Azad's *Ab-e Hayat* led the way, with its forced 'periodization' of literature.[18] Azad imposed on a timeless tradition a linear periodization demarcated by evolution or change in literary practice. He called each of these eras *daur*s and created exactly five of them. His narrative style was intensely readable because he peppered the text with anecdotes. Azad and Hali both subscribed to what can be called a 'reformist' stance towards literature. They may even have shared notes and ideas when they were living in Lahore in the 1870s.

But I suspect that we need to dig deeper into Ghalib's early life rather than simply arguing about the reality of Abdus Samad. There are significant gaps in our information about Ghalib's birth and early years. For example, Hali did not question Ghalib's date of birth any more than Azad did, and later biographers have followed their lead. But can we really be sure that we know when Ghalib was born?

Ghalib's Date of Birth: Was He Born in 1797?

> The date of my birth was expressed in the Realm of the Angels with the words: 'tumult of desire'; 'unknown stranger'.
>
> —Ghalib, *Kulliyat-e Farsi,* 1863[19]

Traditionally speaking, Indo-Muslim children's birthdays, if they were documented at all, were recorded in the hijri calendar. Over the course of a lifetime, the result would be a difference of two or three years in one's age, when compared with the ce reckoning. We have to keep this in mind as we examine the assortment of contradictory evidence about Ghalib's date of birth. Although Ghalib himself has provided much of the evidence, either through his letters, or in the form of biographical notes that were written ostensibly for tazkirahs, the dates often do not match his reminiscences. The first instance of his birthdate is recorded in the initial manuscript version of the *Divan-e Nazm-e Farsi* of 1837. At the conclusion of this volume, Ghalib wrote: 'To this day from the *hijrat* of our last Prophet, one thousand, two hundred, fifty and three years have passed, and my fortune's star through the movement of the skies' messenger has reached forty-one years.' Thus, in 1253 hijri Ghalib, according to himself, was forty-one years old. This affirms that he was born in 1212 hijri (1797 ce).[20]

Ghalib's Persian Divan of 1837 includes a *qasidah-e manqibat* (an ode in praise of the Prophet's companions and descendants) in honour of Hazrat Imam Husain. The manqibat has a section in which Ghalib eloquently describes the conjugation of stars that dealt him misfortunes. A subsequent version of this Persian divan, prepared in 1848, has

Ghalib's horoscope in his own hand attached with the manqibat.[21] The horoscope mentions that Ghalib was born four hours before sunrise on Sunday evening (*yak shambah*), 8th of Rajab, 1212 hijri. But 8th of Rajab, 1212 hijri, was *not* a Sunday; it was a Wednesday (*chahar shambah*). This seems to be a minor mistake, but as we shall see, there are more inconsistencies than just a mere confusion of days.

Maulana Imtiaz Ali Khan Arshi, who saw the horoscope, describes it in his essay 'Mirza Ghalib Ka Za'ichah'.[22] He writes:

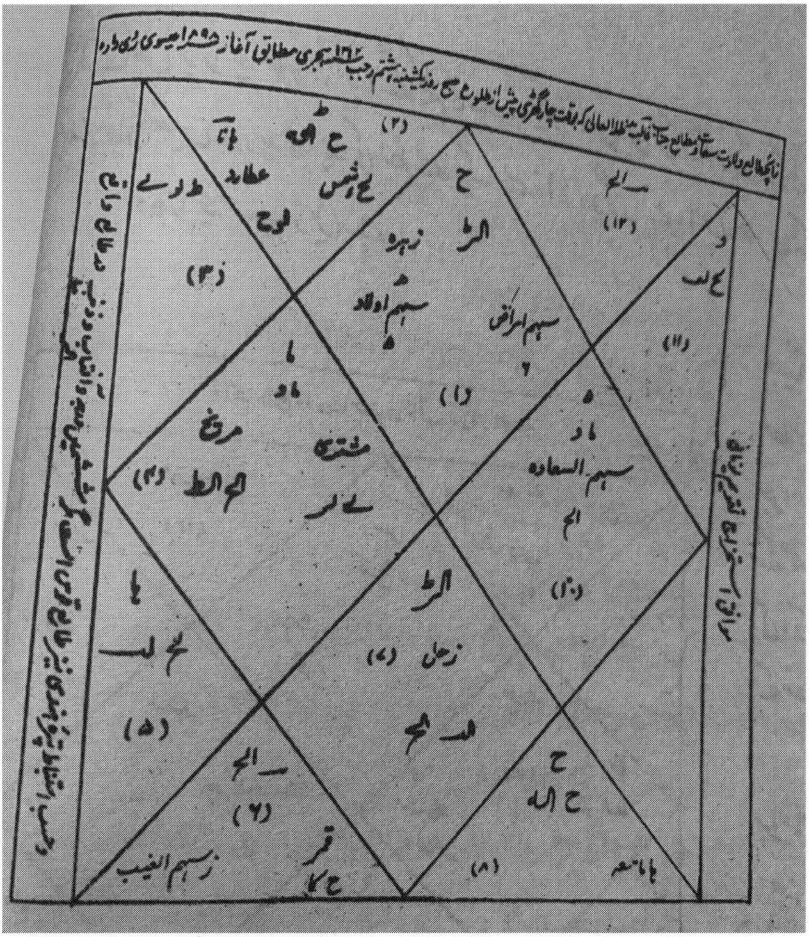

According to this horoscope, Ghalib was born on Sunday, 1212 hijri. This corresponds to the beginning of 1798 CE.

'To my knowledge, this horoscope was made by Ghalib. There is no reason to doubt that the information presented in it was provided by him. He must have reviewed it many times. The information in it is not second-hand.'[23]

Maulana Arshi also recounts that there are two versions of this horoscope. A second, but somewhat different, copy is attached with the third manuscript version of the *Divan-e Farsi*, dated 1278/1861. Ghalib's cousin and pupil, Navab Ziyauddin Khan Naiyar, owned the manuscript. The horoscope is attached on page 40. Although

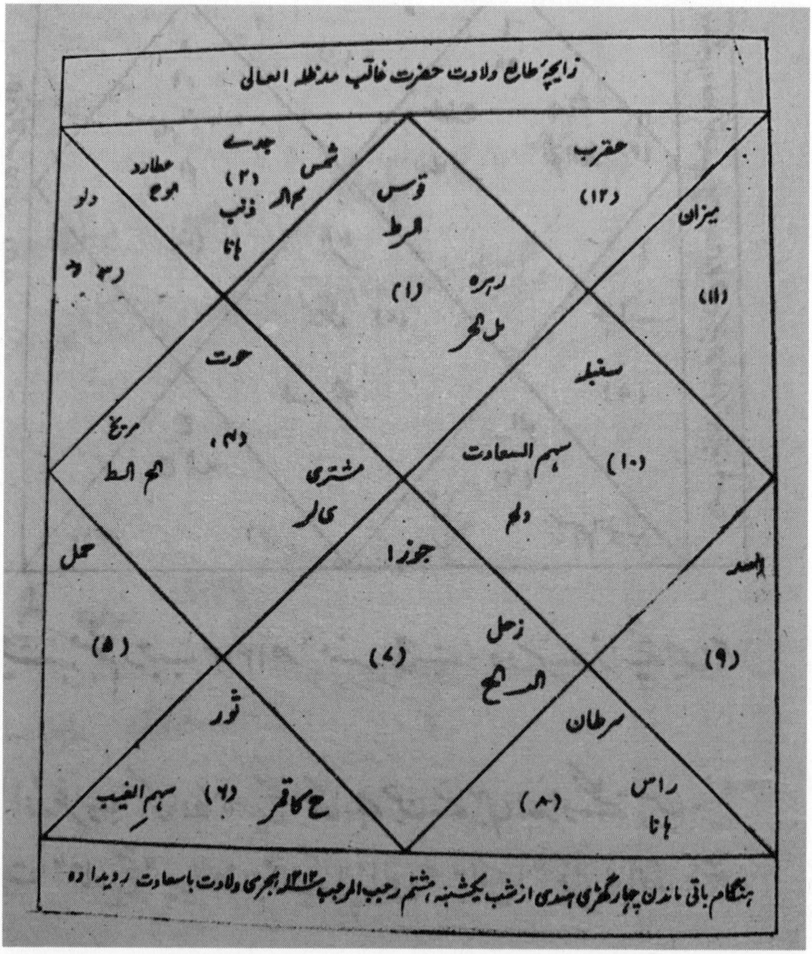

A slightly different version of Ghalib's horoscope.

the second horoscope has the same date of birth—8th Rajab 1212 hijri—the numerals are a bit smudged. The date is qualified with an additional phrase giving the concordance of the hijri with the Christian calendar. Probably due to an error in calculation, it says that 1212 hijri is equivalent to the beginning of 1798 ce.

It is the second version that is published in the Naval Kishor edition of *Kulliyat-e Farsi* of 1863 (pp. 198–99). In this version, the smudged numerals of Ghalib's date of birth erroneously get reproduced as 1214 hijri. There are other differences, too, among the first, second and third versions. The second horoscope mentions that it has been prepared according to the Greek school of astrology. The first does not mention this.

Saiyyid Muhammad Husain Rizvi has interpreted Ghalib's horoscope in his article titled 'Ghalib ki Sahih Tarikh-e Viladat' (Ghalib's Correct Date of Birth).[24] Rizvi begins by elucidating that it is not clear exactly which school of astrology forms the basis for configuring this horoscope. This is strange since the second horoscope clearly mentions it to be the Greek school of astrology. Rizvi, who hasn't seen Maulana Arshi's essay, rightly assumes that 1214 hijri could be a copyist's error, because the two chronograms—*shorish-e shauq* and *gharib*—furnished by Ghalib in a quatrain in the *kulliyat* yield, in the chronogram system, a date of 1212 hijri.

> O Ghalib, because of the useless elusiveness of fortune, I fear the foe, and also covet the beloved.
> The date of my birth was expressed in the Realm of the Angels with the words: 'tumult of desire'; 'unknown stranger'.[25]

Elaborating on the finer details of the inconsistencies in the published version, Rizvi makes the point that if Ghalib was born four hours before sunrise, the day would still be Saturday (*shambah*), not Sunday (yak shambah), as per the Indic system. He reiterates that because 8th Rajab 1212 hijri was a Wednesday, both the day and year mentioned in the horoscope are incorrect. He concludes that the correct date should be 8th Rajab 1211 hijri, which was a Saturday, corresponding to 8 January 1797.

The horoscope, Rizvi explains, is to be read in context with the qasidah-e manqibat in honour of Hazrat Imam Husain. The manqibat, comprising 112 verses, has some eighteen verses that refer directly to the conjugation of planets at Ghalib's birth. Rizvi's Urdu version presents a lucid translation of the eighteen (Persian) verses. In these verses, Ghalib shows how the planetary configuration in his horoscope makes it easy for sorrow to overwhelm his fortune. Each verse elaborates with Ghalibian flair the theme of the role of planets in predicting a miserable life for him. It is not clear how deep Ghalib's knowledge of astrology really was, or how far one should go in assigning any authentic significance to the horoscope. It is possible that Ghalib drew up the horoscope to substantiate what he had been saying all along regarding the day, date and time of his birth, but in the process he muddled the issue. I think Ghalib's horoscope should not be taken literally. It is a poetic flourish meant to further enhance his reputation for the knowledge of the classical arts.

Kamal Ahmad Siddiqi and Hanif Naqvi have published articles containing detailed research on Ghalib's date of birth.[26] Both scholars have presented an exhaustive list of references, gathered from letters and other sources. They agree that the important signposts in the poet's lifespan are the death of his father, the death of his uncle, his marriage and, most important, his move from Agra to Delhi. Sandwiched between Ghalib's marriage and his move to Delhi is a significant but dubious period: the two years he allegedly spent with his Iranian tutor, Abdus Samad. Information about Ghalib's teenage years is so scarce, and so hard to corroborate, that one can either believe in or disbelieve the existence of Abdus Samad in Ghalib's life.

We also don't know exactly when Ghalib took up permanent residence in Delhi. It appears, from a letter that Ghalib wrote to

Munshi Shiv Narain Aram, dated 19 October 1858, that he lived in Agra till he was at least twenty years old:

> When I was a youth [*javan*], I observed Munshi Bansidhar [Shiv Narain Aram's grandfather] with Khan Sahib [Ghalib's maternal grandfather, Kamidan Ghulam Husain Khan]. Munshi Bansidhar was Khan Sahib's petitioner in the claim he had filed with the government for possession of his lands in Kathim village. He was a lawyer who dealt in such cases. He and I were the same age. Perhaps Bansidhar was a year or two older or younger. I was nineteen or twenty; he must have been the same age. We played chess and spent time together, staying up way past midnight. Because his house was not far, he could leave whenever he wanted. Between his place and ours was Machhiyarah, the prostitute's house, with our two plazas in between. On one of the terraces of this plaza, I used to fly kites. Raja Balvan Singh and I used to have kite-fights.[27]

According to this letter, it seems that Ghalib was still living in Agra in his grandfather's home when he was nineteen, and that his grandfather was alive.[28]

Kamal Ahmad Siddiqi takes this letter as concrete proof of Ghalib's age and surmises that he was not married then. He believes that Ghalib was around twenty-four years old at the time of his marriage. Siddiqi provocatively concludes that Ghalib was born between 1784 and 1790.[29] He draws attention to another important document that can help us determine Ghalib's age. It is an affidavit written in Ghalib's hand on behalf of his mother. The document, dated 1804, is preserved in the Maulana Azad Library at Aligarh Muslim University. If Ghalib had been born in 1797, he would have been six years old in 1804. It is hard to believe that a six-year-old child could have written that document, or that it would have been considered valid. Malik Ram contests the date of this document.

He suggests that the correct date for the document is 1840.[30] The document is extremely important because from it we learn of Ghalib's mother's name for the first time, and the fact that the two mansions she owned were mortgaged to Khudadad Khan and Validad Khan as collateral for loans. Ghalib would have inherited these properties after the debts were cleared. According to Malik Ram, the contents of this affidavit leave no doubt that a mature Ghalib drafted the document on behalf of his mother, and that she was alive in 1840.

Siddiqi is more convincing when he argues that it is difficult to believe that a twelve-year-old poet could be included in a tazkirah. The *Tazkirah-e Sarvar* has a fairly long entry on Ghalib, listed under 'Asad', which was his pen name in the early period. This voluminous tazkirah contains entries on 1200 Urdu poets. Sarvar began his tazkirah in 1216/1799 and the last amendments or updates were completed by 1224/1809. Ghalib would have been two years old when Sarvar started the tazkirah, and twelve at the time of completion. Siddiqi could be overreacting when he says that the verses presented in the tazkirah are too polished to attribute to a twelve-year old, but he certainly makes a good argument that Sarvar's description of Ghalib doesn't fit that of a twelve-year-old youth:

> Asad, *takhallus* Asadullah Khan, *urf* Mirza Naushah, originally from Samarqand, was born and lives in Akbarabad [Agra]. He is an accomplished young man [*javan-e qabil*], friend-loving, kind-hearted, and always having lived in luxury. The disposition to write Rekhtah is in his heart. He has been instructed in romantic love [*ishq-e majaz*]. In the art of poetry, he is indebted to the style of Mirza Abdul Qadir Bedil (may God bless him). He writes Rekhtah with a lot of Persian idioms. In a way, his style is unique. This writer knows him. Our friendship [with this writer] is established. His verses are often in difficult, and/or sophisticated meters. Composing in the *khiyal band* style is dear to his heart.[31]

Khwaja Ahmad Faruqi, editor of *Tazkirah-e Sarvar*, notes that our information about Ghalib's life in Agra is very limited and scattered over many sources. It appears that his life in Agra was luxurious; however, his move to Delhi was financially challenging. As per the information in his letters, he could have moved to Delhi any time between 1811 and 1816.[32] Faruqi also alludes to Munshi Shiv Narain Aram's letter (quoted above), which mentions Ghalib's kite-flying matches with Raja Balvan Singh. Balvan Singh had moved to Agra in 1812. Faruqi concludes that Ghalib must not have left Agra before 1814.[33] He also makes the point that the references to Ghalib's lifestyle, and the examples of poetry quoted in the *Tazkirah-e Sarvar*, are from the Agra period. It must be noted that Sarvar does not mention that Ghalib lived in Delhi. Faruqi remarks that Maulvi Karimuddin's tazkirah, *Tabaqat-e Shu'ara-e Hind* (1847), mentions Ghalib's location as follows: 'At first he [Ghalib] lived in Agra, but now, since 1250/1834, he lives in Shajahanabad.'[34] Maulvi Karimuddin gives a wider leeway to Ghalib establishing a permanent home in Delhi. This further strengthens the argument that Ghalib lived in Agra at least till he was nineteen. Other contemporary tazkirahs, such as Khub Chand Zaka's *Ayar ul-Shu'ara*, Mustafa Khan Sheftah's *Gulshan-e Bekhar* and Batin's *Gulshan-e Bekhizan*, do not provide dates or details of Ghalib's move from Agra to Delhi. We can thus conclude that if Ghalib was born in 1797, his permanent move to Delhi happened around 1818, at the age of twenty-one. But if Ghalib was born in 1784, as Kamal Ahmad Siddiqi wants us to believe, he moved to Delhi when he was in his thirties. Siddiqi's assumptions do not match with the dates of Ghalib's later life and are therefore not convincing.

As is the case with everything else related to Ghalib's age, there are many contradictory and imprecise references with regard to how old Ghalib was when he started writing poetry. Depending on his allusions, or what we accept to be his date of birth, he could have begun to write any time between the ages of ten and sixteen. In his letters, Ghalib made whimsical, offhand remarks about his age at the time he began to write poetry. Sometimes he says he was twelve, even ten, and at other times, fifteen. For example, he wrote on one occasion: 'I was twelve when I began to blacken paper with poetry and prose like a testament of my deeds.'[35] On another occasion, he wrote: 'I was fifteen when I began writing poetry. For sixty years, I chattered. I received no reward for my odes, nor praise for my ghazals.'[36]

After sifting through the references to Ghalib's date of birth, we can conclude that he was born in the 1790s, most likely a couple of years earlier than the putative date of 1797.

Ghalib's Genealogy

One of Ghalib's favourite topics was his genealogy, which he traced to the ancient kings of Persia. To begin with, there is a seemingly playful poetic argument, the major premise of which is a matter-of-fact claim that he was a descendant of Pashang and Afrasiyab and, through them, the legendary Jamshed, who is said to have been the inventor of wine in Iran.[37] The illustrious Afrasiyab and Pashang are not historical figures but epic heroes belonging to the borderland between Iranian mythology and prehistory. Perhaps Ghalib did not know this. We don't know if he had heard about his ancestry from his elders as a family tradition, or had invented it to suit his poetic ambitions. To be a descendant of Jamshed, the inventor and owner of the world-reflecting wine cup, which is one of the archetypal symbols of Persian and Urdu poetry, signifying an all-comprehending intellect, is a cause for great pride. Certainly, modesty regarding one's ancestry was not a virtue practised in Ghalib's social circles.

'I am of Turkish origin,' he asserted more baldly in a letter to his dear friend Maulvi Sirajuddin, 'and my ancestry goes back to Afrasiyab and Pashang. My forefathers, because of [their] blood relationship with the Saljuqis, carried aloft the standard of rulership and military leadership during their time. When the fortunes of their patrons declined, some of them took to the highway and others to agriculture. My branch of the family settled at Samarqand in Turan.'[38] No matter who Ghalib's ancestors were in hoary antiquity, it is important that Ghalib believed in them, for, as we shall see, his fascination with the *Dasatir* must have had its roots in his wish to be connected organically to the Persian language.[39]

A more practical description of ancestry and birth is available in Ghalib's own hand, produced for inclusion in a tazkirah, *Mazhar ul-Aja'ib,* to be compiled by an Englishman named Rattigan, which was never published.[40] Although Rattigan's tazkirah has not been found, we do have copies of Ghalib's original handwritten introductory note about himself.[41] The note, written in the third person, was for Rattigan. In this note, Ghalib mentions his paternal grandfather, Quqan Beg, for the first time. The note is useful for our purpose of tracking Ghalib's date of birth. It is interesting that he mentions his date of birth, but it is added in the margin, almost as an afterthought:

> *Sal-e viladat, 8 Rajab, 1212 hijri, yak shambah*
> [Year of birth, 8 Rajab, 1212 hijri, Sunday]

Asadullah Khan, alias Mirza Naushah, is the nom de plume of Ghalib, Seljuqi Turk, the descendant of Sultan Barkiyaruk. His grandfather, Quqan Beg Khan, came to Delhi from Samarqand during the reign of Shah Alam and entered the emperor's service as a commander of fifty horses, with a personal kettledrum and standard. The *pargana* (group of villages constituting a unit) of Pahasu, which was granted by the government to the Begam of Sumro, was given to him as his personal estate. Asadullah Khan's father, Abdullah Beg Khan, left his estate in Delhi and migrated to Akbarabad, where Asadullah Khan was born. Abdullah Beg Khan then took to service under Rao Raja Bakhtawar Singh of Alwar and was killed fighting in a battle when Asadullah Khan was only five or six years old. Asadullah Khan's paternal uncle, Nasrullah Beg Khan, was at that time the *subahdar* of Akbarabad, under the Marathas. When, in 1803, General Lake attacked Akbarabad, Nasrullah Khan voluntarily surrendered the city to him. As reward for this, the general appointed him a brigadier of over 400 horses, on a salary of Rs 1700. Later, when Nasrullah Khan wrested the parganas of Sonk and Sonra from Holkar's cavalry, the general granted the lands to him in perpetuity. But Nasrullah Khan was killed after falling off the back of an elephant ten months later. His estate was taken back by the government, and in lieu thereof an annual pension was awarded to his heirs, of which Asadullah Khan got Rs 750 a year.

As mentioned at the beginning of this chapter, the inconsistencies surrounding Ghalib's early years are many, and so diverse, that it is tedious to track, assimilate and infer conclusively from the material gathered. Although Siddiqi and Naqvi Sahib have compiled a plethora of references, they haven't reached a firm conclusion as to what Ghalib's year of birth was. Naqvi is inclined to think that it could be between 1790 and 1793. He thinks a safe bet would be that Ghalib reduced his age by four years, that he was born in 1208/1793. Siddiqi wants to push the date further back, to 1786.

Ghulam Rasul Mehr, in a series of articles written through the 1950s and 1960s, questioned the inaccuracies, missing information and erroneous assumptions about Ghalib's familial ties. In *Ahval-e Ghalib ki Gumshudah Kariyan* (The Lost Links in Ghalib's Biography), Mehr queries the authenticity of Ghalib's paternal grandfather Quqan Beg's employment at the Mughal emperor Shah Alam's court. If Quqan Beg was employed in Delhi as the commander of fifty horsemen, with the revenue from the estate of Pahasu in Bulandshahr as his salary, why did he move to Agra? Why did Khwaja Ghulam Husain Khan Kamidan agree to marry his daughter into a relatively unknown, lower-ranked family? In 'Mirza Ghalib ki Validah Majidah' (Ghalib's Honourable Mother), a chapter in the book mentioned above, Mehr wonders why we know so little about

Ghalib's other aunts and uncles. Apparently, his father had three sisters and three brothers. Ghalib, however, only mentions his uncle, Nasrullah Beg Khan, who became his guardian after his father's death. Incidentally, Ghalib's paternal grandmother and three aunts were among Nasrullah Beg's dependents and received a share of the pension settled for his dependents. Ghalib's mother, Izzatun Nisa Begam, continued to live in Agra after he moved to Delhi; she was alive until 1824. She must have supported Ghalib, because she would have inherited considerable wealth from her father. Mehr criticizes Ghalib for not writing about his mother's death, especially when he mentions the loss of other close relatives. In a letter to Munshi Nabi Bakhsh, dated 20 December 1853, Ghalib wrote:[42]

> On Tuesday evening, 18th of Rabi ul-avval, my paternal aunt [*phuphi*], whom I loved as a mother, and who loved me as a son, passed away. You should understand that with her death, it is as if nine people have died: three aunts, three uncles, a father, a grandmother, and a grandfather. When she was living, I felt all these nine were living too. With her death, I feel that all nine have died at once.

Mehr concludes that either Ghalib's mother was still alive, or he was only recounting the deaths of his paternal relatives. I think the latter is probably true. (Ghalib had taken full responsibility for the care of Mirza Yusuf, his younger brother, who had suffered from mental illness since the age of thirty. Ghalib mentions him often in his correspondence from Calcutta. Had Ghalib's mother been alive, she would surely have helped with Mirza Yusuf's care.)

Navab Ilahi Bakhsh Khan: Ghalib's Father-in-Law

Ghalib's marriage connected him to a powerful family, but the influence and wealth of his in-laws was a perpetual reminder of his own struggle to maintain a lifestyle that was beyond his means. Ghalib's relationship with his father-in law, Navab Ilahi Bakhsh Khan Ma'ruf, is another neglected area of his biography. Ma'ruf died in 1243/1826; Ghalib is buried close to his grave in the vicinity of Hazrat Nizamuddin.

Navab Ilahi Bakhsh Ma'ruf was a well-known poet with two divans.[43] The younger brother of the wealthy and influential Navab Ahmad Bakhsh Khan, he was not interested in politics or administering the family estate. He was a learned man, well-schooled in the contemporary arts. Khub Chand Zaka, in his tazkirah *Ayar ul-Shu'ara* devotes several pages to describing Ma'ruf's accomplishments.[44] Zaka remarks that Ma'ruf was inclined towards Sufism. Sarvar's tazkirah mentions that he was proficient in the military arts. Muhammad Husain Azad writes at length about him in *Ab-e Hayat,* but mostly from the point of view of Zauq, Azad's ideal, who was at the time a rising young poet.[45] Azad writes that Ma'ruf had shown his work to many ustads but, hearing of Zauq's talent, wanted to get suggestions for improvement from him as well. According to Azad, Ma'ruf's divan was heavily corrected by Zauq:[46]

> Navab Ma'ruf, because of weaknesses from old age, could not make the effort to fit a theme [*mazmun*] into the right words and meter. But he recognized the finer points of composing. At this stage, the venerable ustad [Zauq] would work with the Navab's themes in every detail just as he wanted. The venerable ustad used to say, 'Although I had to struggle a lot with the challenges of perfecting [the Navab's] ghazals, in the process, I became perfect.'

Muhammad Ayyub Qadri has published a collection of Ma'ruf's ghazals that were not included in the latter's published divan. He also argues that Azad's claims of Zauq rewriting Navab Ma'ruf's ghazals are exaggerated.[47] Ma'ruf's ghazals are very lively (*shokh*) and the themes similar to the style (*tarz*) of contemporaries like Momin Khan Momin, Shah Nasir and others:

دل بیتاب کی میرے نہ رکھو آس مٹھی میں
یہ جگنو ہے چمک دامن میں اس کی باندھ کر رکھو
[Don't hold my restless heart's longing in your fist
It's a firefly, hold its glimmer in your garment's skirt]

جو چاہو مہر و مے کو چاندنی میں دیکھئے یک جا
تو پیارے یہ طلسم آ کر شب اپنی بام پر دیکھو
[If you want to see love and wine together in the moonlight
Come to your terrace at night, my dear, and see this magic]

It is disappointing that we don't have much from Ghalib about his father-in-law, the poet, because it would have been so interesting to learn about their interactions.[48] Hali tells us that on one occasion, Navab Ilahi Bakhsh tried to spark Ghalib's interest in Sufi practices. The navab used to host gatherings of young aspirants whom he would initiate into the practical aspects of Sufism. He asked Ghalib to join the assembly and, in order to involve him in the project, entrusted him with the task of making a fair copy of the succession list of Sufis of the order. According to Altaf Husain Hali, Mirza Ghalib readily agreed to do so, but the list was long and Mirza was in a rush. When Navab Ilahi Bakhsh got the fair copy, he was astonished to see that the list seemed considerably shortened. Ghalib had skipped alternating names on the list. When he asked Mirza about the missing names, pat came the reply that to list all the names would be as good as constructing a ladder to the heavens, but that if a person had strong aspirations he could climb the ladder quickly by placing his feet on alternate rungs! Hali reports that this was the end of Navab Ilahi Bakhsh's attempt to draw his young son-in-law towards Sufism.

There is one reference from Ghalib in a letter dated 27 July 1862, written to Navab Alauddin Ahmad Khan Alai, his wife's nephew, who was also his pupil, that Navab Ilahi Bakhsh Khan Ma'ruf had created a new 'ground' (zamin), or metrical arrangement, and asked Ghalib to compose in it as well:[49]

Fifty years ago, the late Navab Ilahi Bakhsh Khan, may God have mercy on his soul, came up with a good zamin for a ghazal. At his imperative wish, I wrote one in it, the worthiest verse being:

پلا دے اوک سے صاقی جو منہ سے نفرت ہے
پیالہ گر نہیں دیتا نہ دے شراب تو دے
[If you find me [my face] odious, pour the drink in my cupped palms
If you don't give me a cup, don't give it—but give me the wine.]

The final verse in this ghazal goes like this:

اسد خوشی سے میرے ہاتھ پائوں پھول گَئے
کہا جو اسنے ذرا میرے پائوں داب تو دے
[Asad my hands and feet swelled with happiness,
When she said, 'Just press my feet a bit.']

According to the date mentioned in the letter, this ghazal was written around 1812, when Ghalib was fairly young. It is always noteworthy when Ghalib points to a favourite verse from a ghazal. This ghazal in particular is outstanding for its edgy rakishness, a quality that one can see in Navab Ilahi Bakhsh's poetry as well. It would have been interesting to compare Navab Ilahi Bakhsh's ghazal in this zamin, but I couldn't locate it. Nonetheless, from the snippets above, we do get a sense that Ghalib and his father-in-law surely exchanged notes on the composition of poetry.

Burhan-e Qati and *Qati-e Burhan*: The 'Cutting' Argument and the 'Cutter' of the Argument

Ghalib did not mention his alleged tutor, Abdus Samad, until late in his life—that too at a time when he was writing a retaliatory, critical review of a prominent Persian dictionary compiled by an

Indian author.[50] In the agonizing months after the Revolt of 1857, Ghalib was virtually confined to his house with (according to him) two books: a Persian dictionary called *Burhan-e Qati* and a copy of the *Dasatir*. During this period of isolation, when all his friends had either been driven away from Delhi or killed on suspicion of abetting the uprising, Ghalib was allowed to remain in his house in Ballimaran under the protection of the Raja of Patiala. Since he had a lot of time on his hands, he decided to compose an account of the rebellion, which was later published as *Dastanbuy*. To make the prose of his narrative more interesting and special, he decided to avoid using Arabic words. He not only took inordinate pride in his command of Persian but also had a low opinion of Indian-born Persian writers. He was also fascinated with pre-Islamic Persian and enjoyed digging up obscure idioms and unfamiliar words, which he would then employ with relish in his writing.

In addition to his narrative of the rebellion, he decided also to write an exposé of the errors in the dictionary that he had on hand, the monumental *Burhan-e Qati*.

Muhammad Husain Burhan ibn Khalf Tabrezi had completed *Burhan-e Qati* in 1062/1652. It had entries for 22,322 words. Ghalib's objections were limited to just 284 words, but he claimed in his preface that these were only a sample of the larger picture. In the concluding pages of his critique, which he called the *Qati-e Burhan*, Ghalib proclaimed for the first time that he had been taught the finer, intuitive usages of Persian by Abdus Samad:

> What I am saying is not my dictum, but the mandate of my ustad. The gentleman [*shat*] named Hurmuzd was a Zoroastrian descended from the Sasanids of Persia; Hurmuzd was the given name of this learned man. After acquiring knowledge and wisdom to his utmost satisfaction he accepted Islam. He chose Abdus Samad as his name. In 1226 hijri, he came to India as a tourist. He came to Akbarabad [Agra], where I was born and brought up,

> and he stayed at my lowly house for two years. I have learned the principles of 'elaboration of meaning' [*ma'ni afirini*] and 'uniqueness of God' [*yaganah bini*] from him. May his being be praised [*afirin*] and his soul prosperous [*abad*]. In this regard, it is relevant to point out that in the Pahlavi language abad, among other meanings, also means afirin. 'Shat' is synonymous with *hazrat*.

In a long letter, in fact a pamphlet, to Mirza Rahim Beg, the author of *Sati-e Burhan*, dated August 1865, Ghalib denigrated Indians who wrote Persian dictionaries, again invoking his ustad:[51]

> There are some very good poets who write beautiful and complicated verses, but which fool would say that these people could claim to write assertive language [*da'vi*]? As for those who write dictionaries, God save us from them . . . all these dictionaries and their writers, the books and the writers together are like an onion, layer upon layer, doubt upon doubt and guesses upon guesses . . . If someone were to say, 'Ghalib, you too, were born in Hindustan,' I would reply that this humble one was born in Hindustan, but his tongue is Persian . . . Expertise in Persian has been my power since eternity; this is a gift from God. Proficiency in Persian has been given to me by God, perfection I learnt through practice with my ustad.

In another letter to the Navab of Rampur, Ghalib reiterated his love for Persian—how he wanted to know the language beyond the level of dictionaries, and how this wish was fulfilled by a tutor from Iran:[52]

> I was naturally attached to the Persian language. I wanted a source better than dictionaries. My wish was granted. A gentleman from among the elite of Iran came here to Akbarabad and stayed at this humble person's home for two years. I learnt the realities and

subtleties of the Persian language from him. Now I feel satisfied in this regard.

Beyond Ghalib's vehement claims that he learned the finer points of Persian from a tutor, who was for all practical purposes non-existent until he decided to name him, let us examine the intensity of his penchant for Persian in detail.

The *Qati-e Burhan* affair ostensibly began as an academic or literary debate but quickly deteriorated into the flinging of insults and the hurling of derogatory epithets. Finally, the matter was dragged into court. Ghalib had offered a scintillating display of his intimate, organic closeness with Persian in the book, but the scathing, demeaning and offensive tone he adopted while discussing the lexical items went beyond a critique of the dictionary itself, to become more like an attack on the compiler of the dictionary. According to Naiyar Mas'ud, it was Ghalib who decided the nature of this fight. Ghalib's piercing, demeaning manner of writing evoked similar responses among his adversaries.[53]

Hali tries to paper over this glaring breach of etiquette on Ghalib's part by saying that even if he had not used such offensive language, his critique of widely respected scholars would have drawn sharp rebuttals. This is a moot point. Most of the objections arose not on substantive grounds, but because Ghalib used such harsh language to attack Indian-born Persian scholars.

In short, Ghalib's critique of *Burhan-e Qati* drew a lot of retaliatory criticism. It has mostly been seen as a consequence of his fierce pride in his Persian. Almost all scholars agree that Ghalib did not know much about lexicography, and that his command over Arabic was weak. Many have pointed to the connection between the humiliation Ghalib suffered in Calcutta for his Persian usage, at the hands of non-native Persian poets, and his critique of *Burhan-e Qati*. Ghalib's Calcutta experience will be examined in another chapter. Here, I am trying to connect the dots in Ghalib's early biography.

Knowledge of his peculiar circumstances will help us understand his behaviour, especially with regard to the vexed question of his severe editing of his early divan. It is generally believed that Ghalib removed verses that were heavily Persianized and/or inordinately influenced by Mirza Abdul Qadir Bedil, the great seventeenth-century Indian-born Persian poet.[54]

Ghalib's Persianized Urdu

In the history of Persian poetry, the so-called 'Indian style' (*Sabk-e Hindi*) has also been called the Mughal-Safavid style, or the *tazah-goi* movement; the scholarly name for this kind of poetry has evolved over time. The style is generally traced to the sixteenth-century poet Baba Fighani, who was a pupil of Jami. By that period, poetic rules for the ghazal had accumulated into a stock of *mazmuns* (themes) that were developed through 'expansion of meaning' (*ma'ni afirini*). At the Mughal court, the traditional mazmuns were given an extra twist of elegance and profoundness. The flurry of artistic endeavour encouraged poets to experiment with metaphor in order to pack more layers of meaning into a mazmun. The resulting pithiness could be a challenge to unpack for those who were not deeply familiar with the traditional tropes. The tightly woven web of words could obscure meaning and require a lengthy explanation. Ghalib's early poetry often displayed this kind of obscurity; Hali gives some examples. Later critics (notably Khurshidul Islam) have shown the correspondence of Ghalib's early Urdu verses with the mazmuns of eminent Indian-style poets such as Mirza Bedil, Mirza Sahib, Ghani Kashmiri, Shaukat Bukhari, Asir and Nasir Ali.[55]

Why did Ghalib so conspicuously choose this highly Persianized style in his early Urdu poetry? Khurshidul Islam writes that Ghalib was interested in Old Persian history and, in his early years, spent much time studying Persian poetry. He was attracted to the Bedil-inflected

Indian style because he found it to be free-spirited and inward-looking; it sought to transcend worldly ties. His earliest poetry, which is mostly in Urdu and has not been exhaustively studied, is the most replete with imagery and metaphor, influenced by this highly Persianized Indian style.

The Persianized literary system in which Ghalib functioned was circular. It put a lot of weight on the assimilation of earlier poetry through a thorough apprenticeship that involved memorizing the verses of the masters. Classical Persian poetry, as represented by Rumi, Hafiz, Sa'di and Jami, was a part of the education of elite north Indian Muslim men. Initiates in the field of poetry showed their prowess by writing verses on themes that had been used by the masters, but tried to go beyond the earlier verse by bringing in new colour, hyperbole or wit. Urdu poetry's rhetoric and poetics were organically connected to Persian. Traditionally, the archetypal themes of the ghazal were love, wine and beauty. The ghazal had to be musical, or at least rhythmic, since its structure was tied to metre, rhyme and refrain. It was meant to be recited or sung, not read silently in a corner. Pre-modern Urdu literary culture was almost entirely oral in terms of the general communication of poetry, and it largely remained that way well into the twentieth century. As Urdu poetry individuated itself from Persian, it still retained the rules of composition, adornment, and so on, which were its inheritance. The ghazal in the so-called Indian style endeavoured to bring new types of artistic imagery to supplement the time-worn descriptions. These innovations passed from Persian into Urdu and strongly influenced the poetics of the youthful Ghalib.

Shibli Nomani, in his monumental history of Persian poetry, *She'r ul-Ajam*, elaborates on how to distinguish, within this poetic tradition, the features of a good verse. His critical apparatus was further developed by Shamsur Rahman Faruqi in *She'r-e Shor-Angez*.[56] Bringing their ideas together, I have identified six broad categories:

1. Verses with a distinctive poetic idea/thought/theme: The finer points of this category can be described as mazmun afirini, *khiyal bandi*, mazmun *sazi* and ma'ni afirini.
2. Verses in which a poetic example is given or quoted to serve as an argument: *tamsil nigari*.
3. Verses constructed with enhanced wordplay and verbal affinities: *ri'ayat-e lafzi* or *munasibat-e lafzi*.
4. Verses that have many layers of meaning, mostly delicate or fine nuances: *nazuk khiyali*.
5. Verses with a high degree of emotional effect: *shorish*. Also verses that evoke an emotional response in the listener: *kaifiyat*.
6. Verses in which the connection between the two lines that make up the verse is meaningful: *rabt*.

Faruqi's restatement of the poetics of the Urdu (and incidentally Persian) ghazal has explicated generic terminologies in Urdu literary practice that were assumed but never elaborated. Within his work, the ideas underlying apparently amorphous terms like *fasahat*, *balaghat*,[57] mazmun afirini, ma'ni afirini, kafiyat, rabt, and many more, have been fleshed out. Using his conceptualizations, we can examine how innovative Ghalib was compared to his peers and to what extent this might be an attribute of his affinity with the Indian style.

Ghalib's immediate predecessor, the masterful eighteenth-century Urdu poet Mir Taqi Mir (d.1810), experimented with a different style of language, one that was closer to common speech. But he stayed within the ambit of the traditional themes. Mir was versatile. His poetry encompassed a variety of genres and a wide range of emotions. Ghalib, in contrast, devised a literary language that reflected his close reading of the seventeenth-century Indian-style Persian poets and was suited to his abstract thought. It was a language within a language. The temperament of his imagination was different from Mir's. So were his favourite themes. Mir's poetry as a whole had a more emotional effect (shorish). Ghalib showed more wit, of a cerebral and metaphysical kind. He deliberately complicated a theme to make it harder to reach the meaning. Ghalib's mind absorbed and reflected the challenges of his times to a much greater degree than Mir's.

The special feature of the Indian style was the artistic construction of a verse with maximum elaboration. Ghalib, as a young acolyte, followed the tradition of the Indian style and tried to surpass the models before him. Khurshidul Islam, in his pioneering work on Ghalib's early poetry, shows how the young Ghalib instilled new colour into old images and intensified the complexity of already-complicated metaphors. I will conclude this chapter by highlighting the workings of Ghalib's mind in the early phase of his career—that is, up till the time he compiled his first divan in 1816.

Generally speaking, much of his early poetry has not received the attention it deserves, because once Ghalib decided to publish a selection, an *intikhab* (art of selection), from his Urdu verses, the verses he did not include in it came to be deemed unworthy. Now, the original, unpublished manuscript divans have been recovered and are available in published form. It is therefore possible to examine each divan individually, in sequence. The very first divan (1816) gives us a clear idea of the themes and images that Ghalib favoured as a young man. This gives us perhaps the best available sense of what might be called his 'literary apprenticeship'. Among the Persian poets whose tarz Ghalib admired, he felt closest to Mirza Bedil, probably because he was unquestionably the best poet in the group.

Bedil was a Sufi whose vision of the world was contemplative. The general goal of Sufism was attaining union with the divine beloved through self-purification and self-transcendence (*be-khudi*). Sufis went through escalating states of aloofness until they were totally free from the bonds of existence. This inward state of being was at once free and constricted. It was constricted metaphorically because the self was withdrawn to the point that it became a dot in the ocean of existence. Bedil's poetic motifs were extremely pessimistic and bordered on non-acceptance of the world—the world is an illusion, its secret is incomprehensible; the world is transitory, all bonds with it should be terminated; intellect and knowledge are snares that draw us towards desire; the only way to cope with the illusory existence of the world is through the power of imagination.

The young Ghalib was no Sufi, but he was drawn to these themes—perhaps because they appealed to his imagination. The complex ideas and exotic imagery of this poetic world excited his sensibilities. The novelty and vigour of the Indian style induced Ghalib to push the envelope to create imagery that was bizarre, or even surreal. Bedil's ideas find only a partial reflection in Ghalib, but there is an unmistakable affinity with Bedil's favourite themes, such as wandering, constriction, loneliness and terror.

Here is an example from a very early ghazal (1816, one not chosen for the published divan) that exemplifies the youthful Ghalib's inventiveness and love for complexity. A Bedilian, Sufistic theme is taken to another level by the young poet:

رفتار سے شیرازۂ اجزائے قدم باندھ
اے آبلے محمل پئے صحرائے عدم باندھ
[Stitch together the elements of your footprints with your speed;
O blisters, prepare for travel to the desert of non-existence][58]

This is a new, almost-grotesque twist on the long-standing theme of blisters and journeys. The blisters will work like bookbinding thread to string together the footprints, which are never too clear and almost always disappear quickly. The fluid from the blisters will be like the thread that binds the footprints to each other. As the fluid leaks, the blisters will disappear, they will go away into the realm of non-being. Blisters appear suddenly and burst quickly; the speaker warns the blisters to keep pace with the traveller. The poignant *shirazah* (binding thread) of blisters will perhaps hold together the narrative of the journey into non-existence.

Another verse from the same ghazal presents a different facet of the blisters theme but lacks the clarity of the previous one:

> اے جادہ بسر رشتۂ یک ریشہ دویدن
> شیرازۂ صد آبلہ جون سبحہ بہم باندھ
> [O pathway, run a string through my blisters;
> Bind them together, like prayer beads][59]

Because the traveller's feet are blistered and the path is as narrow as a thread, the speaker in the verse urges the path to thread the blisters, such that they become prayer beads.

Could Ghalib's affinity with Bedil's themes have something to do with the misfortunes and adversities that stalked him? Most likely not. One can't avoid being speculative here, even though Ghalib's obvious hero worship of Bedil blazes a trail across his two early divans (1816 and 1821). In my opinion, Ghalib's identification with Persian culture has more to do with his preference for Persian as a creative model. Marxist scholars like Khurshidul Islam and Ralph Russell tend to see Ghalib's poetic rendition of miseries as being inspired by real-life circumstances. In their seminal work, *Ghalib, 1797–1869: Life and Letters*, Russell and Islam draw parallels between the poet's life and his work.[60] Indeed, Ghalib so loved to rail against his misfortune in his letters that his biographers cannot be faulted for reading personal allusions into his poetry. Natalia Prigarina's monograph on Ghalib follows Hali's biographical methodology of weaving poetry into narrative, but she steers clear of over-reading into the connection between life and poetry.[61] Because Ghalib's letters provide such a rich, albeit hyperbolic, resource, it becomes impossible to read them separately from his poetry in trying to reconstruct his life. It should be kept in mind, however, that these letters—almost all of them—come from the latter decades of Ghalib's life and thus don't necessarily shed much light on his youthful self.

In Ghalib's ghazals, the lover often comes across as more wilful and individualistic than the prototype in most other ghazals. I will illustrate this point with just one early verse (1816, not chosen for the published divan) to show Ghalib's scintillating use of language:

> عجز و نیاز سے تو وہ آیا نہ راہ پر
> دامن کو اسکے آج حریفانہ کھینچیَے
> [My humility and submissiveness did not bring her into line,
> Let me today tug at the hem of her garment like an adversary-friend][62]

There is a complete, emotionally nuanced story implied by these two lines. The tone is introspective; the lover seems to be thinking aloud. The lover is individualistic—he has initiative. If the beloved is not moved by his entreaties, his declarations of undying love, he plans to grab her attention by tugging at the hem of her dress like an old friend, or an opponent. The masterly touch of *harifanah khainchiye* (pull or tug like an adversary) in the second line elevates the verse above and beyond the theme of the disappointed lover. 'Harif' is a double-edged word that means both friend and opponent. In the context of this verse, it fits like a glove.

Daman is a stock word in the lexicon of the ghazal, with metaphorical associations similar to a garment's hem. One can seize the hem of someone's garment as a show of humility, or as an implicit threat to detain the person. 'Daman *khainchna*', a literal translation from the Persian 'daman *kashidan*', means 'to seize the hem' in either or both of those senses (submissively or demandingly). By adding 'harifanah' to the act of daman khainchna, Ghalib brings a psychological undercurrent to the exchange. Is the lover upset, or is he no longer a lover but a friend, or even a frenemy? Notice the freshness and directness of *aaj*, 'today', which suggests a change from what has gone before.

My effort throughout this chapter has been to highlight the neglected parts of Ghalib's early biography, in conjunction with his intellectual history. Most of the scholarship on Ghalib—and it is both vast and deep—looks at him and his life in bits and pieces. For example, his Persian work (poetry and prose) is viewed separately from his Urdu work. In Urdu, the current published divan is almost the sole focus of attention, even though Ghalib's earlier poetry, which he did not publish, is available. There is a very small number of studies on the poetry Ghalib chose not to include in his Urdu divan. The name of Gyan Chand Jain stands out in this tiny group of four or five. An exceptional, invaluable effort was made by Kalidas Gupta Raza (1988) who compiled a complete collection of Urdu verses, *Dívan-e Kamíl*, organized chronologically. Raza's work made it easy to study Ghalib's poetry from the very early period till the last phase. Ghalib's large corpus of letters in Urdu and Persian has now been organized by various editors. We are indebted to Khaliq Anjum for the best set, in five volumes, of the Urdu letters.

Ghalib's early Divan of 1821 (generally known as *Nuskhah-e Hamidiyyah*) was found in the Navab of Bhopal's library in 1918. It was published in 1921. It has been nearly a hundred years since its publication, but this divan, which contains as many verses as the published *Dívan-e Ghalib*, has remained a neglected area of scholarship. More manuscript divans were subsequently discovered, creating a dynamic textual history. I will treat each divan as an individual entity, a record of the poet's compositions to that date. The divans show a continuity, and a remarkable editorial progression. Maulana Imtiaz Ali Khan Arshi and Kalidas Gupta Raza's commendable efforts in producing scholarly editions of Ghalib have unfortunately fractured his work into segments, according to their individual visions. Maulana Arshi separated the published (*mutadavíl*) divan from the ones that were not circulated by publication (*ghair mutadavíl*); he published them in the same volume, but his arrangement is hard to follow. Raza Sahib has provided invaluable dating for the compositions, but he has arranged the material according to the date of composition. Again, this arrangement fractures many ghazals.

The next two chapters will offer a closer look at the three most significant early manuscript divans: 1816, 1821 and 1826. We will consider the remarkable stories behind their (re)discovery, the particular features of each and some of the idiosyncrasies of Ghalib's editorial choices. The first two divans can be said to represent Ghalib's earliest oeuvre. After 1828, Ghalib basically switched to writing poetry in Persian and did not return to Urdu until the 1850s.

2

The Divan of 1821 and the Divan of 1826

> In my opinion, Ghalib had the right to remove and discard his own poetry. He retained what he liked and took out what he did not like. But we do not have that right. Until this [1821] manuscript was found, the situation was different . . . How Ghalib must have suffered in cutting off these pieces of his heart. He must have endured so much heartache and misery.
>
> —Mufti Anvarul Haq, editor,
> *Divan-e Ghalib Jadid al ma'ruf bah Nuskhah-e Hamidiyyah*[1]

Ghalib's readers would have been deprived of almost half his poetry if the handwritten manuscripts (nuskhahs) of his earlier divans had not been found. The first among these invaluable manuscripts were discovered in Bhopal (in central India) in 1917, some fifty years after Ghalib's death. It is known as the *Nuskhah-e Bhopal* (Bhopal manuscript) or *Nuskhah-e Hamidiyyah* (Hamidiyyah manuscript). For clarity's sake, I will refer to the different manuscript divans in conformity with their colophon; thus *Nuskhah-e Hamidiyyah* will be referred to as the Divan of 1821. The provenance of this manuscript is convoluted. There are intricate twists involving its journey from Delhi to Bhopal, but more important is the debate surrounding the text itself: the corrections, the notations in the margins, the additions of entire ghazals—not to speak of the assorted materials found both in the first few pages preceding the main text and at the end of the manuscript.

Despite much scholarly discussion, many questions remain unresolved. The discussion was complicated by the disappearance of the manuscript sometime before or during the mayhem of Partition. A somewhat flawed edition had been published in 1921.[2] Subsequent editions have been revisions of the first one, supplemented with notes taken by scholars who had seen the manuscript before it disappeared from the public domain. This situation has recently and unexpectedly changed, as we will see.

The manuscript Divan of 1821 was first discovered in the personal library of Faujdar Muhammad Khan, the youngest maternal uncle of Navab Sikandar Jahan Begam, ruler of the state of Bhopal. Begam Sikandar's twenty-one-year reign (1847–68) was the golden period of Bhopal's history. She presided over a dynamic, reform-oriented regime. Resisting pressure from her advisers, Sikandar Begam had the foresight to side with the British during the Revolt of 1857. Hearing of Ghalib's financial difficulties after 1857, she invited him to take up residence at Bhopal. But Ghalib, despite his woes, was reluctant to leave Delhi. Although he did not accept the offer to visit Bhopal, it seems that the Begam sent him monetary gifts through her uncle Faujdar Muhammad Khan. Salim Hamid Rizvi makes a plausible, though unsubstantiated, claim that Faujdar Muhammad Khan acquired the manuscript from Ghalib on one of these visits:[3]

> She [Navab Begam Sikandar] occasionally sent her uncle, Miyan Faujdar Muhammad Khan, to Ghalib with monetary gifts. The result of these comings and goings was that Ghalib presented Faujdar Muhammad Khan a nuskhah of his original divan that

had been corrected in his own hand. This nuskhah became the jewel of Faujdar Khan's library.

Faujdar Muhammad Khan (d.1865) was a learned nobleman—a polymath who took an interest in literature, grammar, prosody, music, logic, Islamic law, mathematics, Unani and geography. He was an avid collector of books.[4] We also know that Faujdar Muhammad Khan was an admirer of Ghalib's work, which is why it is not surprising that such a manuscript divan should be in his library. Apparently, Ghalib and Faujdar Muhammad Khan corresponded, but no letters have survived to prove this claim.

Faujdar Muhammad Khan's son, Navab Yar Muhammad Khan Shaukat (1823–1913), inherited his father's love of literature. Even as a child, he showed an interest in writing poetry. As soon as he was old enough, Faujdar Muhammad Khan took him to Delhi and requested Ghalib to accept him as a pupil. Ghalib was getting on in years. He accepted the special pupil (*shagird*) with the suggestion that Navab Yar Muhammad Khan also show his compositions to Maulana Muhammad Abbas Raf'at.[5] However, according to Abdul Qavi Dasnavi, Navab Yar Muhammad Khan accompanied not his father but his aunt, Navab Begam Sikandar Jahan, when she travelled to Delhi in 1866 to meet Lord Lake. Navab Yar Muhammad Khan met with Ghalib, who accepted him as a pupil and suggested the pen name Shaukat.[6] Although the navab did not benefit directly from Ghalib's mentoring, he did mature as a poet and came to have a published divan.[7]

The details of the manuscript's acquisition by Faujdar Muhammad Khan have considerable historical and anecdotal interest but are not very necessary for its authentication. The Divan of 1821 bears Faujdar Muhammad Khan's octagonal seal on various pages—at the beginning, at the end and randomly throughout the manuscript. Two different seals appear. The larger of the two seals is more ornate, encircled with a traditional, hand-painted design in indigo, green, red and gold. It bears the date 1261 hijri (approximately 1845) (see image below).

Faujdar Muhammad Khan's ornate seal.

The smaller seal has an earlier date, 1248 hijri (approximately 1832) (see image below).

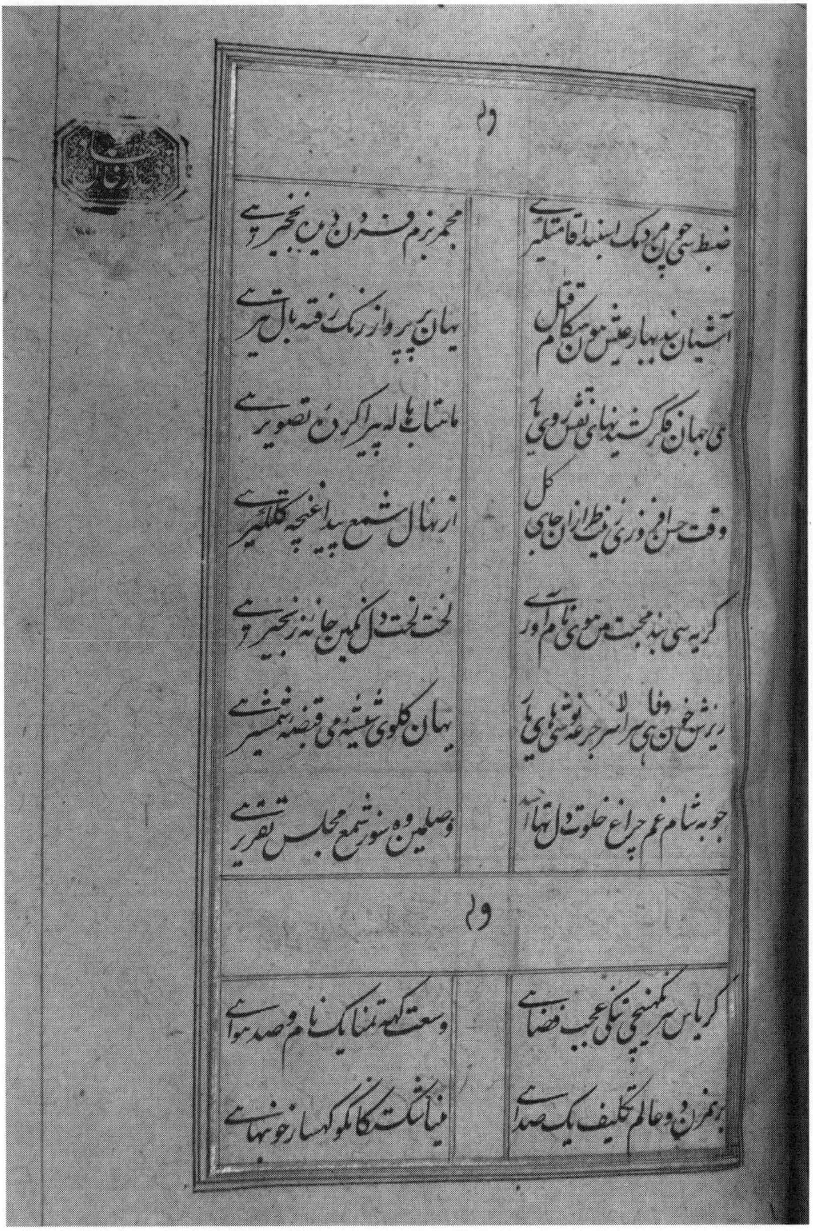

The top-left corner bears Faujdar Muhammad Khan's smaller seal.

Fortunately, the manuscript has an intact colophon giving the date of its completion, 1237 hijri, which corresponds to November 1821. The completion date of 1821 indicates that the manuscript was calligraphed eleven years prior to the library's accession date (1832) on Faujdar Muhammad Khan's seal. The difference in these dates has led to speculations as to where the manuscript was before it reached Faujdar Muhammad Khan's library. Was it with Ghalib or someone else? I will go into these details later in this chapter.

To make things more confusing, as recently as 1969, Bhopal became the site where another earlier, and in some respects more important, manuscript of Ghalib's divan was discovered. This manuscript, apparently in Ghalib's hand, was completed in 1816 when Ghalib was (if we accept the traditional date of his birth) nineteen. Since both manuscripts, the Divan of 1821 and the Divan of 1816, were found in Bhopal, there has been some confusion in discussing the codices. Then, to add to the muddle, both manuscripts, after their initial discovery, disappeared again; fortunately, both resurfaced recently. (Ghalib's bibliographical vicissitudes have proved to be no less extravagant than his ghazals.) The Divan of 1816 will be discussed in the next chapter.

The Divan of 1821, the *Nuskhah-e Hamidiyyah*, is named after Navab Hamidullah Khan who was the secretary of Bhopal in 1918, when the manuscript was found at the Hamidiyyah Library.[8] Its transition from a private to a public library must have made its discovery possible. Navab Hamidullah Khan played an indispensable role in getting it published. At the time, the eminent scholar Abdur Rahman Bijnori had been in the process of compiling an annotated edition of Ghalib's divan for the Anjuman Taraqqi Urdu. He had been collecting numerous editions of the divan to ensure textual accuracy and was on the lookout for rare editions, including manuscripts. Bijnori was alerted that an early divan of Ghalib's had been found at the Hamidiyyah Library in Bhopal. Credit for actually finding the manuscript goes to Maulana Abdus Salam Nadvi.[9] His find was announced in the journal *Ma'arif*, published from Azamgarh in 1918. The discovery of this new manuscript gave an entirely new perspective to Bijnori's ongoing work. He was invited by Maulana Nadvi to undertake the challenging task of editing the newly discovered manuscript. Bijnori had written a stimulating book-length essay entitled *Mahasin-e Kalam-e Ghalib* (Merits of Ghalib's Poetry); it was presumably meant to accompany his forthcoming edition of Ghalib's divan.[10] Unfortunately, Bijnori died in the flu epidemic that swept through India in 1918.[11] He was only thirty-one years at the time; his work on editing the divan had only begun.

But Bijnori would have been happy to know the fate of his long introductory essay. His account of the merits of Ghalib's poetry has become a classic for at least two important reasons. First, it begins with a resounding rhetorical claim, which in one bold stroke puts Ghalib on the same plane as the Vedas. Bijnori wrote:

> India has two divine gospels, the holy Vedas and the *Divan-e Ghalib*. From beginning to end there are barely 100 pages, but what else is there [in this world] that is not present here . . . Poetry is the revelation of existence; just as life is not confined in its appearance, so is poetry unlimited in its expression.[12]

And second, Bijnori peppered his essay with references to Goethe, Kant, Nietzsche, Hegel, Spencer, Rimbaud, Fitzgerald and a host of other European writers. He started a new comparative trend in Urdu critical writing. He demanded that Ghalib's greatness be acknowledged beyond the limits of the Urdu-reading world and claimed that Ghalib's ideas on existence, reality, nature and the endlessness of imagination resonated in Goethe's poetry as well.[13]

Mufti Anvarul Haq's Edition (1921)

With Bijnori's untimely death, the task of introducing and editing the newly found manuscript fell on Mufti Anvarul Haq, the secretary of education for Bhopal state. A scholar of history with a deep interest in science, he wrote notable essays on these subjects. Nonetheless, stepping into Bijnori's shoes was not easy for him. The challenge of editing this complicated manuscript was difficult for a person who was not trained in the field.[14] But he did an exemplary job—one that has not received the recognition it rightfully deserved.

This first-published edition of the Divan of 1821 was entitled *Divan-e Ghalib Jadid, al ma'ruf bah Nuskhah-e Hamidiyyah* (The New Divan-e Ghalib, known as Nuskhah-e Hamidiyyah). The edition has been criticized quite severely, especially for not respecting the integrity of the text. There were also the inevitable errors of copy-editing, which only added to the muddle. Until I saw the edition myself, I went along with the critics and inwardly blamed Mufti Sahib for not attending to the nuances of scholarly editing. On reading his introduction, however, I changed my opinion because Mufti Sahib addresses many questions that are more important than the errors of copy-editing. He also provides a concordance chart that clarifies the ratio between omitted and selected verses. One of the pressing exegetical questions that Anvarul Haq brought up was: What is to be gained by publishing Ghalib's early efforts?[15] Apparently, there was quite a bit of resistance to publishing the poetry that Ghalib had decided not to publish. Haq mentions that one gentleman was so incensed that he referred to the unpublished verses as *muhmilat-e Ghalib* (meaningless verses of Ghalib).[16] To his credit, Haq argued soundly in favour of publishing this newly discovered poetry; in his view, bringing out the early verses showed the evolution of Ghalib's poetic thought and technique. It also highlighted the process of revision and correction that is evident throughout the manuscript—a step-by-step way of perfecting a verse.[17] He reinforced his own arguments by quoting Hali's estimation of the early verses:[18]

> One can call Mirza's early poetry meaningless and absurd, and keep it out of the circulation of Urdu literature; but there can be no

> doubt that one finds in them the precise pointers to his originality and extraordinary creativity. These very convoluted and oblique ways of thinking affirm his lofty, innate, extraordinary intelligence and capabilities.

Hali further argues that although Ghalib omitted many verses that were obscure when he made a selection for the purposes of publishing, his published divan still has many obscure verses, because the process of discarding or rejecting one's poetry must be a painful one:[19]

> There is no doubt that Mirza must have created those verses by squeezing his very life and heart into them. When people like us are saddened at discarding our ordinary verses, then Mirza's heart must have ached in removing or forsaking so much of his poetry.

Mufti Anvarul Haq's introduction is brimming with intelligent, definitive arguments in defence of publishing Ghalib's early work:[20]

> In my opinion, Ghalib had the right to remove and discard his own poetry. He retained what he liked and took out what he did not like. But we do not have that right.

Haq's position on the disputed subject of how the manuscript reached the library of Faujdar Muhammad Khan is quite straightforward, though unsubstantiated. He believes that the manuscript was prepared for the nobleman himself; it was sent back to Mirza Ghalib from time to time for additions. According to Haq, the revisions of text and the writing in the margins are in Ghalib's hand, because who else could have had the temerity to alter the poetry but the poet himself? He suggests that the manuscript was sent to Ghalib on more than one occasion for additions and corrections. However, Anvarul Haq does not address the issue of the other, distinct handwriting(s) that can be seen in several places throughout the manuscript. If we accept Haq's suggestion that the manuscript was prepared for Faujdar Muhammad Khan, and was sent to Ghalib for updating, this still does not explain why the manuscript bears the Faujdar's seal of 1832. Haq does not explain why the manuscript, which was completed in 1821, bears the Faujdar's seals from later years (1832 and 1848).

Haq made an important but highly controversial editorial choice in presenting the Divan of 1821. He decided to insert the verses from Ghalib's published divan into the manuscript, and also to follow the ordering by refrain (*radif*), which is the standard practice in arranging a divan. In other words, he produced what could be called a complete, 'unedited' divan. He demarcated the verses in the published divan from the newly found ones by putting the letter *mim* for *muravvaj* ('customary, prevalent'—that is, from the published divan) in between the two lines of a verse. Where there were revisions, he provided footnotes and supplied the alternate line that differed from the standard version. If there was more than one version of a line, then multiple versions were provided.

As mentioned earlier, one of the characteristics of the Divan of 1821 was the addition of entire ghazals in the margins. Anvarul Haq's edition ignored the boundaries between the actual text and the verses in the margins, incorporating them together into the main body, thus obscuring the historical sequence of the compositions. A useful feature of his edition was a concordance chart provided in the introduction. Looking at this chart, one gets a quick overview of how much Ghalib omitted and what he included in his published divan.[21]

Haq paid tribute to Bijnori's contribution by including *Mahasin-e Kalam-e Ghalib* as the *muqaddamah*, or critical introduction, to this new version of the divan. A hardbound and a softcover edition were produced. Anvarul Haq's edition has various printed versions, a number of them undated. But the first lot published in 1921 did not have Bijnori's lengthy essay; that edition had a different cover. The essay was added to another printing, probably in 1922. The enlarged edition was priced higher.[22]

In his eloquent foreword to Bijnori's muqaddamah, Anvarul Haq described how much he wanted to acknowledge Bijnori's great work and how hard it was to collect the pieces of the essay.[23] His note on Bijnori's essay lends a unique personal slant to this pioneering work.

Abdul Latif Hyderabadi's Incomplete Edition (1928)

Among the few scholars who saw the Divan of 1821 soon after its discovery were Saiyyid Hashmi and Abdul Latif. Hashmi went to Bhopal to view the manuscript on behalf of the Anjuman Taraqqi Urdu.[24] Latif wanted to prepare a historically sequenced edition of Ghalib's divan. Unfortunately, almost all of his work was destroyed in a calamity during the publication process. Only a small portion of the proofs survived.[25] Here is his description of the manuscript when he first saw it in 1928:[26]

> The binding is so worn out that the pages can be easily pulled apart. The text itself is 75 pages; each page 7x11 1/2 inches. On both ends are affixed four pages of the same paper as the main text. The paper seems to be hand-made, of Hindustani manufacture. In addition to the four pages affixed on both sides, there are two pages of English paper on either side. In the beginning of the manuscript these pages are wedged between page numbers three and four. At the end they are between page numbers two and three. The text on each page has 10–11 verses [*abyat*] written in clear *nastaliq* script in Chinese ink. First, there are four qasidahs; the ghazals total 276. At the end there are 11 *rubais*. There are separate, ornate plates [*lauh*] to mark the beginning of the qasidah and ghazal sections. These are embellished in blue lapis and gold work. The full text is enclosed within gold margins.

After the sad loss of his work, Latif did not attempt to bring out another edition. However, he did write several essays on the unique characteristics and peculiarities of the manuscript, especially the notations in the margins.[27]

Hamid Ahmad Khan's Edition (1969)

Mufti Anvarul Haq's edition produced a lot of interest and curiosity about the Divan of 1821. But since his edition merged the new poetry found in the manuscript with the standard, published as *Divan-e Ghalib*, it disrupted the format and sequence of both the manuscript and the published divan. Some scholars who wanted to see the manuscript in its original form travelled to Bhopal especially for this purpose. Maulana Arshi and Hamid Ahmad Khan, on separate occasions, viewed the manuscript and took notes. Khan went to Bhopal in 1938.[28] He examined the manuscript, particularly the ghazals in the margins, because they had obviously been added after the manuscript had been calligraphed. He concluded that the ghazals in the margins were composed after 1821. The importance of dating the ghazals had been overlooked by Haq. Khan made sure that the additions were demarcated. He observed that the handwriting in the margins could be classified as follows:

1. Written in a clear, legible hand (*khushkhat*) with a fine nib.
2. Written in *shikastah* with a broad nib.[29]
3. Written in shikastah with a fine nib. Of the three, the broad-nib shikastah was quite similar to Ghalib's hand, and most likely to be his.

Khan noted that the two blank pages generally attached at the beginning of a bound manuscript, before the text, were covered in bad writing (*bad khat*). Someone had copied Ghalib's letter to Maulvi Muhammad Fazl-e Haq. The letter, originally written in Persian, was an example of dotless composition (*san'at-e ta'til*, the device of composing without the use of dotted letters).[30] It must be noted that neither Abdur Rahman Bijnori, nor Abdul Latif, nor Mufti Anvarul Haq, all of whom had seen the original manuscript, drew attention to this addendum. It is possible that someone scribbled in the manuscript after 1921.

Another feature of the manuscript, not mentioned by either Bijnori or Haq, are the marks of appreciation put against an occasional verse. The first of these happens to be on the second verse of the very first ghazal. In the margin, clearly legible, is the name 'Abdul Ali'. On another page, 'Muhammad Abdus Samad Mazhar' is inscribed in the margin.[31] Hamid Ahmad Khan speculates that these persons could have been associated with Ghalib. Abdul Latif was of the opinion that Abdul Ali had made the notations in the fine, legible hand in the margins. I think it is possible that Abdul Ali and Abdus Samad Mazhar were readers who may have handled the manuscript and left an occasional mark.

Hamid Ahmad Khan questions Anvarul Haq's assumption that the manuscript was prepared for Faujdar Muhammad Khan, that it was sent to Delhi on more than one occasion for additions and corrections. Hamid Ahmad Khan further adds that it is unlikely that the ghazals added in the margins were composed after 1842. According to him, these changes were made between 1821 and 1832. During these eleven years, the manuscript remained with Ghalib. It reached Bhopal with the corrections and additions. Hamid Ahmad Khan also observes that if we compare the Divan of 1821 with the Divan of 1826, it becomes apparent that the ghazals in the margins of the former are incorporated into the main text in the latter. The Divan of 1826 was completed before Ghalib set out for Calcutta. Therefore, the additions to the Divan of 1821 were made before 1826.[32] It may thus be safe to conclude that Ghalib gave away the older manuscript, the Divan of 1821, after another version, the Divan of 1826, was ready. Hamid Ahmad Khan, however, does not offer an opinion about which manuscript Ghalib took with him on his journey to Calcutta.

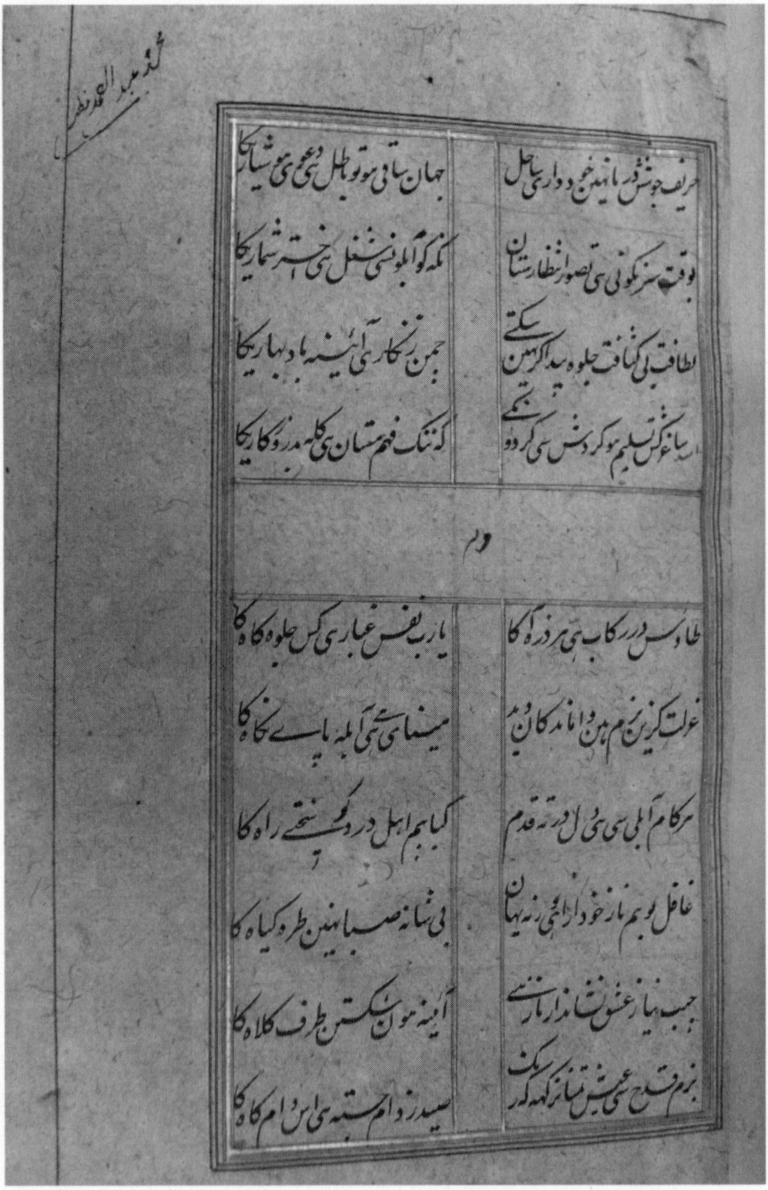

Note the signature of Muhammad Abdus Samad Mazhar on the top left.

Imtiaz Ali Khan Arshi's Incorporation (1958)

On his way back from the all-India Anjuman Taraqqi Urdu Conference in Nagpur in 1944, Maulana Imtiaz Ali Khan Arshi travelled to Bhopal expressly to see the Divan of 1821. He described his impressions in considerable detail.[33] He noted that the dimensions of the manuscript were 8 x 29 x 22 inches, that the paper was a high-quality Kashmiri product. The text was seventy-five-pages long, with eleven lines per page. At the beginning and end were additional blank pages of rough indigenous paper that contained material written after the manuscript was completed. On the first two blank pages was inscribed a copy of a Persian letter of Ghalib's. Then there were two pages of English paper. On the first, inscribed within an ornate medallion, was Faujdar Muhammad Khan's seal. On the second page was the Faujdar's large seal with the date 1261 hijri. On the first page of the actual text were two smaller seals with the date 1248 hijri. On the last page of the text was the colophon with the date 1237 hijri. Below it was Faujdar Muhammad Khan's small seal with the date 1248 hijri. Additions and revisions were scattered throughout the text. These seem to have been done at different times by different people, as is made evident by the clear differences in the ink, nib and handwriting. In some of the corrections, the handwriting resembles Ghalib's; in others it is clearly not his.

Maulana Arshi noted that at the start of some ghazals was inscribed the word *ghalat* (incorrect). In some ghazals, the word's initial letter, *ghain*, was inscribed in such a way that the head of the letter was between the two lines of the opening verse (*matla*), while the body of the letter extended to encompass the full ghazal.[34] These ghazals, he pointed out, were excluded from the Divan of 1826. Some ghazals, meanwhile, had *mukarrar navishtah shud* (rewritten) noted in the margin. These ghazals were among those that had been rearranged by selecting and then merging with them verses from other formally identical (*ham-tarh*) ghazals.

On the blank pages at the end of the manuscript were inscribed ghazals composed at a later date, but all in the refrain of *ye*, the last letter of the alphabet. The handwriting here is, or strongly resembles, the 'bad hand' (bad khat) found in the margins. According to Arshi, this means that these ghazals were added on Ghalib's instructions.[35]

Maulana Arshi admits that he did not count the verses in the manuscript. He observes that Anvarul Haq's tabulation of verses is confusing because we do not know whether he counted the additions at the end of the manuscript. There are other mistakes in Anvarul Haq's tabulation and dating caused by the merging of verses in the margins with the main text.[36] Maulana Arshi's edition, incorporated into his authoritative *Divan-e Ghalib* of 1958, corrects the numeration of verses in the Divan of 1821 with the help of the Divan of 1826 and *Gul-e Ra'na.* He concludes that the corrections in the margins of the Divan of 1821 were done during or after the compilation of the Divan of 1826 and *Gul-e Ra'na* (1828); both these texts will be discussed in later chapters.[37]

Maulana Arshi's was the last recorded description of the Divan of 1821 until very recently—when it was made available to me by Shahab Sattar, who acquired it from a rare-book dealer in London.

The Facsimile Edition (2015)

When I began to research Ghalib's textual history, I wanted to see the original manuscripts and first editions of his published divans. Whenever I presented my research, I always mentioned the loss of the Divan of 1821, which had disappeared from the Hamidiyyah Library in Bhopal, perhaps in the mayhem of 1947. But there were rumours that it was still around somewhere, leading me to hope that it might one day be found. Still, I was amazed to receive an email in 2015 with the subject line 'Nuskhah-e Hamidiyyah'. Shahab Sattar wanted my opinion on a manuscript that was in the art dealers' market, described as the original Divan of 1821. He wanted some authentication before he bought it. I certainly wanted to see the manuscript before giving an opinion. In the course of a visit to the US in May 2015, Sattar visited me in Charlottesville. A week or two later, he sent me convincing digital scans. Eventually, Sattar sent me the manuscript itself to examine, in return for my promise to write an introduction to its facsimile publication.

The Divan of 1821 has had a long, colourful history, the highlights of which I have presented in the preceding pages. There are some unresolved issues that I will attempt to answer. For clarity's sake, I list them here:

1. Where was the Divan of 1821 for the eleven years before it was first registered in the library of Faujdar Muhammad Khan in 1832?
2. Who entered the ghazals noted in the margins? Was it Ghalib?
3. How many different styles of handwriting can be identified in the manuscript?
4. Who copied Ghalib's Persian letter in the san'at-e ta'til to Maulana Fazl-e Haq?
5. Who added the seven ghazals in the refrain of 'ye' in the last pages of the manuscript? Was it Ghalib?
6. The inscription beneath the ghazals on the very last page—دیکھ تو عکسِ قدِ یار لبِ جو پر سے۔ تمام شُد۔ کارِ من نظام شُد۔ ربِ یسر و تمم بالخیر۔ [Look at the reflection of the friend's stature from the ocean's edge. It is complete. My work is done. God is great and the work was finished smoothly]—is in the same hand as the ghazals. The line quoted by the scribe is quite meaningful, especially because these additions are meant to bring comfort or satisfaction (*bahr-e tarvih*).
7. There is a definite process of selection and some deletion going on in this manuscript. Many ghazals are marked as *valahu* (to be carried further).

8. Is it possible that this manuscript was the one that Ghalib brought with him to Calcutta? Did he make the selections for *Gul-e Ra'na*, and for his published divan, from this manuscript?

Note the addition in the margin of two more verses to the ghazal: *naqsh faryadi*. The handwriting is khushkhat.

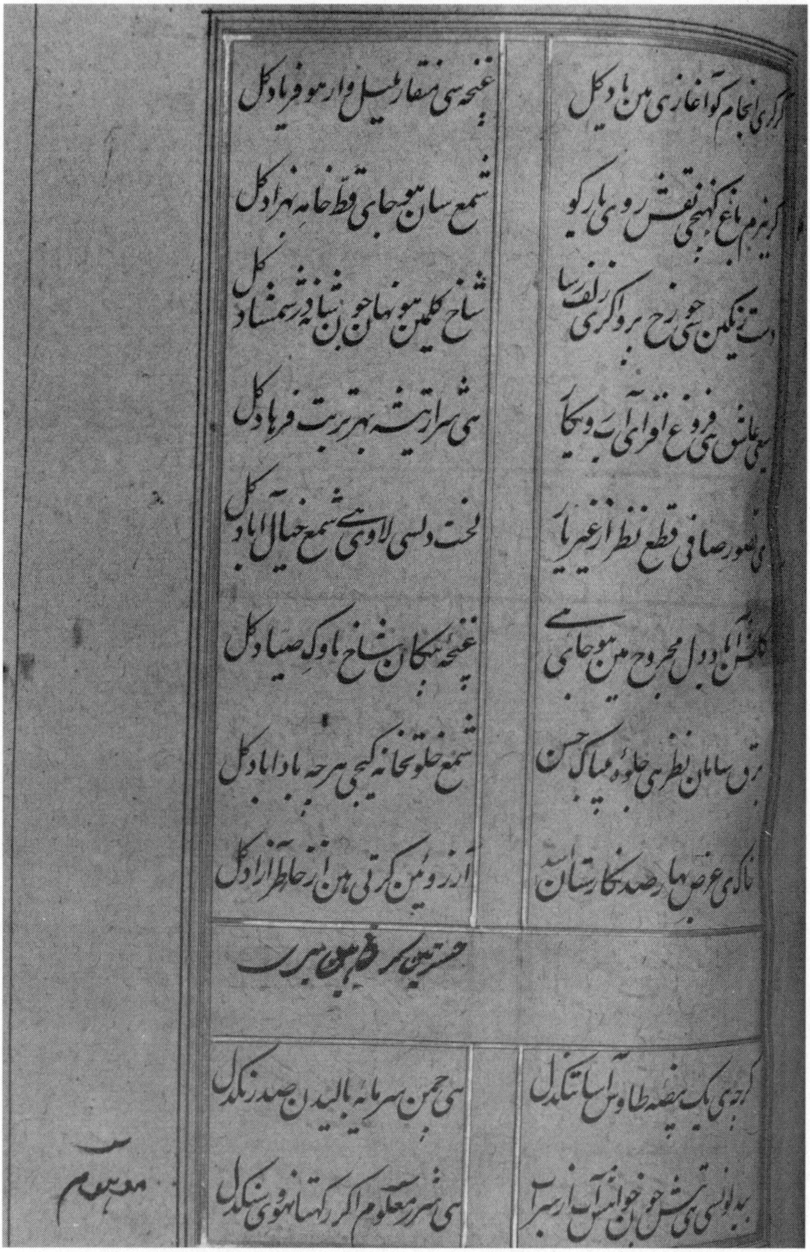

Changes made in Ghalib's hand. He changed *arzu'en* to *hasraten*.

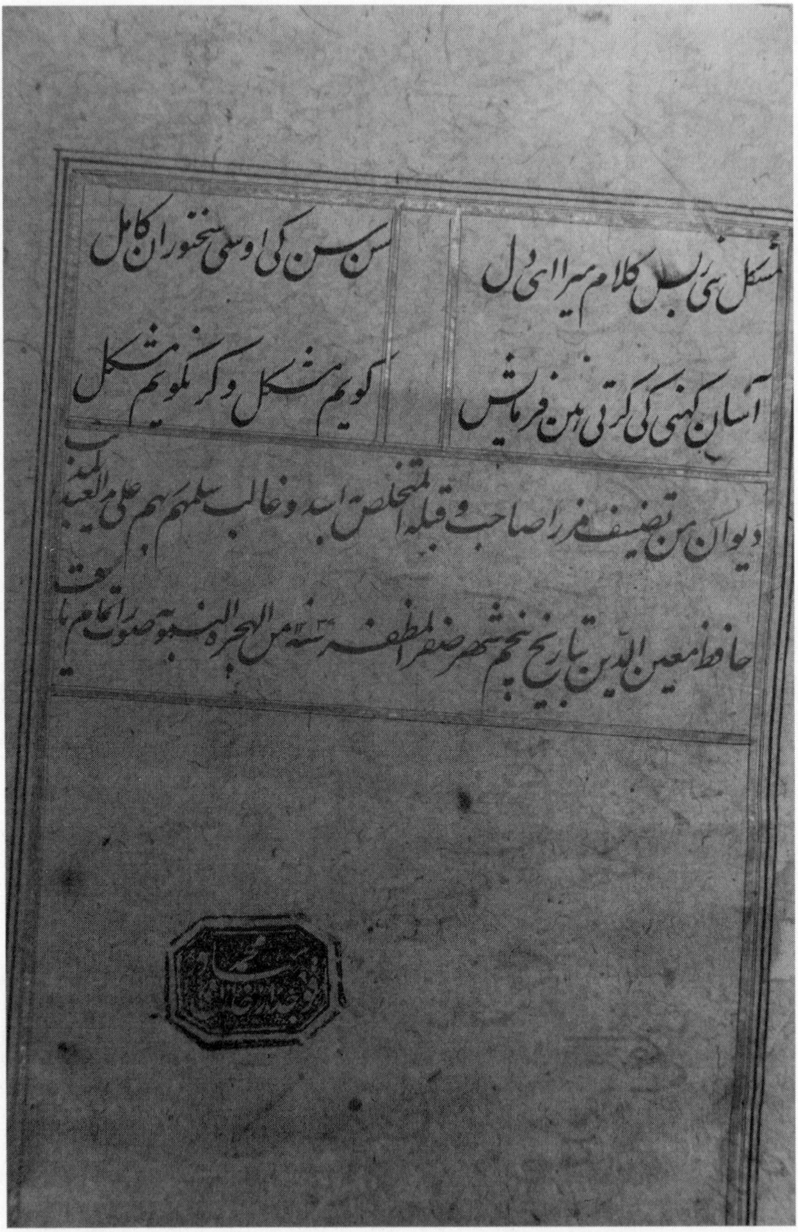

مشکل ہے زبس کلام میرا اے دل — سن سن کے اسے سخنوران کامل

آساں کہنے کی کرتے ہیں فرمائش — گویم مشکل وگر نگویم مشکل

دیوان من تصنیف مرزا صاحب و قبلہ المتخلص اسد و غالب سلمہم ... علی ید العبد

حافظ معین الدین بتاریخ پنجم شہر صفر المظفر سنہ ... من الہجرۃ ...

The last page of the divan. The colophon is inscribed in red ink.

Notable Characteristics of the Divan of 1821

The manuscript has the following arrangement: qasidahs: four, comprising 255 verses; ghazals: 275, comprising 1883 verses; rubais: seven, comprising fourteen verses. Hamid Ahmad Khan's edition (1969) egregiously lists the number of rubais as eleven.[38] The rubais constitute the last verses of this manuscript; they are followed by a colophon in red, which identifies the author, the calligrapher and the exact date of its completion.

The Colophon

The colophon inscribed in red reads:

> Divan of Mirza Sahib, the honourable, known by the pen names Asad and Ghalib, complete and calligraphed by the hand of Hafiz Mu'inuddin, completed on the fifth day of the month of Safar in 1231 hijri [1 November 1821].

The point to note is Ghalib's name. He is mentioned as Mirza Sahib, who is 'known by the pen names of Asad and Ghalib'.

The Qasidah Section

The manuscript has obviously been rebound since it was last seen by Maulana Arshi in a dilapidated condition seventy years ago. The new binding is red leather; all the pages are intact and arranged in proper order.

The text itself is inscribed on burnished, handmade paper that has borne the ravages of time quite well. I found that the two formerly blank pages of the original, somewhat rough, paper at both ends of the manuscript have now been embellished with additions in bad khat shikastah. Two more blank pages of white English paper were added after the manuscript was acquired by Faujdar Muhammad Khan.

On the first formerly blank page, within a somewhat unskilfully drawn gold medallion decorated with indigo floral design, is written:[39]

> This divan, authored by Mirza Naushah Dihlavi, whose pen name is Asad, from the library of the generous, exalted, protector of the world, Miyan Faujdar Muhammad Khan Bahadur, may his worth reach new heights. Calligraphed in the khushkhat style.

The fine quality of the paper, the decorated opening pages, and the delicately executed borders and calligraphy indicate that it was prepared with special care. A novel feature of this manuscript is that it begins with qasidahs. There are four qasidahs in the manqibat (in praise of Hazrat Ali) mode. The first is in Persian—it has also been labelled *fatihah* (prelude)[40]—while the remaining three are in Urdu.

The recovery of the Divan of 1821 has now made it possible to correct various small errors in prior editions.[41]

The final qasidah has an additional ten verses that read like a personal supplication from Ghalib:

Mujhe us se kya tavaqqu bah zamanah-e javani
Kabhi kodaki men jis ne nah suni meri kahani
[What hopes do I have from Him, now, as a youth?
Who never heard my plea when I was a child?]

Yun hi dukh kisi ko dena nahin khub varnah kahta
Kih mere adu ko ya rab mile meri zindagani
[To wish suffering for someone is not a good thing,
Or else I would have said, O Lord, give my life to my enemy]

Yih hi bar bar ji men mere aye hai kih Ghalib
Karun khvan-e guftagu par dil-o-jan ki mihmani
[The thought occurs to me again and again that, Ghalib,[42]
I should invite my heart and mind to poetry's table]

In addition to sections, the arrangement of the poetry in each individual divan must be scrutinized because it reveals several unexplored aspects of its presentation, as the cultural background moves from the predominantly aural audience in mushairahs to another group consisting of poetry readers—the people who have access to the written version of the divan. The different arrangement in each divan discloses the poet's thoughts at the time of presenting his poetry to a target audience. The fact that the Divan of 1821 opens with a Persian *qasidah-e fatihah*, and then moves on to three long qasidah-e manqibats, shows that Ghalib is providing a token of his classical training in Persian and is following a standard of presentation. This arrangement then becomes more meaningful if we observe the segue from the last verse in this section (mentioned earlier) to the opening verse in the subsequent section.[43]

There is no evidence throughout the manuscript that it was produced for a designated patron such as Faujdar Muhammad Khan.

The qasidah section of the manuscript is clean, untouched by corrections, additions or remarks, except for a signature—'Josh Bedad'—in the margin on the top-right corner of folio ten.

There are indicative markers delicately inked in red to signal new headings and proper nouns. The pen name Ghalib appears in red in the last verse, squeezed into a space, seemingly a replacement for Asad, the poet's earlier pen name. Throughout the divan, Asad is used for the most part, while Ghalib appears only a few times. (By my count, Asad occurs 235 times and Ghalib thirty-eight times in ghazals.)

The Ghazal Section

The ghazal section is marked by an ornate plate (lauh) in gold, indigo and red, similar to that of the qasidah section. There is the signature 'Abdul Ali' beside the second verse, with a diminutive mark of appreciation (*svad*).[44] The ghazal section is the longest and obviously the most important section of the manuscript because Ghalib focused mainly on ghazals when he first published his divan. It is, however, more remarkable or unique as a manuscript because of the additions in the margins—some of the tweaks here and there by Ghalib himself—as well as occasional remarks in the main body of the text. The supplementary verses in the margins are inscribed in different handwritings. Starting from the very first ghazal, these additions in different hands have produced conjectures as to when they were added and who the inscribers were. I have noted four distinct types of handwritings:

1) Khushkhat, very elegant, clearly the hand of a trained calligrapher.
2) Shikastah, very similar to Ghalib's writing.
3) Shikastah, written with a fine nib, very elegant.
4) Shikastah, written with a broad nib, can be described as bad khat.[45]

The reappearance of the Divan of 1821 in the public domain facilitates a close examination of the sequence of ghazals in this manuscript and the order in which they were carried forward. I compared the order of ghazals in the Divan of 1821 with that of the Divan of 1826 and the modern, printed *Divan-e Ghalib*. There were many significant changes in the way the ghazals were ordered.[46]

For example, ghazal no. 5 in the published *Divan-e Ghalib* is ghazal no. 50 in the Divan of 1821 and no. 10 in the Divan of 1826. In the Divan of 1821, the ghazal's opening verse is as follows:

Uf na ki go soz-e gham se be-mahaba jal gaya
Atash-e khamosh ke manind goya jal gaya
[My heart burned from pain's heat unstoppably, without a murmur;
So to speak, it burned like a silent fire]

This ghazal has six verses in the Divan of 1821, none of which are included in the published *Divan-e Ghalib*. In the margin, however, written with an elegant and fine nib, five more verses have been added. These verses are in the published *Divan-e Ghalib*.

Dil men zauq-e vasl-o yad-e yar tak baqi nahin
Ag is ghar men lagi aisi keh jo tha jal gaya
[Desire for union with the beloved, even her memory doesn't remain
This house was consumed by such a fire that everything that was
burned]

In the Divan of 1826, this ghazal has ten verses. It begins with the same opening verse as the Divan of 1821, followed by the additional five verses from the Divan of 1821's margin, but with the order changed. The closing verse from the Divan of 1821 is dropped and a new one added. The earlier closing verse read:

Hai Asad beganah ai afsurdagi ai bekasi
Dil ze andaz-e tapak-e ahl-e duniya jal gaya[47]
[Asad is a stranger, O loneliness, O sorrow
The heart burned at the style of 'warmth' of the people of the world]

The new closing verse from the Divan of 1826, familiar today from the published *Divan-e Ghalib* is:

Main hun aur afsurdagi ki arzu Ghalib kih dil
dekh kar tarz-e tapak-e ahl-e duniya jal gaya
[Longing for loneliness—and me, Ghalib, for my heart
Having seen the style of the 'warmth' of the people of the world,
burned]

In the published *Divan-e Ghalib*, this ghazal has only six verses. The opening verse has been modified:

Dil mera soz-e nihan se be-mahaba jal gaya
atash-e khamosh ke manind goya jal gaya
[My heart burned from a secret pain unstoppably
So to speak, it burned like a silent fire]

It is apparent that the modified first line is more sophisticated, and the change from *soz-e gham* (burning of grief) to *soz-e nihan* (hidden burning) adds another layer of meaning. Similarly, replacing *uf nah ki* ('I didn't complain', or more literally, 'I didn't say "ouch"') with *dil mera* ('my heart') imparts a poignant tone to the line. The closing verse, too, has been vastly improved by changes in the first line. These changes might seem like nitpicking, but they show the meticulous attention Ghalib paid to polishing and crafting his verses.

It seems to me that Ghalib was using the Divan of 1821 like a reference notebook. Perhaps it was always by his side. He seems to have made selections from it. He might even have used the end pages to set down new ghazals.[48] The shikastah written with a fine nib appears to have been added after the manuscript was brought to the library of Faujdar Muhammad Khan. It could perhaps be the hand of Abdul Ali, who put in the appreciation marks indicated by the letter 'svad' (short for *sahih*) to mark the verses that he liked.

Ghalib might also have used the extra pages at the front to draft the letter in the dotless composition style. As we have seen, there is a 'copy' of Ghalib's letter in Persian in the dotless composition style on two original blank pages of the manuscript.

This is puzzling for several reasons. The first question that comes to mind is why would anyone want to 'copy' a letter on the pages of such an important manuscript? The second problem is that the letter is not an exact copy of the version in a published version. I compared the text of the so-called copy with other versions of the same letter:

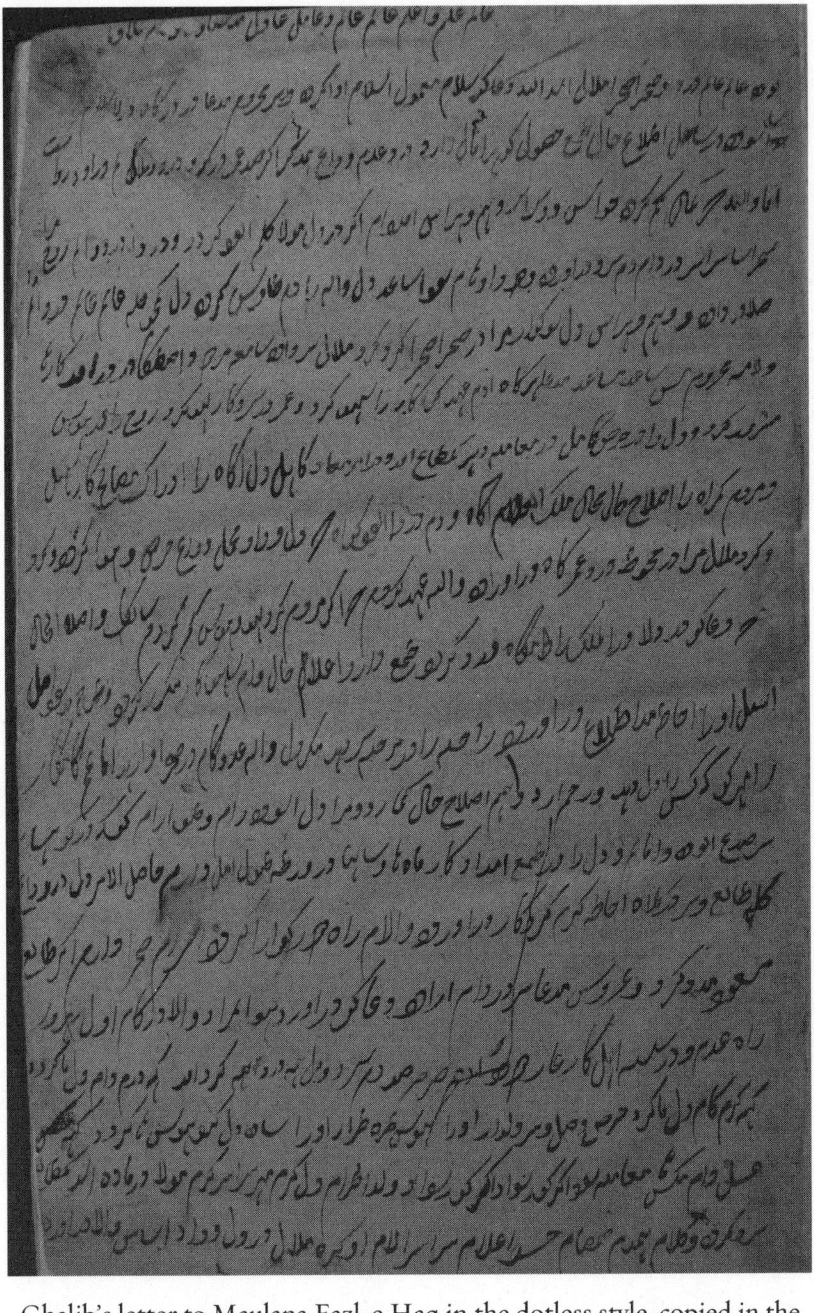

Ghalib's letter to Maulana Fazl-e Haq in the dotless style, copied in the manuscript Divan of 1821 by an unknown hand.

1. The published version in *Panj Ahang*.
2. The versions inserted in the *khatimah* of the manuscripts of *Gul-e Ra'na*. The letter in each of the manuscripts of the *Gul-e Ra'na* has a slightly different text. The 'copy' of the letter in the Divan of 1821 differs significantly from all these versions. There are phrases inserted in the body of its text, missing lines and words, and many errors of spelling.[49]

Furthermore, Ghalib's name is signed as Muhammad Asadullah, and Asadullah is misspelt! Ghalib occasionally used 'Muhammad' with his name, but its addition here is remarkable because the signature is not included in any of the published versions. The last few words on the page: بہرِ ترویح جناب (*bahr-e tarvih janab*) are the opening words of the very first qasidah in the manuscript. This, too, is intriguing. Was this meant to indicate the beginning of the manuscript? The untidiness, wrong spellings and other errors point to a careless copyist. Perhaps Ghalib asked the same person to copy this letter and the additional ghazals on the back pages of the manuscript, because there are striking similarities in the handwriting.

Because this letter to Maulana Fazl-e Haq was written during Ghalib's journey to Calcutta, it seems likely that Ghalib drafted it there.

What Divan Did Ghalib Take to Calcutta?

An unresolved problem is identifying the manuscript that Ghalib carried with him to Calcutta. There is an important document published by S.A.I. Tirmizi that sheds light on this complicated issue.[50] Ghalib wrote that a person from Delhi, who went before him to Calcutta, had informed the governmental authorities that Ghalib was unreliable, that he had a bad reputation and that he had changed his name and pen name.[51] To counter this pernicious allegation, Ghalib presented his divan, which had been completed seven years earlier, embossed with his seal, with the lettering: *Asadullah Khan urf Mirza Naushah, 1231 hijri* (1816).[52]

> دیوانِ ریختہ کہ گرد آوردن آں بیش از ہفت سال گزشتہ و مع ہزا مہری از مواہیر این رو سیاہ کہ اسد اللہ خاں عرف مرزا نوشہ نقش نگین و جلوئہ سال یک ہزار دو صد سی و یک ہجری طرز دامن و آستینش بود بر خاتمئہ اوراق آن سفینہ رقم آخر زباں بندی اعداد داشت، بہ خدمت سر حلقئہ افراد دفترکدہ بہ شہادت فرستادم۔
>
> [I sent my Rekhtah Divan that was prepared seven years ago, along with a *muhr* (seal) from among the muhrs of this wretched Asadullah Khan urf Mirza Naushah that had numerals inscribed with the year one thousand twelve hundred thirty one hijri, like a hem beneath the sleeve at the end of my divan, as a witness for the persons in the office, as testimony]

The passage is difficult to translate because it appears to be ambiguous, at least in my reading. It is not clear if the seal with '1231 hijri' was beneath the colophon or sent along with the manuscript. The question is: Why couldn't this divan be the Divan of 1821? The stumbling block is the mention of a *muhr* (seal). Ghalib had two seals with the date 1231 hijri. The first one was inscribed, *Asadullah Khan urf Mirza Naushah,* and the second, *Asadullah al-Ghalib.*[53] There is no seal beneath the colophon in the Divan of 1821. Ghalib occasionally made careless or casual remarks in letters. After all, memory often plays tricks. Ghalib may have misremembered, or even confused, the attestation of the colophon with the seal.

Ghalib scholars have taken different positions on this matter. The controversy is deeply tied to the question of the provenance of the Divan of 1821. Akbar Ali Khan, editor of the manuscript of the Divan of 1816, is convinced that an updated copy of the Divan of 1816 was made in Ghalib's own hand and completed around 1820.[54] A copy of the 1816 divan was indeed made, but there is no way of knowing whether that copy was the Divan of 1821. It is likely that there were two copies, one made in 1820 and the other in 1821.

Ghalib refers to the manuscript he took with him to Calcutta as 'the second divan' (*divan-e duvvam*).

Unless we find a divan dated 1820, with a seal bearing the inscription 1231 hijri, I will remain convinced that Ghalib was referring to the Divan of 1821 as 'the second divan'. There are several reasons for this assumption. Ghalib had a third divan ready before he left on his journey; this was the Divan of 1826 (discussed below). The Divan of 1826 was left for safekeeping with Maulana Muhammad Ali Khan of Banda. Ghalib often wrote to the maulana during his travels and also sent him the new ghazals he had composed on the way. The Divan of 1826 has these ghazals added in the margins. The Divan of 1821 had clearly been in Ghalib's possession for some time. This is obvious from the modifications in the text throughout, which only Ghalib could have made. All Ghalib scholars agree that these modifications are in Ghalib's own hand. Notations such as 'ghalat' (incorrect), 'valahu' (to be carried forward) and 'mukarrar navishtah shud' (written twice by mistake) are definitely in Ghalib's hand. All these markings are indicative of an ongoing selection being made by the poet. This manuscript was also updated from time to time. Most of the updates seem to be in Ghalib's hand.

When the selections for *Gul-e Ra'na* were made in 1828, it is highly likely that the Divan of 1821 was the basis for this selection. It was most probably the base for the *muntakhab* (selected) divan that was ready by 1832, because Ghalib continued to tweak it and add new verses after *Gul-e Ra'na*.[55] It is possible that after the muntakhab divan was ready, Ghalib gave away the Divan of 1821 to Faujdar Muhammad Khan.

The Divan of 1826

The most extensive, discursive evaluation of the Divan of 1826, also known as the *Nuskhah-e Sherani*, is by Vahid Quraishi.[56] Although the Divan of 1826 does not have a colophon, all evidence points to it being completed after the Divan of 1821 and finished around 1826.[57] The manuscript, conserved at the Punjab University Library, Lahore, is named after Hafiz Mahmud Sherani, who found it in a collection of rare manuscripts.[58] We, however, do not know the exact date of its recovery, or how Hafiz Mahmud Sherani acquired it. Along with the rest of the Sherani manuscript collection, it was bought by Punjab University after Sherani retired in 1942. Qazi Abdul Vadud made a copy of the manuscript when he visited Lahore in 1957.[59]

The Divan of 1826 helps in authenticating and correcting the Divan of 1821. A facsimile edition published in 1969 has made this easier for Ghalib researchers.[60] Unlike the Divan of 1821, this manuscript does not begin with qasidahs, nor does it contain any rubais. Signs of water damage on the edges of the pages suggest that the manuscript was rebound. It is surmised that during the rebinding the order of contents was changed; perhaps the rubais were left out because the last few pages were badly damaged. The manuscript also has notations in the margins. According to Maulana Arshi, the text is emended in several places in Mirza Ghalib's hand.

The Divan of 1826 has fewer verses than the Divan of 1821, mostly because the qasidahs and rubais are missing. There are also some pages missing towards the end, which shows that some ghazals, too, were lost from this manuscript.[61] Because I am interested in the ordering of ghazals within each refrain letter, I checked the Divan of 1826 against the Divan of 1821. The latter contains 2188 ghazal verses (including those in the margins and at the end), 255 qasidah verses and fourteen rubai verses, a total of 2457 verses. The Divan of 1826 contains 2015 ghazal verses (including those in the margins) and sixty-three qasidah verses, a total of 2078 verses.

Comparing only the number of ghazal verses, we see that Ghalib dropped 132 verses. These verses were identified as belonging to those ghazals that have 'ghalat' inscribed at the top in the Divan of 1821. Maulana Arshi regarded the Divan of 1826 as a clean copy (*mabaizah*) of the Divan of 1821. This view, however, is not correct because there are additions in the main text of the Divan of 1826 that are not to be found in the Divan of 1821.[62] Also, the order of ghazals in the two manuscripts is quite different. Nonetheless, there is a dynamic connection between the two manuscripts. It is quite possible that once the Divan of 1826 was available, somebody sat down and added some of the new material to the margins of the Divan of 1821. The ghazals that Ghalib composed during his travel to Calcutta were added to the margins of the Divan of 1826, yet the number of ghazal verses in this manuscript does not exceed the number in the earlier Divan of 1821. This is evidence that Ghalib was writing more in Persian after 1827.

When Ghalib set off for Calcutta, whom did he trust to safeguard the Divan of 1826? There are a couple of entries in the margins of the text saying 'received from Banda' and 'sent from Banda'. These clearly refer to the ghazals Ghalib must have sent from Banda where (as we will see in Chapter 4) he spent months recuperating. According to Maulana Arshi, the manuscript was in the safe hands of Navab Ziyauddin Khan. But Navab Ziyauddin does not mention the Divan of 1826 in any of his writings on Ghalib. Besides, he was born in 1821 and would have been only six years old at the time Ghalib left for Calcutta. Quraishi has conducted a thorough inquiry into the possible guardians of this manuscript but was unable to reach a definite conclusion.[63]

Thus, the Divan of 1826 has its own mystique and its own mysteries. An interesting example of Ghalib's process of editing is provided by those ghazal verses obviously written for Navab Ghaziuddin Haider, the ruler of Avadh, from whom Ghalib expected a generous award. These are noted in the margins of the Divan of 1826. Ghalib emended the verses later because he was disappointed at not being able to meet the navab:

> The reason for visiting Lucknow is not apparent, Ghalib
> I am not one who lusts for travel and fun

If there isn't enough strength to endure the hardships of travel
I am also burdened by the sorrow of separation from friends
I am drawn here in the hope that Mu'tamid Daulah's
'K' of kindness will be the thread of my path.[64]

In Ghalib's published divan, the verses appear as follows:

The reason for visiting Lucknow is not apparent, Ghalib
I am not one who lusts for travel and fun
This city is not the closing-verse of a sequence of ardour
I have resolved to go to Najaf and circumambulate the Ka'bah
Ghalib, a single hope leads me
That the 'k' of kindness will be the thread of my path.[65]

Ghalib's reference to Najaf opened a discussion among Ghalib scholars, such as Malik Ram and Maulana Arshi, regarding the dating of the ghazal. When did Ghalib emend these verses? In Calcutta or later? This question leads to the interesting speculation about Ghalib's wistful desire to travel to Iran (discussed in Chapter 9). From Quraishi's essay we get insights about the manuscript that Ghalib took with him to Calcutta.[66] If Ghalib had the Divan of 1826 with him in Calcutta, it would surely contain evidence of his new compositions recorded in his hand; but it does not. There is a favourite verse of Ghalib's in *Gul-e Ra'na* that is not part of the Divan of 1826:

Sadgi par us ki mar jane ki hasrat dil men hai
Bas nahin chalta kih phir khanjar kaf-e qatil men hai. [67]
[The heart longs to die for her simplicity
I have no control, for the dagger again is in the hands of the slayer][68]

While we may not be able resolve the question regarding the divan that Ghalib brought with him to Calcutta, these hair-splitting details show how minutely scholars have examined his manuscripts. Quraishi perceptively observes: 'A comparison of the texts of *Nuskhah-e Hamidiyyah*, *Sherani* and *Gul-e Ra'na* (i.e., the 1821, 1826 and 1828 manuscript divans) shows that Ghalib made specific, focused efforts in making selections from his existing corpus for every divan, and added the newly composed ghazals in their entirety. We can see that in the *Gul-e Ra'na* he presents the new ghazals almost in their entirety.'[69]

In the next chapter, we will consider Ghalib's earliest extant manuscript divan. It was completed sometime before 1821, most likely around 1816. It was recovered in 1969, nearly fifty years after the Divan of 1821. This Divan of 1816 is in Ghalib's own hand.

3

Ghalib's Earliest Divan: The Divan of 1816

Having written this divan, the longing for earning a name for myself is fulfilled. In the search for other themes [*mazamin-i digar*], I now turn to the spirit of Mirza Bedil, may God shower him with beneficence.

—Ghalib, colophon to the Divan of 1816[1]

Khulta kisi pah kyun mere dil ka mu'amilah
She'ron ke intikhab ne rusva kiya mujhe
[Why would anyone have known the matters of my heart?
My selection of verses exposed me]

—Ghalib, Divan of 1816[2]

The most unbelievable, serendipitous and propitious discovery of Ghalib's early work happened as late as 1969, the year his birth centenary was being celebrated across the Indian subcontinent with great fanfare. The story, as narrated by Ghalib scholar Malik Ram in his essay 'Divan-e Urdu ki Kahani', is worth retelling.[3]

Taufiq Ahmad Shahid Chishti, an antique-books dealer in Amroha, Uttar Pradesh, collected books by touring cities, searching for rare finds. In April 1969, when he was in Bhopal, he met Shafiqul Hasan, a rare-book aficionado. Hasan showed him what he called a rare gem; a divan of Ghalib's, which he claimed was written in the poet's hand. His asking price was Rs 25. After some intense bargaining, Taufiq Ahmad bought the divan for a mere Rs 11. He then brought it to Delhi and placed an advertisement in the newspaper *Al-Jami'a*, offering up the rare manuscript for Rs 6000. People thought it was a joke. Taufiq Ahmad received no offers, but he was not going to give up easily. He showed the manuscript to Ghalib scholar Nisar Ahmad Faruqi, who confirmed that it was indeed authentic and probably in Ghalib's hand.[4] Malik Ram heard about it, too, and affirmed that it was authentic. He offered Rs 10,000 for it. But by then Taufiq Ahmad had learned that the British Library had acquired two letters of Ghalib for a large sum of money. He decided to negotiate for the 'rare gem' with the Raza Library in Rampur. The Rampur library already owned some rare manuscripts of Ghalib's divan.[5] The newly discovered manuscript was supposedly acquired by Akbar Ali Khan Arshizadah,[6] who, realizing the importance of the document, quickly brought out a facsimile edition. In the meantime, Nisar Ahmad Faruqi had also made a copy of the manuscript and sent it for publication to Muhammad Tufail, the editor of the Urdu journal *Nuqush*, which was published from Lahore. It appeared as a special edition of *Nuqush* in 1969, along with illustrations by master painter and calligrapher Sadequain[7] and a portrait of Ghalib by renowned artist Abdur Rahman Chaghtai.[8]

How such a rare manuscript reached the bazaar is also a fascinating story. It was originally in the possession of Navab Yar Muhammad Khan Shaukat Bhopali, son of Miyan Faujdar Muhammad Khan, the owner of the Divan of 1821.[9] Its last owner was Mujahid Muhammad Khan, whose house servant sold it along with other discarded papers and books to a scrap dealer (*kabari*), Haidar Sher Khan, who then sold it for Rs 2.5 to Shafiqul Hasan.

As mentioned earlier, there are two published versions of the 1816 manuscript. Both editions have their idiosyncrasies. Because the material was so novel, controversial and exciting, the editions were prepared as quickly as possible.[10] The *Nuqush* special edition has the advantage of providing a facing nastaliq (standard Urdu script) version of Ghalib's shikastah penmanship. This is very useful, as it makes the original easy to access while retaining the fascinating presentation of the original. The *Nuqush* edition has a scholarly introduction by Nisar Ahmad Faruqi. He begins by giving a short history of its discovery, which is similar to Malik Ram's account, but with some additional, noteworthy sidelights. Since it was 1969, the year of Ghalib's centenary celebrations, the appearance of a manuscript, allegedly in Ghalib's hand, was treated with suspicion. According to Nisar Ahmad Faruqi, Taufiq Ahmad Chishti, the antique-book dealer, had expected Hakim Abdul Hamid Khan to buy the manuscript. Hakim Sahib had established the Ghalib Academy in the same year, with a pledge of Rs 10 lakh.[11] However, no one at the academy thought it worthwhile to make the trip to nearby Amroha to look at the manuscript.[12] The manuscript was authenticated by Muhammad Jalaluddin, an official from the State Archives at Allahabad, who happened to be visiting Amroha at the time. The news of the discovery was published on 16 April 1969 in all the major newspapers and in the news bulletin of All India Radio. I have reproduced below the announcement by the Press Trust of India (PTI):[13]

> Rare Poems by Ghalib Found
> Lucknow, April 16 (PTI)
>
> A rare collection of Ghalib's *gazals*—about 1000 verses—written in his own hand has been found with a dealer in old manuscripts,

> Taufiq Ahmad of Amroha. An official of the UP Archives, Allahabad, said no collection of the poet's works had been found before. He said the collection, which included 13 Persian and 11 Urdu '*rabais*' appeared to be Ghalib's work up to the age of 23. About 100 verses in it had been scored off by the poet himself [sic].

The news clip has several inaccuracies, the most glaring one being the assertion that 'no collection had been found before'. Probably the report meant to emphasize that it was the first manuscript in Ghalib's hand, and also the earliest. The inaccuracies notwithstanding, the news coverage(s) adds to the provenance of the manuscript, for as we shall see, this manuscript, too, disappeared from circulation after its spectacular, coincidental appearance in 1969. We are fortunate that Nisar Ahmad Faruqi recorded every detail of it.[14]

Nisar Ahmad Faruqi's Edition

Faruqi's edition was published as a special Ghalib number of *Nuqush*. In this edition, he referred to the manuscript as *Nuskhah-e Amroha* and titled it *Bayaz-e Ghalib*. The same introduction was also published separately as 'Divan-e Ghalib, Nuskhah-e Amroha' in his book *Talash-e Ghalib*:

> This rare manuscript has thirty-six folios; the dimensions are 7.5x5.5 inches. On Page 1, the title is inscribed in red, the rest of the nuskhah is in black ink. In the first few pages, a space has been left blank for the pen name, perhaps the intention was to write it in red, but was not done. The paper is of high quality, handmade. Although it is 150 years old, there are no marks of water damage or insect damage.[15] There are some ghazals inscribed in the margins that appear to have been added later by another hand.[16] Some

verses from these have been sliced off in the binding process. Every word in Ghalib's hand is legible. Generally, each page has three columns with nine lines, but the number of lines or columns can vary. On some pages the verses have been arranged in fives or fours. Some pages are larger in size and their corners are folded. Some new ghazals are inscribed in another hand on these folded spaces.

Nisar Faruqi describes the unusual dedication on the frontispiece:

Ya Ali al Murtaza Ilaiha wa Ali Auladas Salwat wa salam
Ya Hasan Bismillah al Rahman al Rahim Ya Husain
Abul Ma'ali Mirza Abdul Qadir Bedil Razi'allah anha[17]

[O Ali, the Chosen one, prayers (praises) and peace be upon him and his sons.
O Hasan, In the Name of Allah, the Most Beneficent, the Most Merciful/ O Husain
Abul-Ma'ali Mirza Abdul Qadir Bedil, May God be pleased with him.]

This is a Shia Muslim invocation. Ghalib's veneration of Hazrat Ali, an inclination towards Shi'ism, and his admiration for poet Mirza Bedil are topics that Ghalib scholars have dissected over and again. Discussions on whether or not the handwriting was Ghalib's continued for decades after the folios were published. Both Faruqi and Akbar Ali Khan highlighted the distinctive features of Ghalib's writing; both were convinced that the manuscript was indeed in Ghalib's hand.[18] There are some characteristic irregularities in some of Ghalib's spellings—irregularities that are acknowledged to be present in the manuscript.

A characteristic feature of this manuscript, according to Nisar Ahmad Faruqi, is the exclusive use of the pen name Asad. The change of the pen name from Asad to Ghalib happened soon

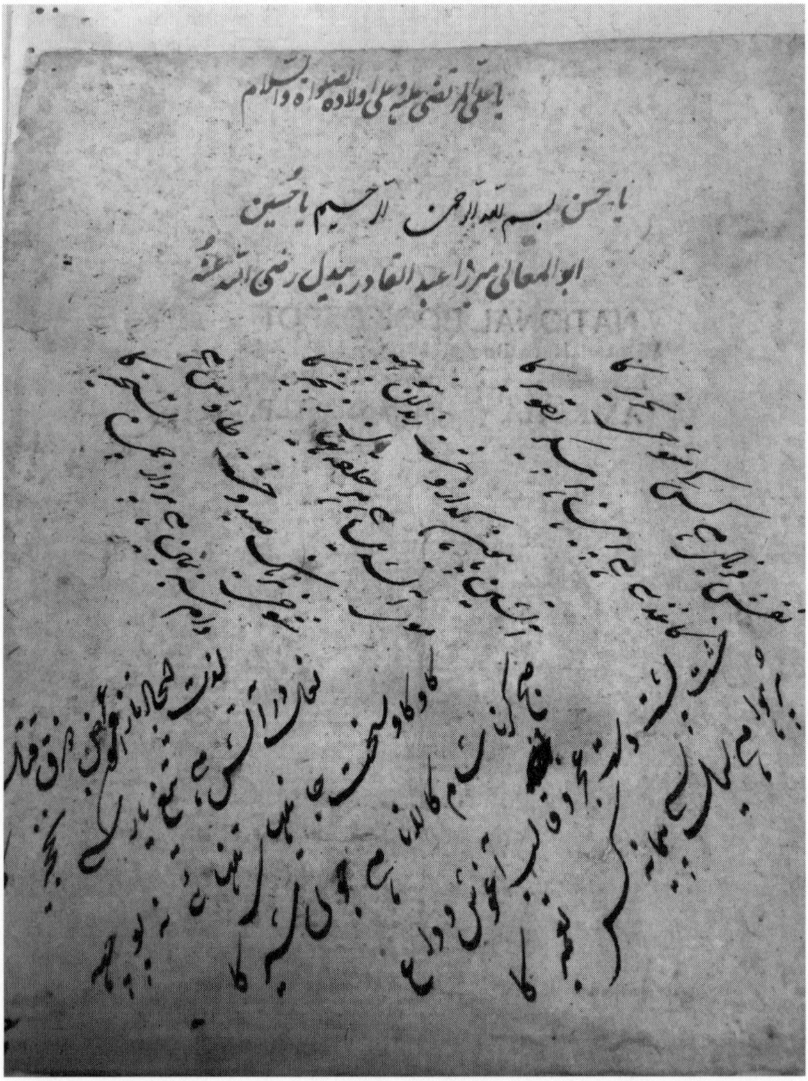

The first page of the Divan of 1816. The manuscript is in Ghalib's hand.

after this manuscript was completed. In subsequent revisions of his manuscript divans, Ghalib changed Asad to Ghalib in several places and made appropriate metrical adjustments. Faruqi makes an important observation when he explains how the Divan of 1816 was useful in correcting or emending the scribal errors in the Divan of

1821. Almost all manuscripts and printed texts suffer from scribal and/or copyist's errors. These unforeseen errors can easily make a two-line verse unintelligible, especially if the poetry, like Ghalib's, is obscure to begin with.

> Many verses in the Nuskhah-e Hamidiyyah [Divan of 1821] that seemed meaningless [*muhmal*] are now emended and have meaning.[19]

One of Ghalib's verses in the *Tazkirah-e Sarvar*, which had puzzled commentators because it was meaningless, has now been restored:[20]

Jigar se tute hu'e mu ki hai sinan paida
Dahan-e zakhm se akhir hu'i zaban paida
[A broken hair from the liver becomes a spear
At last the wound's mouth has a tongue]

The first line as per the Divan of 1816 should read:

Jigar se tuti hu'i ho gayi sinan paida
[A piece broken from the liver has become a spear]

In the first version, the word *mu*, which means 'hair', is perplexing because it refers to the liver. The emended version drops 'mu', producing a better sense of meaning. The verse builds on the conceit of the tongue being shaped like a spearhead. A wound or a gash in Urdu–Persian poetry is seen to resemble a mouth because it is open and red in colour. The wound needs a tongue to express its agony. Here, the spear as a tongue serves a double purpose, because it is a weapon as well.

It is worth noting that, as with all of Ghalib's known manuscripts and published divans, the first ghazal is always *naqsh faryadi*. Ghalib had not written any *masnavis* or qasidahs at this point.[21] The ghazal section in fact concludes on page 61. It is followed by a section of rubais. It is remarkable that there are thirteen rubais in Persian because none of them are included in the Divan of 1821.[22] However, Ghalib retrieves one later for his Persian divan. The remaining twelve remain unpublished.[23]

The Persian section is followed by eleven rubais in Urdu. All the Urdu rubais have been included in the published divan, except the last one:

Gulkhan-e sharar ihtemam-e bistar hai aj
Ya'ni tab-e ishq sho'lah parvar hai aj
Hun dard-e halak-e namah bar se bimar
Qarurah mera khun-e kabutar hai aj
[A burning stove is my bed today
That is, love's fever is aflame today
I am ailing from the pain of losing my messenger
My wine glass is filled with pigeon's blood today]

Indeed, the imagery in this rubai seems excessive and somewhat repugnant.

The Colophon

The colophon follows the rubai quoted above and seems straightforward until one realizes that the year of completion is not mentioned:

> Completed on Tuesday afternoon of 14 Rajab, in the hijri era. I remain, the humble follower of Bedil, Asadullah Khan Ghalib, also known as Mirza Naushah, pen name Asad, may God bless him [*afi allah anha*]. Having written this divan, the longing for earning a name for myself is fulfilled. In the search for other themes [*mazamin-i digar*] I now turn to the spirit of Mirza Bedil, may God shower him with beneficence.

The manuscript is bound along with another manuscript, *Qissah-e Laila Majnun* (The Tale of Laila Majnun). Neither Nisar Ahmad Faruqi nor Akbar Ali Khan provide details of the second manuscript because it is irrelevant. Nonetheless, it is interesting that at some point the two manuscripts become separated.

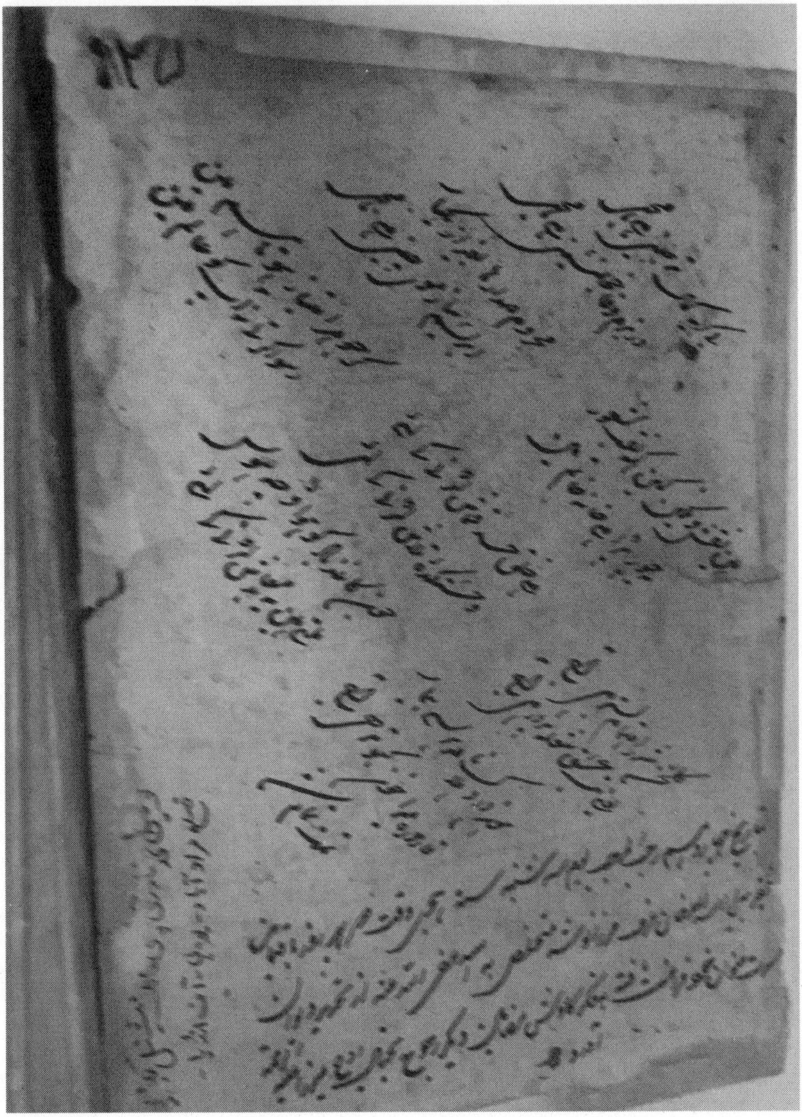

The colophon is at the bottom of the page.

Mirza Bedil is conspicuous in both the dedication and the colophon, which reinforces the well-known fact that Ghalib was influenced by Bedil's style of poetry. The peculiarities of the dedication aside, the manuscript is controversial because there were some doubts: first, about whether it was in Ghalib's hand, and second, about the actual year of its completion.

The First Controversy: Is the Manuscript Actually in Ghalib's Own Handwriting?

According to Nisar Ahmad Faruqi, there is no doubt that the Divan of 1816 is in Ghalib's own hand. There are many samples of Ghalib's handwriting that have come down to us over the years. Because this manuscript is from his early years, it would make sense to compare it with a sample from, or as close as possible to, that time. The earliest example we have of Ghalib's handwriting is a letter addressed to Khudadad Khan and Validad Khan, two businessmen from Agra. The year on the letter, 1804, seems incorrect, because that would mean—if we accept the traditional birthdate—that Ghalib was only six or seven at the time it was written.[24] Ghalib's seal is affixed to the letter, bearing the date 1231 hijri, which corresponds to 1816. Thus, it is likely that the letter was written in or after 1816. Whatever the correct date might be, there is no doubt that it is an early example. And the handwritings in the letter and in the Divan of 1816 are very similar.

Ghalib's handwriting had distinctive characteristics that are easy to identify. One was to connect *alif* and *dal*, and *alif* and *re*, and write them together. This can be seen in words such as *bahadur*, *faryadi*, etc. He also connected *dal* and *va'o* together in words like *do*, *dost* and *duri*. Sometimes he joined two words together: for example, *mahfil men* would be written as *mahfilmen*, *josh men* would be *joshmen*.[25]

The Second Controversy: What Was the Actual Year of Completion?

We do not know how old Ghalib was when he started writing poetry. The confusion around this has been aggravated by Ghalib's own statements scattered throughout his letters about when he began to write poetry. On one occasion, he mentioned he was ten; on another, twelve; on yet another, fifteen. The general opinion among scholars is that Ghalib began writing poetry in or around 1807 or 1812, which means that he was probably writing from the age of ten or fifteen.[26]

In the colophon of this manuscript, Ghalib mentioned the day, date and time but (presumably) forgot to add the year to the colophon. Fortunately for us, on page 41, there is a note by Ghalib that brings us close to the possible year in which the manuscript was completed:

> Lal Khan, Safar 1, 1230 hijri, two rupees, eight annas.

This note can be interpreted in two or three ways: Lal Khan was hired on Safar 1, at a salary of two rupees and eight annas, in 1230 hijri; or Ghalib owed Lal Khan the amount mentioned; or Lal Khan borrowed the money from him.[27] Since the note is close to the end of the manuscript, it can be assumed that the manuscript was almost complete by then. We know that Ghalib stopped using the pen name Asad after 1235 hijri/1820 CE because all the ghazals in this manuscript have Asad as the pen name. It is safe to assume that this divan was completed between 1230 and 1235 hijri, which corresponds to 1816–1820 CE.

Working with 1230 as a possible starting point, it was possible to approximately calculate as to when 14th of Rajab fell on a Tuesday. According to Nisar Faruqi, it was 1231 hijri.[28] However, he didn't settle on a particular date or year. Ali Akbar Khan came up with a concrete date: 11 June 1816.[29]

The Third Controversy: Is the Divan of 1816 a Fabrication?

Kamal Ahmad Siddiqi is sceptical about the authenticity of this manuscript and calls it a forgery. He alludes to a number of minor discrepancies in the manuscript, the most glaring one being the omission of the year in the colophon.[30] Why did the author inscribe the symbol to indicate the year, write 'hijri' next to it and then not put in the numerals? It does seem anomalous. The explanation offered by Nisar Ahmad Faruqi and Akbar Ali Khan is that perhaps Ghalib meant to put the numerals in later, in red ink. It was not unusual for calligraphers to leave blanks to be filled later. Mirza, too, is spelt out in two different ways in the colophon. The word 'Mirza' in Mirza Naushah is spelt without a 'ye'; but when referring to Bedil, it is spelt with a 'ye'.

The charge that the Divan of 1816 was fake does plant a seed of doubt in my mind. But the question is: What was to be gained by this audacious forgery? What could the forger's motive be? A few pages forged in Ghalib's hand with the 'newly discovered ghazals' would have been enough to cause a stir. Creating a whole divan, complete with additions in the margins, revisions, notations, even scribbles, in different hands, sounds like an incredible overkill—especially because the persons behind this so-called forgery were never identified. Who then composed the 'new' ghazals and rubais?

Presumably, archivist Muhammad Jalaluddin, who first authenticated the manuscript, knew what he was doing. We don't know whether the handmade paper on which the manuscript was written was ever tested. Kamal Ahmad Siddiqi squarely blames Malik Ram and Maulana Arshi for their hasty and 'sloppy' conclusions regarding the manuscript's authenticity.[31]

A Description of the Ghazals in the Manuscript

As mentioned earlier, the manuscript has additional ghazals noted in the margins in another hand. This shows that updates were made, probably at Ghalib's behest, because these are new ghazals. There were 1533 verses in the original version. The thirteen new ghazals account for 122 verses, for a final total of 1654 verses. The new ghazals have 'Ghalib' as the pen name. Nisar Faruqi provides the details (the closing verses, number of verses and page numbers) of these ghazals in the form of a very useful tabular analysis of the entire contents of the manuscript; a separate index of the closing verses is also provided. Faruqi has also used asterisks to mark the ghazals that do not appear in any other manuscript, or in the published divan; there are nineteen ghazals and thirteen rubais that are not carried forward to subsequent divans.[32] Such meticulously edited scholarly publications are of invaluable help to researchers.

Special Features of Akbar Ali Khan's Edition

Akbar Ali Khan chose a name for his edition of the Divan of 1816: he called it *Dívan-e Ghalib bah Khatt-e Ghalib* (The Divan of Ghalib in Ghalib's Handwriting). The lettering of this title was designed to represent Ghalib's handwriting and was inscribed in gold on the cover of the expensive, hardbound limited edition. The edition itself was published on heavy, cream-coloured art paper with artistic flourishes throughout. Ghalib's seal (Asadullah al-Ghalib), with the date 1231 hijri, is used as a watermark for the forty pages of introductory material. The seal is alternated with the older seal that bears the inscription 'Mirza Naushah urf Asadullah Khan, 1231 hijri'. It is an innovative idea because the date marks the significant declaration of the transition to the new pen name. This is also the putative date of completion for the Divan of 1816. But the watermark of this date, in saffron yellow, is intrusive for the reader, not to mention that having two separate seals with the same year is muddling in itself. We can only speculate about Ghalib's reasons for having two seals, but using them as watermarks is distracting.[33]

Akbar Ali Khan's dimensions of the manuscript are slightly different. He tells us that the original folios must have been 9.2 x 6.7 inches, which was reduced to 7.6 x 5.5 when the manuscript was rebound.[34] Khan writes that the new binding sliced off words from the margins of at least eight pages. When rebound yet again by Khan, the folio size was further reduced to 6.4 x 4.2 inches. The paper is desi, the first page is blank and the text begins on the second page, with the header in red. The text is arranged in three, sometimes four, columns. In some cases, one has to turn the book upside down to read the second column. On some pages, the verses are arranged in a zigzag pattern, while other pages have diamond patterns. According to Khan, this is typical of Ghalib; it is the same in his copy of the manuscript of *Gul-e Ra'na*. This is a traditional, ornamental style of writing found in poetry notebooks, which Ghalib retained even in his old age.[35]

According to Khan, eleven ghazals are marked for deletion (*qalamzad*) in this manuscript, and they don't appear in any other version. There are thirteen others that were ultimately not carried forward to the Divan of 1821. Two others were marked for deletion with the sign 'ghalat', but were nevertheless carried forward into the Divan of 1821. There are notations in the margins, some in Ghalib's hand and longer ones in another hand, distinctly different from the one in the Divan of 1821.[36]

An aspect of this manuscript, which has been overlooked by Nisar Ahmad Faruqi but noted in Akbar Ali Khan's observations, is the presence of several verses on the very last page. One verse is attributed to Sarvar, a second to Nishat, while a third is not attributed.[37] These verses are in the unknown scribe's hand, which matches the hand that inscribed the fourteen complete ghazals added in the margins. Incidentally, that scribe made plenty of errors in spelling throughout the additions.[38]

Akbar Ali Khan's introduction also has a section titled 'New Findings'. In this section, he discusses the likely possibility of there being at least two more manuscripts; one, perhaps the poet's notebook or *bayaz*; and the other, a version or copy of this divan that could have been complete before 1821. Among the reasons for this conjecture are two notes in the margins in Ghalib's hand: one says 'Copied till here', while the other says 'Begin from here'.[39]

Another unresolved issue is regarding the manuscript Ghalib carried with him to Calcutta in 1827.[40] Khan is convinced that an updated copy of the 1816 manuscript was made in Ghalib's hand, which was completed around 1820.[41] Khan speculates on the possibility of Ghalib carrying an updated copy of the 1816 manuscript to Calcutta. This discussion seems off point, except for the fact that Ghalib's change of pen names was used by his opponents in the pension case to show that he was unreliable.

Reappearance of the Divan of 1816 in 2016

In the previous chapter, I described how the Divan of 1821, the *Nuskhah-e Hamidiyyah*, was reintroduced. After being lost for seventy-odd years, it became available for sale through a dealer in London in 2015;[42] it has now been digitized and published.[43] In the spring of 2016, I was travelling on a fellowship and was based in New Delhi. I was making the usual rounds of libraries, searching for material on Ghalib. The library of the Ghalib Institute is an exceptionally rich resource; among other valuable items, it houses the collection of the eminent Ghalib scholar Kalidas Gupta Raza. On one of my visits, I was poring over the handsome print edition of the 1863 *Divan-e Ghalib*, wishing for a scanner to facilitate material collection. Raza Haider, the director of the institute, came to my table and mentioned a manuscript that had arrived by post around a year ago and which might be of interest to me. He was kind enough to bring out the package from its secure location. When I saw the contents of the package, I could not believe my eyes. The unbound pages were so familiar. It was the Divan of 1816, the manuscript that we believe to be in Ghalib's own hand.[44]

As we have seen, Ghalib's textual history is complex because we have so many versions of his Urdu divan, both published and

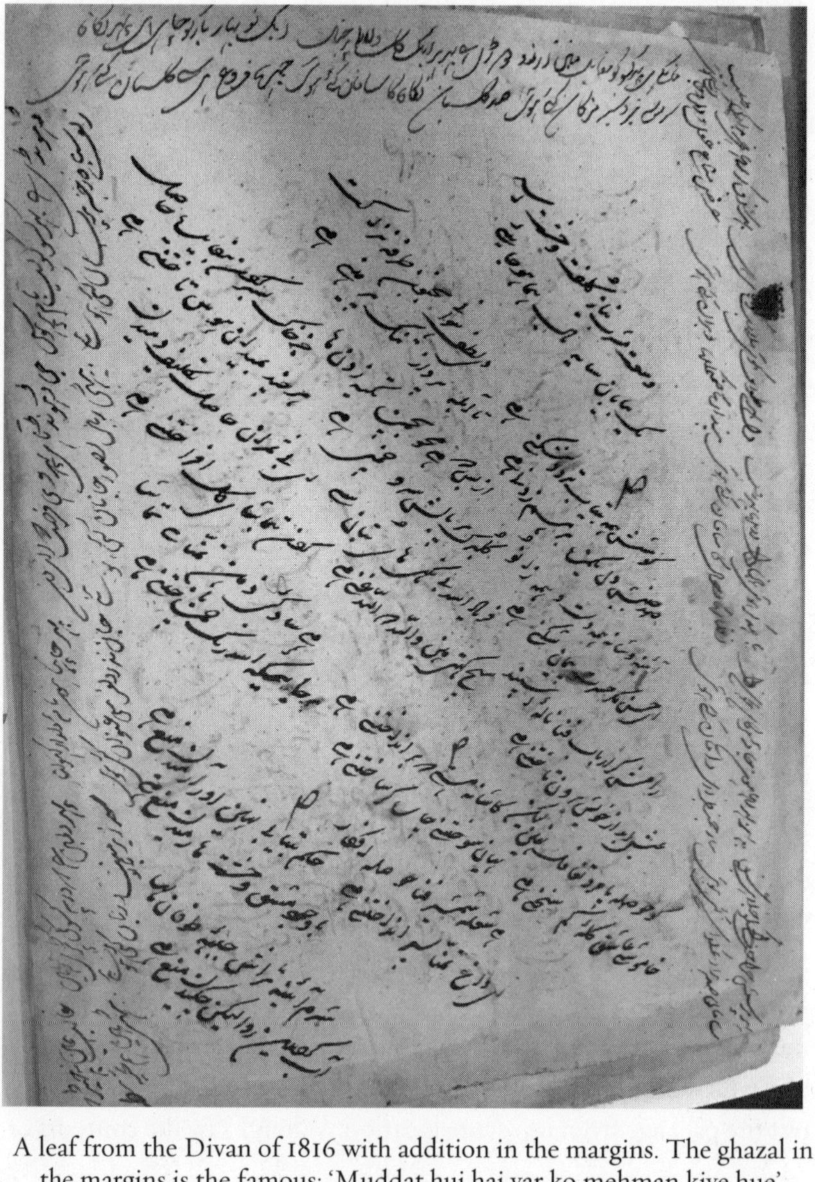

A leaf from the Divan of 1816 with addition in the margins. The ghazal in the margins is the famous: 'Muddat hui hai yar ko mehman kiye hue'.

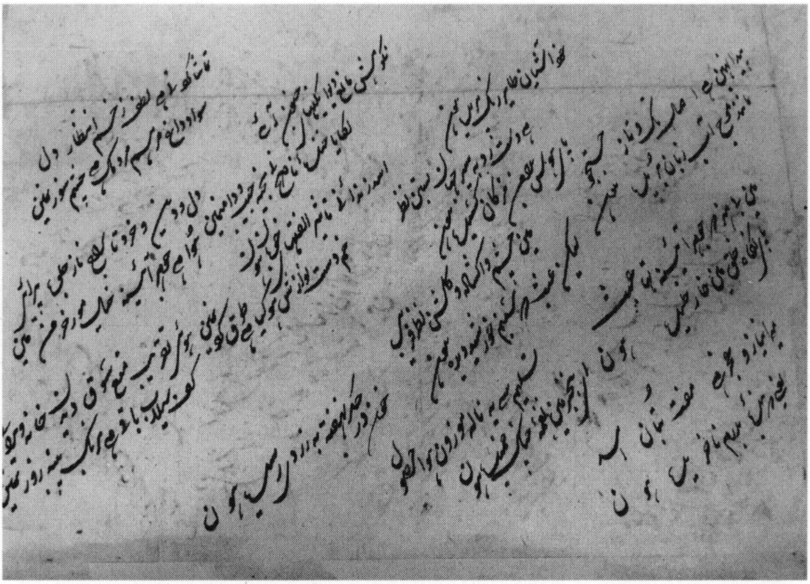

A leaf from the Divan of 1816. Many elements of Ghalib's calligraphic style are evident here.

unpublished. I have only scratched the surface here. The divans were recovered at different times, sometimes fifty years apart, as was the case with the divans of 1816 and 1821. The third divan, the Divan of 1826, or *Nuskhah-e Sherani*, was published in 1969. In between the discoveries, *Gul-e Ra'na*, Ghalib's selection of Persian and Urdu poetry, which he completed in Calcutta in 1828, was recovered in 1955. Each divan thus comes to us with its own convoluted history—taken in sequence, each of them also offers an editorial history of Ghalib's poetic choices and priorities over time.

In each of these divans, the first ghazal has an opening verse specially framed as an introduction, while the last ghazal has a closing verse specially framed as a kind of envoi.[45] There is also a deliberate (but not haphazard) arrangement of ghazals within each alphabetic refrain letter. What is more striking is that each individual ghazal has a sequence of verses more finely tuned than simply their enclosure between an opening and closing verse. Both these claims may sound

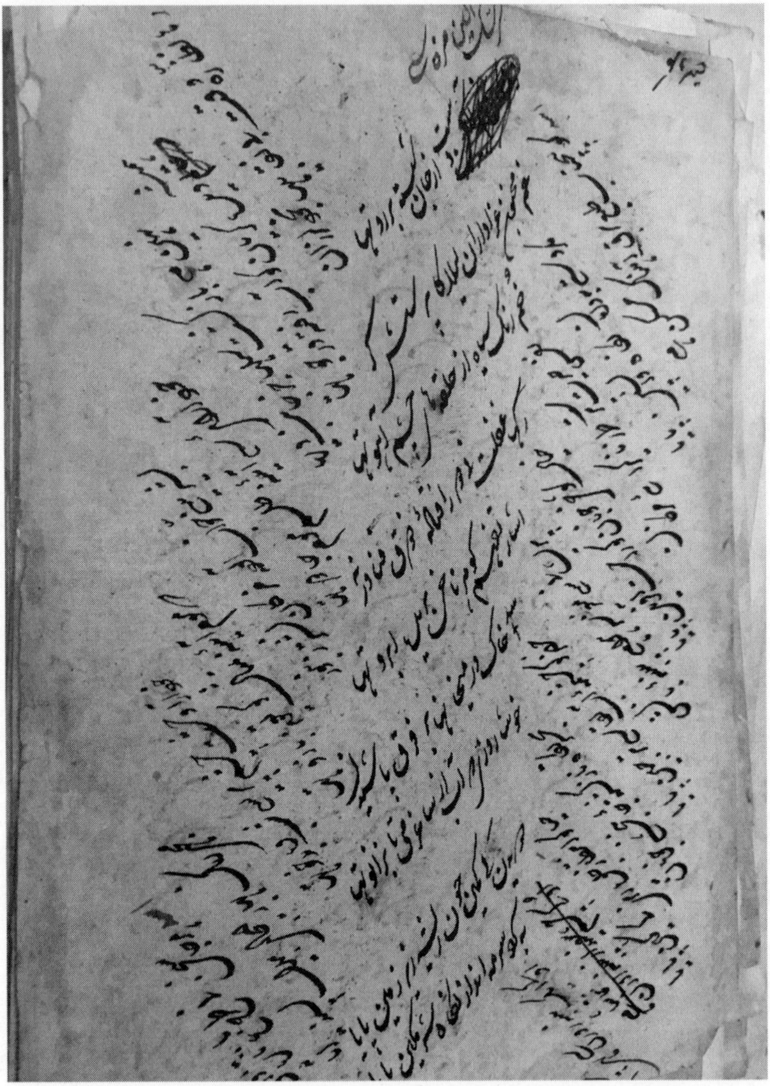

Another leaf from the Divan of 1816, illustrating a different pattern of presentation.

extraordinary to Ghalib scholars, and I will need to document them carefully and justify my conclusions. I propose to undertake this fairly elaborate project in another volume.

Throughout this study, I try to weave the history of the significant divans into the story of Ghalib's poetic journey. His earliest poetry

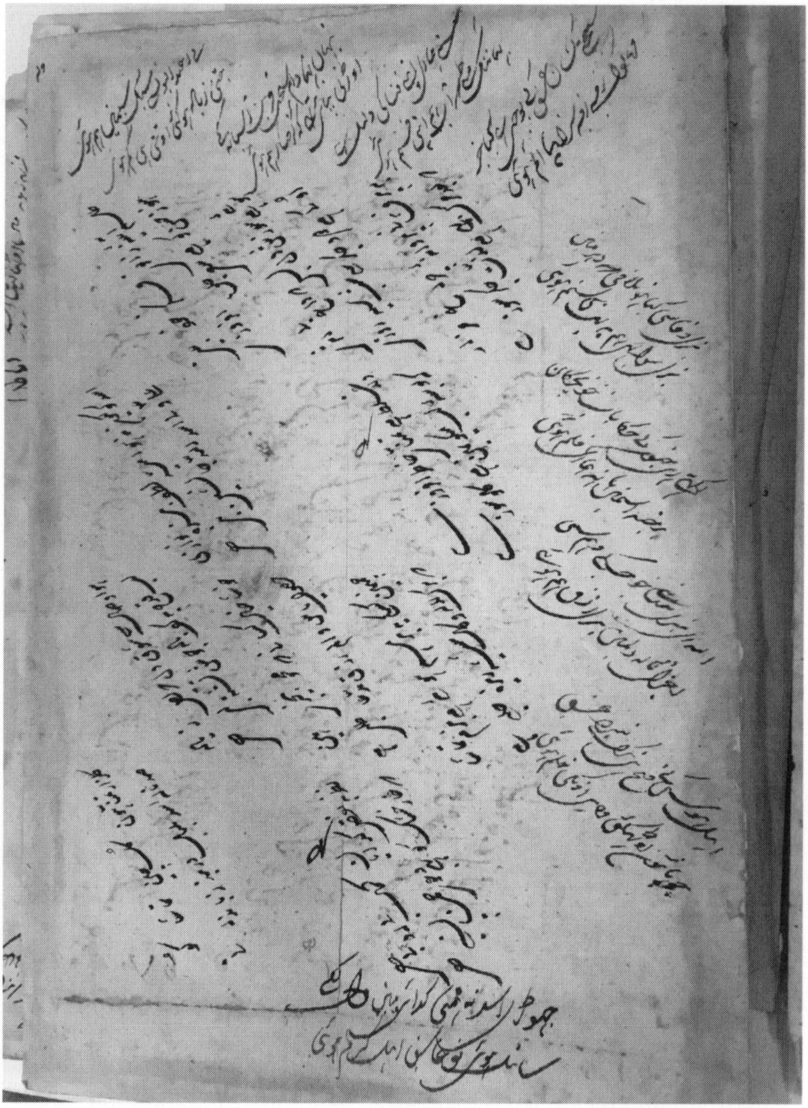

Another leaf from the Divan of 1816. Notice the marks of appreciation indicated by the letter 'svad' on two of the verses.

was in Urdu; he composed mostly ghazals, along with some rubais. The move to writing more in Persian happened over the course of his thousand-mile trip to Calcutta and during his sojourn there. Ghalib began to expand his repertoire, composing masnavis and qasidahs in Persian. For roughly twenty years, from 1830–50, he wrote mostly in Persian; he turned again to Urdu only in the 1850s, when he became closely associated with the Mughal court.

Beginning with *Gul-e Ra'na*, his first intikhab, Ghalib wrote a foreword (*dibachah*) to each divan. These forewords contain valuable insights into Ghalib's ideas about his own poetry vis-à-vis that of his predecessors. They are in many ways the frame within which the poetry is presented. In the chapters that follow, I will analyse Ghalib's literary trajectory with an eye on his self-presentation. What does Ghalib accomplish when he edits his Urdu divan? What are the exigencies of severely editing the Urdu and not the Persian divan? Why does Ghalib write more in Persian? Where does Ghalib stand in the canon of Indian-Persian poetry? Did Ghalib privilege his Persian over his Urdu?

In 1837, Urdu replaced Persian as the official language of administration for India's colonial regime. Persian scholarship was on the decline in British India, yet Ghalib's most bitter battles were fought over questions of correct usage in Persian. His remarkable dedication to the Indo-Persian Sufi poet Mirza Bedil, repeatedly expressed in the Divan of 1816, might surprise us. Why does the young Ghalib so rarely praise, or even allude to, Mir Taqi Mir, his great predecessor in Urdu poetry? Mir, too, belonged to Agra; Mir also made his career in Delhi. He died in 1810 in Lucknow. Ghalib did admire Mir, but he didn't seem to be genuinely inspired by his style. Ghalib's real admiration and devotion were for Bedil. In the early Urdu divans, this admiration was expressed as conspicuously as possible; later, it remained mostly unexpressed but still evident.

When he began to write obscure, highly Persianized poetry in Urdu, Ghalib knew that he was swimming against the current. But he was not as individualistic and unique in this respect as his biographer Hali makes him out to be. There were other poets who wrote in a style similar to Ghalib's. They were Shah Nasir (1755–1838) and his pupil Sheikh Ibrahim Zauq (1788–1854). The rivalry between Ghalib and Zauq is well known. In Lucknow,

Sheikh Nasikh (1777–1838) wrote in a cerebral, non-emotive style that revelled in abstract, far-fetched themes similar to Ghalib's. Despite the fact that Ghalib was more sophisticated and stylistically more convoluted than these poets, the similarity between Ghalib and these poets, particularly Nasikh, cannot be denied.[46]

But more important is the fact that Ghalib primarily thought of himself as a Persian poet. Literary practices such as *istiqbal* (salutation to poets and poetry, a kind of shout-out), *javab* (a reply, an explicit evocation of and response to a poem) and *tatabbu'* (following in the footsteps of a predecessor) were common to Indo-Persian poetics sixteenth century onwards. In his Persian poetry, Ghalib made unabashed use of these precedents. In his letters, he frequently referred to many classical Persian poets whom he admired; for Urfi, in particular, he had unbounded admiration.

Ghalib's published Urdu divan looks slender when placed next to his thick Persian divan. But we must remember that the Urdu divan is an intikhab with no pretensions to being the entire body of his work. Over the course of our inquiries, we will pay close attention to the reasons that led Ghalib to prune his Urdu divan but not his Persian one.

4

Contrary Winds: The Journey to Calcutta (1826–29)

Calcutta is remarkable! It is a world where everything except a remedy for death is available. Every task is easy for its talented people. Its markets have an abundance of everything, except the commodity of good fortune.

—Ghalib, in a letter to Mirza Ali Bakhsh Khan, 1248/1833[1]

After all attempts to get his just share from Navab Ahmad Bakhsh Khan failed, Ghalib undertook the long, arduous journey to Calcutta to present his pension case before the British Governor General.[2] This journey was a big turning point in his career for several reasons. The most important was the change from writing poetry mostly in Urdu to writing in Persian. The second was his exposure to a world more cosmopolitan than Delhi. He now had opportunities to meet Iranians and people from Central Asia who were in Calcutta for trade and diplomatic purposes.[3] The literary gatherings in Calcutta were not of the courtly type: instead, the ambience tilted towards a greater openness, with more freedom to disagree. Print was in evidence, in pamphlets and newspapers, its effect quite palpable. Separation from his familiar haunts in Delhi and north India prompted Ghalib to write many letters describing what he saw and experienced. The letters, written in Persian to friends, relatives and acquaintances, constitute a valuable archive that shines light on the north Indian literary culture in the first quarter of the nineteenth century.

From our perspective, the most significant outcome of the journey was Ghalib's intikhab of his Urdu and Persian poetry, the *Gul-e Ra'na* (to be discussed in Chapter 5) and its dibachah. This selection, as we shall see, formed the basis of his choice for the Urdu Divan of 1841. The other remarkable products of the journey were two masnavis in Persian. The first was *Chiragh-e Dair* (Lamp of the Temple), regarded as the finest poem of its kind on the allure of India's Mecca, Banaras; and the second, *Bad-e Mukhalif* (Adverse Winds), was a sharp retort in verse, deriding the rude behaviour of the Calcutta audience. Ghalib initially called it (ironically) *Ashtinamah* (letter of conciliation); he published it as a pamphlet and claimed that it had reached 5000 people.

The early death of his father put Ghalib under the official care of his paternal uncle, Nasrullah Beg Khan,[4] who was married to Navab Ahmad Bakhsh Khan's sister. Thus, Ghalib's uncle was Navab Ahmad Bakhsh Khan's brother-in-law. Navab Ahmad Bakhsh Khan was the scion of an important family who represented the interests of the Maharaja of Alwar. The navab and Nasrullah Beg Khan had fought for the British, under the command of Lord Lake, in the Anglo-Maratha conflict of 1802–03. In recognition of their service, Lord Lake had awarded the navab a permanent jagir in the district of Firozpur-Jhirka. The Maharaja of Alwar gave him the pargana of Loharu. Nasrullah Beg, too, was awarded a permanent jagir by Lord Lake, which yielded an annual income of Rs 1 lakh.

Unfortunately, just three years after his father's death, Nasrullah Beg Khan died unexpectedly after falling off his elephant. He had no children of his own, but he left behind his mother, three sisters and two nephews—Ghalib and his younger brother, Mirza Yusuf. Ghalib was around nine years old at this time. The British government confiscated Nasrullah Beg Khan's estate and disbanded his cavalry of 400 horsemen. Fortunately, the astute Navab Ahmad Bakhsh Khan was able to negotiate a stipend in lieu of the jagir, ostensibly for the dependents. The sum settled upon with the British was Rs 10,000 for the dependents and Rs 15,000 for the maintenance of troops to be supplied, if needed. The whole transaction was conducted without any money being exchanged. A total of Rs 25,000 was to be deducted directly from the revenues of the navab's estate.

Meanwhile, taking advantage of the situation, Khwaja Haji, a relative and employee in the household of Nasrullah Beg Khan, commandeered the disbanded horsemen and brought them to Navab Ahmad Bakhsh Khan.[5] The navab, pleased with the additional retinue, requested Lord Lake to permit Khwaja Haji to be included among the 'official' dependents of Nasrullah Beg Khan. He also reserved Rs 5000 from the stipend for his own use. In June 1806, the distribution of the family pension from Nasrullah Beg Khan's estate was settled as follows:

1. Khwaja Haji: Rs 2000 (as the commander of a contingent of fifty horsemen)
2. The mother and sisters of Nasrullah Beg Khan: Rs 1500
3. Mirza Ghalib and Mirza Yusuf: Rs 1500

At the time of the settlement, Ghalib was too young to protest.[6] The allocation remained unchanged four years later, after Ghalib's marriage to Umrao Begam, the daughter of Mirza Ilahi Bakhsh, Navab Ahmad Bakhsh Khan's younger brother. The marriage was expected to strengthen the ties between the two families, but it seemed to have complicated matters when Ghalib alleged that Khwaja Haji had no right to be included among the dependents. It was difficult for him to actually petition in court against Navab

Ahmad Bakhsh Khan's decision. Ghalib repeatedly protested to the navab himself against this injustice, with the latter assuring him that Khwaja Haji's share would cease after his death. In 1822, Navab Ahmad Bakhsh Khan appointed his eldest son, Navab Shamsuddin Ahmad Khan, as his heir and the manager of his estate. Ghalib's relations were already strained with Navab Shamsuddin Ahmad Khan owing to both political and personal reasons.[7] When Khwaja Haji died in 1825, his share of the pension was not suspended but transferred to his surviving heirs. This was an apparent breach of the promise made by Navab Ahmad Bakhsh Khan. Ghalib was greatly affected by these developments because his creditors, who were aware of the new arrangement, began to clamour for money. The situation was so dire that Ghalib could not leave his house during the day for fear of being arrested.

Following Khwaja Haji's death, Ghalib appealed to Navab Ahmad Bakhsh Khan many times, reminding him of his promise to revert the stipend. He made more than one trip to Firozpur-Jhirka to pursue the matter. But as we learn from his letters to Rai Chajja Mal, his last trip to Firozpur-Jhirka left him feeling so frustrated that he felt like he was destined to die and be buried there.[8] The navab was on a prolonged trip to Alwar, and when he finally returned, he was still recovering from his serious injuries.[9] It appears that transferring the stipend was not entirely in the navab's hands; the British Resident had to sign off on it as well. It was therefore important that Ghalib meet Charles Metcalfe, the newly appointed Resident of Delhi and agent of the Governor General.[10] When Metcalfe reached Delhi from Calcutta, he had plans to settle the affairs at Bharatpur first. With the Governor General's permission, Metcalfe led the siege of Bharatpur in December 1825. At this point, the navab persuaded Ghalib to travel to Bharatpur with him so that he could meet Metcalfe.

One can only imagine how miserable and troubled Ghalib was in those days. His younger brother, Mirza Yusuf, whom he loved dearly, seemed to have lost his mind. Ghalib needed money for his brother's treatment. His father-in-law, Mirza Ilahi Bakhsh, died that year, too. Laden with debt, his cup of misery overflowing, Ghalib set out for Bharatpur with Navab Ahmad Bakhsh Khan. But the trip was unsuccessful; the navab did not introduce Ghalib to Metcalfe. Ghalib returned empty-handed. Though the navab was an ailing, dying man, he was very shrewd. He kept making empty promises, stringing Ghalib along and encouraging his hope of meeting Metcalfe. Since returning to Delhi without resolving the issue was risky, Ghalib stayed on in Firozpur-Jhirka for three months, till January 1826.

Eventually, he decided to meet Metcalfe without the navab's intercession. When he heard that Metcalfe would be going to Kanpur to welcome the Governor General, Ghalib decided to try his luck there. Since it was not feasible to return to Delhi, because his creditors would hound him, Ghalib wanted to proceed directly to Kanpur. It is not clear if he secretly went to Delhi to arrange for funds, but in his petition dated 28 April 1828, he mentions that he sold off all the valuables in his possession to partially appease his creditors.[11] With the remainder of the proceeds, he returned to Firozpur-Jhirka and then left for Kanpur via Farrukhabad.

These last-minute arrangements to raise money must have been terribly stressful, so it is not surprising that Ghalib fell very ill on reaching Kanpur. Since a doctor couldn't be found, he had to be carried across the Ganga to Lucknow. In Lucknow, he spent five long months recuperating, and enjoying the company of friends.[12] At the time, Navab Ghaziuddin Haider was the ruler of Avadh and Saiyyid Muhammad Khan Agha Mir was his close associate.[13] Agha Mir expressed a desire to meet Ghalib. In preparation for this meeting, Ghalib composed a qasidah of 110 verses and a petition in Persian, crafted in the san'at-e ta'til style. The meeting, however, did not happen because Ghalib set some conditions that Agha Mir declined. Ghalib did not send him the qasidah or the petition.[14] Any hopes that he may have had of receiving a gift from Agha Mir, which would defray his travel expenses, were shattered. His experience of Lucknow was embittered as well, and he wrote about it in unflattering terms.[15] This was yet another case of wasted opportunity. The meeting with Metcalfe did not materialize, but Ghalib decided to continue his journey, albeit with a slight change of plans. He now wanted to go to Calcutta to petition at the Governor General's court, but the question of adequate funds for the journey was still unresolved.

It was most likely the need for financial support that prompted Ghalib to leave Lucknow and go to Banda, where an affluent cousin of his lived.[16] Banda, in the southern part of modern-day Uttar Pradesh, is now known as Bundelkhand. Ghalib arrived in Banda via Kanpur in late June or early July of 1826 and promptly fell ill again. Because his cousin was a close family member of the Navab of Banda, Ghalib was taken care of at the behest of Navab Zulfiqar Ali Bahadur himself. Ghalib stayed in Banda for at least six months, in the navab's guest house.[17] In addition to this cousin, Ghalib had other relatives and friends as well in the city. The *sadr-e amín* (civil magistrate) of Banda, Navab Muhammad Ali Khan, was a poet of repute. A deep, abiding friendship developed between the two poets. Eventually, Muhammad Ali Khan arranged to finance Ghalib's trip. The many letters that Ghalib wrote to him during the journeys to and from Calcutta, detailing his experiences of the city's milieu, are particularly important. Ghalib perhaps also left with him for safekeeping his most recent Urdu divan, the Divan of 1826.

The journey to Calcutta began from Banda, as Ghalib made his way from there to Allahabad and onwards. The details of the first leg are narrated in Ghalib's letters to Muhammad Ali Khan.[18] It was slow going because the mule that drew the baggage cart (*chíkra*) was scrawny and sluggish, and could not travel more than 25 miles a day. After spending a night in an obscure village, the party reached Chilla Tara on the banks of the Jumna (Yamuna). They decided to abandon travel by land and take a boat instead. It turned out that the boat was just as slow. After a week or so, they arrived in Allahabad, on 27 November 1826.

Allahabad didn't prove to be very hospitable. Perhaps Ghalib's host was Ghulam Imam Shahid, a pupil of the Persian poet Mirza Qatil (whom Ghalib despised).[19] Malik Ram and Qazi Abdul Vadud speculate that some unpleasant incident may have triggered Ghalib's dislike for Qatil. Khaliq Anjum writes that Ghalib and Shahid may have exchanged some sharp words at a gathering. Whatever the case may have been, Ghalib did not tarry at Allahabad for more than a day. In an oft-quoted letter to Muhammad Ali Khan, Ghalib described Allahabad as a desolate place where nothing was available. The people were uncultured and inhospitable. Allahabad was like hell.[20] It wasn't long before Ghalib left the city by boat; his spirits were buoyant as they approached Banaras.

Banaras seemed to be the city of his dreams. Another long, scintillating letter to Muhammad Ali Khan describes the wonderful ambience of the city in exaggerated poetic terms: 'The air is so refreshing that it breathes life into dying souls. The flowing river is like a sea whose waves touch the sky.' The second part of the letter goes into the actual challenges of travel, of the five days spent at an inn for no reason except to recoup his energy, of finding a house on rent that was 'darker and narrower that a miser's grave'. Ghalib clearly was in a dilemma about what to do next. Should he travel by land or by boat? These uncertainties, coupled with ill health and no money, bothered him considerably.[21] Ultimately, he stayed on in Banaras for a month. This seems like an odd choice, given that he had no friends or mentors, no pupils or followers in Banaras. Perhaps he was waiting for funds to arrive, for some additional help from Muhammad Ali Khan.

Meanwhile, he poured his frustrations out into a beautiful masnavi on the city, calling it *Chiragh-e Dair* (Lamp of the Temple).[22] This masnavi, consisting of 108 Persian verses, is a masterpiece. It is adorned with unusual similes and metaphors. Banaras is personified as a beautiful woman with the enchanting face of a fairy who can see her reflection mirrored in the Ganga. The masnavi builds on this idea of reflection from many charming, poetic aspects: how the city's image in the water is like revealing the face of a new bride; how the reflection creates a duplicate of the city, protecting the original from the evil eye; how Banaras's wildernesses are gardens, as flower-filled as if spring were eternal; how it is the Mecca of Hindustan; how its inhabitants are saving the rest of humankind from the Day of Judgment![23] A noteworthy point is that this masnavi may bear the influence of three masnavis by eminent Indian Persian poets (who, as we shall see, ceased to captivate Ghalib later): Mirza Bedil's *Tur-e Ma'rifat*, Munir Lahori's *Dar Sifat-e Bangalah* and Ghanimat Kunjahi's *Nairang-e Ishq*. For his masnavi, Ghalib adopted a well-known metre used by Jami (in *Yusuf–Zulaikha*), Nizami (in *Khusrau–Shirin*) and by the above-mentioned Indian Persian poets as well.[24] This is one of the sweetest, most mellifluous of all metres. It creates an aura of untrammelled feelings, bubbling freedom and unsuppressed passion. Ghalib was longing to be home, but he also wanted to air his feelings about the hard-heartedness of his compatriots, about his hurt pride and pain at being ignored. He expressed his thoughts not as a lament but as a protest:[25]

Dil az shor-e shikayat ha bah josh ast
Hubab-e be nava tufan kharosh ast
[My heart is seething with the fervour of complaints
It's like a silent bubble in a thunderstorm]

Ze dihli ta birun avurdah bakhtam
Ba tufan-e taghaful dadah rakhtam
Kas az ahl-e vatan ghamkhvar-e man nist
Mara dar dahr-e pindar-e vatan nist
Mago dagh-e firaq-e anjuman sokht
Gham-e be mihri-e ahl-e vatan sokht

[Fate brought me away from Delhi
I threw my baggage to the storm of neglect
Nobody from my homeland shares my pain
In these times I don't have pride in my homeland
Don't say I am burnt by wounds of separation from those gatherings!
I am burnt by the unkindness of my countrymen]

When Ghalib describes the beauty of the women of Banaras, he creates the most eloquent picture of their loveliness: shining faces, tall stature, rosebud lips and long eyelashes that pierce their lovers' hearts; how their gait makes waves fall still in wonder, and when they step into the water of the Ganga, it creates havoc; how lovers' hearts writhe like fish; and how oysters' pearls turn into water because they cannot compare with the glow (*ab*) of the beautiful women of Banaras. In his letters from Banaras, Ghalib declares himself to be completely in love with the city:

> I felt like giving up religion, tossing away the prayer beads, putting a vermilion stripe on my forehead, wearing the sacred thread, and sitting by the Ganga, purged of the trappings of the dust of existence and merging with the ocean like a drop of water.[26]

He carried away rosy memories of Banaras. Late in life, he wrote to Miyandad Khan Saiyyid:[27]

> Banaras is beyond words. Such cities are seldom created. I happened to be there at the height of my youth. If I were young now, I would go and live there and not return.

While Ghalib's Banaras experience seems to be at odds with his fastidious nature on one hand, on the other it seems like he needed a peaceful space where he could be removed from the cares and sorrows of life. Tahseen Firaqi writes that this masnavi shows the conflict between Ghalib's poetic and real self. The attraction for Banaras contains his love for Delhi as well. The beauty of Banaras pierces his heart and reminds him of Delhi, and the heartless compatriots.[28] The masnavi is a journey of the poet's self. In the concluding section, Ghalib talks about the genuineness of passion *(junun)*, how if his passion is true, then the distance between Kashi and Kashan is merely a short step, and how he needs to get out of the confines of his body and float like fragrance.[29] In this heavenly place (Banaras), he should think of his dear ones who are in the wilderness. He should not let the flowers of Kashi beguile him but should think of the scars on the hearts of those he loves. Ghalib also mentions how Banaras is only a stopping point and that he should move on. His passion must melt his heart, he must prepare to roam and seek. He must become free.[30]

After a month of anonymity in Banaras, during which he claimed to have put behind his ill health and misgivings, Ghalib set off for Patna. He had wanted to travel by boat, but the demands of the boatmen went beyond his straitened finances. One hundred rupees was the price to sail to Calcutta. Since Ghalib could not afford even Rs 20 for Patna, he abandoned the idea and opted to travel by land, on horseback.[31] In his letters, Ghalib described the hardships he had endured during the journey. He wrote in a letter to Khwaja Fakhrullah:

> In short, I wanted to succeed; for this crime, I had to go through such terrible days. I wanted to comb the tresses of the Laila of my desires; for this crime, I had to suffer indescribable hardships. Moaning and groaning against the power, influence, and reach of my enemies, walking and crawling with my chest on a sword's edge, I reached Calcutta.[32]

Ghalib arrived in Calcutta on 19 February 1828.[33]

When we think of the challenges of a 3000-kilometre journey that was interrupted by long episodes of illness (five months spent recovering in Lucknow, six months in Banda, one month in Banaras), we have to admire Ghalib's tenacity of purpose. It almost seems like a miracle that he reached his destination. Meanwhile, Ghalib kept pouring his heart out in letters. He wrote Persian in an elaborate but emotional style, creating a wonderful archive of the sojourn in elegant prose. From his letters, we learn that in Calcutta he rented a comfortable house that was amenable in every way. It had a big courtyard, a well with sweet water, a delightful room on the terrace and a spacious lavatory! The rent was a mere Rs 6 per month.[34] The address was: Haveli of Mirza Ali Saudagar, Gol Talab, Shimla Bazaar. Calcutta's vibrant ambience made a deep impression on Ghalib's alert mind. He wrote to Mirza Ali Bakhsh Khan:[35]

> Calcutta is remarkable! It is a world where everything except a remedy for death is available. Every task is easy for its talented people. Its markets have an abundance of everything except the commodity of good fortune. My house is in Shimla Bazaar. I was easily able to find a house within a day or two of arriving here. In short, it is God's grace that a careless one like me, who had awakened from a deep sleep, and who went to the durbar without washing his face, was given a place in the heart of the rulers, and was awarded a position higher than I expected in the assemblies. I was blessed with a kind-hearted mentor, a member of the Council, Mr Andrew Stirling, who is willing to listen to the plea of this broken-hearted one and put healing ointment on his wounds.

Ghalib's letters from Calcutta cover a large canvas that can be tantalizingly fragmented and frustrating because the documents are distributed across separate collections. Many letters have dates missing, so events cannot be arranged in chronological order. The earliest letters are those that constitute the fifth section of *Panj Ahang*;

they were published during his lifetime.[36] Another collection of forty-eight letters, found in Lucknow, contain the letters he wrote to the friends he made in Calcutta, notably Maulvi Sirajuddin Ahmad.[37] Equally important is another clutch of thirty-two letters found in the private collection of Hakim Habibur Rahman of Dacca (now Dhaka). These are addressed to many of his friends in Calcutta and have been published as *Ma'asir-e Ghalib*.[38] Last in the series is the unique manuscript preserved by the National Archives of India. It is dated 1839 and contains thirty-two letters and two prose narratives, which elaborate on the literary combat that played out at the Calcutta mushairahs between Ghalib and his critics.[39]

It didn't take Ghalib long to establish himself among the important people in the city. He travelled to Hugli (Hooghly) by boat to pay his respects to Navab Ali Akbar Khan Tabataba'i, who received him cordially and soon became a friend. On 28 April, armed with a freshly composed qasidah, Ghalib called on Andrew Stirling, Persian secretary to the Governor General, and apprised him of the pension case. Stirling had a taste for fine Persian poetry and was soon among Ghalib's well-wishers.[40] Next, Ghalib called on Simon Fraser, officiating secretary to the Governor General, who greeted him cordially by rising up to receive him, and even offered him perfume and betel leaf, the customary welcome for friends. Fraser had known Ghalib's uncle, Nasrullah Beg Khan. Ghalib submitted his petition to Fraser, feeling quite optimistic about the outcome.

Meanwhile, Mirza Afzal Beg, the brother-in-law of Khwaja Haji, had been busy spreading canards about Ghalib.[41] Beg had been appointed to the post of vakil, or agent, of Emperor Akbar Shah II, in September 1827; he had arrived in Calcutta much before Ghalib.[42] Afzal Beg, who wielded considerable influence in the official circles, began to spread the story that Ghalib was an unreliable man who changed his pen name every now and then. It is well known that Afzal Beg made every effort to malign Ghalib among the religious scholars and literati of Calcutta. He informed the Shias that Ghalib was an atheist; the Sunnis were told that he was a heretic (*rafizi*). Not content with this, Mirza Afzal Beg spread a rumour that Ghalib had publicly disparaged Mirza Qatil, the noted Urdu and Persian poet who had many followers in Calcutta. Ghalib responded to the allegation about him changing his pen name by producing a copy of his Urdu divan that was compiled seven years ago, which bore his seal dated 1231/1815 and also the legend 'Asadullah Khan urf Mirza Naushah'.[43] This could have been the Divan of 1821, or a copy. Although the manuscript as it presently exists does not bear the seal mentioned by Ghalib, its colophon declares in no uncertain terms that it is the work of Mirza Sahib, who uses both Asad and Ghalib as pen names.[44]

Ghalib's petition to the Governor General, dated 28 April 1828, is an elaborate document that details the history of his case from the time his uncle, Nasrullah Beg, died in 1806 to the death of Khwaja Haji in 1825. It is a history of injustices, unfulfilled promises and consequent hardships.[45] Its main argument is that Khwaja Haji was not a relative but a hanger-on and that thus Khwaja Haji's share should now revert to Ghalib and his dependents, rather than to Khwaja Haji's heirs. Although Simon Fraser accepted Ghalib's petition, and assured him of taking action, the fact is that the petition was in the wrong hands. The council wanted Ghalib to submit the petition to the Resident in Delhi, after which it would be forwarded to Calcutta. Poor Ghalib had made the arduous journey in vain. The prospect of journeying back empty-handed was terrifying.

However, it was possible to arrange for the petition to be submitted in Delhi while Ghalib remained in Calcutta. A lawyer, Pandit Hira Lal, was commissioned in Delhi by Ghalib's dear friend Maulana Fazl-e Haq Khairabadi. A whole year went by before Ghalib heard that his petition had been received at the Delhi court. Meanwhile, the Governor General announced that the government, with the members of the council and other officials, would move from Calcutta to Meerut in preparation for a shift of operations to Delhi.[46] Francis Hawkins replaced Colebrooke, the British Resident in Delhi. Colebrooke had been sympathetic towards Ghalib. With the new twist, Ghalib realized that staying on in Calcutta would be of no use. In August 1829, he left Calcutta. He reached Delhi in November 1829. In Delhi, Ghalib met the new Resident, Francis Hawkins. He brought along the qasidah he had composed for Hawkins, which was read out and approved. But there was no further sign of approval beyond this. On 5 May 1930, his petition was dismissed.[47]

Over the year and a half in Calcutta (February 1828 to August 1829), Ghalib had led a life that oscillated between the highs and lows of literary and social experiences. The most energizing moments perhaps were the monthly mushairahs attended by the literati of various persuasions, from Persian and Urdu backgrounds. In Ghalib's Delhi, mushairahs were dominated by Urdu poets. Here in Calcutta was an opportunity for Ghalib to flaunt his (self-proclaimed) native fluency in Persian. But the path was not smooth. A small but significant factor was the indirect involvement of Ghalib's adversary, Afzal Beg, in these mushairahs. Afzal Beg was connected to Munshi Abdul Karim of the governmental Persian department, who was influential in literary circles and active in the organization of the mushairahs that were held on the first Sunday of every month.[48] Ghalib's experience of his first mushairah, in June 1828, was positive. The ghazal that dragged him into a raging controversy was the one he composed for the second of these mushairahs, which he attended on 8 July 1828. The pattern-line (*misra-e tarh*) was from Hakim Hamam's ghazal.[49]

Ghalib composed a ghazal on the proper pattern-line (which, as usual, had been specified beforehand) and presented it at the mushairah. In the following week, news began circulating that one of Ghalib's verses was grammatically flawed. We have an account of the incident in Ghalib's words:

> ده دوازده بیت در ہمین ردیف و قوافی از رگِ کلک فرو ریختم و بہ مشاعره بر خواندم۔ پس از ہفتہ خبر رسید کہ بی دانشی بیتی از ابیاتِ مرا خرده گرفتہ و خود را از اہلِ معنی رسوا ساختہ۔
>
> [Ten or twelve verses in that refrain came out from the veins of my pen, and I recited them at the mushairah. After a week, I heard that some stupid, ill-advised persons caught the one verse from my verses, and declared themselves to be the dispensers of meaning][50]

This is the verse that drew disapproval in the second mushairah:[51]

> جز وِے از عالم و از ہمہ عالم بیشم
> ہم چو موئیکہ بتاں را زمیاں بر خیزد
> [I am a part of the world, and better than the whole world
> I am like the hair that grows from the beloved's waist]

Three objections were raised: *hamah alam* (ہمہ عالم) should not be used in conjunction with *alam* because the latter is a collective noun, *bish* should not be used in the form used by Ghalib but as *bishtar*; the verb *barkhastan* is not suitable for *khat* or 'mu'.[52] The critics provided Mirza Qatil's *Char Sharbat* to substantiate their arguments.[53] By the time the third mushairah took place, Ghalib's well-wishers had asked him to be cautious in responding to criticism. Fortunately, the ambassador from Iran rose to Ghalib's defence, praising his poetry, quoting verses from Hafiz, Sa'di and Zuhuri, which illustrated each one of the usages Ghalib was being attacked for.[54] The ambassador's defence of Ghalib appeared to annoy, not appease, the gathering. The quibbles were dispelled but never forgotten.

In the third mushairah, Ghalib's adversaries found another verse to criticize:

> شورِ اشکِ بہ فشارِ بُنِ مژگاں دارم
> طعنہ بر بے سرو سامانیِ طوفان زدئہ
> [I have the salt of tears in the roots of my eyelashes
> They taunt me for being homeless in a storm]

The objection was over the use of زدئہ. The arguments spilled beyond the gathering; complaints reached Navab Akbar Ali Khan about Ghalib's rude behaviour at mushairahs.[55] Navab Akbar Ali Khan and Maulvi Sirajuddin Ahmad advised Ghalib to maintain his equilibrium and apologize to the Calcutta poets.[56] While Ghalib does not mention the names of his detractors, except Afzal Beg, further research into this incident has revealed the names of two or three others. Maulana Abul Kalam Azad tracked them down.[57] The episode triggered a series of pamphlets and some columns in the weekly Persian newspaper *Jam-i Jahan Numa*. Ghalib was advised by his friends to patch up. He wrote the *Ashtinamah* by way of reconciliation; it was printed and distributed as a pamphlet. But the anger, distress and pain of his peers' criticism haunted Ghalib even after he had poured it out in poetry. Certainly, the *Ashtinamah* is a piquant poem, passionate and pain-filled. It can be interpreted literally, or with some allowance for rhetoric.

A careful reading of the *Ashtinamah* is warranted here because Ghalib's responses to his adversaries need to be judiciously studied with a view to the impact they might have had on his self-determined criteria of selection for his future divan(s). Although Ghalib did not entirely change his style—as has sometimes been claimed—after he began to disparage Indian poets writing in Persian, he did tone down his public expression of admiration for Mirza Bedil. He certainly did not include many of the verses in which he eulogized Bedil in the published Urdu divan.[58] Ghalib's apologia in the *Ashtinamah* was full of self-righteousness. Once the Calcutta sojourn was over, he made some pertinent revisions to it and changed the title to *Bad-e Mukhalif* (Adverse Winds). The poem must be read as an assertion of Ghalib's superiority in Persian; it is a manifesto, staking out a claim that he would keep making and defending for the rest of his career.

The poem itself comprises 155 verses.[59] Composed in the free-flowing metre used for masnavis, it has both momentum and style in equal measure. The first ten verses are addressed to the poets of Calcutta (*sukhanvaran-e Kalkattah*), praising them for their felicity with words. In the next twenty verses, Ghalib reminds them that he is their guest, a traveller who has been forced to visit their land by the vagaries of fortune. He implies that they have been harsh and unkind, instead of welcoming:

> بر غریبان کجا رواست ستم
> رحم گر نیست خود چراست ستم
> [Cruelty towards strangers is not the custom
> If you are not kind, why be cruel?]

With this strikingly emotional build-up, he dives into the controversy regarding his Persian with casual but hard-hitting clarity:[60]

> Who said first that *hamah alam* was incorrect?
> Who spoke in that manner first?
> Who said first that *bishtar* is better that *bish*?
> Who spoke ill of me in front of me?
> Who said that a hair from the waist was incorrect?
> Who said that this verse from top to bottom was incorrect?
> Now you have seen the objections were baseless,
> Whatever Ghalib has written was right.

The next twenty or so verses express how hurt Ghalib is by this unjust criticism. Then he begins an explanation of the finer details of his Persian usage. At this point, Ghalib brings up syntactical issues:[61]

> These objections have burned my soul,
> And singed the marrow in my bones.
> When I wrote *zadah* the *he* in it did not imply *kasrah-e zarafat*
> It's not an *izafat* either, but a marker of singular *ye*
> I did not invent this style,

> This blame should not be laid at my door.
> Others have written in this manner too.
> . . .
> *Mai zadah, gham zadah, sharab zadah*
> *Mai zadah* and *gham zadah*, are in this humble one's opinion
> inherent *izafats*
> Just like wax in honey
> One gets the meaning with a bit of effort
> But in some cases, its meaning can be
> 'afflicted with', but not always.

Ghalib then goes on to defend Mirza Bedil, whom he admired and venerated despite the latter not being an Iranian. After another twenty-some verses, in which he reiterates his responsibility towards representing Delhi at the Calcutta gathering, he slyly slips in Mirza Qatil's inability to write good Persian. Ghalib accuses Qatil of not being 'one of those with the language' (*ahl-e zaban*) because he does not have an ingrained understanding of Persian usages. Ghalib once again displays his own ease with the so-called controversial manipulations of language. He flourishes a string of names of great Persian poets: Sa'ib, Urfi, Naziri, Sa'di, Talib, Fughani and Zuhuri, all masters of style and meaning. These are the poets who should be emulated, not Qatil. After all this fist-shaking, sabre-rattling and posturing, Ghalib's masnavi concludes on a pseudo-conciliatory note, seeking forgiveness for excesses, because he is blameless!

Masud Hasan Rizvi Adib has compared the text of *Ashtinamah* with *Bad-e Mukhalif* and made important observations. Ghalib deleted several verses and added new ones. He also changed the order of verses. In fact, the changes are more pronounced towards the end of the masnavi. The verses in praise of Qatil, inserted for the sake of appeasement, are so exaggerated that they sound like disguised disparagement.[62]

While Ghalib's response to his critics produced one of his most sparkling pieces of poetry, his adversaries took the whole affair to unpleasant lengths. Besides publishing nasty columns about his poetry, they hurled abuses at him in the bazaar. They stooped so low as to attack Ghalib's pension petition. Ghalib's friends feared for his personal safety. Maulvi Sirajuddin Ahmad asked Ghalib to move out from the Shimla Bazaar house and take refuge in his house, an offer Ghalib delicately refused. In a lengthy letter to Maulvi Sirajuddin, he wrote:

> The barking of dogs doesn't diminish the daily bread of fakirs. But because birds can fly on the powerful wings of eagles, and rivers flow on the energy from the ocean, I have become disillusioned with this city [Calcutta]. My heart is deeply pained. I have rubbed my forehead on the dust of humility, but did not find acceptance. I took the path of apologies. They did not approve. I wonder what kind of service I should render, that the elders and notables of the society may consider me worthy of praise. This is my heart's blood that is flowing from my throat and lips. I don't see any purpose in going further. [What] I want to say is that it is well-known among astrologers that the adverse gaze of fortunate people doesn't do any harm, and the loving gaze of unfortunate ones doesn't do any good.[63]

The battles that Ghalib fought did not discourage him. Instead, they made him determined to succeed. During his year in Calcutta he was very prolific in Persian, writing some twenty-seven ghazals and many masnavis and qasidahs. The *Ashtinamah* has been singled out because of the circumstances in which it was written. I suggest that it be read as a text that illustrates how fastidious and fussy critics in this literary culture could be, and how much importance they assigned to grammar, usage and clarity. While Ghalib disproved all the objections that were raised, it must have heightened his awareness of his own propensity to reach for remote, obscure themes such as 'the hair that grows from the beloved's waist'.

Ghalib's sensitivity to his critics' nitpicking is illustrated in another incident from this time. A friend, Mirza Abul Qasim Khan, sent him a dish of dal and achar, with a *qita* (a short poem), by way of thanks for suggesting a remedy for a stomach ailment.[64] Ghalib responded to this gesture with a spontaneous qita praising the dal and achar. Later, he worried that this hastily written poem might fall into the wrong hands, that more faults might be found. He worried so much that he wrote a second qita and sent it off with a note that the first one was written in haste and should be destroyed.[65]

The Calcutta chapter in Ghalib's life planted the seeds for his prolonged clashes with critics and his lifelong series of victories and defeats in these linguistic wars. From belittling Indian poets of Persian, he went on to denigrate Indian lexicographers. His letters are full of harsh, unsavoury comments about Indian poets, especially Qatil. Ghalib's onslaught on Indian Persian reveals a deeper layer of insecurity that afflicted the nineteenth-century Urdu-Persian literati. As Shamsur Rahman Faruqi shows, the decline of Persian learning went hand in hand with the valorization of native Iranians over Indian writers.[66] This is a remarkable departure from the eighteenth century, a time when poets such Mirza Bedil, Mirza Mazhar Ali Jan-e Janan, Nasir Ali, Ashna, Faizi and Ghani were regarded as the authorities of correct usage.[67] The great lexicographer-poet Siraj Ali Khan-e Arzu led the way in endorsing Indian Persian usage as being on par with that of Iranians. Tek Chand Bahar's prodigious dictionary, *Bahar-e Ajam*, was regarded as the most complete work of its genre.[68] Sheikh Ali Hazin (1692–1766), an Iranian poet who had settled in Delhi and was a contemporary of Arzu, had started the trend of denigrating Indian Persian poets. He wrote savage satires making fun of Indian usages. Arzu and the others responded scathingly to these criticisms, but these episodes, coupled with the declining use of Persian, did create a doubt in the minds of the Indians about their own competence.

Ghalib composed almost entirely in Persian for nearly twenty years (1828–48), amassing a sizeable divan that was published in 1845. His focus on Persian, combined with his belligerence against Indian Persian, is a subject that bears down on the reception of his poetry in both Urdu and Persian by his peers, and also on how he was judged by posterity. Ghalib filled the breach in Persian composition at a time when the language had begun to languish in India. After centuries of literary domination, Persian was falling behind Urdu, whose literary efflorescence from the eighteenth century onwards was phenomenal. The rise of regional languages or modern vernaculars pushed Persian to the back seat. Its restricted use by Indians ultimately disconnected them from colloquial or native fluency. A group, or even a gang, of specialists or purists began guarding Persian from becoming corrupted. These purists exclusively privileged Iranian usage over Indian Persian and refused to accept the authority of Indian Persian poets/lexicographers.

While it is disturbing that Ghalib, a third-generation Indian, was at the forefront of those who denounced Indian Persian, we can surmise that perhaps there was a plan. We must remember that Ghalib was still quite young (in his early thirties), but mature as a poet, when he switched over entirely to Persian. After enjoying moderate success with Urdu poetry (heavily studded with Persian), he might have sensed a clear field in Persian. In his tirade against Indian Persian, he seems to have gone to extremes. Later in life, he went to the extent of denouncing the great Mirza Bedil, who was once his hero. In a letter to Abdul Ghafur in April 1859, he wrote:[69]

> Nasir Ali and Bedil and Ghanimat, of what worth is their Persian? Examine each one's poetry with the eye of justice. One doesn't need a mirror to see the bracelet on one's arm. Minnat and Makin and Vaqif and Qatil, their names are not even worth mentioning . . . Their poetry doesn't have that taste, it doesn't have the style of Iranians.

Ghalib considered his own Persian poetry to be his 'real' accomplishment, above and beyond his Urdu:[70]

> Go look at my Persian, so that you may find
> Paintings of many hues and colours;
> Pass over my Urdu collection, for it is only
> An initial drawing, devoid of colour

Ghalib flatly refused to accept Qatil, Vaqif or any other Indian Persian poet and linguist as an arbiter when it came to questions about Persian language and poetry. He continued to challenge other poets and linguists, all the while projecting himself as the only one in his generation fully schooled in colloquial and literary Persian. Ghalib was aware of the difference between idiomatic speech and a highly metaphorical and complex literary style, but he refused to accept or concede that creative licence was the right of anyone who knew a language. He saw himself as the sole standard-bearer of Persian poetry. In Calcutta, Ghalib spent considerable time with the Iranians who had shown an interest in his compositions. He even began to dress in the Iranian fashion. Persian clearly had a broader reach, a fact that had perhaps not dawned on him in Delhi, where Urdu was ascendant. Dreams of becoming known in Isfahan and Herat, in a literary culture that had produced the master poets he revered, were enticing. He saw himself as the conduit that connected Urdu and Persian thought through the genres of poetry.

It is not possible to hypothesize about Ghalib's poetic journey without taking into account his extensive Persian oeuvre. Upon his return from Calcutta, his mind was made up regarding his future path. He was going to be the leading exponent of Persian in India. Ghalib was at the top of his form at this point, and Persian flowed from his pen. He kept trimming his Urdu divan, even as he wrote increasingly in Persian. Meanwhile, over the next ten to twelve years, good fortune continued to elude him. He was arrested on charges of running a gambling den at his house (1841). Imprisonment followed; it was a test of endurance.

But better times awaited. He had submitted his Urdu divan to Saiyyid Muhammad Khan Bahadur's Press in Delhi (the Persian divan was ready, too). A comparison of the Persian and Urdu divans at this time is very instructive. The Urdu divan contained a total of 1090 verses, while the Persian divan had over 6000. The Urdu divan was published in 1841, while the Persian divan was brought out in 1845. Over a span of ten or fifteen years, Ghalib had composed a great deal in Persian. As a poet of Persian, Ghalib found a field that was open and devoid of challengers. The great age of Persian in India was over, but the language was becoming a haloed one that could not be trifled with. There was a hierarchy in place. At the top was Iranian Persian, the language of the poets who lived in Iran. Then there was Indo-Iranian Persian, whose exponents were Iranians residing in India. At the bottom were the Indian Persian poets who were third- or fourth-generation Indians, but of Iranian descent.[71] Although Ghalib was a third-generation practitioner of Persian, his self-confidence was luminous. He smugly looked down upon Indian Persian, to the point of disapproving the Iranians' using a word coined by Indians:

> The word '*be-pir*' is a coinage of Indian-born Turks . . . Mirza Jalal-e Asir—God's blessing be upon him—is pluripotent, and his usage is authoritative. How can I say that a word used by him is wrong? But it's a surprise, again, it's a surprise that an Iranian nobleman should use such a word.[72]

Ghalib's stance seems exaggerated. But it was a part of his self-proclaimed agenda to be recognized as the greatest authority on Persian in India. At the time he wrote the letter cited above, Ghalib also composed a pamphlet titled *Namah-e Ghalib*, in which he said:

> There are some among the poets of India who write well and who find new, attractive themes. But what fool would say that it behooves them to claim competent knowledge of the language? Now as regards the lexicographers, may God free us from their snares.[73]

In the same pamphlet, Ghalib went on to boast that he had a native capability for Persian, that it was a special gift from God. He claimed an intuitive grasp of the subtleties of Persian. He boasted that he stood above all Indian writers of Persian. While these claims may not have convinced everyone, they certainly pleased Ghalib.

By 1845 or so, Ghalib's star was ascending. Emperor Bahadur Shah Zafar entrusted him with the task of writing the history of the Mughal rulers. A stipend of Rs 50 per month was settled. The decade after 1845 was prolific. When the first Persian divan was published in 1845, Ghalib wrote to Maikash:[74]

> My Persian divan has reached from Delhi to Madras and Hyderabad; and from Lahore to Herat and Isfahan.

The Persian divan was followed by a collection of Ghalib's Persian prose works: *Panj Ahang* (1849), *Mehr-e Nim Roz* (1854), and many more.[75] A second enlarged edition of his Persian poetry was also under way. A large number of pupils flocked to his doors in a bid to improve their Persian verses.[76] As Ghalib turned to Persian to make his mark, the market for his Urdu poetry rose as well. It is impossible to understand Ghalib's success in Urdu without knowing the full story of his victory in Persian. The Calcutta sojourn was a catalyst for him making the switch from Urdu to Persian. We will now turn to the *Gul-e Ra'na*, his first intikhab of Urdu and Persian poetry, which he prepared in Calcutta in 1828.

5

The Two-Coloured Rose: *Gul-e Ra'na* (1828)

الٰہی ایں گلِ رعنا را بگوشۂ دستارِ قبول جا دہی و ہر کہ ایں را گرامی نہد سِپاسے
از وے بر من نہی

غالب- دیباچہ گل رعنا

[Lord, let this two-coloured rose find place in the sleeve of the turban of acceptance. Let thanks be due from me to him who looks upon it with favour]

—Ghalib, foreword, *Gul-e Ra'na*[1]

Ghalib made both friends and enemies in Calcutta. His dearest friend, with whom he remained in touch for the rest of his life, was Maulvi Sirajuddin Ahmad.[2] The maulvi was a scholar of Persian and an influential personality who edited the Persian weekly *A'inah-e Sikandar*. Sirajuddin Ahmad was from Lucknow but had been living in Calcutta when he met Ghalib. Their friendship blossomed: Ghalib published his poetry in *A'inah-e Sikandar*. It was at Sirajuddin Ahmad's request that he put together a selection of his Urdu and Persian poetry and called it *Gul-e Ra'na*.[3]

Bah Sirajuddin Ahmad charah juz taslim nist
Varnah Ghalib nist ahang-e ghazal khvani mara
[There is no recourse except to oblige Sirajuddin Ahmad
Otherwise Ghalib has no interest in reciting ghazals]

The letters Ghalib wrote to Sirajuddin Ahmad after returning from Calcutta constitute a large chunk of the *Panj Ahang* corpus.[4] His affection for Sirajuddin Ahmad is obvious in the manner he addresses him: 'my lord, my object of devotion, my ruler' (*aqa-e man, qiblah-e man, maula-e man*). An excerpt from his letter shows how highly he regarded the *A'inah-e Sikandar* and how much he valued the friendship:

> My lord, reading *A'inah-e Sikandar* illumined my eyes; the sharpness of its lettering strung pearls in the thread of my sight. It has good narratives, concise news, pleasing rhetorical points, and alluring illustrations. Your command governs my heart and soul. I will try my utmost to introduce this paper [in Delhi]. The people here are irritated with the unreliable news published in *Jam-e Jahan Numa*. They also do not have the proper taste for reading newspapers.[5]

Ghalib undertook the preparation of an intikhab soon after his friend made the request and finished it on 11 September 1828. He decided to give the selection a name. In poetry's colourful garden, what would be more appropriate than *gul-e ra'na*, a beautiful two-coloured rose? Ghalib had plucked a title that reflected his extraordinary felicity with words and would also appeal to those *ada shinasan* (connoisseurs) who had a taste for the complexity of language. Most people familiar with Persian would assume that 'gul-e ra'na' meant a beautiful rose or flower; but in fact it was a very specific kind of flower. In Maulvi Muhammad Lad's sixteenth-century dictionary, *Mu'idul Fuzala*, the gul-e ra'na is defined as a flower that is yellow and red (*zard-o-surkh*).[6] *Bahar-e Ajam* offers more details: it is a two-faced flower (*gul-e do rui*);

the inner part is red and the outer yellow (*andarunash surkh-o birun zard bashad*). The dictionary also suggests that 'two-coloured' could be used to imply 'two-faced'. The following delightful verse by Vahshi (Yazdi Kirmani) is quoted:

> *Bulbul an bih kih fareb-e gul-e ra'na na khurad*
> *Kih du-roze ast vafadari-e yaran-e du rang*
> [Better that the bulbul is not deceived by the two-coloured rose;
> Because the loyalty of two-faced friends lasts only a few days][7]

The tazkirah *Gul-e Aja'ib* quotes a verse by the Urdu poet Bedad:

> *Sar pe dastar-e basanti bar men jamah qirmizi*
> *Khub gaya dil men hamare us gul-e ra'na ka rang*
> [Head adorned with a yellow turban, and dress a wine-colour red
> My heart was delighted with the colourful style of that *gul-e ra'na*][8]

Not only did Ghalib choose a rare, beautiful name for this collection, he also wrote a thought-provoking dibachah and khatimah to go with it. It turned out that these prose pieces saved the *Gul-e Ra'na* from being lost to posterity. The intikhab itself was not published in Ghalib's lifetime. Also, I didn't find any discussion on the subject in his letters to Maulvi Sirajuddin. But because the dibachah and khatimah were published in the collection of Ghalib's Persian prose, scholars were aware that a manuscript of that name existed. I have often wondered why Maulvi Sirajuddin did not publish it, especially since Ghalib prefaced it with such a formal foreword in baroque, elegant prose, in a passionate tone and with a strong message.

In this crucial foreword, he talks about being away from his home and facing the challenge of a new environment. He justifies including Persian with the Urdu, calling it a poetry garden with two doors. More importantly, he directly appeals to the taste of Persianists:

> The second door to this colourful garden named Gul-e Ra'na is presented to the Persian taste, [whose poetry is] a wine that brings down enemies and that vanquishes the one who is a [full] man[9]

Perhaps I am overreaching in suggesting that this collection was meant to be published. Perhaps it was not, because Ghalib had other, grander plans for his Persian poetry. In any case, *Gul-e Ra'na* was seemingly forgotten once the Urdu divan was published in 1841 and the Persian in 1845.

The story of the recovery of its first full manuscript is told with inimitable flair by the well-known Ghalib scholar Malik Ram.[10] Forever in pursuit of rare books, Malik Ram was one day presented with an inconspicuous-looking manuscript by his friend and mentor Saiyyid Naqi Bilgrami. Its cover bore the title *Mutaffariq Kalam-e Ghalib* (An Assortment of Ghalib's Poetry). This rare manuscript had been in the library of Saiyyid Karam Husain Bilgrami, a wealthy nobleman from Bilgram (in present-day Uttar Pradesh) known for his patronage of poetry. Saiyyid Karam Husain often visited Calcutta and had been introduced to Ghalib there by Maulvi Sirajuddin Ahmad. Ghalib and Saiyyid Karam Husain became good friends.[11] When Ghalib compiled the *Gul-e Ra'na*, Husain requested a copy and even arranged for a scribe. The manuscript stayed in the Bilgrami family and was passed down the generations until it was gifted to Malik Ram in 1957. For various reasons, Malik Ram could not publish an edition of the manuscript until 1970, but he wrote two important articles introducing the newly discovered manuscript.[12]

Meanwhile, two other manuscripts of the *Gul-e Ra'na*—one of them in Ghalib's own hand—were found in Lahore (edited and published in 1969). The one in Ghalib's own hand is now known as the *Nuskhah-e Khvajah*, named after its present owner, Khwaja Muhammad Husain. At present, there are, including Malik Ram's, four known manuscripts of the *Gul-e Ra'na*.[13]

Abidi's Edition

Vazirul Hasan Abidi, the editor of the two Lahore manuscripts, has an interesting account of his pursuit of the *Gul-e Ra'na*. He first saw the manuscript of the *Nuskhah-e Khvajah* in 1952, in Khwaja Muhammad Husain's private collection. Since this had been Ghalib's personal copy, its owner considered it to be very special. It took sixteen years for Abidi to convince Khwaja Muhammad Husain to allow him to examine the manuscript closely. Meanwhile, Abidi learnt of another manuscript of the *Gul-e Ra'na* in the personal library of Hakim Muhammad Nabi Khan Jamal-e Suvaida. This manuscript, known as the *Nuskhah-e Suvaida*, according to Abidi, had been prepared by Ghalib's contemporary Izzatullah Dihlavi, from Ghalib's personal copy. Hakim Nabi Khan allowed Abidi to make a copy of this rare manuscript.[14] Access to the two manuscripts gave Abidi the opportunity to compare them. He made note of the idiosyncrasies, the major and minor differences in the text, all of which are detailed in his 1969 edition.

Abidi's edition has a long introduction running into eighty-odd pages, divided into sections. Each section has a title which has the word *gul* in it, such as *bazm-e gul, rang-e gul, daman-e gul, barg-e gul*, and so on. The information is dense; the titles are very distracting, and even confusing. Sifting through meticulous details, two important points are worth noting: first, the foreword of the *Gul-e Ra'na* included in *Panj Ahang* has some sentences deleted from the text, presumably by Ghalib himself.[15] Second, Abidi reports that the *Ashtinamah*, written in a cramped, hasty shikastah, is included as an addition on the last few pages of the *Nuskhah-e Khvajah*. The *Ashtinamah*, Ghalib's response to his critics in Calcutta is not included in all the manuscripts.[16] Abidi provides a concordance of the *Gul-e Ra'na* with the Divan of 1821, the Divan of 1826 and the published divan, in an attempt to throw light on the editorial trail of the selections in their historical context.[17] The multiplicity of references, and some errors in this comparison, make it difficult to grasp his research entirely, but it does help us somewhat in following the convoluted path of Ghalib's process of selection.

Abidi has examined the *Gul-e Ra'na*'s foreword and afterword, mostly for textual accuracy and historical fact-checking. For example, he has reported that the date inscribed at the end of the foreword, in Ghalib's hand, is September 1828. The date is relevant because in the *Nuskhah-e Suvaida* the date at the end of the foreword is May 1830. Abidi avers that the two forewords are otherwise exactly the same. The version with some important sentences deleted first appears in the manuscript of *Panj Ahang*, which is dated 1838.[18] Moving on to the selection itself, Abidi finds it peculiar that Ghalib did not arrange the Persian ghazals in the proper traditional order by refrain (radif), but he does not speculate why this unusual choice might have been made. I, too, find this puzzling. Arranging twenty-seven ghazals is a lot easier than arranging the 117 that form the Urdu section. I will return to this important issue later in the chapter.

Ghalib's afterword, too, has oddities that are alluded to, but not described, by Abidi. Since Abidi's edition has many sections (as mentioned earlier), in which he appears to go over the nuskhah with a fine-tooth comb, I am surprised that he did not translate the dibachah and khatimah into Urdu for the benefit of his readers.[19] Ghalib's Persian prose is intricate but delightful. It seems unlikely that he wrote those pieces in such an ornate style only for a personal notebook meant for a friend. As I noted earlier, Ghalib later included the dibachah and khatimah in his published Persian prose writings.

Malik Ram's Edition

Malik Ram's edition of the *Gul-e Ra'na* (1970) brings out new facets of this important work. In his manuscript, presented to him by Naqi Bilgrami, the date at the end of the foreword has been left blank by the copyist.[20] The text also has blank spots where the copyist apparently could not decipher the word in the original. In his introduction, Malik Ram has discussed the contentious issue of Ghalib's pen name, because it pertains to the bureaucratic hassles in the presentation of the pension case in Calcutta.

Malik Ram accepts the possibility that the afterword in his manuscript could have been copied at a later date from the *Panj Ahang*, or some other collection of prose works. The reason is that the scribe erroneously wrote *khatimah divan-e farsi* (end of Persian divan) at the very end.[21] This shows that the text of the afterword was copied later from a collection of Ghalib's Persian works. In my opinion, it is a minor point because the main text, that is the *Gul-e Ra'na* itself, is intact. What it does show, however, is that in the manuscript edited by Malik Ram, the source from which the copy was made did not have the afterword. Malik Ram's manuscript also did not include the *Ashtinamah*. However, the details are pointers in studying the manuscript history of Ghalib's work.

In the last section of his introduction, Malik Ram broaches the subject of the making of an intikhab by quoting a famous passage from Muhammad Husain Azad's *Ab-e Hayat*, in which Azad claims that the selection process for the published divan was delegated to Ghalib's friends. Malik Ram rightly observes that because Ghalib personally did the intikhab for *Gul-e Ra'na*, he would surely have done the same for his Urdu divan.[22] He also notes Ghalib's steadfast allegiance to Mirza Bedil's poetic style, such that Ghalib's style did not undergo any major change from youth to old age. His poetry was always a mixture of complex, obscure and deceptively simple verses. He provides a sampling of popular ghazals from the early and later periods to substantiate this claim. Malik Ram does not offer a translation or any comments or analysis of Ghalib's foreword and afterword. Once again, Malik Ram's not offering a translation shows lack of rigour in the critical tradition.

Naqvi's Edition

The final edition of *Gul-e Ra'na* is Saiyyid Qudrat Naqvi's (1975).[23] This manuscript, too, has an interesting history, recounted by Naqvi in great detail. Noted Urdu scholar Mushfiq Khwaja, who had found the manuscript in the library of Saiyyid Vasi Bilgrami, brought it to his attention. It had been copied by Har Narain urf Umrao Singh.[24] Bilgrami was the grandson of Ghalib's pupil Safir Bilgrami,[25] whose maternal grandfather (Sahib-e Alam Maraharvi) was close to Ghalib.[26] The manuscript, however, did not belong to the Bilgrami family. It was a gift from Mir Saiyyid Askari Hasan Jafri on the occasion of Eid in 1945. The manuscript apparently belonged to one Maula Bakhsh, whose name appears with the date of 1255/1839, which is some eleven years after the original was first written. It was sold to an unknown buyer in 1310/1905. Jafri acquired it in 1924.

An important feature of Naqvi's edition is that it provides a facsimile version of the manuscript. Also, Naqvi's edition is fastidious. He has painstakingly compared the published editions with his own manuscript to establish the authenticity of the text, as well as the date of the copy. Naqvi is critical of Abidi's edition, blaming him for patching together a text from different sources. The foreword in Abidi's edition is taken from the *Nuskhah-e Suvaida* and the afterword from *Panj Ahang*, because the former does not have an afterword. Nor has Abidi noted the differences in the text of the *Ashtinamah*. According to Naqvi, it is apparent that Abidi depended mostly on Malik Ram's descriptions of his manuscript because his access to the original, the *Nuskhah-e Khvajah*, was limited.[27] Naqvi, on the other hand, provides readers with information about the *Nuskhah-e Khvajah* from the brief article by Mu'inur Rahman, in the special Ghalib volume of the journal *Nuqush*.[28] According to Rahman's description, the selection begins with its title as an invocation: *ya asadullah al-ghalib* (O lion of God, the victorious).[29] At the end, it is signed 'Muhammad Asadullah'. Abidi made no mention of these special features. In Naqvi's afterword, there are two paragraphs and five verses missing from both Abidi and Malik Ram's editions.[30] Naqvi rightly concludes that in the Abidi and Malik Ram manuscripts, the afterword was copied from *Panj Ahang* (1835). Thus their text is established as a version appearing much later than the original.

Naqvi also tells the story of the *Ashtinamah* with all its twists and turns.[31] The point he wants to emphasize is that the *Ashtinamah* must have been composed after the *Gul-e Ra'na* selections were made, or else it would have been a part of the Persian section of that text. The thread of Naqvi's story goes back all the way to Mirza Afzal Beg, who had spread the canard that Ghalib was not trustworthy because he had changed his pen name. Afzal Beg was connected to Munshi Abdul Karim of the governmental Persian department; he was influential in literary circles and was certainly active in the mushairahs. Naqvi gives details of three mushairahs, as we saw in the previous chapter.[32]

Dibachah (Foreword) to the *Gul-e Ra'na*

The three editions of the *Gul-e Ra'na*, with their elaborate introductions and discussions of the textual variations, offer virtually no comments on Ghalib's substantial foreword and afterword that accompany the formative text. Although all three editions are for an Urdu audience, the editors have not translated or summarized Ghalib's complicated Persian prose, denying the non-Persianist reader access to these vital sections.[33] The foreword shows that Ghalib hoped for wide circulation of this manuscript, and that he spent time thinking about the interrelationship between Urdu and Persian poetry, and their audience.

The foreword is a piece of literary baroque, speckled with delightful phrases and unexpected turns, almost like poetry, with a dazzling display of metaphors. Of course, we have to look beyond the screen of sophisticated language to understand Ghalib's intent or purpose in writing it. He begins in a somewhat traditional mode, begging for indulgence from God for his boldness in expressing himself poetically:

> O Lord, despair of your beneficence has emboldened my sins. Crush the arrogance of my madness with the power of your kindness; my desolate heart has become cold from the autumn of deprivation of your bounty. My longings have stoked a fire; don't extinguish it. The fire of my suffering condition is the igniter of the harvest of the future. I have burns from the fires of the hell of non-achievement, don't aggravate them. My life is spent in being a spectator of the eternal glories of springtimes past.

After some more of the same, Ghalib gets around to introducing himself and his poetry:

> As one of those who mix freedom and restraint, I am at the crossroads of doubt and joy, a desirer of illness and pain, with a world of sorrow in my heart. I, Muhammad Asadullah of Samarqand, was born in Akbarabad [Agra], and am a resident of Delhi. As a traveller on the carpet of claim in search of praise, I am creating language from the fabric of my heart, and the unfulfilled lament, washed with tears from my heart, has reached the ears of friends. Those who understand both the depths and the shades of poetry, and those who are aware of the perfections and flaws of this art, know very well that I have not gotten up from the carpet of claim, nor have I made a show of superior intellect. For a long time now, my heart-melting poetry has been searching for hearts that can understand it. I have sprinkled it with the dust of the nuances of words, and with the meaning of the dark-inked letters.[34]

There are several points to be noted in this passage. The first is that Ghalib connects himself to the Persian cosmopolis by mentioning his alleged 'Samarqandi' heritage. Second, he craves for 'hearts' that can understand the depths and nuances of his poetry. Third, he speaks of 'nuances' and the 'meaning' of words, signifying his claim of taking language to its highest capacity in expressing thought. He also makes a point of being 'a resident of Delhi' and a 'traveller', which shows that Ghalib was anxious about the reception his work would receive in Calcutta.

However, the most striking section of the foreword is the clarification that Ghalib gives regarding his engagement with Urdu and Persian:

> Observe the reach of my capabilities, such that I have taken Hindi [Urdu] from Delhi to Isfahan; and applaud the strength of the thread of my thought, that I have brought Persian from Shiraz to Hindustan. I regret the exaggerated praise that I have bestowed on myself in showing my face, having removed the veil of modesty. *They say that the blood of two languages is on my head, and the corpses of the two I have killed are on my shoulders.* So what if one of the languages by my side has become a stranger in its own homeland, and the other due to my ill-fortune is being estranged in its own homeland? Where is that silence that would remove me from the vengeance being sought from me for these languages, and would also free me from the ups and downs of acceptance and rejection by listeners?[35]

The big question that Ghalib addresses here is the literary status of the two languages—Urdu and Persian—including their geography and their cultural currency. The second, more complex, question concerns the pitfalls of writing in two languages. The sentence I have italicized can be given alternative readings. At one level, it implies that Ghalib has not succeeded in either language, an exaggeration that could also imply the opposite. Or else it could be taken to imply that he had no business to put the two together in one volume, thus doing an injustice to both. I am making an educated guess about what

Ghalib might have meant—the language that 'has become a stranger in its homeland' is Urdu; the language that 'is being estranged' is Persian—and he could have meant the opposite, too. The point I would like to emphasize is the poet's concern about the acceptance of his work.

Indeed, Ghalib was at a crossroads. He had been writing mostly in Urdu until 1828, but in Calcutta he found a culture where Persian was thriving, and so he began to write more in Persian, and also to valorize Persian over Urdu. Ghalib had supreme confidence in his ability to craft unique metaphors. He was also keen to impress a host of Persian connoisseurs, a scenario somewhat different from the one in Delhi. It is very clear that he wanted to emphasize his status as a traveller who was exploring new ground both literally and metaphorically:

> In this garden, I am like a bird that has lost its nest; from head to toe I am burning with the flame of my own voice. My lament has made my breath like sparks of lightning; my heart is melting. The colours and fragrances of those who inhabit this garden, and those who are intoxicated by this joyful gathering—their heart-searing voices have awakened the music of understanding in me. With every breath, the lightning of the pain of my lament takes the measure of my being. People are unaware that my heart is in pieces, that my liver is broken to bits, that a blood-soaked voice emerges from my throat. Fear of my listeners makes my breath heave in my chest like a wave in a wine glass. Hostility from my rivals causes the blood from my broken heart to drip like water from a broken earthen cup.

The poetic quality of Ghalib's prose is not surprising; it was the trend of the time. However, he succeeded in going beyond the formal trappings to communicate his trepidation about sharing his precious poems with a new audience:

> Friends have created gatherings and have insisted that I light the candle of poetry. Amazement has made me catch my breath, and shyness has stitched my eyes to my feet.

In the last section of the foreword, Ghalib thanked Sirajuddin Ahmad profusely for encouraging him to prepare this selection:

> He is like shade and spring water to the heart-burnt travellers in the valley of desire, like the shade of friendship of the tree of Tuba and the stream of Kausar in Paradise. He has the qualities of Jupiter; he is courageous by nature, with an angel-like face and God-like temperament.

At the end, Ghalib again referred to his new approach of bringing Urdu and Persian poetry together in one collection. He called the intikhab a 'two-coloured curtain' hung on the window of the 'single-coloured' (*yak-rang*) and entirely perceptive audience.[36] The powerful closing lines emphasized the contiguity of Urdu with Persian, and brought the metaphor of an attractive poetry garden to a graceful conclusion—with the two-coloured rose finding what he called 'a place in the turban of acceptance':[37]

> Every gate in this garden has doors that open face to face. The first I have adorned with the pearls of Hindi (Urdu) poetry. Since the second door is for those who love Persian, and who appreciate style, I have named this notebook (*bayaz*) Gul-e Ra'na. Lord, give this 'two-coloured rose' a place in the turban of acceptance. Whoever accepts this, may thanks from me accrue to them. God alone is enough; the rest have lost their path.[38]

Khatimah (Afterword) to the *Gul-e Ra'na*

The afterword is even more showy and exaggerated than the foreword, but it is mostly rhetoric and yields a lot less information.

However, it is very interesting from the perspective of style. It begins with a prelude of sorts: a visitation from Ghalib's muse, who praises him for creating a new style but chides him for not taking full advantage of the treasures she has to offer. The style of this long passage is delightfully glitzy and airy, with sentence upon sentence of rhymed prose and extravagant poetic language:

> The night when the writing of this pearly document reached its height, after much pushing and pulling, my wayward thought became satisfied. The pen left my hand, as the lament left my heart. My head found my pillow, just as a scar finds a place in the heart. Sleep surged; drowsiness took me away. Suddenly, before my sight, which was waiting to arise and travel in the early morning, a bolt of lightning struck the curtain of imagination. A shining visage came to view as the dust cloud lifted from my consciousness. Her eyes were dark without collyrium, like those of the enchantresses of the desert; her face was rosy like those of the village belles, but without any make-up. Her neck and ears were not adorned with jewels. Her lips were smiling, her eyes shining. She was tall like ambition. Her tresses were as tangled as my days and nights. Her forehead blossomed as beautifully as a wild rose. Her walk was as carefree as spring's flood. Her long hair floated down to her feet in intoxicated coquetry. She removed the veil from her face. Biting her lip as lovers do, she approached me.[39]

After two more paragraphs of verbal baroque, the muse finally asks Ghalib: 'How will you adorn this afterword? With what designs and decorative borders will you embellish this afterword?'[40] To this, Ghalib responds with a long passage of elaborate, elegant prose, at the end of which he announces that he will decorate the afterword with a sample of dotless prose (san'at-e ta'til): 'I will produce such prose that you will find the "high point of the selection" (*nuqtah-e intikhab*) wherever you please.'[41] Since the device of dotless prose requires that no letters with 'points' or dots (*nuqtah*) be used, Ghalib's banter is right on the mark. To provide an example of this dot-free prose, Ghalib resorts to a dotless letter he had earlier written to Maulvi Fazl-e Haq, explaining the exigency of leaving without bidding farewell.[42] The letter is remarkable not so much for its contents as for a glimpse of the rigours of the literary culture that took pride in crafting complex writing, and did not regard prose as being different from poetry in the art of eloquence. The afterword includes not one but two such dotless letters. The second letter was addressed to Navab Agha Mir of Lucknow. There is a qita in the dotless mode included in it. The afterword ends rather abruptly with this letter.

It seems to me that the purpose of the afterword was to demonstrate Ghalib's ingenuity with prose. Since the Persian section of the volume was not as extensive as the Urdu one, sumptuous prose in Persian perhaps compensated for this limitation. Although up to this point Ghalib had composed mostly in Urdu, and very little in Persian, it's striking that the selection in *Gul-e Ra'na* is evenly split between Urdu and Persian. Was this Ghalib's choice or Maulvi Sirajuddin Ahmad's suggestion? The number of both Urdu and Persian verses here is 455.[43] However, the Urdu verses have been selected from 117 ghazals, while the Persian ones are from only twenty-seven. The bulk of the Persian verses are from a qasidah (written for Andrew Stirling), two qitas and the masnavi on Banaras, *Chiragh-e Dair*.[44] This set of verses from longer poems includes 207 verses.[45] The Persian ghazals are not arranged by refrain and are presented in full. Thus, it's clear that up to that time, Ghalib had been writing mostly Urdu poetry. Moreover, he had an Urdu divan with him, properly arranged according to the refrain. The Urdu divan, most probably the Divan of 1821, made the Urdu choices easier to organize; the Persian ghazals were copied from a notebook.

The Evolution of the Urdu Divan

A puzzle that has engaged some scholars is the identification of the manuscript Ghalib brought with him to Calcutta. Was it the Divan of 1821? Is there another manuscript waiting to be found? As we saw in Chapter 3, this is a very difficult question to answer. I will try to do so by examining the text of the Divan of 1821, in comparison with the divans of 1816 and 1826. The possibility of Ghalib having the Divan of 1826 with him can be ruled out because fresh verse entries appear in its text, in the margins, with notations that show that the verse was sent by the poet during the course of his travels. I will also examine the first ghazal in the three manuscript divans (1816, 1821 and 1826), as well as the published *Divan of 1841*, to illustrate its varying versions and to determine what was available to Ghalib when he made the selection.

For *Gul-e Ra'na*, Ghalib selected the following three verses from this ghazal:[46]

Naqsh faryadi hai kis ki shokhi-e tahrir ka
Kaghazi hai pairahan har paikar-e tasvir ka
[The picture is a plaintiff of whose mischievousness of writing,
Every figure in the picture wears a paper robe]

Jazbah-e be-ikhtiyar-e shauq dekha chahiye
Sinah-e shamshir se bahar hai dam shamshir ka
[The wild rush of ardour—you ought to see it
The sword's breath is drawn out of its breast]

Kav-kav-e sakht-janiha-e tanha'i nah puchh
Sub'h karna sham ka lana hai ju-e shir ka
[Don't ask about the digging of the toughness of solitude;
Getting through night to morning is (like) cutting through stone]

The second verse selected for the *Gul-e Ra'na* is not included in the main text of the Divan of 1821, but it is duly noted in the margin along with:

Agahi dam-e shunidan jis qadar chahe bichha'e
Mudda'a anqa hai apne alam-e taqrir ka
[Awareness may spread its nets as much as it can
The meaning of my speech's state is an Anqa]

Thus, the Divan of 1821 has seven plus two, i.e. nine, verses for this ghazal. But it is obvious that the two verses in the margin were composed later. The Divan of 1816 has seven verses; it does not have the two noted in the margins in 1821. The Divan of 1826 has both these verses in the main body, with one addition in the margin, bringing the total to ten:

Bas kih hun Ghalib asiri men bhi atash zer-e pa
Mu-e atash-didah hai halqah meri zanjir ka
[Even in bondage, Ghalib, my feet are on fire,
The link of my fetter is a fire-singed hair]

The verse above is included in all three early divans, though in varying forms:

Atashin-pa hun gudaz-e vahshat-e zindan nah puchh
Mu-e atashididah hai har halqah yan zanjir ka
[My feet are aflame, don't ask of the heat of restiveness in bondage;
Every link of my fetter is a fire-singed hair]

It is clear that Ghalib modified the verse above and then dropped the earlier version from what later became his published divan. The published divan has five verses for this ghazal: the three included in *Gul-e Ra'na*, plus the two noted in the margins in 1821.

The next entries in *Gul-e Ra'na* are three verses chosen from two ghazals that share the same formal structure and metre (*tarh*):

1.
Tha khvab men khiyal ko tujh se mu'amilah
Jab ankh khul gayi nah ziyan tha nah sud tha
[In dreams my thought associated with you;
When I opened my eyes, there was neither loss nor gain]

2.
Leta hun maktab-e gham-e dil men sabaq hanuz
Lekin yihi kih raft gaya aur bud tha
[I take lessons still in the school of the grief of the heart;
But only that: *raft* is 'went' and *bud* 'was']

3.
Dhanpa kafan ne dagh-e ayub-e barahnagi
Main varnah har libas men nang-e vujud thā
[A shroud covered the stain of the flaws of nakedness
Otherwise, in every garment I was a disgrace to existence]

These verses appear in the divans of 1821 and 1826, but not in that of 1816. There is a slight but interesting modification in the second line of the first verse, as it appears in the *Gul-e Ra'na*. The earlier divans have the following:

Mizhgan jo va hu'i nah ziyan tha nah sud tha
[When eyelashes parted, there was neither loss nor gain]

Apparently, Ghalib altered and improved the line when making the selection for *Gul-e Ra'na*. The change from *mizhgan jo va hu'i* (when the eyelashes parted) to *jab ankh khul gayi* (when the eyes opened) is striking and accords another level of meaning to the verse. *Ankh khul jana* is an idiomatic expression that means to wake up, to become acutely aware of one's failings or shortcomings (compare to 'his eyes were opened' in English). 'Ankh khul jana' in common speech also means to wake up; here both senses are fully and enjoyably operative. Moreover, thinking of the beloved in a dream is more complex than simply thinking of the beloved. Daydreaming can be brought into the mix of ideas floated here. Because the 'association' (*mu'amilah*, which can also imply intimacy) happened in a dream, nothing was gained or lost. Ghalib's editing here is a good example of his fastidiousness.

The double-ghazals (*do-ghazlah*), from which the verses were chosen, had a total of fourteen verses. In the published divan, Ghalib presents six verses—the three selected for *Gul-e Ra'na* and three more, merged together as one ghazal.[47] Although there were two opening verses available to him, Ghalib decided to do without one. Below are the three verses (selected from the original fourteen) that were added to the three from *Gul-e Ra'na* to make up the six that appear in the published divan:

1.
Juz Qais aur ko'i nah aya bah ru-e kar
Sahra magar bah tangi-e chashm-e hasud tha
[No one but Qais came into the field of action;
The desert perhaps was narrow like a jealous eye]

2.
Ashuftagi ne naqsh-e suvaida kiya durust
Zahir hu'a kih dagh ka sarmayah dud tha
[Anxiety fixed up the black spot in the heart,
It became apparent that the wealth of the scar was smoke]

3.
Teshe baghair mar nah saka kohkan asad
Sar-gashtah-e khumar-e rusum-o-quyud tha
[Farhad couldn't die without an axe, Asad,
He was dizzied by the hangover of customs and traditions]

A total of eight verses from these two ghazals were left out of the published divan, and at least four of these are splendid. There is, surprisingly, no difference in style, complexity or ambiguity which can explain why the ones that were selected were preferred over the others. There was something other than complexity that was driving Ghalib in the selection process. Here are the four verses that I think are worth including in any selection of Ghalib's poetry:

1.
Alam jahan bah arz-e bisat-e vujud tha
Jun subh chak-e jeb mujhe tar-o-pud tha
[When the world was awaiting the dawn of creation,
Like dawn, a ripped collar was all I had as my warp and weft]

2.
Alam tilism-e shahr-e khamoshan hai sar bah sar
Ya main gharib-e kishvar-e guft-o-shunud tha
[The world is an enchantment, a city of ghosts from end to end
Or I am a stranger, to the realm of speech and hearing]

3.
Tangi rafiq-e rah thi adam ya vujud tha
Mera safar bah tala-e chashm-e husud tha
[Whether in the state of existence, or non-existence, constriction was my constant companion;
My life's journey was under a star that was narrow like a jealous eye]

4.
Gardish muhit-e zulm raha jis qadar falak
Main pa'imal-e ghamzah-e chashm-e kabud tha
[However much the revolving sky was an ocean of tyranny upon me
I was crushed by the sidelong glance of an azure eye]

I have explained the above verses at length in my commentary on the 'unpublished' verses of Ghalib.[48] One can even make the argument that these verses (except the fourth one) are Bedilian in style. The last verse is in fact a great example of Ghalib's innovative genius. Blue is considered to be an inauspicious colour among the Iranians. Thus, the blue sky is blamed for tyranny and inflicting cruelty upon human beings. The sky (or the skies, for there are seven, or nine) is supposed to spin (which explains the changes in the positions of the stars). The sky keeps spinning, that is, it constantly keeps piling on new afflictions. Because the stars change their positions, and it's the stars that govern the destiny of men, the sky is the author of all misfortune. A point of theology: since it is not possible to blame God for human misfortunes, the sky (or the skies) become an easy scapegoat, since its rotation affected the position of the stars. A delightful point: the poem's speaker was unfazed because he was captivated by the azure eyes of the cruel, beautiful beloved. In spite of the heavy Persianisms, the theme is unforcedly romantic.

The Beginnings of the Persian Divan

Gul-e Ra'na's Persian section begins with a fifty-five-verse qasidah in praise of Andrew Stirling.[49] Although we saw in Chapter 4 why Ghalib wrote this qasidah, the beauty of its composition is exceptional. It is unusual to find a qasidah (as opposed to a ghazal) brimming with emotions as personal as this one:

I.

مرا دلےست ز درد شکستگی لبریز

نہ آرزوی امیری نہ حسرت خانی

[My heart is bleeding with the pain of being broken

I don't have desires to be an Amir or Khan]

2.
کجاست جیب کہ چاکے درو توانم کرد
مگر جگر بہ دریدن دہم ز عریانی

[Where is the collar that I can tear?
But I can tear my liver and bare it]

Two qitas follow the qasidah. The second presents Ghalib's peregrinations in a very lively question-and-answer form, and concludes with his observations of Calcutta, its literary scene and other delights.[50]

3.
ساقی بزم آگہی روزے
راوقے ریخت در پیالہء من
[One day, the Saqi of the gathering of awareness
Poured wine into my cup.
When that wine hit my brain
I became as fearless as a cavalryman]
[. . .]
He [the Saqi] asked, 'What was the reason for travel?'
I said, 'The cruelty and disloyalty of my people.'
He said, 'Tell me, what is Delhi?'
I said, 'It's a soul, and the world its body.'
He said, 'What is this Banaras?'
I said, 'A beautiful beloved, engrossed in plucking flowers.'
He said, 'How sweet is it?'
I said, 'It is sweeter than sweets.'
He said, 'What is Azimabad?'
I said, 'More colourful than a thousand gardens.'
He asked, 'Tell us about Calcutta then.'
I said, 'It is one of the seven skies.'

He asked, 'Do humans reside there?'
I said, 'From every place and of every profession.'
He said, 'What are you doing there?'[51]

The masnavi on Banaras follows the qitas.[52] The ghazal section in the *Gul-e Ra'na* is very special because most of the ghazals are new, composed by the young Ghalib as he rose to the challenge of competing with an unfriendly group. Abidi's comparison of Ghalib's ghazals with those of the great masters of Persian shows that most of the ghazals are in tarhs (rhyming elements plus metre) used by Naziri, Zuhuri, Sa'ib, Urfi, Faizi, Talib, Hazin and Bedil.[53] Abidi thus suggests that Ghalib is no less than these masters. Comparison with master poets is a time-honoured critical lens for the classical ghazal, since the same theme is often repeated with new nuances. Writing new ghazals in the same metre as well-known ones makes such comparison easier. Here is an example of comparison with Ghalib's opening verse:

4.
شبہای غم کہ چہرہ بہ خوناب شستہ ایم
از دیدہ نقش وسوسہء خواب شستہ ایم
[The nights when I wash my face with tears of blood
I am washing from my eyes the tumult of dreams]

From Zuhuri:

درد ورع زدل بہ مے ناب شستہ ایم
وز جوش داغ سینہ بخوناب شستہ ایم
[The pain of temperance/cowardice in my heart I wash with wine
And the festering scar on my breast I wash with tears of blood]

From Faizi:

> ما لب زنوشدا روی سہراب شستہ ایم
> ساغر بہ زہر و شیشہ بہ خوناب شستہ ایم
> [Our lips we refresh with ruby-red water
> The wine with poison and glass with tears of blood]

The *Gul-e Ra'na* is an invaluable text because it helps us understand Ghalib's logic behind his selection process, both here and later for his published Urdu Divan of 1841, which he undertook presumably after the *Gul-e Ra'na*. Since the selection for the Urdu Divan of 1841 was made so close to the episode of his denouncing Indian Persian poets, he may have avoided including she'rs that were very Bedilian in style. While Ghalib was sensitive to criticism, he set exacting standards for himself, too. From the very beginning, he edited and constantly revised his poetry. This is evident when we compare the existing manuscripts. He excluded many ghazals and rubais from the 1816 manuscript when the Divan of 1821 was prepared. They were mostly his earliest ghazals and, presumably, lacked the finesse of his later work. Many of the verses quoted in tazkirahs such as *Tazkirah-e Sarvar, Bagh-e Mihr* and *Tazkirah-e Zaka* were not included in his published divan. This indicates that he had distanced himself from, and did not care to look back on, his earliest work. But it also shows that he was not careful about preserving all of his poetry. It appears that he did not keep personal copies of each subsequent divan as it was updated. But we can follow the fascinating trail of corrections and updates in the margins of the manuscript divans available to us.

There is a vital connection between the Calcutta journey and Ghalib's trajectory that I want to emphasize here. In Calcutta, Ghalib began to embrace Persian in a manner that was conspicuously absent before. We must remember that Ghalib's Persian kulliyat comprises 10,000 two-line verses, while his entire Urdu corpus is not much over 4000 verses.

From examining three early divans in the previous chapters, we know that Ghalib regularly modified verses, besides enhancing and pruning his ghazals. He also made new additions in the margins of manuscripts; he scored through or marked verses that he wanted to remove. He did this carefully, over a period of time, with each new copy of his divan. In the early phase of his poetic career, when he was quite young—in fact, by modern standards, only a teenager—he wrote mostly in Urdu.

So the overarching point to be gleaned from looking at the various manuscripts is that for Ghalib, the making of an intikhab was a specific practice. With a light-hearted and self-reflexive tone, Ghalib introduces us to the Urdu section of his last intikhab prepared in 1866:[54]

Khulta kisi pah kyun mire dil ka mu'amilah
She'ron ke intikhab ne rusva kiya mujhe
[How would anyone have known the matters of my heart?
My intikhab of verses brought me out into the open]

6

The Culture of Book Publishing and the Divan of 1841

I hope that [the] literati, and also those who appreciate my work, would not declare the scattered pages [*abyat*] which are not included in this divan to be the result of the ink from my quill, and would not oblige the collection of my writings with praise of those verses, nor would they lay blame on me for their adaptations.

—Ghalib, dibachah to the Divan of 1841[1]

Chand rangin nuktah-e dilkash takalluf bar-taraf
Didah am divan-e Ghalib intikhab-e besh nist
[A few colourful, delightful nuances, let's put aside formalities—
I have seen the *Divan-e Ghalib*, it's no more than an intikhab]

—Ghalib, intikhab of 1866[2]

In the previous chapter, we discussed Ghalib's unique Urdu and Persian intikhab *Gul-e Ra'na* (1828). It wasn't published, but after this Ghalib apparently began the process of putting together a selection to be published as a divan. This new intikhab was ready by 1833; however, it took eight years before it was published (1841). With this, Ghalib became the first Urdu poet to publish an intikhab of his poetry. In the process of selection, he chose, out of the 2000 verses he had composed thus far, only 1084, or just a little over half of his Urdu compositions.[3] What could have been the exigencies that prompted Ghalib to cut his own oeuvre into half its size? To what extent was the idea of reducing the size affected by the cost of publishing? Who were the readers Ghalib had in mind when he decided to print his divan? Were these readers different from those who had access to manuscripts? Did the new readership alter the relationship with the text, in the sense that instead of a predominantly aural reception of poetry, was book culture likely to encourage silent reading practices? Was the idea of 'ownership' transformed in the sense that the purchase of a printed book changed the way the public thought of literature, so that it became a commodity one possessed and displayed and consumed? The biggest question is whether Ghalib's popularity was in some ways connected to the size of his first published divan and its wider circulation in print. A public sphere as opposed to an elite literary circle?

In this chapter, I will discuss the publication of Ghalib's divan in the backdrop of the complicated relationships in reading practices, ushered in by the popularity of print in mid-nineteenth-century north India. The transition from manuscript to print was gradual, in that the tradition of producing as well as copying manuscripts continued simultaneously, with book printing. Certainly, manuscript copies were limited in number when compared to even the smallest print runs. But as Ulrike Stark's work on Naval Kishor has shown, despite the continuities between manuscripts and print, there were some instant effects of print on the literary world of northern India in the nineteenth century.[4] Print opened the possibilities of wider recognition for writers, new markets for printers, publishers and booksellers and also increased the availability of texts for readers. In the beginning, patronage played a large role: a large proportion of books were published by the author or by order of a wealthy patron. This suggests that, in most cases, authors sought out printers, rather than printers seeking authors. Thus, the initiative came from patrons or authors who wished to see a work in print and not in manuscript form. When printers took the initiative, they relied on texts that were already known and thus would be sure to find readers.[5]

Stark makes a convincing argument about the radical shifts in structures of patronage generated by print. A new source of patronage was the reader. Mass printing technology changed the function of the book. Publishers became important literary patrons. The emergence of the low-priced book from the 1850s made books an affordable commodity for a large section of the urban literate classes.[6]

Print in the early stages did not produce new books as readily as it did old books. For example, grammars, etc., were published anew, but it must be reiterated that they had been written and transmitted before print. And yet, print changed attitudes towards language and literature: this shift was not simply because of print but due to new literary practices that accompanied it, such as script reform and more varieties of discursive prose. Print enabled change by allowing certain texts to spread more quickly and widely than was previously possible using speech or writing. Print increased literacy. It accelerated the number of copies and the distribution of traditional texts.

As far as we know, none of Ghalib's eminent contemporaries—Imam Bakhsh Nasikh in Lucknow (d.1838), Shah Nasir in Hyderabad (d.1839), Atish in Lucknow (d.1847), Momin in Delhi (d.1852) and Zauq in Delhi (d.1854)—took the initiative to get their work published. This brings us to the importance of print as an influential factor in explicating the literary history of nineteenth-century India. It played a role in conferring status on one linguistic register over another, and in establishing a literary canon. One reason why Ghalib towers over his contemporaries, as well as famous eighteenth-century poets such as Mir Taqi Mir, could be due to the power of curated publishing. Although Mir's collected divans (kulliyat) were published by Fort William Press in 1811, perhaps their huge and unedited size did not make them a popular commodity. It is possibly that because of the pervasiveness of print, Ghalib's intikhab became current as his only divan, and people quickly forgot that he had composed more than what he had selected for publishing.

It is conceivable that Ghalib's modest success in mushairahs and the absence of a 'known' or reputed ustad to offer *islah* (suggested improvement) on his compositions may have driven him to become a vigorous, vigilant editor of his own work. We may take his frustrations with his audience with a grain of salt, but we cannot disregard them. We must accept that he was apprehensive about the reception of his poetry, especially in his younger days. The 1821 divan ends conspicuously with a rubai in which Ghalib says that the *sukhanvaran-e kamil*, or accomplished poet-critics, ask him to write simpler verses. Notice how the last line in which he makes the exasperated appeal is in Persian:

Mushkil hai kalam mera ay dil
Sun sun keh use sukhanvaran-e kamil
Asan kahne ki karte hain farma'ish
Goyam mushkil va gar na goyam mushkil
[O heart! My poetry is difficult.
Accomplished literary critics, having heard it,
Ask me to compose simpler verses.
I say, 'It is difficult. If I don't, it is difficult too'][7]

It is *mushkil*, or difficult, for him to write anything except that what is 'mushkil'. An earlier version of this rubai had this contemptuous line: *hote hon malul usko sun kar jahil*, instead of the one quoted above, meaning, 'uneducated or unschooled people are irritated by his verses'.[8] Later, Ghalib changed the line with the offending adjective, *jahil*, to *kamil*, implying a more sarcastic but subtle indictment of his critics. His reputation of being a 'difficult' poet, however, bothered him enough to prompt him to allude to it in his poetry quite often.

There are relatively few examples of an Urdu poet producing his own intikhab. When Shah Hatim ostensibly set out to purge the Urdu language of desi (Indic) vocabulary, he prepared a smaller version of his original divan, which he called *Divanzadah* (Son of the Divan). The reduced version was not free of Indic vocabulary, but that is another issue altogether, beyond the scope of this book. The process and purpose of preparing the *Divanzadah* was entirely different from Ghalib's intikhab. The preparation of an intikhab is a critical method by which a sample, large or small, is culled for a readership the selector has in mind, or, sometimes, to endorse a thematic narrative. The act of intikhab-making has a purpose, a method, even an agenda. Usually, representative selections were made by tazkirah writers in the classic Perso-Arabic literary tradition.[9] The tazkirah, though written in Persian, was a popular genre in the eighteenth-century Urdu literate world. Historically, the literary tazkirah grew out of the bayaz that the literate elite carried with them for recording verses that they particularly liked.[10] At mushairahs, gatherings where poets were invited to recite before an active and participatory audience, enthusiastic listeners wrote down the verses they appreciated. These personal notebooks formed a kernel for a more detailed, critically nuanced sharing of poetry. As Frances Pritchett notes, the tazkirah genre both defines and embodies the parameters of this literary culture; tazkirahs are excellent tools with which to understand it. They can illustrate for us this highly formalized, remarkably coherent vision of poetry.[11] The poetry notebook also explains the idea behind the intikhab—a personal approach to poetry that expresses the selector's personal taste.

The great eighteenth-century Urdu poet Mir Taqi Mir's tazkirah, *Nikatush Shu'ara* (Fine Points about Poets), is among the earliest. True to its title, Mir's tazkirah not only gives us a selection of poets but also literary judgements about their creation. Mir was aware of the pioneering nature of his work. His introduction defines Rekhtah, which is poetry in a mixed or cobbled-together language, consisting of large chunks of Persian alternating with similar chunks of Urdu. It then goes on to describe six different kinds of Rekhtah. The ultimate form is the style that he adopted, enriched with poetic devices such as *íham* (ambiguity), *ada bandí* (romantic dialogue), fasahat (rhetoric), and so on, that distinguish good poetry. Mir applied his critical judgement in discussing the poets selected in the *Níkatush Shu'ara*. Although Mir claimed that his own poetry illustrated the whole repertoire of verbal devices, he did not make a selection from his own multi-volume oeuvre. In fact, Mir became the first Urdu poet whose voluminous kulliyat was typeset and published from Fort William College, Calcutta, in 1811.[12] Comparing Mir and Ghalib is a long-standing, ongoing debate in Urdu literary culture. My question here is not the hackneyed 'Who is a better poet?' Instead, I am curious why Mir did not prepare an intikhab from his multi-volume poetry collection, while Ghalib pursued the task of stringent editing throughout his poetic career, producing several intikhabs of both Urdu and Persian poetry and prose.[13]

Ghalib's Calcutta sojourn brought him into direct contact with the world of print: he experienced the power of publishing. In the 1820s and 1830s, Calcutta, serving as the capital of British India, was a different literary milieu from Ghalib's Delhi. It had a vibrant literary culture that valorized print as a medium of preserving classical knowledge, while simultaneously going forward with new literary practices. As Graham Shaw's work has shown, Calcutta rapidly developed into the largest centre of printing in the subcontinent since its first printing shop opened in 1777.[14] While the presses in Madras remained in the hands of the government and the missionaries, the Calcutta presses saw a proliferation of commercial printing shops and newspaper offices. Weekly newspapers laden with advertisements were the lifeblood of the early trade. Much of the printing was for practical consumption. Printing was not cheap, but nevertheless, enthusiasts such as Khwaja Haji Mustafa laboured to publish translations from Persian classics. John Borthwick Gilchrist's two-volume dictionary of English and 'Hindostanee' was published in 1798. In those days, it appeared that the patronage of the East India Company was essential for a publication to be really successful. With the establishment of Fort William College in 1800, to train the Company's officials in the Indian languages, the scope of printing widened further. Gilchrist acquired his own press in 1802 to provide much-needed material to the students at Fort William. The press produced many celebrated works of Urdu literature, such as the *Divan-e Mir Soz* (1810), *Intikhab-e Sauda* (1810) and *Kulliyat-e Mir Taqi Mir* (1811).[15] While printing was a colonial tool of control and education, its benefits for writers cannot be ignored. Ghalib embraced printing and its advantages, and wanted his work to be published.

Ghalib returned to Delhi in November 1829 after an absence of three years. He had spent a considerable amount of borrowed money during his trip and was in dire straits. His journey had failed to augment his pension but marked a turning point in his poetic career. He returned with new ideas and plans for the future. He was, of course, keen to get his work published as soon as possible. The printing technology in Delhi was still in a tentative stage. Ghalib needed a patron to finance his publication. The fact that it took eight years to find a financier attests to the enormity of the task. A draft of the Urdu divan was ready in April 1833. This is verified by the date on the foreword that Ghalib wrote for it. At this time, his language was more practical and less creative than it was in the earlier foreword he had written for the *Gul-e Ra'na*. He called the divan an intikhab and promised to deliver one for his Persian poetry as well. Navab Ziyauddin Ahmad Khan wrote the formal introduction (*taqriz*). More importantly, in his revised foreword, Ghalib inserted the paragraph in which he said in no uncertain terms that he absolved himself of responsibility for the quality of any verses attributed to him, those that were found outside of this divan.

I was searching for surviving copies of Ghalib's 1841 Urdu divan. Rampur's Saulat Library has a copy of the same, but the library was

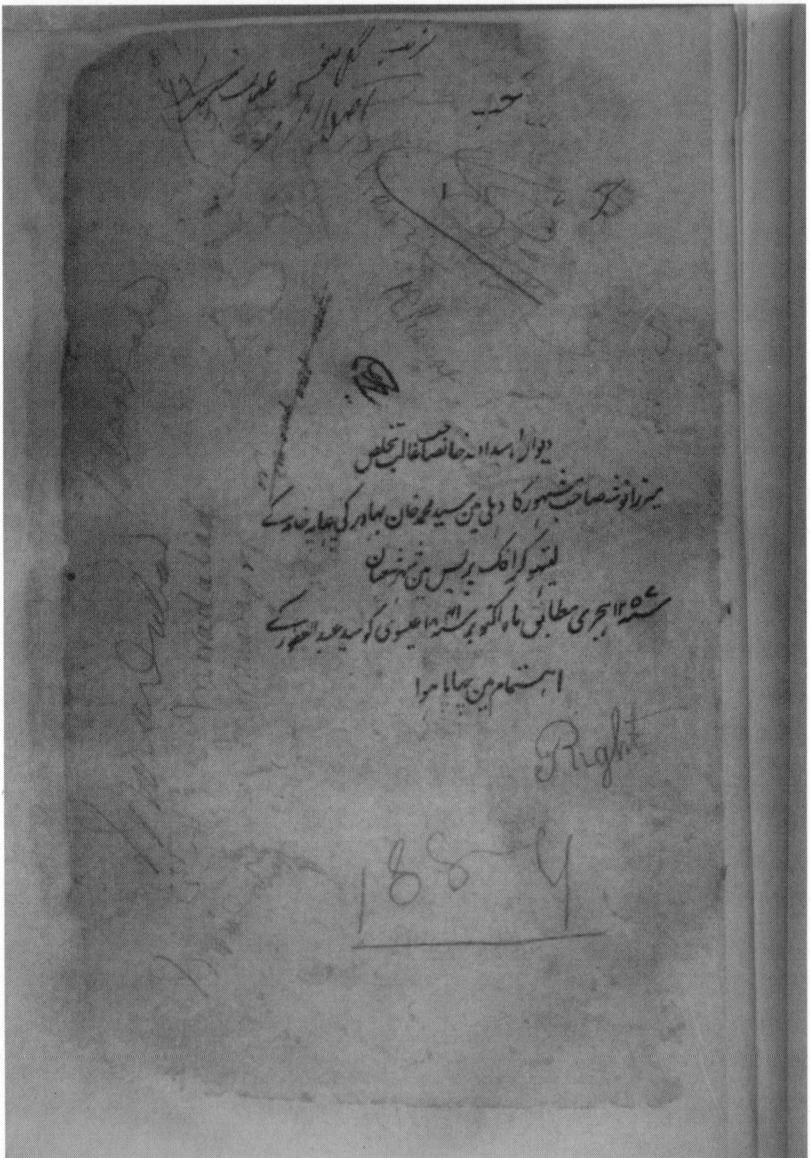

Cover page of the first published edition of Ghalib's Divan of 1841. It bears the publisher's signature and the affirmation: *Divan-e Asadullah Khan Sahib Ghalib Takhallus.*

closed for renovations when I visited in December 2015. Fortunately, I found a copy of this prized first edition in the manuscript section of Jamia Millia Islamia library.[16] The historic 1841 divan is a slender, nondescript little book.

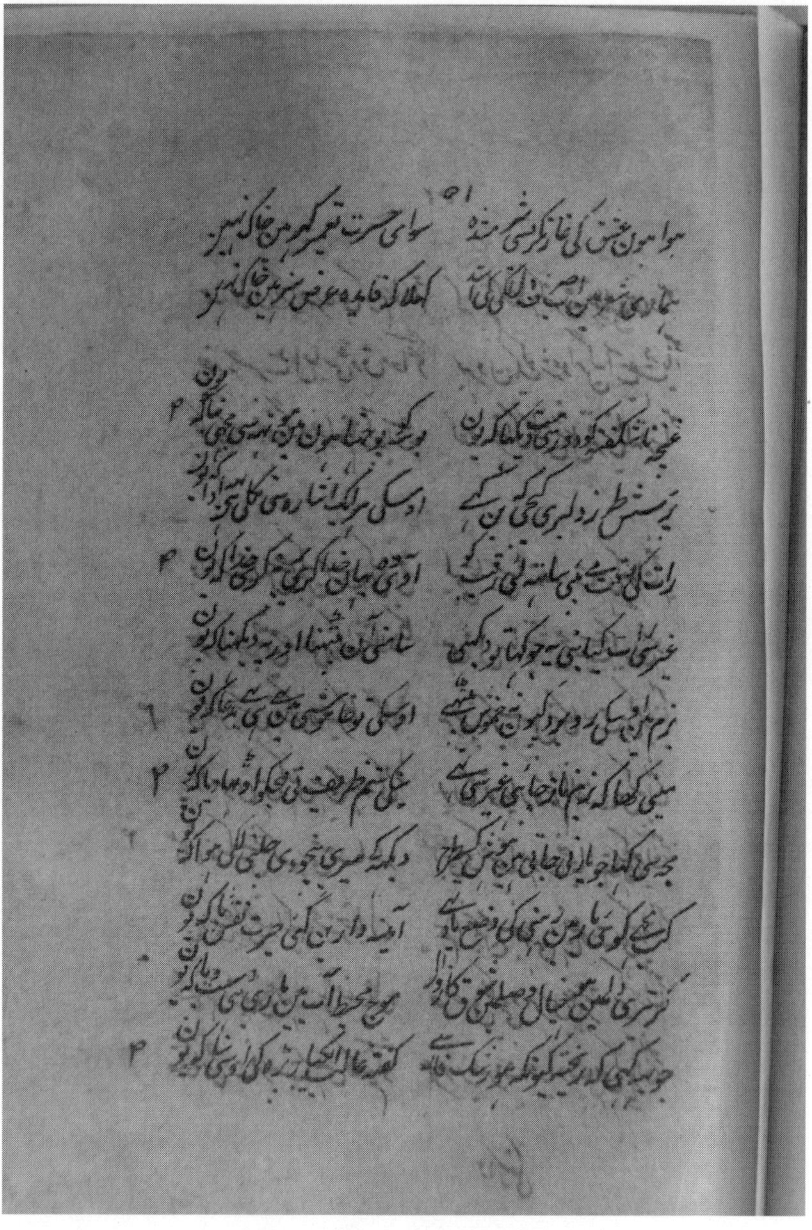

A page from the Divan of 1841. Notice its plainness and lack of decorative margins.

It has none of the rich, decorative beauty of the manuscripts of Ghalib's earlier divans, such as the Divan of 1821 or the Divan of 1826. Ghalib's foreword, in Persian, is reproduced with many errors. The ghazals are arranged without any frills, shockingly plain. There are no margins or other decorative artwork of the kind deployed in manuscript divans. The orthography sometimes varies within a single ghazal.

Yet, the importance of this little book cannot be exaggerated. Saiyyid Muhammad Khan (Saiyyid Ahmad Khan's elder brother), who owned a small lithographic press, was the publisher.[17] There is no way of determining what the print order was, or the price—generally 200 copies was the norm for high literature. It is remarkable that a small, ordinary-looking book like the 1841 divan survived the arson and pillage of 1857. It shows that the divan was a prized possession, a unique testament to the importance of print culture in revolutionizing the circulation of texts.

Ghalib's Foreword to the 1841 Urdu Divan

As mentioned earlier, Ghalib wrote a short foreword (dibachah) for this intikhab in 1833, but he inserted a small, seemingly ambiguous but crucial paragraph before the book was published in 1841:

> I hope that [the] literati and also those who appreciate my work would not declare the scattered verses [*abyat*], which are not included in this divan, to be the result of the ink from my quill and would not oblige the collection of my writings with praise of those verses, nor would they lay blame on me for their adaptations.[18]

This paragraph was invoked in the 1920s when Ghalib's previously lost early Divan of 1821 was identified in the library of the Navab of Bhopal. There was a debate as to whether publishing verses that Ghalib had not included in his published divans was appropriate

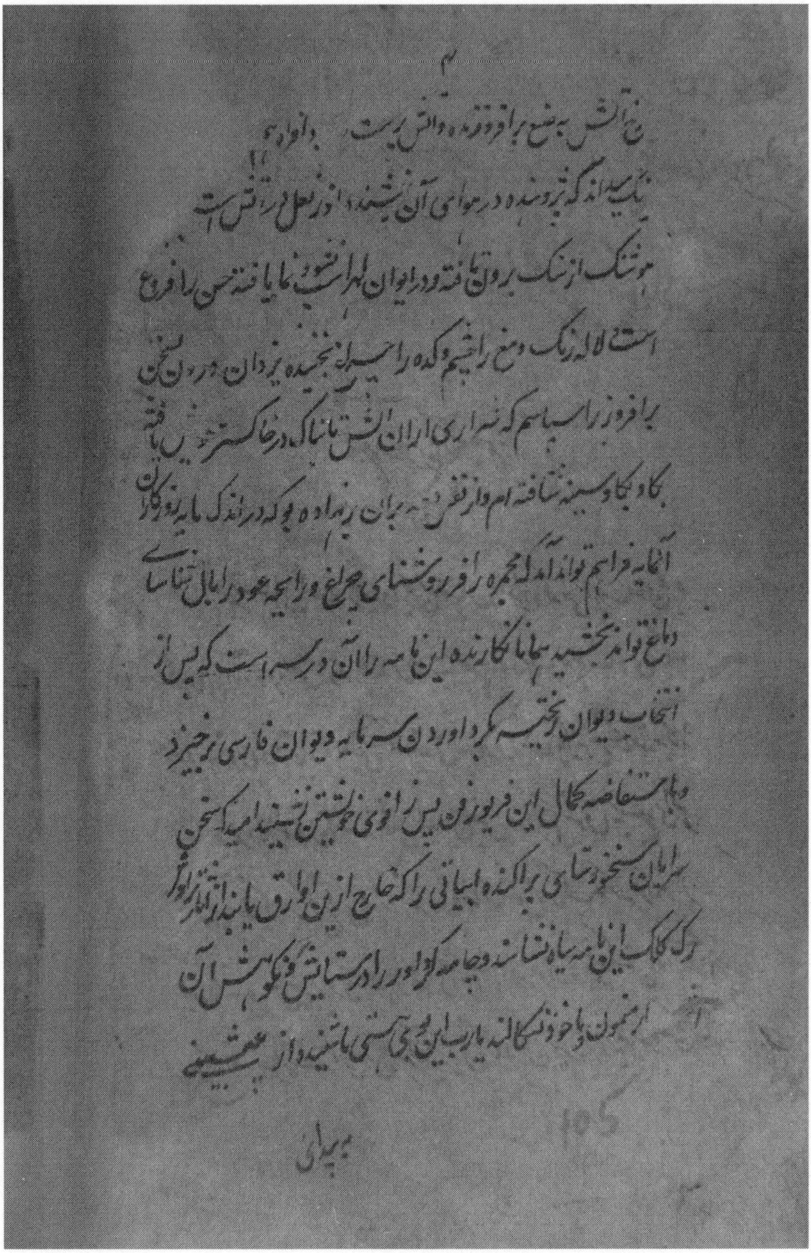

Ghalib's dibachah to the Divan of 1841 with the paragraph (the last five lines from the bottom of the page) attesting a proto copyright. Ghalib inserted this in preparation for publication.

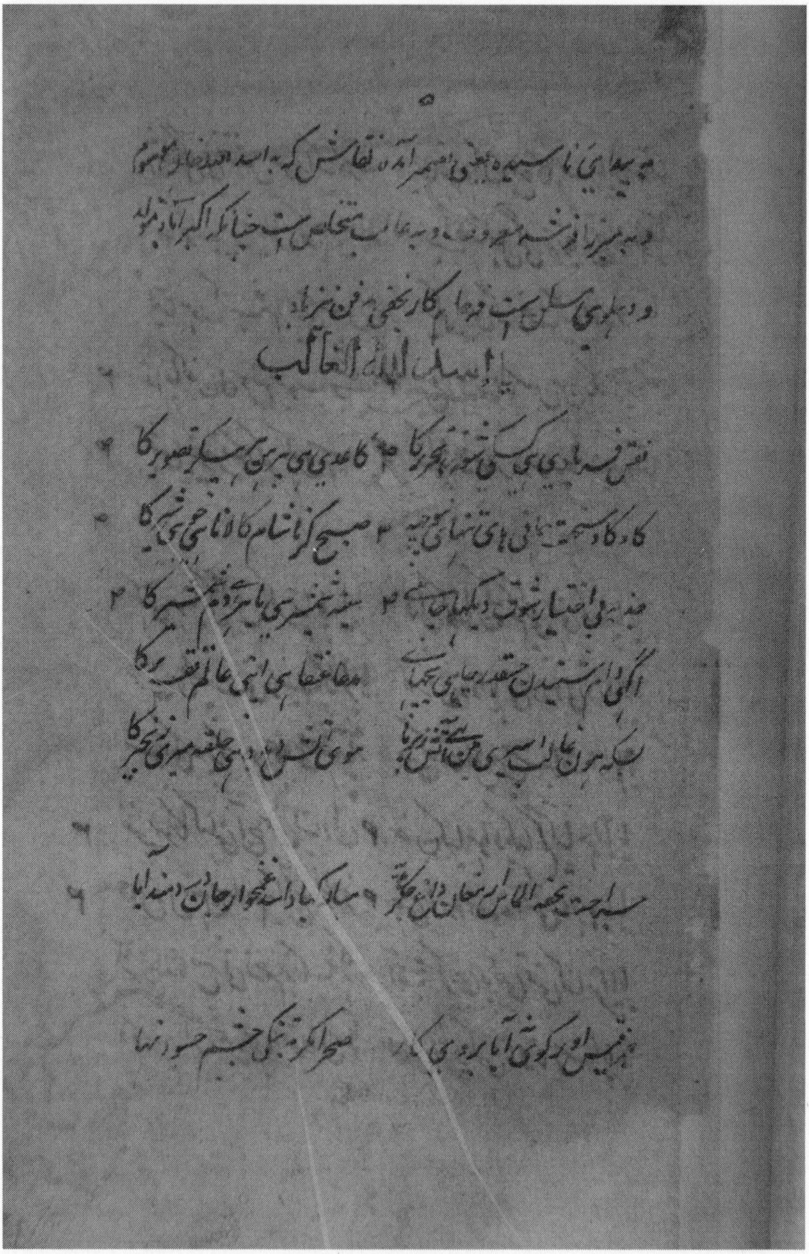

The closing sentences of the dibachah and the first ghazal of the Divan: *Naqsh faryadi hai kis ki shokhi-e tahrir ka.*

or not. There was speculation as to what exactly Ghalib meant by the *paragandah abyat*, or scattered verses, which were not included in this divan (*kharij az in auraq*). Was the reference to stray verses found in early tazkirahs or did he mean earlier compositions that did not meet his criteria for the intikhab? Fortunately, the Divan of 1821 did get published in 1921 as the *Nuskah-e Jadid.* Details of its publication have been outlined in Chapter 2.

Ghalib had on several occasions in his letters referred to the verses in his early divans, in relation to his wayward, obscure style at the beginning of his poetic career, and how he had scored through those verses with a stroke of his pen. While this hyperbolic claim is an exaggerated one, it pertains more to his so-called change in style rather than a rejection of those verses. The claim of a change in style is also incorrect. I combed through the early divans and found many ghazals that are as good as the ones that he included in the Divan of 1841.[19] Any intikhab is bound to be coloured by personal preferences. A poet's intikhab of his own verses is as subjective as a literary critic's. Ghalib's intikhabs, too, tell us something about his personal preferences, because he produced several. The last one, in 1866, towards the end of his life, was made at the request of the Navab of Rampur.[20]

The question that we must not lose sight of is whether Ghalib, in his foreword, was disowning almost half of his Urdu poetry, or only the 'scattered verses'. A point that is sometimes overlooked is his claim that he must not bear the blame for the adaptations (*chamah kardan*) of his work. Earlier discussions around this question have failed to notice that this is in fact an assertion of copyright. Ghalib had realized that printing practices were quite different from the manuscript culture. Printing imposed a certain fixity on the text. It provided standardization. It also permitted rapid circulation. Ghalib wanted to put an authorial seal on his compositions. He wanted the published divan to be an authoritative presentation of his poetry, selected and put forward by himself; this is why he inserted the passage that declared he did not want to accept praise or blame for verses outside of the published divan. I suggest that we should regard Ghalib's language in this crucial paragraph as a precursor to copyright assertion, a disclaimer or warning of sorts to imitators, rather than a pronouncement of disassociation with his early poetry. There are, of course, some stray verses attributed to Ghalib whose authenticity is entirely dubious.[21]

Taqriz by Navab Ziyauddin Ahmad Khan Naiyar

The Divan of 1841 includes a critical introduction, or taqriz, by Ghalib's young, and powerful, pupil, Navab Ziyauddin.[22] The navab was the younger son of Navab Ahmad Bakhsh Khan and only eighteen at the time of writing this taqriz.[23] A taqriz was not just an ornamental piece of writing; it worked critically. It presented the work to readers. In doing so, a taqriz was an effect, a corollary to the aural appreciation of ghazals in a mushairah. I will quote extensively from the taqriz because it also provides an incisive and direct experience of the literary culture and Ghalib's position in it.[24] Navab Ziyauddin's taqriz begins with a traditional reference to the radiant, poetic muse from the household of thought:

> In the name of God: There is a straight-statured beloved from the angelic household of thought, who has appeared, and is now engaged upon making her radiant beauty apparent. It is this hidden beauty who saunters in a carefree manner, having lifted the veil from her face, who has now readied herself with her skirt tucked up and tied at her waist in the style of one who tears open the curtain.[25]

After the curtain has been drawn, a glorious picture gallery emerges: a narcissus garden where houris lose their senses, a sky full of pearl-like stars, a lamp to which *paris* (fairies) are drawn like moths. Above all, Navab Ziyauddin asserts, poetry is sacred—it is a continuous tradition that flows from Persia to India:

> It is a house of God, a place of worship, whose key has been given into the hands of proper understanding. And whose door has been opened for those who are intent upon visiting the wide plains of the heart. It's Somnath,[26] where a whole city of beautiful idols of thought, wearing the sacred threads, put their foreheads on the ground. It's a picture gallery whose exhibition of rare paintings causes [the famous Persian painters] Mani and Arzang to touch the back of their hands on the ground in obeisance.[27] Every page in this book is a Magus reading from the [Zoroastrian text] Avesta. It is a mirror where the whole world is reflected.[28]

The next paragraph is about the 'beloveds' of imagination who inhabit the divan. They are saucy-eyed and endowed with hearts filled with knowledge. They are salamanders capable of drinking away the whole ocean: 'They are Indian idols that roam Iran. They are Delhi-born but brought up in Isfahan.'[29] This deliberate reference to Persian standards of composition for an Urdu divan underscores both the rivalry and the literary dialogue between the two cultures. Here, we find a glimpse of the cosmopolitanism of the Urdu-Persian literary world that we will explore in the next chapter. Meanwhile, Navab Ziyauddin goes on to heap praise on Ghalib in well-wrought prose:

> Now this is the selected divan in the Urdu language, which has dropped from the pen of the holder of Jesus-like revelations, who serves the balance of wisdom, who has the power of sight and determination of the astrolabe and who is the substance of creation's mirror, who is the standard of the value of all things of value, who is the ultimate stair of the ladder of high station, who is the hero of the dominion of the nurture of meaning, who is the

> rule giver and regulator of the land of poets and poetry, who is the master of the land of the new style of writing, who is the leader of fresh discourse . . .[30]

The crucial point here is the allusion to a new style of writing and a fresh discourse. Navab Ziyauddin's taqriz is an early endorsement of what Ghalib scholars have supported all along, namely, that Ghalib's poetry is unique in the inherent punniness, unexpected metaphors and intricate meaning. Many Urdu critics, following Hali's lead, regard these features to be distinctive and individualistic enough to merit the badge of creating a new style. This style was loosely defined as *mushkil pasandi*, or the predilection for writing 'difficult' poetry. The eighteenth century had produced many notable Urdu poets such as Mir Dard, Mirza Sauda and Mir Taqi Mir. Mir's genius for writing accessible poetry on complex emotional–mystical subjects was recognized as exemplary. Strangely enough, when young Ghalib began writing poetry in Urdu, he did not follow the path of Mir. Instead, he chose to emulate the Indian-Persian poet Mirza Bedil (1644–1720), who was known for his intellectual scepticism and exotic, obscure wordplays. The question one needs to ask is: Why did an Urdu poet follow in the footsteps of this particular Persian poet? I will quote two such verses here to show how much Ghalib esteemed Bedil:

> Writing Rekhtah in the manner of Bedil
> My God, Asadullah Khan, what an enormous thing it is![31]

> O Ghalib, I have no fear of going astray in poetry's journey:
> Bedil's pen is the guiding staff of Khizr in poetry's vast, wild spaces.[32]

Ghalib took a great risk in swimming against the current and earned scorn, and even derision, from his peers. His conscious departure from Mir's style points to a linguistic shift that Hali failed to notice, for Ghalib's language register reveals a cultural–political change in the literary climate of Delhi. When Persian was no longer the official language, its stature as a classical language (free of geographical boundaries), superior to Urdu, began to take root. Since languages are always perceived to have geographical, or rather, national, ties, Persian's displacement as the 'official' language had far-reaching consequences that I will discuss in another chapter. Although Ghalib's poetry in Urdu presented the working of a mind attuned to new ways of thinking, his language register is not the de-Persianized Urdu of Mir Taqi Mir. Ghalib had begun to compose mostly in Persian at this stage. Perhaps he felt that Persian's transregional reach enabled a conversation with the Persophone (Persian-speaking) literary world. Ghalib thus freely indulged in the creative appropriation (*tasarruf*) of Persian masters.

To return to the vexed question of Ghalib's criteria for editing his divan, I would like to revisit the controversy apparently stoked by Muhammad Husain Azad's claim that Ghalib's divan was edited by Maulvi Fazl-e Haq and Mirza Khan Khani, the chief kotwal of Delhi, who took out all the obscure verses. This apocryphal justification of putative editorial advice became popular, as did many of Azad's anecdotal stories in *Ab-e Hayat*.[33] I maintain that Ghalib would not have trusted Mirza Khani to decide which verses should be discarded, because the latter was a pupil of Mirza Qatil, the Indian Persian poet Ghalib disliked.[34] I had thought that Ghalib probably did the intikhab all by himself. However, after scrutinizing the taqriz, I am persuaded that Ghalib might have taken advice from Navab Ziyauddin, his cousin and pupil who was so dear to him.[35] The paragraph below indicates that Navab Ziyauddin helped Ghalib in putting the divan together, at least in the final stages. The navab mentions the 'toil and travail of digging and collecting'. Apparently, he also counted the number of verses in the divan, although his number is a bit inaccurate.

> For a long time, Muhammad Ziyauddin Naiyar of humble and lowly thoughts had been concentrating and weighing the gravity of

> his own lightness of worth [to express an opinion] on the project, that these honorable offspring of my brother, each one of whom is a true child of the house of the unapparent but is in fact the grandparent of heart-pleasing themes, should, for the purpose of educating the new learners who at present are unable to distinguish the good from the bad. And these valued gems, of which each is like a bracelet on the silver body of wisdom, and the earring for the beautiful form of sensibility, should be brought out and hung in the niche of the dome of recognition and acknowledgement. So finally, a thousand praises for the Great Lord and Maker of things, that at this time, which is the sacred year of the emigration of the Prophet, on the master of which [the Prophet himself] the greatest of salutations and the most perfect of greetings, the year 1254, the long-standing and heart-pleasing desire, due to the favourability of the straight-moving time, and the guidance of the awakened fortune, has turned into reality, even better than what I had desired. Happiness took its seat in my heart and the toil and travail of digging and collecting went away.[36]

The final sentences of the taqriz are also noteworthy because they warn backbiters who might make fun of the small number of verses:[37]

> O you of strong senses, attend; and O you with ears to hear, pay attention! It is now necessary for us to walk on the highway of the ample recognition of beautiful themes and not indulge in taunting and backbiting on the smallness of the quantity of the verses. As that great master through these words, in fact, narrates his own discourse in the form of Persian, and his command is quite true.[38]

A verse by Ghalib is quoted here:

> I don't write if it is not sweet, O Ghalib
> So what if my verses are few in number.[39]

A comparison of Ghalib's Urdu Divan of 1841 with the Persian divan published in 1845 is inevitable, and not only because the latter contained more verses (6000). This area needs much more scholarly attention than it has received. Ghalib valorized Persian over Urdu. His self-exaltation and assertive boasting is far more evident in Persian than Urdu. But above all, a comparative analysis is needed because Ghalib's idioms in Persian are grammatically straightforward and not as exasperatingly inaccessible as they tend to be in Urdu. In Persian, Ghalib is conscious of adhering to a cosmopolitan idiom, following the path of canonical masters while reaching for new imaginative possibilities. At first blush, it might seem contradictory for a poet to both follow the path of the classical masters and to lay claim to new themes or freshness. Yet this is entirely possible, because freshness or innovation in ghazal poetry was largely based on using established themes, but with a new twist. The artistry involved in heightening the theme showed inventiveness.

Thus, while one can make the argument that the exigencies of print culture prompted Ghalib to hone his critical apparatus of selection, or that his sensitivity to being labelled 'mushkil pasand' determined what he wanted to circulate to a wider readership in Urdu via print, it does not adequately explain why he did not follow the same stringent rules of selection for Persian. Apparently, Persian, despite its waning importance in nineteenth-century British India, still had more lustre than Urdu because of its classical stature. Ghalib made it clear that he accorded more weight to his Persian compositions.

Ghalib's Trajectory of Publishing

With the publication of his Urdu and Persian divans, Ghalib's reputation as the leading poet of the time began to soar. Although Ghalib was unhappy at the way scribal errors and poor proofreading marred the production of his books, he took to print like a fish to water. His publication history was admirable; volume upon volume of Persian and Urdu poetry and prose were printed.[40] We must pause here to examine Ghalib's relationship with the printed text and his relations with the publishers of those times. First and foremost was Saiyyid Muhammad, who had published the first edition of the Urdu divan (1841). He ran one of Delhi's first presses, which also published one of the earliest newspapers, *Sayyidul Akhbar*, founded in 1836/37.[41] Saiyyid Muhammad was the older brother of the famous Saiyyid Ahmad Khan, a name associated with Islamic 'modernism', who took over the press after the death of his brother in 1841. The paths of these two towering intellectuals—Saiyyid Ahmad Khan and Ghalib—crossed often. Khan asked Ghalib to compose a critical introduction (taqriz) for his monumental edition of *Ain-e Akbari* (1855–56). Ghalib's response to Khan was surprising, to say the least. He urged Khan to focus on the present and be more forward-looking.[42] Ghalib's taqriz was not included in the *Ain-e Akbari*. Consequently, relations between the two remained strained for many years, until they reconciled nearly a decade later.[43] Both of these nineteenth-century intellectuals had notable publishing trajectories.[44] Khan produced remarkable works in Urdu prose. It would be useful to compare their attitudes towards the classical and the modern forms of language usage. However, this is outside the scope of the chapter.[45]

The most successful publisher of the time was Munshi Naval Kishor (1836–95) of Lucknow.[46] He launched *Avadh Akhbar*, the first Urdu weekly published in northern India, in 1858.[47] While the newspaper claimed broad news coverage, it also functioned as a literary journal, promoting both poetry and prose writing. It also covered literary events, announced new publications and provided a forum for literary debate. The paper's role in the development of a modern Urdu prose style was facilitated by a number of eminent editors from the literary world. Ghalib was an avid reader of newspapers and began perusing *Avadh Akhbar* almost as soon as it started publication. The paper carried advance notices of his forthcoming books, as well as new poetic compositions from his contemporaries. He used to borrow the paper from Navab Ziyauddin Ahmad Khan before Munshi Naval Kishor began mailing him a complimentary copy.[48] Ghalib later regretted handing over his Urdu divan to publishers other than Kishor. He even praised the distinctive production of Kishor's Lucknow Press.

Kishor's first letter to Ghalib, written perhaps late in 1859, was in Persian. He solicited Ghalib's poetry for publication and also asked him to subscribe to the paper. The letter is lost, but we have Ghalib's reply, also in Persian, agreeing to send his work and also to buy the paper. The extensive correspondence between Ghalib and Kishor, and some other publishers, is one of the best sources of author–publisher dynamics in nineteenth-century Urdu literature. By the time Ghalib and Kishor established contact, in the early 1860s, several of Ghalib's Persian prose works had been published. The publications were, however, disappointing, riddled with errors. When Kishor approached Ghalib, it was the case of a publisher approaching an author and not vice versa. Ghalib decided to authorize Naval Kishor to first reprint his Persian prose works: *Panj Ahang*, *Mehr-e Nim Roz* and *Dastanbuy*. Soon after, Ghalib decided to give his Persian kulliyat, as well as *Qati-e Burhan*, to Munshi Naval Kishor.[49] The announcement of the forthcoming titles was published on the front page of *Avadh Akhbar*. Advance subscriptions for the kulliyat offered readers discounted rates of Rs 3 and Rs 4, as compared to the selling price of five rupees. News about Ghalib was published regularly in the paper. The announcement of Ghalib's recognition in the form of new titles by the lieutenant governor of Delhi was prominently placed, too. The relationship between the author and the publisher was one of mutual trust and cordiality. Ghalib sent his pupil Qadar Bilgrami to Lucknow with a recommendation letter, to seek employment with Naval Kishor Press. Bilgrami was hired in the editorial office and stayed in Lucknow for some years, although he was not happy with his salary.

Ghalib's controversial *Qati-e Burhan* was first published by Naval Kishor in 1862. In his taqriz to it, Ghalib heaped high praise on Kishor:[50]

> Well, finally the human regard and the practice of love from the pupil of the eye of that practitioner of love who is the son of the sky of humanness, he who is heavy in property by wisdom, and he whose station is high on account of honour, he who behaves and deals with arrogant people as Faridun did with Zahak and who, with the humble people, is like Solomon to the ant, he who is wisdom from head to foot and insight embodied, that is, Munshi Naval Kishor, came to the conclusion and took a decision to buy from a shop which really had no goods, so that the impressions of the scattered pages in print became proper and correct. Had this brave and chivalrous person who is awake of heart not decided to get these scattered pages bound and put together, that paper which constitutes the manuscript of the *Qati-e Burhan,* would have been taken to the paper maker, washed with water and pounded into pulp; or this paper would have bought by the coal seller for making spills. After all, my truth-submitting pen at the end of the printed copy of this manuscript decided to create another impression in the form of a taqriz, and a new stamp [mohur] so that no one else should ever be able to pour this manuscript into the body of print without the permission of the owner of the *Avadh Akhbar* press.[51]

The one and only meeting between the poet and the publisher happened in 1863, when Naval Kishor visited Delhi. On 3 December 1863, Ghalib wrote to Navab Alauddin Ahmad Khan Alai,

> My kind and considerate benefactor, that man of kindness incarnate, Munshi Naval Kishor came by the mail coach [dak].

> He met me, and your uncle [Navab Ziyauddin Ahmad Khan] and your cousin, Shihabuddin Khan. The Creator bestowed upon him the beauty of Venus and the qualities of Jupiter. He is himself the conjunction of two auspicious stars. I hadn't mentioned this to you, and accepted that ten hardbound copies of my Persian collected verse would cost fifty rupees. But now when I mentioned this to him, he agreed to accept the price that had originally been advertised in the newspaper—three rupees and four annas per copy. At this rate, ten copies come to thirty-two rupees and eight annas, and thirty-two rupees and eight annas are what you are to pay. In all, sixty-five rupees will have to be sent to the *Avadh Akhbar* Press.[52]

When Munshi Naval Kishor returned from Delhi, he published an account of his meeting with Ghalib in *Avadh Akhbar*. In the account, he expressed his admiration for Ghalib sincerely. The Naval Kishor Press published Ghalib's works with special regard, which reflected Ghalib's stature. Clearly, Ghalib was sought after by the leading publisher of the time, but the poet was equally anxious to please his publisher.[53] We do not know what the terms and conditions were for the copyright. From the above passages, it seems that Ghalib had given the copyright to Naval Kishor. The press continued to publish Ghalib's work long after the poet's death.

The Final Intikhab of Persian and Urdu (1866)

> جو یہ کہے کہ ریختہ کیوں کہ ہو رشک فارسی
> گفتۂ غالب ایک بار پڑھ کے اسے سنا کہ یوں
> [If someone would say: Why would Rekhtah be the envy of Persian?
> Read out Ghalib's verse, just once: 'Like this!'][54]

In the last few years of his life, Ghalib prepared separate Persian and Urdu intikhabs, in manuscript form, for the Navab of Rampur.[55]

While the Persian one was carefully preserved, the Urdu manuscript languished among the heaps of papers at the Rampur Raza Library. Maulana Imtiaz Ali Khan Arshi, the distinguished editor of Ghalib's Urdu divan, recovered the manuscript and published it with a scholarly introduction in 1942.[56] The brilliant Persian and Urdu scholar Alessandro Bausani, in his article 'The Position of Ghalib in the History of Urdu and Indo-Persian Poetry', drew attention to this remarkable intikhab. Bausani is, to my knowledge, the only reputable scholar who has compared Ghalib's Persian and Urdu verses, albeit within a restricted field that he terms Ghalib's 'Bedilism'.[57]

The Persian and Urdu intikhab(s) of 1866 were undoubtedly a compilation of Ghalib's preferences and deserve a close scrutiny. Bashir Husain Zaidi, in his foreword to the published edition of these intikhabs (1942), says that the Persian intikhab was added to the library's collection of divans in 1866 itself, while the Urdu manuscript ended up in the wastepaper pile, from which it was rescued by Maulana Arshi.[58] Eventually, Maulana Arshi put together both the Urdu and the Persian intikhabs in the 1942 edition. Bashir Husain Zaidi makes a crucial observation in his preface to this edition:

> If we think about the issue of the lack of appreciation [*nah maqbuliyat*] of the Persian compared to the Urdu, a factor behind the scenes could be that Mirza Sahib did not present a selection [*muntakhib majmu'a*] of his Persian poetry for the perceptive audience/readers. As a result, the priceless pearls of his Persian verses remained buried in the heap of less-valuable jewels. Fortunately, this selection is being made available through the high offices of the Rampur Library. It was a commendable work carried out by Mirza Sahib in the most mature years of his life. Now this shortcoming [of not having a Persian intikhab] has been surmounted.[59]

Nonetheless, the publication of the volume with the two intikhabs, along with a learned introduction, seems to have gone unnoticed in the mayhem of the 1940s. Since the *Gul-e Ra'na* had not been discovered yet, here was an opportunity to read Ghalib synchronically in both languages.

However, the literary climate had changed with the times. Urdu, despite its short literary history, had made big strides. It was promoted as a modern vernacular; its literature was taught in schools. While in 1866 the Urdu intikhab had been discarded in favour of the Persian by the staff at the Rampur library, the Persian intikhab was largely ignored in 1942. The focus of Maulana Arshi's introduction is primarily on the Urdu selection.

The manuscript of the Urdu intikhab, Maulana Arshi tells us, was calligraphed in a single hand. It was riddled with spelling mistakes and other corruptions that were then corrected by Ghalib. Apparently, Ghalib made the selection on a copy of the Nizami Press edition of the Urdu divan. That edition itself was littered with errors, which the calligrapher had not bothered to correct. The Nizami Press edition has a total of 1799 verses (inclusive of ghazals, qasidahs, rubais, qitas and masnavis). Ghalib selected a total of 868 verses, the bulk of them—673—from ghazals. The Persian intikhab was apparently made from the *Kulliyat-e Farsi*, the Naval Kishor edition of 1863. This edition has 3606 verses from ghazals and 208 rubais. Ghalib chose 1060 ghazal verses and eighteen rubais. It seems to have been copied in three different hands, a small portion of which were done by Ghalib himself. There are some errors that have been rectified in Ghalib's hand.

Maulana Arshi makes a common but fallacious argument about the progression of Ghalib's views on poetics. He writes that Ghalib's literary tastes changed over the years:

> There are two aspects to poetry [*guftar-e mauzun*]. One has to do with [arrangement of] words, the other with meaning. Mirza Sahib at first paid attention to the aspect of meaning and ignored

the beauty of words. In regard to the verses in the Nuskhah-e Hamidiyyah, he explained this in a letter: 'poetry is *ma'ni afirini*.'[60]

Maulana Arshi's point is that Ghalib's intikhab of 1866 generally avoids complicated verses.[61] He writes:

> Upon scrutinizing the intikhab, one realizes Mirza Sahib elected directness of words (simplicity of structure) and meaning as the criteria for selection. Therefore, all the Persian and Urdu verses that had tasteless imaginative flights, unappealing and far-fetched metaphors and similes, or unfamiliar Persian idioms and phrases, were not included.[62]

Maulana Arshi thus sought to use these intikhabs to strengthen his own argument that Ghalib began to eschew complexity in favour of the simplicity in later years. The explanation, however, does not suffice because Ghalib's intikhab for the *Gul-e Ra'na*, made in 1828, is quite similar to the one he made in 1866. In 1866, he had more verses from his mature years to choose from. Nonetheless, he left out many beautiful, well-known verses from Persian and Urdu. Maulana Arshi has given examples of the most glaring omissions. It is far more plausible to assume that Ghalib's selection for the navab was made with a view to the latter's taste, not his own. For example, Ghalib included his masnavi on mangoes (*masnavi dar sifat-e ambah*), obviously, for its general appeal. In any case, intikhabs tend to be idiosyncratic rather than logical.

The Urdu and Persian Selections of 1866

فارسی بیں تا ببینی نقش ہائ رنگ رنگ
بگزر از مجموعۃ اردو کہ بیرنگ منست
[Look at my Persian so that you may see different colours,
Pass over my collection in Urdu because it doesn't have my colour][63]

The Urdu section of the 1866 intikhab opens with two verses culled from the famous opening ghazal of the published *Divan-e Ghalib: Naqsh faryadi hai kis ki shokhi-e tahrir ka*. The path of this ghazal can be followed, as we saw in Chapter 5, by looking at its earlier versions. Ghalib had pared it down from nine verses in the Divan of 1821 to five for the Divan of 1841. The order of verses was also changed as new ones were added.[64] For *Gul-e Ra'na,* Ghalib had selected only three verses from this ghazal, including the opening verse.[65] The verses selected for *Gul-e Ra'na* do not show the alleged simplicity and directness. In fact, there is no way of determining why Ghalib chose them, except to say that they are masterpieces:

جزبۂ بے اختیار شوق دیکھا چاہَے
سینۂ شمشیر سے باہر ہے دم شمشیر کا

بسکہ ہوں غالب اسیری میں بھی آتش زیر پا
موئ آتش دیدہ ہے حلقہ میری زنجیر کا

[The wild rush of ardour—you ought to see it.
The sword's breath is drawn out of its breast.

Ghalib, even in bondage I'm so aflame with restlessness,
Every link of my chain is a fire-singed hair][66]

Overall, the 1866 intikhab is highly suited for the purpose it was made for: a contribution to a bayaz for the navab. With the Persian and Urdu selections in one volume, it is an invaluable resource for comparing the poet's selected work in the two languages.

We know that Ghalib valorized his Persian over Urdu, but did he really mean that his Urdu divan was colourless or that it should be bypassed? To what extent can one read the author's intent into verses which are idiosyncratically or haphazardly culled throughout a poetic career? For example, Ghalib prefaced the 1866 Persian intikhab section with the following verse, which seems to apply more to his Urdu poetry than Persian:

چند رنگیں نکتۂ دلکش تکلف بر طرف
دیده ام دیوان غالب انتخابی بیش نیست
[A few colourful, delightful nuances, let's put aside formalities—
I have seen the *Divan-e Ghalib*, it's no more than an intikhab][67]

While the verse is appropriate for this intikhab in a witty, culturally suitable, self-deprecating manner, it cannot be applied to Ghalib's Persian divan. Likewise, the Urdu intikhab section is prefaced with the following verse that is amusing and appropriate for this context:

کھلتا کسی پہ کیوں میرے دل کا معاملہ
شعروں کے انتخاب نے رسوا کیا مجھے
[How would anyone know the matters of my heart;
My intikhab of verses exposed me][68]

But this verse was written before 1821 and is a part of a ghazal that has an introspective, self-searching and somewhat melancholic mood.[69] The refrain (*mujhe*) adds an intensified personal tone to the ghazal. Its opening verse deserves to be quoted here:

ہے آرمیدگی میں نکوہش بجا مجھے
صبح وطن ہے خندہ دنداں نما مجھے
[In repose, scorn is appropriate to me;
The dawn of the homeland is a teeth-baring smile to me]

The teeth-baring smile is a taunting smile. The sarcastic laughter of his peers floats into the thoughts of the speaker in the verse.

The verse that follows the one about the selection of verses is notable as well:

تا چند پست فطرتی طبع آرزو
یارب ملے بلندی دست دعا مجھے

> [To what extent can the lowliness of the temperament of longing be;
> O God, may I acquire the loftiness of the hand of blessing]

The point I want to emphasize is that the same verse(s) can be quoted to support two opposing arguments. But it helps to know its textual history, if it is available, before reaching conclusions. In my work on Ghalib's textual history, I demonstrate that the position or ordering of verses in the ghazal is significant. The mood of the ghazal as a whole, and the placement of each verse, does have the intent of the poet behind it. The practice of intikhab-making can be contrary to the ordering of verses. The making of an intikhab is a cultural practice connected to the evaluative criticism of javab-goi, as well as the competitive ambience of mushairahs. Javab-goi could be spontaneous, as in a mushairah, or take the form of a focused, polished response as a chain of ghazals composed in the same strain as master poets. The performative aspect of the ghazal lends itself to intikhab, too. Ghazal singers typically select verses and string them into a sequence to please audiences.

Examining Ghalib's purpose behind producing an intikhab of his Urdu poetry expressly for publishing, and whether this editorial finesse has played a role in Ghalib's popularity, I think that there is a positive correlation between the two. First, as we have seen in this chapter, there are two prominent models of presentation of poetry—kulliyat (complete works) and intikhab (selection). Ghalib prepared at least two notable intikhabs of his Urdu and Persian poetry; first in 1828 and then in 1866. Both were prepared at the behest of influential friends and patrons. But the Urdu Divan of 1841 is an intikhab that Ghalib undertook for the purpose of sharing his poetry in print with a wider audience. Its popularity is attested by the subsequent editions.[70] It was a successful model. Therefore, Ghalib did not retrieve the verses and ghazals he had left out in 1841 from his early divans. He added new verses composed after 1841. Again, we must remember that in this period Ghalib was writing more in Persian and less in Urdu. His focus on publishing his larger divan in Persian, in the tradition of the kulliyat, may have to do with his perception of the readership. Persian readers, as Ghalib has reminded us, are *sukhan shinas*, they know the marks of good poetry. However, the limited success of Mirza's Persian poetry is apparent from the fewer editions, as well as the lacklustre reception of his Persian intikhab in 1866.

A selective reading of Ghalib's poetry can be misleading. Indeed, to not be aware of Ghalib's Persian poetry while assessing him is to present an incomplete picture of his poetic genius. Ghalib deserves to be read in both languages. If we can read Amir Khusrau across his putative Hindvi and Persian, we can at least read Ghalib's selections of Persian and Urdu to get a better sense of his style in the two languages. Reading Ghalib's work as a whole, that is, his Persian and Urdu poetry and prose, one is struck by a curious stylistic contradiction. The Urdu verse, as a whole, is remarkably obscure, strewn with unfamiliar compounds and dissonances that resonate with Bedil and other Persian poets of the so-called Indian style. It is very complicated. The Persian poetry is definitely more approachable; its language is more direct, though the sensibility or character is culturally more Indian than Persian. Ghalib's Persian prose is the opposite of his poetry. His prose is intricate, hyperbolic and formal; its structure is complexly decorative. His Urdu prose is lively and dramatic.

Ghalib's Persian poetry was composed at a mature age, with an awareness of a connection with a deep historical and literary tradition. He had studied the various styles, or *rangs*, of Persian masters. He was careful to follow the lexical, idiomatic and grammatical characteristics of the 'pure' Persian language, which he believed had been sullied by Indianisms. He felt he knew Persian grammar and syntax like a Persian, not an Indian, and this led him to follow 'good' Persian models. In the oft-quoted letter to Sahib-e Alam, Ghalib sums up the three styles of Persian poetry:

> Summing up, there are three styles (*tarzen*) current: that of Khaqani and his peers, that of Zuhuri and his followers, that of Sa'ib and those like him. Now tell me truly, in which of these styles is the poetry of Mumtaz, Akhtar, etc., composed? You will no doubt answer that they write in another style, and that we will have to consider it a fourth one. Well, it may be a style, perhaps even a good one; but it is not a Persian style. It is Indian.[71]

Although Persian in the nineteenth century was being edged out by modern vernaculars like Urdu, it still held a position of privilege and was synonymous with aristocracy. In the next chapter, we will examine the importance of Persian and the transregional poetic conversation that it invited.

7

Prefacing the Poetry: Ghalib's Self-Presentation

O God, after me, create someone like me who would go through the entirety of speech, so that it would be understood how very high and palatial the wall of my [*sukhan*] speech/poetry is, and the thread of the lasso of my imagination is tied to the high points of that palace.

—Ghalib, dibachah to the Persian divan[1]

Ghalib was both a Persian and Urdu poet, and a prose stylist, yet his Persian and Urdu contributions are almost never viewed or discussed together. While we can attribute this to the decline of Persian in India from the nineteenth century onwards, Ghalib's pride in his own Persian, and his insistent denigration of Indian Persian poets, is a subject that cannot be ignored. In this chapter, I will scrutinize Ghalib's dibachahs to his Urdu and Persian divans, to interpret his 'theory' of the language of poetry. Is his theory of *sukhan* intimately bound with his subsequent self-conception and self-projection?

The dibachah to the Persian divan is expansive, more than five times the length of the one he wrote for the Urdu divan. It also has a khatimah, which again extols Ghalib's genius in Persian. Why does Ghalib give more weight to his Persian poetry? What exactly is the newness that Ghalib mentions in his dibachah?

Prefacing the Poetry

The dibachah is a critical but somewhat neglected category of Persianate literature.[2] There is no real equivalent for the term in English. Translating dibachah as 'introduction' is incorrect because the dibachah does not always refer to the contents. Its role might be more limited to the purpose of praising God, the Prophet and the patron. Neither 'introduction' nor 'preface', in their current usage, perfectly convey the function of this introductory text. Ideally, some neologism could be found to unite the senses of the two and convey the idea behind the alternating terms, but I prefer to use the original.[3] Another form similar to the dibachah is the *muqaddimah*.[4] Often, these two literary forms are used interchangeably. In visual-art books or albums, a clearer distinction can be found. The dibachah is a text written in a florid style, often with an illuminated double-page frontispiece.

Dibachah compositions were a common practice at the courts of the Safavids, Ottomans and Mughals, as was the art of historical–biographical writing (tazkirah). In Persian literature, particularly in the dibachah, figurative discourse predominates even in those passages of the text that refer to specific experiences and judgements. Tropology (a theory of figures of speech and of thought) is ubiquitous in Persian literature. The response to the trope, in particular, is to understand it as a normative linguistic habit that by its ubiquity might lose the power to convey the originality of experience or thought. Julie Scott Meisami has argued for the power of this literary phenomenon as an analogical mode: 'Metaphor transcends the status of trope to become a consistent means for signifying the inner substance of things.'[5] In a world in which everything is a figure, it is a sign testifying to the unifying order of creation.

As Chander Shekhar affirms, there is much information that can be culled out of the thickly knitted rhetorical language of dibachahs. Broadly speaking, there are three categories:

1. The dibachahs of poets and writers.
2. The dibachahs to historical works or chronicles.
3. The dibachahs by princes.

Poets explained the formal reasons behind their compositions, their style and the possibility of its criticism at the hands of the readers.[6] The best examples of dibachah writing prior to the Mughal period are from the pen of Amir Khusrau. The prefaces to Khusrau's first two divans—*Tuhfatul-Sighar* (Gift of Young Age) and *Wastul-Hayat* (Divan of Middle Age)—are short but important literary pieces. Both prefaces are great examples of literary style and full of information about his literary ambition and the milieu. The dibachah to his third divan, however, surpasses the first two and is of immense significance in delineating the history and poetics of Persian literature.[7] Moving on to the Mughal period, a cluster of dibachahs is collected in *Majma'ul Afkar.* In the eighteenth century, Indo-Persian writings became more assertive or definitive of the 'Indianness' in language use. A group of lexicographers, grammarians and exponents of prose *(insha)* took up the cudgels to compete with the mother-tongue speakers. Under the genre of insha writing, dibachah writing, too, continued to be practised as part of the Indo-Persian curriculum, to explore the various facets of language and literature on the one hand and court culture on the other.[8] Ghalib had several precedents in the art of dibachah writing to draw upon. Since he admired Khusrau, and after him, Faizi, he must have read their dibachahs.

When we look at Ghalib's dibachahs, we encounter a rhetorical mode of discourse that uses tropes to organize modes of perception. Their literary make-up is so complex and challenging that it often defies translation and comprehension. The language is loaded with cultural allusions, multiple meanings, puns, plus an inherent ambiguity which produces a textual structure that is not easy to comprehend. The static wordplay makes it difficult to bring out meaning. Perhaps this is why Ghalib's Persian dibachahs haven't attracted scholarly attention, let alone translation. Nonetheless, I found that in spite of the challenges of interpretation, Ghalib's dibachahs are filled with critical perceptions that are not simply figurative but can be interpreted to derive an understanding of his poetic self. I deploy the method of comparison to elucidate a relationship and make explicit the terms of which it is constitutive. My method of comparison reveals Ghalib's relationship with his Urdu and Persian poetry.

Dibachah to the Urdu Divan of 1841

Although Ghalib's Urdu divan was published before his Persian, and it was undoubtedly a momentous event for our poet, because he had been preparing it for a long time, its dibachah is not even a pale shadow of the anguish and brilliant rhetoric that he packed into the dibachah for the Persian.[9] A comparison of the two dibachahs reveals Ghalib's intellectual and emotional attitude towards his poetry in the two languages. The dibachah for the 1841 Urdu divan (written, of course, in Persian) is brimming with conceit and confidence. Let us look beyond the rhetoric and examine the opening paragraph of this short, purposeful document:

> Minds aware of fragrance are invited, and those who are used to sitting in gatherings are given the good news that some material for burning in the brazier has become available; some Indian aloe bark [*ud-e Hindi*] has come to hand. This aloe bark has not been splintered with a stone, or chopped inappropriately, or carved with an unskilled hand. In fact, it has been cut with an axe, then divided into small pieces with a knife and sculpted with a whittle.

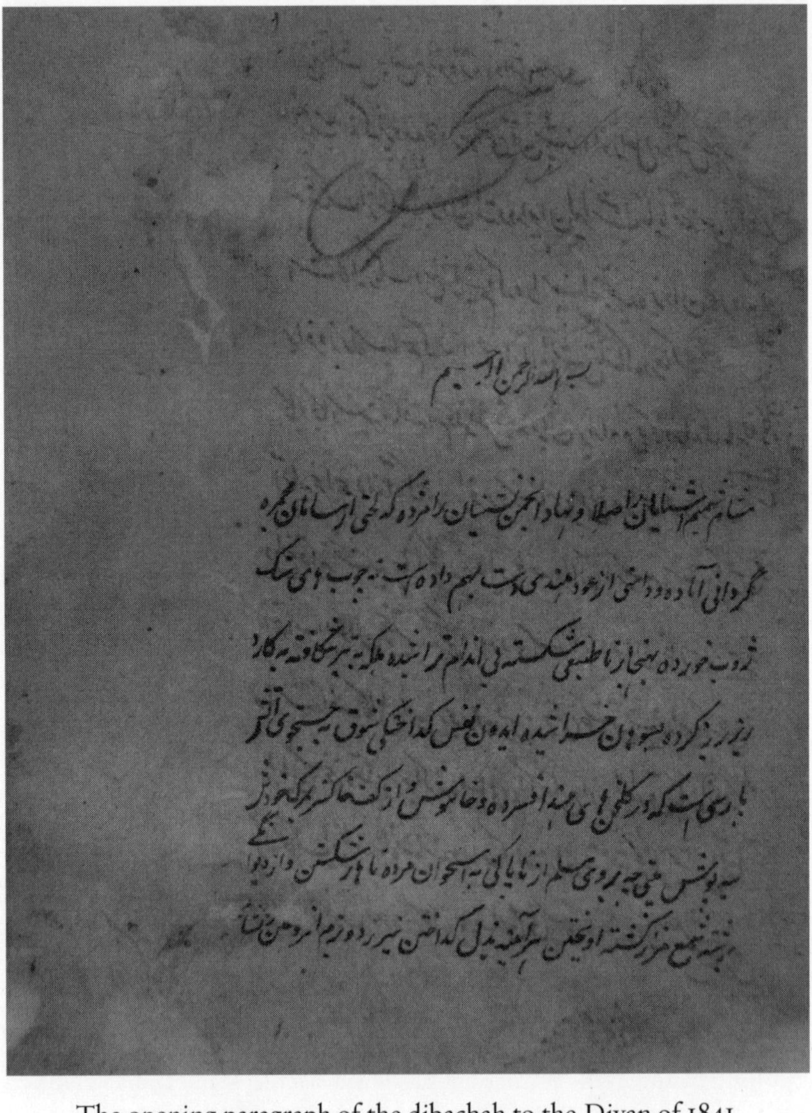

The opening paragraph of the dibachah to the Divan of 1841.

> The breath-burning power of desire is now looking for the Iranian fire. Not the fire that has now become dead and burnt to cinders in the Indian hearth, which you now see clad in black on account of its own death having become a handful of ashes. Because it is quite clear that it is unclean to breakfast with dead bones and it is proven madness to hang by the string that is the pendant of the snuffed-out candle of a grave. In any case, it is not proper to use a dead lamp for the purpose of melting one's heart, or for lighting up an assembly.[10]

The first point to note is that the dibachah, except for the standard 'in the name of God who is the most kind and merciful', does not commence with extensive praise of God, or the Prophet, or any other personality venerated from early Islamic or theological history. Instead, it opens with an invitation to those with awareness. The good news, as Ghalib writes above, is the emergence of some strikingly new material that has been carved and pared to perfection with a highly skilled hand. This bark is the distinctive, fragrant Indian aloe. Ghalib does emphasize the Indianness of the material. The second point is the reference to the Iranian fire. But the old Iranian fire has now become dead and burnt to cinders in the Indian hearth. Ghalib is not going to 'breakfast with dead bones', or 'use a dead lamp' for lighting this assembly. What Ghalib has to offer in the Urdu divan then is to bestow a new brilliance to the few sparks that he salvaged from the ashes. Ghalib's Urdu poetry is a phoenix rising from the ashes of a nearly dead Persian fire that is reinforced with Indian aloe wood.

In the subsequent paragraph, Ghalib explains the metaphor of the Iranian fire dying in the Indian hearth and how he reignited it with pickings from his heart:

> I am full of thanks to the lord, the bestower of poetry to the inner self, that I have in the ashes found a few sparks from that brilliant

> fire and have quickly engaged by picking at my heart, and have produced bellows from my breath for that fire, so that in the circle of the people of the world, which has scant capital of its own, some capital may be made available. Such that it may bestow on the brazier the brilliance and glory of the light of a lamp, and may vouchsafe fragrance of aloe bark the power to fly to the nose and thus make the brain fully saturated with its perfume.[11]

Ghalib thus claims to have brought freshness, both literal and metaphorical, to Urdu poetry. He will breathe passion to stoke the fire. I presume that the fire he is referring to, which has now burnt to ashes, is the Indo-Persian trend of tazah-goi. Mirza Bedil was the last great poet in that style. He assures his readers that he will publish his Persian divan next, and it's only then that he would rest, or, as he puts it, 'after having broken his feet'.[12]

In a small but crucial paragraph added to the dibachah at a later date, presumably inserted after some rumination, Ghalib declares the scattered verses found outside of this divan to be inconsequential. I make the case in Chapter 5, that it is an assertion of copyright. This paragraph became pivotal when Ghalib's 1821 divan was found in 1918 and Ghalibians were reminded that there were almost as many verses outside the authorized divan as were included in it. The paragraph lent itself to the argument that was circulated to show that Ghalib did not care about the large number of verses that he did not include in the Urdu divan. That part of his oeuvre is known as 'rejected' (*mustarad*). The paragraph also drew attention away from the more meaningful assertions that Ghalib was making in the dibachah.

The closing paragraph draws attention to the momentous act of publishing his poetry:

> Lord, these [texts] which have not yet smelt the fragrance of being nor have reached the level of the apparent from the unapparent,

> that is, the paintings which are still within the inner self of the painter whose name is Asadullah Khan, who is known as Mirza Naushah with the pen name of Ghalib. Such that may God grant, that just as he was born in Agra and has made Delhi his home, he may be buried in Najaf.[13]

With this concise dibachah, the Urdu divan is presented with the self-assurance of a poet who knows the singularity of his work. I will now compare the dibachah of the Urdu divan to that of the Persian divan to illustrate the differences in tone, as well as the specific audience that Ghalib is addressing in the two texts.

Dibachah to the Persian Divan of 1845

The Persian divan has a lengthy dibachah that is profoundly moving and self-assertive, written in the delectable, though convoluted, literary prose style that an educated native Persian speaker of Ghalib's time would be expected to thoroughly enjoy.[14] This is undoubtedly his most challenging piece of prose, filled with metaphorical compounds that may seem either meaningless or distracting to a casual reader. The divan's publication was supported by the generosity of Navab Aminuddin Ahmad Khan of Loharu. Ghalib praises him generously in the dibachah's concluding pages, both in prose and in an elegant masnavi that is stamped with Ghalib's poetic genius.

Over the course of this dense narrative, Ghalib broaches several questions that connect with the continuity and transregionality of the Persian tradition of ghazal poetry, and its practice in northern India. Although Ghalib's musings, or even assertions, can be perceived as being synchronic with the broad idea of contemporaneity or timelessness in the Perso-Urdu tradition, I would venture to say that Ghalib was aware of the spatial, geographical and historical reach of Persian. He frequently mentions Zartusht, Azar, the fire temple and even Ahriman and other imaginary and mythic characters associated with pre-Islamic Iran. Yet, more significant is his allusion to new Persian and his own affinity with it.[15] The prickly problems of language currency and literary use are embedded in the text, couched in metaphors that need careful untangling. Prashant Keshavmurthy's work on Persian authorship and canonicity in late Mughal Delhi provides an exposition on the networks of patronage that made such literary self-fashioning politically effective.[16] I will return to the discussion on poetry and polity later in this chapter. Let us first look at the continuum of this dibachah with an eye on Ghalib's specific claims in composing poetry.

In a typical, symbolically charged mode, the dibachah begins with the play on *zaban*, which means both tongue and language, the instrument with which the poet composes, and for which he is grateful to God:

> In the name of God, who has blessed me with the tongue, I am thankful. For what business do I have to praise Him? I, who cannot differentiate a word from a pot shard [*harf-khazaf*].[17]

In the second sentence, the brilliant wordplay turns on the orthography and calligraphic practice. If one writes *khazaf* (خزف) without the dots (as was the traditional calligraphic practice in the times), it could easily be mistaken for *harf*. One can, of course, dig deeper to excavate Ghalib's implied meaning of the relationship between clay and creativity (clay-pot shard). The next sentence builds further on the orthographic–calligraphic theme:

> That same Power has miraculously removed the veil from the face of this beautiful youth whose facial hair [*khatt*] is just sprouting, that earlier intellects called a divan.[18]

By referring to *khatt* (خط), which means both the newly sprouted facial hair of young boys and the script or style of writing, Ghalib alludes to his divan as a beautiful, newly sprung piece of writing. Words, Ghalib goes on to say, are the ancient scars of madness scratched on paper by the nails of his breath. Hot, steaming blood oozes from the wounds, from the depths of his being. These words are clothed in the garb of paper; they are silent and mute like painted pictures because of the astonishment caused by being. These words are blazing and black from the heart's smoke. The blackness of ink is a timeless metaphor deployed to emphasize that inscription makes the words glow, giving them a lasting lustre. Moving on, Ghalib creates another fantastic picture of the unveiling of his divan. There is lightning-like ardency, there is the pain of ecstasy and the tumult of brilliance:[19]

> I don't say that it is smoke and lamp, or, tulip and scar, but rather [collection/divan] burning and breaking apart. I don't say it is lightning or the mountain of Tur, or Jannat and houri, but pride is its kingdom, and a place of repose and relaxation, its environs or outskirts [*savad*]. It is the magical illusion of the flame and the smoke, and the magical illusion is traced back to the Zartusht of thought. The flame is hidden and the smoke apparent. The heart is the tablet of the magical illusion and the tongue [*zaban*] its revealer [of the illusion]. It is an assembly of cloud and wind, stirred up by the magic of the thought of the pearl-filled clouds and the diamond-scattering breezes, and thought is the deceptive scroll of colours and lips that incant magic.[20]

The stage for the divan's unveiling is suffused with miraculous illusions drawn from nature. An awareness of the zaban revealing the ideas encrypted in the poetry builds on the organic relationship between thought and language. The sentence that follows further expands the connection between the magic of thought and its capture through words (scroll) and utterance. A lot of ghazal imagery is woven into the description in a foreshadowing of what the reader can expect in the poetry itself. Because of the cryptic nature of language in the ghazal, there is a dynamic relation between the writer and the reader-listener in ghazal poetry. Using nature imagery is a perfect way of describing the divine effulgence, and is also a reflection on creation. In nature's beauty one sees God; for God is manifested in nature. Continuing in this vein, Ghalib ingeniously points towards competitors who cannot bear to recognize his talent:

> I am scarred by the short-sighted jealous ones who cannot be thrilled by the blossoming of a fresh rose in the meadow, of the lightning that flashes in the dark night.[21]

After sharing his concern about his rivals, Ghalib moves on to the first of several long poems embedded in the dibachah. The first of these is an enthralling masnavi in praise of God:

> O You who bestow [upon man] what is hidden, and who is
> munificent to all that is apparent.
> You, who give weight and gravitas to the heart by sorrow, and to
> the body, by life.
> You, who makes the heart feel grief, and the body life force.
> The spark that is in the heart of the stone, because of You,
> Is the sparkling appearance of colour on the ruby's face.[22]

As the poem develops, it uncovers Ghalib's manipulations of religio-cultural affinities. The fragrance of monotheism permeates the breeze perfuming the dawn. God releases the musk sac from the veins of spring and unveils the essence of Beauty. With a flourish of his pen, Ghalib identifies the Creator with *nur* (Light) that permeates both the Ka'bah and the Zoroastrian temple. There is only one God, and God subsumes everything.[23]

> O You, in whose ocean the heavens are mere bubbles,
> And the earth is the lees from Your wine cup.

O You, from whose cask of pure wine
The strainer of wine in the Zoroastrian temple scatters stars.
You are the bestower of being on the good, and the evil.
You are the splendour of the Ka'bah and the temple.
. . .
O God, you have bestowed upon me the splendour and the voice of Khusrau[24]
You have given to Persian newness through me.[25]
. . .
I am silent and patient, in submitting to You,
It's from Your blessing that I sing in my own praise,
Being infirm is the foundation of many strengths,
Ostentation of one's self is ostentation of God [because knowing oneself is knowing God].[26]

By proclaiming that it is the same God whose light shines in the Ka'bah and the fire temple, Ghalib smooths the path to drive home a prickly issue, the blessing to give Persian newness. He claims affinity with and descent from the Iranian king Khusrau. In this masnavi, he avoids mentioning the Iranian poets that he generally looked up to, such as Sa'di or Urfi, because he wants to emphasize his connection to, and benediction from, Iranian kings. In fact, throughout his career, Ghalib claimed that his felicity in Persian was God's gift. Since he was fortified by God's grace, no one could touch him. Here, he is boasting that though a mere Indian, he does better than the Iranians. His precursors and peers may not tolerate his boasting, and some of it is routine in this style of writing. The qita below is a good example:

Don't be awed by Urfi because he is from Shiraz
Don't be captivated by Zulali because he is from Khwansar
Come into the Somnath of my imagination, so you can see,
My brow brightens the soul, and the sacred thread adorns my shoulder.[27]

Ghalib's reference to the legendary temple of Somnath and the sacred thread worn by Brahmins is to emphasize the Indianness and plurality of his imagination's heights. Somnath stands for all of India because it represents the lure for its seductive treasures. It is a very strong assertion of the richness of cultural metaphor in Indo-Persian poetry, as well as Ghalib's advantage in having access to it. Shiraz and Khwansar cannot compare with Somnath.[28] As if this qita wasn't enough, perhaps because it is a challenge, Ghalib, unabashed, heaps more praise on himself in another, lengthier qita:

> Since no one else in the age is worthy of praise,
> I praise myself.
> Since no one understands my language,
> What is it that I could submit before the people of this place?[29]

Ghalib takes recourse in poetry to make oblique comments on the capabilities of his precursors and competitors because one can be subversive in poetry and get away with it. In the long qita, an excerpt from which is quoted above, Ghalib's aggressive boasting takes many interesting turns.[30] Ultimately, he broaches the vexed subject of (a) new Persian poetry. While he is contemporaneous with his precursors, how does he assert his own voice? How does one make a mark in a tradition where themes are commonly shared? I think Ghalib wants to explain that his style is not a break from tradition but a regeneration. He invokes Sheikh Ali Hazin on this complicated thread of community and continuity of tradition.[31] According to Ghalib, Hazin's poetry is the supreme point of desire [*intiha-e arzu*] of the ancients, as well as the beginning of the glory [*abru*] of the contemporaries.[32] To explain this abstract, abstruse idea, of how the ultimate point of desire could be the self-annihilation from which a new glory begins, Ghalib brings in the familiar trope of the moth. He refines and reinterprets the self-destructive yearning of the moth. According to my interpretation, Ghalib suggests that the moth has an intense desire pulsing in its veins to scatter its existence, to foster a new beginning.[33]

This sentence comes at the end of a convoluted paragraph about the unevenness of custom and religion, and how much sifting and straining goes on in the process of creating the wine of poetry. Read in conjunction with the verse that follows (quoted below), I interpret this to mean that Ghalib acknowledged the depth of pain as an essential for great poetry, such as of the great masters; but when the creative desire reaches its apogee comes the time to pass on the light; to carry it further. Here, Ghalib could be echoing the critical literary exposition on the fine split between theme (mazmun) and meaning (*ma'ni*). While themes are shared, new twists to well-worn themes are possible through creative fashioning. He praises Hazin as *intiha-e arzu-e mutaqaddimin*, that is, the ultimate (in poetry), that the precursors would have wished for; but he is also the *ibtidaa-e abru-e mutakhirin*, that is, the commencement of the honour and pride of the contemporaries. At this point, Ghalib quotes a verse from Hazin:[34]

> I brought back many candles of truth from the graves of the Martyrs
> Because they [the Powers of Destiny] gave me a heart and eyes that scatter blood.[35]

The 'I' in the verse is now meant to be read as Ghalib, to whom the torch is being passed on by Hazin. In an oblique style, which is characteristic of this form of writing, Ghalib has presented himself as the chosen one. The excessive self-praise, however, is tempered in the very next paragraph with the realization that it may not go down well with his detractors. Nonetheless, Ghalib delights us with every turn of phrase:

> Justice is above obedience. The desire with which I beat my wings in hyperbole, and in the style with which I praise myself, half of it

> is love of the beautiful ones [*shahid bazi*] and the other half is windy boasting. Look at the injustice, that wherever the comb tries to straighten the hair of curly-haired people, calamity emerges in my heart, so that I bind my thoughts with the twists of that lock . . . On the one hand I am happy that I have been allowed to compose much poetry in the style of the *ishq bazan*, but I am also in anguish of the greed that caused me to blacken so many pages for those in power.[36]

The enigmatic sentence with which this paragraph opens—'Justice is above obedience'—and what follows after it can be interpreted in at least two ways. The first is that the culturally ingrained virtue of obedience is not above justice, which could imply that disobedience, or straying from the path, can be tolerated from the view of justice. The curly-haired people could be the wilful beloveds whose locks can never be straightened. But the metaphor can be interpreted differently, too. One can never be sure what exactly is the meaning hidden in these complexly crafted sentences. The beauty of such a style is that it is loaded with allusions; in Ghalib's case, the tropes are often allusions to his going off the beaten track in pursuit of newness or freshness in poetry.

Sukhan: Ghalib's Thoughts on Poetry and Poetics

Just as zaban means both language and tongue, sukhan is a multivalent word with several meanings, the two important ones being speech and poetry (poetic utterance). Throughout the dibachah, Ghalib has demonstrated his crafting of language. Finally, the narrative gets to the point where, couched in a language charged with tropes, we get pointers about the qualities of good poetry (sukhan). Ghalib lists the following: virginity or originality (*doshizagi*) of nature and bent of mind, sweetness and chastity of nature, burning-ness (being full of strong emotion), especially of pain and of theme, the heart-melting tenderness of spirit, the pleasurable taste of submission and utterance, tastefulness in complaint (against the beloved, or God), the joy of song and the anguish of lament, the flowing-ness of the action (of poetry), *ravani* (flowing-ness), the attainment of fruition, the unveiling of mysteries, the presentation of good tidings, the suitability of praise, the heart-rending-ness of blame or reproach, the smoothness of sound, the harshness of dismissal and the submission for the following—of promise, of the transmission of message, of the rule and formula for the setting up of assemblies and for the attainment of results from assemblies and wars.[37]

While many of the qualities Ghalib listed may be perceived as the accepted standard for poetry described in the tazkirahs, I want to emphasize the order in which these are listed. Notice that the virginity of mind comes first, followed by the burning-ness of the theme.[38] But Ghalib adds a piquant note by adding that the poet needs to have access or invitation (*barnamah*) to gatherings where poetry is presented. These gatherings (mushairah) were battlegrounds for literary sparring, wordplay and witty repartee. The success or failure of poets in mushairahs was measured through the response of the audience. Ghalib craved audiences, and also readers, who could understand his abstractions. But he felt that many people did not know the difference between the warp and woof of silk and rough cloth. Ghalib wrote that the struggle for a poet was to capture and communicate the meanings of forms through the images he paints with his pen. To understand the nature of existence, one has to have faith in God:

> The forms of things before they existed in the world are in God's realm. Colours are the drawings on the wings of the *anqa*. With all these images that poured out of the pen, the thinker has a hundred colours and a thousand modes of music. Every manifestation from the veil of speech that flaps its wings is the natural movement of the wave, and everything that is apparent in the mirror of sight

rotates in the lantern of thought. Those, whose minds are light, and who hang on the wind, what can they understand of speech (poetry) except wind? Those who have weighty souls, who are aware of the existence of things, what can they discover in the stories except stories. Therefore, the veil lifter of this burning and making, the author of *Gulshan-e Raz*, has said:

Whoever has a heart that is free of doubt
Is convinced that existence is naught but Unity.[39]

A critical aspect of Ghalib's poetry is the significance he gives to forms and the slippage between form and illusion. Perhaps we could add imagination to this play of form and illusion. As a poet who captures the meanings of forms, he also questions what one sees or imagines. The images (*naqsh*) that flow from the poet's pen are at one level imaginary because of the singularity of perception. A similar nuance is Ghalib's perception of colour(s). Colour is a vital component of imagination, especially when painting images of emotions. The ideas expressed in the above paragraph touch on facets of Ghalib's poetics. How can speech and sight be crafted into poetry? Speech is drawn from thought; and thought has a connection to forms of things. Mirror is an essential trope through which the abstraction of form is expressed in classical ghazal poetry. The image that is reflected in the mirror is perceived as a reflection of thought. Another essential trope is the veil, the invisible curtain that falls between us and reality. Thus, poetry, which is the highest form of expression, needs minds equally aware to understand the mysteries of existence.[40]

In the paragraph that follows, Ghalib speaks of the slippery slope-like challenges a poet faces to survive in the world. He has blackened pages and pages with poems praising patrons, but time is running out and he has to prove his worth. He mentions his imaginative prowess and how he is different from those who court worldly honours.

Finally, in the last paragraph, Ghalib gives up any pretence of humility or diffidence. With exemplary self-aggrandizement, he declares:

> So. Why should it not be that a person of my capabilities does have honour and pride of superiority, and the dress of my being does have the property (prize) of being decorated with perfection?
>
> No, the tunes of grammar and etymology, and derivatives from root words, are not on my lips. Nor do I have the song of the negative or the positive on my tongue. The blood of no Surah (صراح) [a famous dictionary of Arabic] is on my head; nor is the corpse of a Qamus (قاموس) [another famous Arabic dictionary] on my shoulders. My feet have no blisters by walking the path of figures of speech, nor do I string the pearls of rhetorical devices. I am the kabab roasted on the heat of the smokeless fire of Persian. I am drunk on the strong, pungent wine of new themes. I am the salamander [a mythical creature which thrives only in the fire] of the fire-temple of the Magis of Ajam [Persia]. Ask me about my song. I am the bulbul [songbird] of the garden made by the gardeners of Persia.[41]

This last paragraph makes several critical points that need careful unravelling. Why does Ghalib mention dictionaries of Arabic (the Surah and the Qamus)? He also repudiates figures of speech and rhetorical devices in his poetry! Instead of stringing the pearls of rhetorical devices, he prefers to be the kebab roasted on the 'smokeless' fire of Persian, drunk on the wine of new themes. All these pretentious claims point to the rivalry between Indian Persian and Iranian Persian. The poetry of the Indo-Persian school was loaded with stylistic devices, metaphors with cultural allusions, and sometimes (as in the poetry of Mirza Bedil) the diction was more Indian than Persian because of regional expressions. Ghalib claimed his Persian was free of Indianisms, that his Persian was not weighed down by Arabic words. The language of his song was a Persian nightingale's, and nothing less.

'I Am the Moon Ten Times Over': What the Qitas in the Persian Divan Reveal about Ghalib's Self-Presentation

The Persian divan opens with an arrangement of sixty-one qitas, followed by masnavis and other miscellaneous genres.[42] I will now examine the first ten qitas in the divan because they are illustrative of Ghalib's engagement with issues of language ownership. I see a strong message in the deliberate arrangement or sequence in the presentation of qitas. They are not arranged alphabetically, that is, they are not arranged according to the last letter of the refrain.

The first qita is all about ethnicity:

Ghalib, I am from the sacred land of Turan;
Doubtless, I have superiority and precedency by virtue of my ancestry.
I am of Turkish extraction, and am by birth
One with the high and powerful of my community.
From among the Turks, I am of the community of the Aibaks;
In fullness, I am the moon ten times over.
My ancestors' occupation was agriculture and husbandry;
I am from Samarqand, a child of landowners.
And if you ask about my true reality
What can I say about myself, that I am such and so much?
I am the meanest apprentice at the flowing bountifulness of the Lord:
Choicest child of that sole Mentor called Gabriel.
It's because of his refulgence that I am friend and companion to lightning.
It's because of his munificence that I am like the cloud.
I am triumphant, by virtue of the pursuit that is mine.
I am happy, by virtue of the livelihood that I don't have.

I weep copious tears at what I am;
I laugh wholeheartedly at what the times are.[43]

As an introduction through a poem, Ghalib delivers a lot of information. Then, having established his ethnic lineage—Turkish ancestors from the Aibak community, Ghalib moves to his Turko-Persian literary (*adabi*) lineage. In the second qita, he claims descent from legendary heroes Pashang and Afrasiyab; he is the true inheritor of Jamshed's wine.[44] The subsequent qitas are about his pen's prowess, the originality and newness of his themes and the jealousy of his rivals. He then delivers a longer qita (no. seven), which seems to be addressed to his rivals (of which there were many), where he makes a compelling case for the superiority of his Persian:[45]

O you, who stated in the assembly of the poetry-discerning King of Kings:
'As far as profuseness of composition goes, so-and-so is of equal weight to me in poetry.'

Well, you spoke true, but you don't know that there can be no occasion for taunt,
If the tune from my harp is less than the loud report of a drum.

There's no harm, if my writings in Rekhtah are just a quire or two;
For that is no more than a leaf from the oasis of my literatures.[46]

Look into the Persian, so that you may see paintings of myriad shades and hues.
Pass by the collection in Urdu, for it is nothing but drawings and sketches.

Look at the Persian, so you'll know that in the realm of imagination;
I am both Mani[47] and Arzhang;[48] and that manuscript, my angel-inspired Artang.[49]

The third and fourth verses from this qita are widely quoted as a testimony of Ghalib's great pride in Persian and his low opinion of his own Urdu divan. It often happens that verses are plucked from poems to suit an argument. This poem is not about brushing past the Urdu for the Persian. In fact, it calls attention to both. It appears from the qita that Ghalib is being mocked for his low output in Urdu, and he scathingly strikes back saying that the harmonies of his Urdu are beyond the capability of a lesser poet. Ghalib continues:

Enmity needs a vocation shared by two, and you know that's not the case here;
The harmonies that are in my harp are impossible for you to produce.

Since you do not play the same music nor speak the same tongue as I,
Why then is your heart tied into the knot of perplexity, envying my song?

Towards the end of the poem, Ghalib deftly connects the Persian and Urdu traditions:

Perspicacious master and law-giver Siraj-ud Din Bahadur Shah, he,
Who can divine the spark buried in the veins of my granite.

King with Jamshed in his entourage, who, when his armies are
Inspected by him, can count Darius among his foot soldiers—

I am Anvari and Urfi and Khaqani to my King,
And the King is my Tahmurs, Jamshed, and Hoshang.[50]

The last Mughal emperor, Bahadur Shah, wrote Urdu poetry under the pen name Zafar. His court was famous for mushairahs, which the emperor himself would preside over. Literary controversies were played out between rival factions. Ustad Ibrahim Zauq was the emperor's tutor. Ghalib's recognition from the court came in 1850, when he was appointed to write the history of the Mughal rule. After Ustad Zauq's death in 1854, Mirza Ghalib was appointed the royal tutor. As is evident from the qita quoted above, there must have been a discussion around Ghalib's oeuvre in Urdu, and how the Persian was much more than the Urdu. Ghalib had returned to Urdu composition after two decades of writing mostly in Persian. He had picked up the challenge of taking Persian to new heights, in spite of its declining popularity at the court, because he believed in the wider scope and prestige of the language and its literature.

In the verses quoted above, Ghalib's argument delivers a double blow. Not only is he as great as Anvari, Urfi and Khaqani, his king (Bahadur Shah) is the mythic Jamshed. Like almost every poet in this classical tradition, Ghalib had no qualms in projecting himself as the leading Persianist of his age who was on par with the 'nightingales' of the Persophone world.[51]

The tenth qita is both delightful and unusual. In this qita, Ghalib is apparently talking with his muse, the cup-bearer in the assembly (*bazm*) of awareness. The Saqi has added something to the poet's cup that heightens awareness and loosens the tongue. Thus, the poet begins to ask questions ranging from the existential to the mundane: What is the basis of creation? What are worldly accomplishments? What should I do with those who oppose me?

The focus then moves to the cities Ghalib has travelled, from Delhi to Banaras and Patna and, finally, Calcutta. The pleasures of these cities are deftly described. Ultimately, the poet asks the Saqi what path he should follow. The Saqi responds that he should give up the world of pleasure and make the pilgrimage to Karbala.[52]

From the preceding description, we can see how creatively Ghalib has arranged the first ten poems in the divan. This illustrates my earlier point about the pains he took in ordering his poems in a divan.

The Khatimah (Afterword) to the Persian Divan

> There are ten thousand, four hundred and twenty verses (10,424), each one of which is powerful enough in its sharpness of effect, to be like the ornament of the throat of a slaughtered [*bismil*] one, and in elegance of speech, like a pearl pendant in the ears of the heart.[53]

Altaf Husain Hali, whose work is indispensable in reconstructing Ghalib's trajectory, is puzzled by Ghalib's zealous pursuit of Persian.[54] He wonders why Mirza Ghalib was so obsessed and focused on perfecting an art that didn't have many appreciators. According to Hali, Ghalib's patrons were mostly British government officials who hardly knew the Persian language and were strangers to its poetry and literary culture, or the Mughal king and his nobles who didn't have the time or desire to read his qasidahs. Hali might be romanticizing the unappreciated genius here: the mute Milton, the unsung Mozart. The myth of the unappreciated Ghalib continues down the ages. Ghalib did have many friends who believed in his poetry but, according to Hali, that cannot be enough to keep a poet going. Hali goes on to say that although Persian was languishing in India, but like the proverbial sputtering lamp in its last phase, there were some first-rate scholars in Delhi who also had an appreciation for its poetry. Hali mentions Maulana Fazl-e Haq Khairabadi, Maulana Mufti Muhammad Sadruddin Khan Azurdah, Maulvi Abdullah Khan Alavi, Maulvi Imam Bakhsh Sahbai, Hakim Momin Khan Momin, Navab Mustafa Khan Hasrati, Navab Ziyauddin Ahmad Khan Naiyar and Ghulam Ali Khan Vahshat.[55] The presence of these people in Delhi as the contemporaries of Ghalib gave him reason to hone his Persian. Some of them, Hali hints, were his rivals and critics, which is why Ghalib had to be careful in his usage of Persian. Maulana Azurdah disliked Ghalib's style, something which Ghalib alluded to on several occasions. Maulvi Sahbai and Maulvi Alavi (who composed in Bedil's style) also disapproved of Ghalib. Hali concludes that Ghalib had to constantly strive to improve his poetry because of his critics, and that was the reason for his extraordinary felicity.[56]

Hali further makes the point that Ghalib's early Persian ghazal was in Mirza Bedil's style. He composed a large number of ghazals in that style and on similar themes, but he gradually moved away from Bedil and ultimately matched the great Persian ghazal poets such as Urfi, Zahuri, Naziri and Talib Amuli. But Hali's great error is to believe everything Ghalib says about himself. The poetry of Talib, Naziri and Urfi is quite similar to Bedil's, in that it is deeply saturated in tazah-goi. It may be that Hali didn't appreciate or understand the subtleties of the new style.

> Much as my [poetic] temperament is from divine inspiration, from the very beginning [of my literary career] it was inclined towards composing poems worthy of being chosen [among the best], and it also inclined [only] towards [the manner] what appealed to me most. Yet mostly [in the beginning], it didn't. Because of extravagance and waywardness, [it didn't] follow the footsteps of those who knew [the turns and twists of] the paths, and fancied that the plenitude and abundance of elegance in their way of walking was actually the stumbling of the drunk. Yet, in all this running and speeding about, the kindness and affection of previous travellers came in action, because of the worth and virtue of the kinship (similarities) that they found in me; their hearts filled with pain because of shame [at my wayward ways]. They were sad at my wandering aimlessly about and they looked at me with the eyes of a teacher.
>
> Shaikh Ali Hazin, by his soft half-smiles, made me see my wanderings from the true path, Talib Amuli's angry look and the lightning-eye of Urfi Shirazi burnt off all that source and material which caused absurd and frivolous movement to my journeying

> feet. Zahuri, most promptly, by the power of his poetry, tied an amulet upon my arm and travel provision to my waist. Naziri, who walked uncaring and unafraid of all else, brought elegance to my gait by his personal laws and rules.[57]

We must note that Ghalib acknowledges Naziri (1560–1612/14), Zuhuri (1537/8–1591), Urfi (1555–1591), Talib Amuli (1585–1637) and Hazin (1691–1766) to be among the forbears who 'guided' him towards the right path. But the two poets he does not mention, Sa'ib and Bedil, are the ones closest to his own style, and whose influence on Ghalib is noticeable.[58] While one has to take lightly Ghalib's dramatic rhetoric regarding the so-called guidance he received from the selected forbears, even taking these lines at their face value shows that Ghalib wanted to pay homage to the important Iranian names among the cluster of poets celebrated for tazah-goi, as he went on to claim his own distinctive status. It is in these rivalries, emulations and improvements on existing themes and ideas that the continuity of the poetic tradition thrived.

In the closing lines of the khatimah to this monumental divan, Ghalib once more emphasizes the 'newness' of his contribution, at the same time expressing genuine concerns about depredation by other poets. He mentions the exact number of verses in the edition to be 10,424.

Finally, he closes with the ultimate, hyperbolic claim on the art of poetry:

> O God, let these goods and merchandise, having been left on the open plain, and this door-opened treasury be safe from the depredation of those who steal [elegant] themes [from other poets] and from the marauding horsemen who don't understand and write properly; and let the high-watered pearls from this collection be so remembered by heart and be on the tongues with such swaying [i.e., desirable and elegant] gait that whichever

> [pearl], because of its brilliance, stumbles during the measuring of the threads of discourse [study and recitation] should not cease rolling and tumbling until it touches the very depth of the hearts.

Rubai:

> If a taste for poetry was the law of the land,
> My poems would have fame like the Pleiades;
> And, Ghalib, if this art of poetry were a religion—
> This book of poems would be its Revealed Book.

Ghalib's Conscious Aesthetic Goal

From my reading of the dibachah and khatimah of Ghalib's Persian divan, many questions regarding his affiliation with Persian are clarified and a clearer picture of the Persian literary cosmopolis emerges. There is no doubt that Ghalib aspired to reinvigorate classical Persian poetry with innovative and fresh ideas. His literary world was in a state of rapid transition from the courtly culture that had nurtured talents from across the Persianate to a utilitarian, colonial one where cosmopolitan languages were making space for the modern vernaculars. Ghalib, a bilingual poet, was at a crossroads. There was Urdu, his first language of poetry, and there was Persian, the language of his forbears in which he enjoyed innate felicity. He chose the cosmopolitan path because it afforded a deeper conversation with the tradition and transregional connection.

Shamsur Rahman Faruqi, in his erudite and widely read essay on nineteenth-century literary culture, asked why users of Indian Persian began to privilege all Iran-born writers above the Indo-Iranians and Indian Persianists. It seemed to be a strange case of 'unprivileged power'.[59] Ghalib led the charge against Indian Persianists with scornful barbs. The disputes mostly revolved around the use of Persian words by Indian writers but spilt into

Persian use in Urdu as well. I have discussed the objections over Ghalib's Persian usages on the subject of the authority of Mirza Qatil (1747–1818), which happened during Ghalib's sojourn in Calcutta (1827–29), earlier in the book. Eventually, Ghalib wrote the masnavi *Ashtinamah* by way of conciliation. But even in the conciliatory poem, he declared his affiliation to Talib, Naziri, Urfi and Zuhuri, and not Bedil, who had been his ideal thus far in both Persian and Urdu poetry. In Calcutta, Ghalib realized that the reach of the Persian cosmopolis was far more extensive compared to the narrower world of Urdu.

The geographical qualification implicated in the metonym 'Sabk-e Hindi' suggests a discernible 'Indianness of style', generally sidestepping the poets' own claims that such inventiveness was fresh and new rather than merely Indian. Rajeev Kinra, in his recent book, makes an arguable point that quibbling about the Indianness of the style bypasses the question of early modernity altogether. Kinra cites Paul Losensky's path-breaking work as the only book-length study in English that examines the poetics of tazah-goi in terms of the poets' own literary claims and vocabulary, rather than retroactively imposing the anachronistic Sabk-e Hindi model on them. Kinra's argument is refreshing even though it underplays the debate on Persian language as used by Indians, which is an essential part of the debate as well. In the last decade of his life, Ghalib took his aggressive claims of fasahat (language usage or linguistic purity) in Persian to the ultimate degree by writing a critique of Muhammad Husain Tabrizi's well-known dictionary, *Burhan-e Qati*. Ghalib went on to publish *Qati-e-Burhan* in 1860: a compendium of his nasty quibbles with some two hundred of Tabrizi's entries in *Burhan-e Qati*. The publication triggered an unpleasant sequence of rejoinders and counter-rejoinders. Still, Ghalib stuck to his assertion of superiority in language use.[60] In his dibachah to *Qati-e-Burhan*, he claimed to have had a native Iranian tutor, Abdus Samad (way back in Agra in 1811), who amended his

Persian to make it contemporary and colloquial. We know that the immigration of intellectuals from Iran had tapered off in the nineteenth century. This created a void that Indian Persianists could fill, except for their own complexes about correct usage, as well as the perceived obsessive necessity to maintain the purity of the language. Ghalib's Persian oeuvre suffered not only because of the fading of Persian and the rise of the vernaculars in colonial India but also because poetry in tazah-goi by Indian Persianists was associated with a politically enfeebled Mughal Delhi. With the trend for 'nationalist' literatures gaining momentum, Indo-Persian became a marginalized subject.

I find Ghalib's dibachah to his Persian divan brimming with observations on poetry, which give us his perspective on both newness and its so-called Indianness. Ghalib is aggressively engaged in showing that it is possible to belong to multiple heredities, especially in the world of *adab* (literature). He emphasizes the importance of new themes in poetry and the inability of the 'jealous ones' who cannot think imaginatively:

> The beauty of the new spring (*tazah bahar*), with its scattered colours, cannot be tolerated by every discerning person (*didahvar*), and the fineness of the transparency of the linen cloth cannot be perceived by every stylish person (*adashinas*). If the particle can cover its nakedness with the sun (wear the sun), what envy would then be for those who wear those elaborate golden turbans. If the wilderness, because of its burning heart, drinks the moonlight, what can those who sleep inside know about it?[61]

I read the 'new spring' that Ghalib mentions here as an indicator of his innovative literary ingenuity that goes a step beyond his peers or precursors. But to what extent can one accept rivalries mentioned in poetry to be literally true? These protestations of superiority, the tradition of javab-goi, seem to be an exercise that opens an ongoing dialogue between those that have gone before and the present group of poets. In the Persophone world, this dialogue is complicated by the implications of regional metaphor. In the short qita quoted earlier in the chapter, Ghalib playfully alludes to these regional prejudices while adding his own distinguishing cultural–regional marker.

As we have seen, Ghalib distanced himself from Bedil and other Indian poets because of the unpleasant quibbles over Persian usage. Yet, Bedil's poetic philosophy was deeply ingrained in Ghalib's mind. More recently, Keshavmurthy's work on Bedil's poetics helps understand the extent to which Ghalib was influenced by the Sufi master. In Bedil's Sufi poetics, sukhan, or poetic utterance, came to designate the spirit of creativity, boundless imagination and intuitive knowledge. In Keshavmurthy's telling, Bedil's interpretation of sukhan translates as the practice of working language, of ingenious poetic artifice that is harmonious with Islamic orthopraxis as one of the several spiritual practices by which to testify to the distance between the world, or creatures, and what is most real. Sukhan, the verbal witnessing of the gap between the creator and the creature, formed part of one's preparation for the recognition of the true self.[62] Ghalib's Urdu poetry is suffused with these themes from Bedil's tazah-goi style.[63] In fact, the greatest impact of Persian tazah-goi is seen in his Urdu poetry. In Urdu, Ghalib is acknowledged and celebrated as a great classicist with a modern mind. Ghalib is modern because he questions the authenticity of things and perspectives. In Persian, too, Ghalib comes across as a modern mind sensitive to the historical dynamics of his time.

The evaluative mode of literary criticism, which was the standard in Persian and Urdu literary practice of the time, searches for both emulative and creative features of poetry. The conventional practice is to compare two (or multiple) poets' composition of a theme that is common to all them, with a view to examine the nuances of ma'ni afirini, mazmun afirini and other elements of style. Often ghazals that share a zamin (metre, rhyme and refrain) are selected for the sake of equivalence. For example, Hali sets two of Ghalib's ghazals against model ghazals composed by two of his eminent precursors, Naziri and Zuhuri.[64] Although, initially, the pairing could be seen as arbitrary, Hali matches the two poets verse for verse and offers interesting intertextual analysis. He wanted to demonstrate which poet's handling of a particular theme or phrase was better and pronounced his personal verdict on each verse's appeal.[65] Although the method is effective as an element of mazmun afirini, this method of evaluative comparison presumes that the verses were deliberately written to match or outdo one another. It relies inordinately on personal preferences and ignores the effect of the ghazal as a whole. Nonetheless, evaluative criticism is an essential part of cultural, critical poetics because of the timelessness of the important themes in ghazal poetry. It is possible to collect the verses of different poets connected by a certain theme, for example, the pain of separation, or the cruelty of the beloved. Following through on Hali's comparative exercise, I realized that Ghalib's ideas almost always had a little extra twist, a tinge of scepticism and passion that signified his approach. Below is an example from the ghazals Hali compared:

Zuhuri:

Beh shukr-e didah-e tar tar zabani-e daram
Keh zahr-e giryeh taravat deh-e shakar khand ast
[Thanks to my tear-filled eyes that give me eloquence of speech,
For the poison of my tears makes her laughter sweet]

Ghalib:

Nigah-e mehr beh dil sar neh dadeh chashmah-e nosh
Hunuz aish ba andazah-e shakar khand ast

[Her looks of love haven't produced a spring of sweetness in my heart
I am simply revelling in her apparently sugary laughter]

Zuhuri's verse is a classic in the layered use of language. *Didah-e tar* means eyes glistening with tears. *Tar* has many meanings: new, fresh, tender, moist, gladdened, steeped, shining. *Tar zaban* means one who is skilled in the use of language, one who has a way with words. *Taravat* shares affinity with 'tar'; it means freshness. Thus, in Zuhuri's verse, pain sharpens or makes language glisten. The beloved laughs and exults in the poet's pain. There is a play between *zahr-e giryah* (the poison of tears) and *shakar khand* (the sweetness of laughter). Tears give freshness to her laughter. Ghalib's verse, however, contains cynicism. In his verse, the beloved's flirtatious looks of love don't produce a swell of emotions. Nonetheless, the lover enjoys the sweetness of laughter.

Hali could have compared Ghalib with Bedil, or he could have selected Sa'ib because the latter is known for his innovative intricate style. But because Ghalib preferred Zuhuri over every other poet of this style, praising him above all Mughal-era poets, a comparison with Zuhuri may seem logical.[66] For example, in the masnavi *Ashtinamah*, Ghalib names Talib, Urfi and Naziri as his models, but describes Zuhuri's poetry to be the acme of creativity. Not just this, he praises Zuhuri in many verses scattered throughout the divan:

Ghalib, I am living because of the prose and poetry of Maulana Zuhuri
I have made the binder's thread of his book my jugular vein.[67]

To respond to the question of Ghalib's passion for composing in Persian, I scrutinized his creative engagement with the poets of the classical past and those that are described to stylistically represent tazah-goi. In itself, tazah-goi is new or fresh, perhaps as much as any innovative creative urge could be. The element of Indianness that supposedly made the poetry obscure seems to have more to do with temporality than geography. The Mughals' pursuit of Persian was intricately tied up with the overlapping Indic linguistic–literary traditions. The extensive translation of Indic works from Sanskrit to Persian produced a legacy of appropriations. For example, the rasa of Sanskritic traditions, particularly the *sringara* rasa, or the erotic–aesthetic mood, came to heighten the mood in erotic–aesthetic temperament associated with *firaq*, or separation, in the Persianate poetics.[68] Iranian émigrés at the Mughal court were bound to have a subjective engagement with cultural aesthetics that coloured their metaphorical use of language. Indian Persian poets' tropological dialogue, or exchange with the Iranian poets, produced startling similes and unexpected images, and even unfamiliar meanings, which widened the limits of expression.[69]

Rajeev Kinra makes an important point when he interprets Abul Barakat Munir Lahori's (1610–44) sharply worded essay titled 'Karnamah' (Book of Deeds), in which Munir upbraids four major poets of the age—Urfi Shirazi, Talib Amuli, Zulali, Khwansari and Zuhuri—all Iranian émigrés, not because of ethnic–professional rivalry, but specifically in terms of defending classicism against the excesses of tazah-goi, for which he blames the Iranian poets and not the Indian poets. Munir's point is precisely that literary competence in a cosmopolitan language like Persian should not be region-specific. He cites the popularity and gracious reception of Indian poets like Masud Sa'd Salman, Abul Faraj Runi, Amir Khusrau Dihlavi, Hasan Dihlavi and Faizi in the wider Persianate world. The problem in his era was the privileging of Iranians as native speakers. Munir's argument was that even Iranians were not infallible when it came to questions of grammar, usage and literary taste.[70] This criticism of tazah-goi from the champions of classicism needs more scholarly attention. Tazah-goi, it seems, is not as full of Indianness as a departure from the classical canon, or evidence of modernist tendencies in poetry.

I began the chapter by comparing Ghalib's dibachahs to his Urdu and Persian divans. Studying Ghalib as a bilingual poet in nineteenth-century colonial India intersects with the dynamics of late Mughal literary culture and print capitalism, to name two of several interstices. A thread that we have followed is Ghalib's presentation of his poetry and its reception by his peers. Then there is the question of Persian in the nineteenth century—its slow death. But Ghalib was not alone or anomalous in his preference for Persian at this time. Texts were still being produced in Persian from all over nineteenth-century north India and the princely states. When Persian was replaced by Hindustani-Urdu as the language of bureaucracy, its classical status continued unblemished. Urdu was a colloquial, popular language with an admirable corpus of poetry rising on the wings of modernity. Hali exaggerates when he writes that there were not many readers of Ghalib's Persian. The question is not so much why he was using Persian, but why he was so combative and defensive when most writers from the eighteenth century onwards had comfortably accepted an Indo-Persian brand of the language?

Ghalib's discursive comments on sukhan are not limited to his dibachah. In the letters written to his pupils, especially those seeking islah in Persian, Ghalib holds forth on sukhan in lyrical language:

> Sukhan is a beloved's fairy visage [*maishuqah pari paikar*]. Metricality is her dress and themes her ornaments. Discerning people have found this beautiful sukhan dressed in these clothes and ornaments to be like the full moon.[71]

Explaining the idea of sukhan and its reception, or performativity, Ghalib writes:

> Metrical composition [*guftar-e mauzun*] that is called poetry has a different place in every heart, and a different colour in every eye, and gives to the reciters, a different wound with every twist, and instrument a different rhythm [*ahang*].[72]

In one of his letters to Chaudhri Abdul Ghafur, Ghalib puts forward a *mizan*, or criterion, for the assessment of poetic style, chiefly in Persian but also in Urdu. The letter refers to a long discussion between Ghalib and his friend Sahib-e Alam about the new style (*tarz-e jadid*) of Persian poets in India.[73]

> In this letter, I shall take the liberty of expounding a standard of poetry . . . here is the standard. A first group of poets is that which goes from Rudaki and Firdausi up to Khaqani, Sana'i, Anvari, etc. The poetry of these personalities, notwithstanding differences of small account, is based on the same style. Then Sa'di was the founder of a special style. Sa'di, Jami and Hilali; such personalities are not numerous. Then Fighani is the inventor of another special art [of poetry] bringing delicate images and sublime meanings. Perfection in this kind of art was achieved by Zuhuri, Naziri, Urfi and Nau'i. God be praised! It was as if life itself were poured into the body of speech [*qalib-e sukhan*]. This style was then given the slickness [*charbah*] of a fluid simplicity [*salasat*] by other poetical dispositions such as those of Sa'ib, Kalim, Salim, Qudsi and Hakim Shifai. The style of Rudaki and Firdausi was abandoned in the time of Sa'di. On the other hand, Sa'di's art being 'inaccessible simplicity' never found large diffusion. It was Fighani's style that spread widely, and in it, new and original refinements [*nae, nae rang*] emerged. Summing up, there are three styles [*tarzen*] in existence: that of Khaqani and his peers; that of Zuhuri and his followers; that of Sa'ib and his parallels. Now tell me in sincerity, in which of these three styles is the poetry of Mumtaz, Akhtar, etc., composed? You no doubt will answer me that they write in another style, and that we have to consider it as a fourth one. Well, it will be

a style, perhaps even a good one, but not a Persian style. It is Indian. It is a coin, not coined in the Royal Mint, but a false coin. Be just![74]

. . .

Do not deny that in the poems of these people [Persian ethnicity] there is 'something else' [*chize digar*] beyond the poetry. That something else has been given to these Persians. Yes, in Urdu, the Indians have been given that 'something else'.

Ghalib then quotes Mir Taqi Mir, Sauda, Qaim Chandpuri and Momin as possessors of that 'something else' in Urdu. He writes that Nasikh and Atish also have similar capabilities, but he couldn't recall a verse from them at that moment:[75]

Mir:
Bad nam hoge jane bhi do imtihan ko
Rakhe ga kaun tum se aziz apni jan ko
[Forget about the test! You'll earn a bad name
Who would hold their life dearer than you?]

Sauda:
Dikhlaiye le ja ke tujhe misr ka bazaar
Khvahan nahin lekin koi van jins-e giran ka
[Let us show you the bazaar of Egypt
But no one there wants an expensive item]

Qaim:
Qaim tujh se talab bose ki kyun kar manun
Hai tu nadan magar itna bad amoz nahin
[Qaim, why would I believe the request for a kiss from you?
You are naive but not so badly taught]

Momin:
Tum mere pas hote ho goya

Jab koi dusra nahin hota
[You are near to me, so to speak,
When no one else is near]

What stood out to me in the verses quoted by Ghalib was the directness, in that the verses are not heavy with metaphor. These are great examples of the inaccessible simplicity that is a mark of poetic craft. They also present a dialogue between the lover-beloved (*muamilah bandi*), a style that was both popular and admirable in Urdu ghazal poetry. I assume that the *chize digar* Ghalib refers to has something to do with the free and flowing use of language, as one sees in dialogue.[76] Ghalib's Urdu poetry, even after repeated intikhabs, cannot be described as flowing (*ravan*). Much has been written on Ghalib's choice of metaphor-laden language in Urdu poetry. Ghalib acknowledged Amir Khusrau and Faizi (somewhat half-heartedly) as the greatest Persian poets of Indian origin. Both Khusrau and Faizi wrote influential dibachahs to their poetry collections, elaborating on ghazal poetics. Ghalib does not engage with them in his own dibachahs, or in the mizan mentioned above. The mizan, or criterion, that Ghalib presents in the letter does not apply to his own Persian or Urdu poetry. It is the voice of Ghalib's older self, where Ghalib speaks as the ustad, as the teacher. However, his point about the chize digar, the intangible touchstone that distinguishes a native fluency in language from a non-native one in the pursuit of Persian, is what characterizes his personal goal for Persian.

Before closing, I want to revisit the quote at the start of this chapter, about Ghalib's self-presentation regarding the uniqueness of his sukhan:

> O God, after me, create someone like me, who would go through the entirety of speech so that it would be understood how very high and palatial the wall of my [*sukhan*] speech/poetry is, and the

thread of the lasso of my imagination is tied to the high points of that palace.

The contemporariness of the Persianate tradition made Ghalib compete with the canonical poets, and he also had to proclaim his own uniqueness in relation to them. He therefore asserts the entirety of his sukhan, that is, he has accomplished what the great masters would find hard to rival. In other words, only another poet as involved in sukhan as Ghalib could surpass him.[77] Ghalib's position as a nineteenth-century Persian poet, in what became colonial India, is wrought with issues of his engagement with the preceding literary canon. What could a poet seek to accomplish in a tradition that valorized the notion of literary community? Themes or, to be more specific, tropes, as we have seen, belonged to a shared poetic sensibility. Yet themes are embedded with possibilities of meaning that have to be excavated with deliberation and contemplation. One could excel as a poet by perfecting an idea that was used by a predecessor.

As an Urdu poet, Ghalib drew strength from the imaginative conceits of the Indo-Persian style to create intricate meaning. He revelled in abstraction. As a Persian poet, he preferred to carve his own path, branching out from the classical tradition but not straying too far from it. He has a distinct authorial voice, but he did not create a new style. The newness he speaks of throughout the discourse of his dibachahs is the twist or colour (*rang*) he gives to themes. He claimed an organic, nativist connection with the Persian language. Ghalib's anxiety is perhaps related to his desire of being accepted in the Persian tradition. Did he possess the chize digar that marked the poetic language of the Persian speakers, the *ahl-e-zaban*? Did he arrive too late in the long, venerable tradition of Persian poets?

Ghalib went to great lengths to prove his mastery of Persian. Ironically, it was the younger tradition of Urdu that gave him everlasting fame. As a traveller on the wide path of poetry (he uses this trope throughout the khatimah), he learned from those who went before him, and he pushed forward to newer heights of imagination:

> I left behind all that came before me in my journey:
> I saw the Ka'bah, I named it the travellers' footprint.[78]

8

Transregional Sensibilities: The Case of Ghalib's Persian

I, Muhammad Asadullah of Samarqand, was born in Akbarabad (Agra), and am a resident of Delhi . . . Observe the reach of my capabilities that I have taken Hindi from Delhi to Isfahan and applaud the strength of the thread of my thought, that I have brought Persian from Shiraz to Hindustan.

—Ghalib, dibachah, *Gul-e Ra'na*[1]

I only have one desire, that I could tour the land of Iran and see the fire temples of Shiraz. And, if my aging limbs don't falter, my final destination would be to somehow reach the glorious Najaf and see the mausoleum of that being who evicted me from the religion of my ancestors, yet included me in spirit in his group. Then happily [I would] give my life and put my head on the pillow of nothingness.

—Ghalib, letter to Imam Bakhsh Nasikh[2]

Ghalib's passionate engagement with Persian plainly draws attention to his Persianate identity and his sense of belonging to a larger world. Nowadays, in modernity's logic, origin is often welded to birthplace. But in the pre-modern literary world, belonging was viewed as a gradient, or a multiplicity of lineages that encompassed origin in conjunction with inherited status, station, trajectory and position. Origin in Persianate adab was a shifting truth, not a self-evident natural fact. Literary influence in Persianate adab is wound up in intertextual dialogue (javab-goi), intertextual appropriations (*tazmin nigari*), direct quotation (*iqtibas*) and linguistic appropriation or innovation (tasarruf). But literary historiography cannot easily escape the clutches of national narratives, and in the process, the larger cultural continuity occasionally gets obscured.

The Dasatiri Movement

In their narration of Biblico-Quranic and Persian myth-histories, early Muslim historians were concerned with coordinating the claims of the origin of the two traditions. Reconciling the originary claim of Adam and Kayumars proved to be the most challenging aspect of historical synchronization. According to Zoroastrian sources, Kayumars, an androgyne, appeared in Iran *vij* (the homeland of the early Iranians), and upon death, a seed from his/her back impregnated the earth's rhubarb plants which grew into the first human couple, Mahryag and Mahryanag.[3] There are several versions of this myth of origin but all agree that Kayumars is the progenitor of pre-Islamic history.

Mohamad Tavakoli-Targhi said in his exemplary work that the allegorical meaning of pre-Islamic Iran was altered radically by the pioneers of a late sixteenth- and early seventeenth-century exilic movement known as Azari, Kayvani or Dasatiri. This movement was led by Azar Kayvan (1533–1618) and his disciples who migrated to Mughal India in response to the repressive religious policies of the

Safavids (1501–1722). According to Tavakoli-Targhi, the architects of this neo-Mazdean intellectual movement wrote themselves back into history by projecting an Iran-centred universal historical narrative that subordinated the Biblico-Quranic myth-history to its own all-encompassing framework.[4] In the generative texts of the *Dasatir*, notably *Sharistan-e Danish va Gulistan-e Binish* and *Dabistan-e Mazahib*, human history begins not with Adam but with the pre-Adamite Mahabad. Linking the history of Iran to pre-Adamite times, the Azaris reframed the Islamicate historiography that was imposed by early Muslim historians on the accounts of pre-Islamic Iran. This reframing also enabled the Azaris to reconfigure the textual traces of Iran's ancient past that had been subordinated to the Islamic narrative. The non-biblical framework of these texts inspired the protoscientific endeavours of early Orientalists, Zoroastrian Khushnumists and Iranian nationalists. It also enabled William Jones and other Orientalists to construct new theories about the origins of languages and races.

The religious policies of Emperor Akbar (1556–1605) provided a suitable intellectual environment for an active reconstruction of Mazdaism. By incorporating the medieval Islamic Illuminationist philosophy (*hikmat-e ishraq*) into a Mazdian cosmology, Kayvan and his cohorts constructed a world view characterized as Zoroastrian Ishraqi.[5] Kayvan identified sixteen pre-Islamic sages or prophets, beginning with Mahabad and ending with Sasan Panjum (Sasan V). The presumed epistles of these sages, collected in the *Dasatir*, constituted the foundational canon of the neo-Mazdian resistance.[6] They claimed that these epistles were written in a celestial language (*zaban-e asmani*) but were translated into Persian with added commentary by the fifth Sasan, who was considered to be a contemporary of Prophet Muhammad and the Sasanian ruler Khusraw Parvez (who ruled from 590–628). Dating the commentary back to a period immediately preceding the Arab conquest of Iran was intended to serve as evidence for the unique and exemplary prose of the *Dasatir*, which was devoid of Arabic terms and concepts and included many obsolete Persian terminologies. The Dasatiri terminologies were liberally incorporated in Muhammad Husain Tabrizi's *Burhan-e Qati*, an influential Persian dictionary compiled in 1651 (it was widely circulated among poets and writers in India and Iran). On account of its lack of Arabic words, the *Dasatir* became an inspiring text for generations of Persian purists from Abul Fazl Allami to Ghalib, who were searching for ways to express complex thoughts, or simply as a testimonial for their native Persian sensibilities.

The *Dasatir* diverged from the historiographic-Mazdian tradition of acknowledging Kayumars as the first human by ascribing the first four epistles to sages who predated Kayumars. This framework was designed to counter the hegemonic Islamic historical imaginary that had marginalized and distorted Persian myth-history. According to Mohsin Fani, the author of *Dabistan-e Mazahib* (who was probably Azar Kayvan's son, Kaykhusraw Isfandiyar), the eras of the sages were astronomical and measured through a temporal expansion of time notated through terminologies encompassing billions of years.

Arab–Persian Ethnic and Linguistic Rivalries

The eloquence of Arabic compared to the Persians and their language was significant to the followers of Azar Kayvan.[7] The *Dabistan-e Mazahib* went further in supplementing the claims of Bahram ibn Farhad's *Sharistan*. The author of *Dabistan-e Mazahib*, Mohsin Fani, used a particular rhetoric that became the pervasive trope of historical discourse in the nineteenth century. He depicted the Muslim conquest of Iran as the winter of Arab oppression and repression. He projected the Qajar dynasty as the beginning of a new season of justice and fairness. As an Indian Parsi, Fani argued that Persians had fled from Iran in the winter of Arab oppression just like migratory birds, but now, with the new season, they had begun to return to their ancestral home. Most nineteenth-century Iranian historians accepted this view. Linking the end of pre-Islamic enlightened times to origins identified with Iran through Mahabad or Kayumars, a new memory, identity and political reality was fashioned. This politics of creating cultural memory, and its de-Arabizing projects of history and language, prompted the emergence of a schizophrenic view of history and the forming of social subjects who were conscious of their belonging to two diverse, and often antagonistic, times and cultural heritages.

Restyling the Persian Language

In Tavakoli-Targhi's analysis of the Dasatiri movement, the invention of a glorious past was concurrent with a thorough restyling of the Persian language. This restyling was achieved through a dialogue with Iran's Arabs and the non-European other, but also with its often-ignored Indian other. In fact, the relationship with the Persian-knowing Indian other facilitated the renaissance and canonization of classical Persian literature. The fear of European colonization, particularly in the case of India, where Persian had served as the official language until the 1830s, led to a desire for neologisms, the promotion of lexicography and the writing of grammar texts. The Iranian nationalists wanted to restore the 'sweet' Persian language by purging the influence of the difficult language of the Arabs.

The rise of a Persian print culture in the eighteenth century strengthened a literary style that resulted from a dispute among the Persian poets of Iran and India.[8] During the seventeenth and eighteenth centuries India had been a centre for the development of Persian art, culture and literature. It was the locus of the emergence of a new style, *tarz-e nau*, or the tazah-goi (Mughal–Safavid) of poetry. The tarz-e nau poets created new conventions and significations by altering poetic tropes and coining new compounds.

The Iranian literati viewed this as a sign of their unfamiliarity, even incompetence, in the Persian language. This issue was the foundation of intense debates and bitter disputes. Sirajuddin Ali Khan Arzu (1689–1756) defended Indian Persian and its use as markers of creative rhetoric and poetic–linguistic identity. The modification of idioms should not be seen as errors, he stated.[9] Mir Saiyyid Ali Mushtaq (1689–1757) and his disciples negated the innovations of the Indian school and formulated a programme explicitly aimed at returning to the images and language of the classical poets. Mushtaq believed that poets must follow Sa'di in ghazal, Anvari in qasidah, Firdausi and Nizami in masnavi, Ibn Yamin in qita and Khayyam in rubai, otherwise they would be on the path to falsity.[10]

Notwithstanding the animosity of Iranian poets, the development of print culture in eighteenth- and nineteenth-century colonial India did provide a strong textual resource for the formation of authoritative canons as well as the dissemination of seminal texts in Persian. Printed copies of the Dasatiri texts were also widely circulated and contributed to the vernacularization of the Persian language.[11] Directly, or indirectly, Dasatiri texts were instrumental in privileging the pre-Islamic usages in Persian. Obsolete Persian words were reintroduced and neologisms found their way into dictionaries. The *Burhan-e Qati* embraced Dasatiri words which then got disseminated among poets and literati, many of whom owned personal copies of the dictionary.[12] The proliferation of these words, despite their suspect origin, signifies the passion for the pure Persian. The displacement of Persian as the official language in India in 1837 did not go unnoticed in Iran. It in fact intensified the need for model lexical resources. Persian dictionaries published in India served as models for lexicographers. Iranian neologists like Ismail Tuysirkani, Mirza Aqa Khan Kirmani and Ahmad Kasravi didn't shy from incorporating many of the controversial terms from *Burhan-e Qati*.[13]

Ghalib's fascination with the *Dasatir* is not limited to his delight in creating new expressions or neologisms. It also is wrapped up in his claim of literary lineage with what he thought was pristine Persian. When Urdu replaced Persian as the language of bureaucracy, Ghalib, who saw himself as a part of high Persianate culture, was dismayed at the prospect of the possible impact on his position as the leading Persianist in Delhi.

Ghalib, keen to claim native competence in Persian, rejected all lexicographers who didn't actually write their dictionaries in Iran, or were not actual, practising Iranian poets. He wrote to his disciple Hargopal Taftah: 'Lexicographers rely on analogy and opinion. Each one wrote what he thought [was] correct. Were there a dictionary compiled by Nizami or Sa'di, it would be binding on us. How and why can one regard Indians to be of proven incontrovertibility?'[14] Around the same time that he wrote to Taftah, Ghalib wrote in a pamphlet called *Namah-e Ghalib* (Ghalib's Letter), addressed to one Mirza Rahim Beg, as follows:[15]

> There are many among the poets of India who write well, and who find [new and attractive] themes. But what fool would say that it behooves them to claim competent knowledge of the Persian language? Now as regards the lexicographers, may God free us from their snares. They put the verses of the ancients before them and marched along the path of analogy and opinion. On top of it all, they travelled the path alone, with no guide or companion, or rather, entirely lost and undone. Were there a guide, he'd teach them the right way, were there a teacher, he'd expound to them the meaning of the verse. [. . .] Keep on removing the veils from the face of the lexicographers, you'll see only raiment, the real person doesn't exist. Keep turning the pages of the dictionaries, you'll find mere pages. The meanings are imaginary.

In both, the above epistle to Beg and the letter to Taftah, Ghalib used almost identical words for himself, to the effect that a competent knowledge of Persian was his native capability, a special gift from

God; and also that he had an intuitive grasp of the subtleties of Persian, thus putting him above all Indian writers of Persian.

In the discussion that follows, I want to read Ghalib's claim of a 'connection' to a language in concurrence with the wider, exegetical parameters of the ethnic–linguistic rivalries between Iranian and Indian Persian poets in the nineteenth century, the restyling of the Persian language and the reimagining of Iran's pre-Islamic history through linguistic and prophetic claims of the Dasatiri movement of Azar Kayvan and his cohorts. I also want to draw attention to the multiple identities or linkages that were commonplace among the elite who travelled in the Persianate space. Ghalib claimed to belong to Samarqand, Agra and Delhi. His ancestors were from Samarqand; he was born in Agra and lived in Delhi.

Ghalib and the *Dasatír*: *Dastanbuy*, a Definitive Attempt to Write in 'Pure' Persian[16]

> I am the source of the heavenly secrets
> That is why I am always free-flowing
> My book is a chapter of the *Dasatír*
> By virtue of my knowledge and expertise I am Sasan the sixth.[17]

In *Dastanbuy*, Ghalib describes the events unfolding in Delhi during the fifteen months of the 1857 revolt (May 1857–July 1858).[18] Noted Persian and Ghalib scholar Khwaja Ahmad Faruqi, in his introduction to the English transition of *Dastanbuy*, elucidates the reasons why Ghalib felt compelled to write a so-called diary of the events of the Revolt of 1857 in 'pure' Persian:

> True to his Central Asian descent and Turkish seed, Ghalib was always vacillating between tearful piety and excessive pride, between mysticism and materialism, between convention

> and liberalism, and between despondency and hope. With his conception of courtesy, he could not dispense with his extreme formalism of Turko–Persian origin, already cooled into set responses and prescribed attitudes. This formalism was motivated by a semi-conscious urge for [the] preservation of artistic solidarity with his ancestral world, with which he had lost direct touch. Moreover, in those feudal days all emotions required a rigid form, for without such form, passion would have made havoc of life. The contradictions and paradoxes had to be wrapped up in veils of fancy in order to exalt and refine them and thereby to obscure the cruel reality.[19]

Ghalib's loyalties were undoubtedly with the Mughal emperor Bahadur Shah Zafar, who had first appointed him to write the history of the dynasty's rule in 1850 and then engaged him as his preceptor in poetry in 1856. He attended the court frequently and presented a qasidah to the emperor on 13 July 1857, on the triumphant occasion of the fall of Agra to the rebels. He contributed another qasidah in August 1857. But in September, when the British forces recaptured Delhi, all hell broke loose. A general massacre followed. Ghalib stayed in the city drowning in the ocean of blood. He was reduced to poverty without money, food, water or clothes. His poems were destroyed in the general loot and conflagration perpetrated on the extensive library of Ziyauddin Ahmad Khan Naiyar, who was also the custodian and a collector of Ghalib's poetry. His mentally ill brother was shot dead by the British. Ghalib himself was suspected of treason. His meagre English pension was stopped. In this situation, Ghalib did what he could do. He had written a qasidah for the queen, and now he penned a commentary describing the events of 1857 in Delhi with a view to disproving the charges against him and making a plea for royal patronage.

The first edition of *Dastanbuy*, with a print run of 500, was published from Agra in November 1858. It was sold out within five months. A second edition was brought out by the Literary Society, Rohilkhand (Bareilly), in 1865 and a third by the same press in 1871. There is a chain of correspondence between Ghalib and his two pupils—Munshi Hargopal Taftah and Munshi Shiv Narain Aram—under whose supervision the first edition was published. Some eight volumes were specially bound and embossed for presenting to exalted patrons. The letters show Ghalib's fastidious attention to detail in the publication process. He emphasized his keenness to write in pure Persian, avoiding Arabic words. In several letters, Ghalib mentions the special pains he took to keep out the Arabic lexis and write in the Dasatiri diction:

> I have tried my best to write in the Dasatiri mode, that is old Persian, and it does not use Arabic words. The verses embedded in the prose are also without Arabic words. Of course, I couldn't change the names of persons. They have been retained as Arabic, English, Hindi.[20]

In the first letter of the series, dated 18 July 1858, addressed to Munshi Shiv Narain Aram, Ghalib wrote:

> I have written my account [*sarguzasht*] after much preparation, [and] editorial formalities [*tauqi' o tamhid*]. I have recounted events. The style is that of 'old Persian' [*qadim*] of which there is no trace now in Iran, let alone Hindustan. I have completed forty pages. Meanwhile, the hope is that the pension case be resolved or I get a [favourable] response [from the English] and I may get a position somewhere. Till that time, whatever I can gather from acquaintances I will put down in writing. If you permit, I will send you the manuscript upon completion so that a thousand copies may be published and distributed in the devastated land of Hind.[21]

To Taftah, Ghalib wrote a similar epistle:[22]

> Now listen to this matter: I have written down the events in the city [of Delhi] and my personal account [*sarguzasht*], a period of fifteen months, from 11 May 1857 to 1 July 1858. I have ensured that the text should be in the Dastiri style, that is, old Persian; no Arabic words should intrude. The verses that are embedded in the prose are also devoid of Arabic words. Yes, people's names can't be changed. I have kept them as they are: Arabic, English or Hindi. For example, your name, Munshi Hargopal; but 'munshi' is an Arabic word, so I took it out and replaced it with 'sheva zaban'.

Ghalib went on to specify the layout of the manuscript, the number of lines per page, the number of copies to be published, the prospective buyers, the pricing, how the glosses should appear in the margins, and so on. In subsequent letters to Taftah, Ghalib meticulously gave minute instructions on the layout of a page, especially if it contained verses that needed to be glossed.

In the letter dated 31 August 1858, to Munshi Shiv Narain Aram, Ghalib underlined details of the layout, the quality of paper and the placement of the glossary:

> The paper should be Shiv Rampuri, white and [*mohra kiya hua*] supple. The glosses in the margin should be inscribed in an attractive, appealing manner [*nazar fareb*]. The font used for the glosses should be distinct from the main text.[23]

Ghalib's anxiety for *Dastanbuy's* production to be as perfect as possible is reflected in this exhaustive letter to Munshi Shiv Narain, dated 3 September 1858:

> There is one other task you have to do. Maybe at the bottom of page three or at the top of page four, is this phrase: *agar dardam digar ba nahib mabash baham bar zanad.* 'Nahib' is an Arabic word, I wrote it by mistake; please erase it and replace it with 'navae mabash'.[24]

Not satisfied with writing to Munshi Shiv Narain alone, Ghalib dashed off a stronger letter to Taftah:[25]

> At the bottom of the third page or at the top of the fourth is this phrase: *agar dardam digar ba nahib mabash baham bar zanad*, please change 'nahib' to 'navae'. 'Nahib' is an Arabic word, if it is left in, people will criticize me. Scratch 'nahib' out with the tip of a sharp knife and write 'navae' in its place.

But despite Ghalib's diligence in trying to get the error fixed, it did anyway creep into the printed text:[26]

> My dear brother, how many double pages (*do varqe*) are there with 'nahib', four hundred or five hundred? Please change them all. Whatever loss is incurred in the price of paper, I will pay for that. If this word remains, my entire book will be a failure. My reputation of perfection will be stained. This is an Arabic word. Although I had fixed it in the manuscript, the calligrapher ignored it.

Finally, after multiple efforts, the error was taken care of, much to Ghalib's satisfaction:[27]

> 'Nahib's' replacement with 'navae' has soothed my heart. Brother, I am a learned scholar [*muhaqqiq*] of Persian. The calligrapher is a Persian expert [*alim*] of the elements of copy-writing. He is more learned than Ghiyasuddin Rampuri and Hakim Muhammad Husain Dakani.[28]

The correspondence around the writing and production of *Dastanbuy* uncovers many layers of the literary and personal complexes surrounding Ghalib. The desperation for financial support and recognition from patrons is the most obvious one. Queen Victoria and her administrative cohorts couldn't be bothered with the technicalities of current Persian, let alone obscure or pure Persian. In fact, Persian was no longer the language of day-to-day official business in British India. Yet Ghalib presents his narrative in a Persian that is not only rare but is tied up with claims of a pre-Islamic linguistic heritage. We have several leads to the nagging question as to why he wrote *Dastanbuy* in pure Persian, or what to him was the Dasatiri mode. It must be noted here that it was in the course of his quest for pure Persian words, for writing *Dastanbuy*, that Ghalib combed through *Burhan-e Qati* (The Cutting Proof), the highly regarded Persian dictionary by Muhammad Husain Tabrizi. In the dictionary, Ghalib found many words that he believed to be peculiarly Indian, or non-Iranian deviations from the original Iranian idiom and usage. Ghalib made a list of these words in the form of a small book sharply titled *Qati-e Burhan* (The Cutter of the Proof).[29] Completed in 1859 and published in 1862, Ghalib's *Qati-e Burhan* ignited a furious, acrimonious controversy that raged until his death.

An important thread in this tangle of language ownership is connected to the circulation and embedding of Dasatiri words into current or regular Persian. Eminent literary historian Mohamad Tavakoli-Targhi shows how Dasatiri words began to be absorbed slowly in the wake of the movement in the sixteenth century but began circulating at a faster pace in the nineteenth century with texts and dictionaries being printed.[30] Muhammad Husain Tabrizi's dictionary had a fair number of such words. Noted linguist and lexicographer Nazir Ahmad has clarified that there are numerous Persian dictionaries that contain pure Dasatiri (*sirah*) words. Notable among them are *Farhang-e Qavvas*, *Sihah al Furs*, *Lisanush Shu'ara*, *Farhang-e Jahangiri*, *Farhang-e Sarvari*, *Surmah-e Sualimani*,

Farhang-e Ja'fari and *Burhan-e Qati*. It is doubtful if Ghalib consulted all those dictionaries for his choice of words; most likely, he found them in the *Dasatir* translation itself.[31]

In a letter to Navab Alauddin Ahmad Khan Alai, dated 2 July 1860, he wrote:

> You ask to borrow books from me? Please recall what I have mentioned to you earlier, that, except for *Dasatir* and *Burhan-e Qati*, I have no other books. The aforesaid, *Burhan-e Qati*, I have already sent to you. *Dasatir* is my faith and heart's refuge [*hirz-e jan*].[32]

The back and forth between Ghalib and his cherished relative and pupil Navab Alauddin Ahmad Khan Alai is perplexing, but it does help us understand some of his fascination with Dasatiri vocabulary, as well as his conviction that Dasatiri Persian was the 'sweet Persian' of pre-Islamic Iran. In another letter to Navab Alauddin, dated 1 June 1861, Ghalib makes a request for the glossary to the *Dasatir*:

> What can I say about your fancy literary footwork, your artful dodging of the issue? You have the Glossary to the *Dasatir*. I asked you for a copy of it. You in turn have asked me for a copy of the *Dasatir*. Well, I swear by everything that's holy that I don't have it. Now, you might well wonder why I should ask you for the Glossary of the vocabulary of a work that I don't have at hand? The fact is simply that I don't recall the vowel markings of some of the words that appear there.[33]

Ghalib's Critique of *Burhan-e Qati*

Although he had nurtured an animosity towards Indian practitioners of Persian since his undeserved humiliation at the mushairah in Calcutta in 1828, Ghalib didn't ever mention or report having a Zoroastrian tutor for Persian. Abdus Samad Hurmuzd was brought into the picture when Ghalib wrote his fierce critique of *Burhan-e Qati* in 1858/9.

Ghalib's half-baked critique of Tabrizi's dictionary is viewed by scholars as a glaring flaw in the poet's egoistic personality. He was not a scholar of Arabic, or even a Persian linguist like Sirajuddin Ali Khan Arzu. There is nothing to indicate that he studied Persian or Arabic dictionaries, or consulted them during the course of this work. Qazi Abdul Vadud's erudite comments on Ghalib's glossing errors proves that Ghalib was largely ignorant of philology (or historical linguistics, as it is now termed).[34] Nazir Ahmad's book-length examination of *Qati-e Burhan* shows sympathy, even admiration, for Ghalib's creative interpretations of words.[35] Yet he never pretends to gloss over Ghalib's errors. Qazi Abdul Vadud and other Ghalibians believe that Ghalib's knowledge of the Dasatiri movement and the language was not deep enough. It was limited to Mohsin Fani's *Dabistan-e Mazahib* and perhaps a translation of the *Dasatir.*

Ghalib believed the *Dasatir* to be authentic, instead of a fabricated account in a made-up language that claimed to be pure Persian. It is interesting that Tabrizi, too, believed the Dasatiri texts to be authentic and incorporated hundreds of Dasatiri words in his dictionary unconditionally, without any acknowledged source. Thus, Ghalib and Tabrizi both believed in the same source, but Ghalib did not trust Tabrizi merely because the latter did not have the credentials of a native speaker-scholar of the Persian language.

Ghalib's Ancestry

Ghalib's ancestors came to India from the territory around the Oxus, a boundary of tradition rather than history. To be precise, his ancestors came from Samarqand, the cradle of civilization, steeped in Persian traditions. It was from the legends, supposedly of Sasanian times, enshrined in the pages of historians and made popular by the national epic of Firdausi, that the Oxus came to be regarded as the boundary between Iran and Turan. Through all the centuries of invasions, the region of Oxus remained, in essence, Iranian, preserving Iranian speech and institutions. Literature preserved the collective memory of the past and gave an element of continuity and meaning to the fleeting realities of the present. Ghalib's ancestors apparently carried with them their inheritance of Turko–Persian traditions.

Ghalib's pride in knowing the standard Persian (Iranian) usages and his interest in pre-Islamic Persian is perplexing until we re-examine his affiliation with a literary lineage that is distinct, though not separate, from his Turko–Persian–Indic one. One of Ghalib's favourite topics was his genealogy, which he traced to ancient kings. To begin with, here is a seemingly playful poetic argument, the major premise of which is a matter-of-fact claim that he descended from Pashang[36] and Afrasiyab[37] and, through them, from the legendary king Jamshed, who is said to have been the inventor of wine in Iran:

> Oh Saqi, since my lineage is of Pashang and Afrasiyab
> Know that the true root of my seed is from the House of Jamshed.
> Jamshed's heritage is wine: so, give it to me.
> After this comes Paradise which is Adam's patrimony.[38]

'I am of Turkish origin,' he asserts more baldly in a letter to his dear friend Maulvi Sirajuddin, 'and my ancestry goes back to Afrasiyab and Pashang. My forefathers, because of their blood relationship with the Saljuqis, carried aloft the standard of rulership and military leadership during their time. When the fortunes of their patrons declined, some of them moved away and others to agriculture. My branch of the family settled in Samarqand in Turan.'[39]

We don't know if Ghalib learned of his ancestry from his elders or 'invented' it to suit his poetic ambitions and to establish himself as a nobleman of high antiquity. To be a descendant of Jamshed, the inventor and owner of the world-reflecting wine cup, which is one of the archetypal symbols of omniscience in Persian and Urdu poetry, signifying an all-comprehending intellect, is surely a matter of great pride. Certainly, modesty regarding one's ancestry was not a virtue practised in Ghalib's social network. The illustrious Afrasiyab and Pashang or Jamshed are not historical figures; they are epic heroes belonging to the shadowy no man's land between Iranian myth and prehistory. Ghalib probably knew them from the *Shahnameh*. Here, we must note that Ghalib chose Turkish (Turanian) military commanders from the *Shahnameh* as his ancestors. He seems to have disregarded the fact that there was prolonged and bitter enmity between Iran and Turan, specifically Afrasiyab and the Iranian kings as depicted by Firdausi. Both the Turanian and Iranian were the stuff of legend, not history, anyway.

No matter who Ghalib's ancestors were in hoary antiquity, it is important that he believed in them, or pretended to believe in them. As I mentioned above, Ghalib's insistence on Iranian idiom as the only authentic one predates his claims to ancient lineage. As we shall see, his fascination with the *Dasatir* must have had its roots in his wish to be connected organically to the Persian language and not to the legends of Iranian antiquity.

Nazir Ahmad has divided the pure Persian words that Ghalib uses in *Dastanbuy* into four categories:

1. Those that are commonly used or are current in Persian.
2. Those that were rarely used in Ghalib's time.
3. Those constructions (neologisms) that Ghalib may have invented or found in obscure verses.
4. Dasatiri words.

Ghalib's contemporary and acquaintance Maulvi Najaf Ali Khan, who wrote *Waqia-e Hizyan* (or *Dafi'-e Hizyan*) in support of Ghalib's *Qati-e Burhan*, also produced a work titled *Safrang-e Dasatir*, which is a rare commentary on the Persian translation of the *Dasatir*.

Safrang-e Dasatir was published in 1864 with an introduction by Ghalib.

Indian Persian and Iranian Persian: The Issue of Ahl-e Zaban

Scholars of what is generally known as the Indian style of poetry (tazah-goi) have shown that the distinctiveness of this style did not go down well with Iranian cultural sensibilities.[40] Muzaffar Alam's illuminating work on Persian in precolonial India has drawn up the trajectory of literary Persian from Ghaznavid times (977–1186) to the nineteenth century. Among the important authors that Alam mentions, who shaped the canon of new Persian, is eminent poet and writer Nizami Aruzi Samarqandi (d.1164). Nizami was at the court of Alauddin Jahan Soz in Ghur. He was the author of *Chahar Maqalah*, an important treatise dealing with poetics, among other subjects. Nizami placed emphasis on the choice of words. In his opinion, poetry should use words in harmony, creating a pleasing effect. Alam researches the question of the expanding territory of Persian and its gradual Indianization. Questions about *lahjah* (manner of speech) and *ravish* (style) were identified by the time of Afghan rule (1450–1626). The proliferation of dictionaries, Alam clarifies, indicates the dissemination of the Persian language, as well as attempts to standardize usage.[41] An important issue that he raises is the space of Indian Persian in the larger world of Ajam.[42] In charting its own course, the new poetry of Ajam diverged from the Arabic tradition, establishing its own aesthetic and literary canon. Notable in this regard is the poetry of Firdausi, whose poetry was fired with the experiences and emotions of a poet witnessing the predicament of the subordination of national culture to Arab literary culture. He wanted his poetry to infuse new spirit into the soulless body of Ajam.

The rise of the Mongols halted the triumphant march of Ajam in the thirteenth century. India, too, reeled under the impact of Mongol incursions. The Delhi Sultanate barely survived it. The

Mongol ravage caused many families from the Perso–Turkic area to migrate and settle in north India. Their presence refreshed Indian Persian, bringing the influences of Rumi and Sa'di. Amir Khusrau's poetic brilliance assimilated the agony and ecstasy of pain and triumph. Khusrau incorporated indigenous imagery; he glorified the Indian tradition in Persian, claiming it to be as rich as that of Central and West Asia. In fact, he asserted that the Indian usage of Persian was superior because it conformed to the same standard everywhere in India, as against the so-called Iranian Persian that changed drastically from place to place.

By the late fourteenth century, however, the linguistic diversity of the different parts of the Persian world became more pronounced.[43] But with the establishment of Timurid power in Iran, the desire to resist the Turkish–Timurid domination also grew. The Iranians craved a distinct political self-definition. As a consequence of these political developments, Persian was increasingly represented as the exclusive language of Iran. Once the Iranians had reclaimed Persian, other regions linguistically and culturally associated with Persian were perceived as secondary. However, in India, under the Mughals, Persian poetry and prose witnessed the most extraordinary efflorescence and level of excellence. Nonetheless, Mughal Persian literature was not incorporated into the Ajamite (Iranian) Persian literature. It remained circumscribed in its own category; it was marginalized in Iranian tazkirahs. It was later embroiled in the raging controversy around Indian usage and the definition–assessment of good poetry.

Persian poetry in the Mughal age was marked by a spirit of innovation and experiment largely within the literary heritage from Iran and Central Asia. The style of the group of poets whose poetic imagination invoked new themes and transcended the ordinary tropes was known as tazah-goi. It integrated many themes and ideas from pre-Islamic Persia with the diverse religious traditions of India.

While the most sublime Persian poetry was produced in India in the sixteenth and seventeenth centuries, the richest and most varied poetry was produced in the eighteenth century. Sirajuddin Ali Khan Arzu's tazkirah, *Majma'ul Nafais*, describes some seventy-seven poets of Persian who lived in the first half of the eighteenth century. Although Persian poetry in the style of tazah-goi made a distinctive mark, the Iranian idiom continued to be the reference point of literary composition. Lexicographers and philologists were concerned about verifying non-Iranian words and expressions that had been incorporated in dictionaries. Several important eighteenth-century dictionaries, such as Arzu's *Siraj ul Lughat*, Anand Ram Mukhlis's *Mirat ul Istilah*, Siyalkoti Mal Varastah's *Mustalahat-e Shuara* and Munshi Tek Chand Bahar's *Bahar-e Ajam* were consciously updating the vocabulary. Arzu used his tremendous authority in asserting that non-Iranians could be as authoritative as the Iranians. He put forth a curious argument in support of this: he said that Iranians (native speakers) also make mistakes; it therefore follows that if the Indian makes mistakes, it doesn't mean that he can't write perfect Persian. He also said that poetic usage was not always the same, or based on colloquial native speech: one had to be well versed in the literary language as well before claiming proficiency as poet. Arzu thus supported and legitimized Indian–Persian usages.[44]

The high qualities of the Mughal poets were seen in the context of the masterful tazkirah of Kishan Chand Ikhlas (d.1748 or 1754). In his *Hameshah Bahar*, compiled in 1723, Ikhlas provided a wide range of features that he considered to be marks of good poetry.[45] Notable among the list are: *ma'ni afirini* (to create a new idea or meaning), *ma'ni yabi* (to unfold or discover a new idea/meaning), *ma'ni nigari* (to depict an idea in writing), *ma'ni bandi* (to weave, contrive and compose an idea), *ma'niha-e gharib va badi'* (far-fetched and novel ideas), *ma'ni ha-e ba'idulfahm* (ideas difficult to comprehend), *mazamin-e tazah* (new themes), and so on. Ikhlas's criteria reflect the qualities that one finds in the tazah-goi style.[46] But these incisive measures of good poetry failed to impress Sheikh Ali Hazin Lahiji who arrived in north India around that time and settled in Banaras. Hazin disliked Indian poets, describing them as crows rather than nightingales, presumably because the language of their poetry was not sweet and their themes, too, were incomprehensible, at least for him. Hazin's invective was echoed by other critics, notably Riza Quli Khan Hidayat (d.1872) and Malikul Shu'ara Muhammad Taqi Bahar (d.1951), who used punitive expressions such as 'spineless', 'nonsensical' or 'feeble' to describe tazah-goi.[47]

It is ironical that Ghalib shared this contempt for non-Iranian writers. This landed him in acrimonious literary battles with his peers. Ghalib rejected all lexicographers who didn't write their dictionaries in Iran or were not actual practising Iranian poets. Ghalib claimed that he stood above all Indian writers of Persian, that he had an intuitive grasp of Persian and its literature, that his Persian was a special gift from God. Later, this contempt rebounded on him when purists like Shibli Nomani (1857–1914) and Saiyyid Ali Haider Nazm Tabataba'i (1852–1933) found fault with some of his Persian.[48] Shibli once wrote that he wouldn't accept Ghalib's usage of 'andaz' (a very ordinary Persian word) because Ghalib was not 'ahl-e zaban'.[49]

9

Return to Urdu

They ask: 'Who is Ghalib?'
Will someone tell them? What can I say?

—Ghalib, *Divan-e Ghalib*[1]

In 1847, Ghalib served a prison term of three months for allowing his house to be used for petty gambling.[2] Mirza was fond of playing *chausar* and chess, and whenever he played, he liked to bet small amounts to add excitement to the game. The kotwal who ordered the raid on Ghalib's house did so out of hostility. Apparently, he disagreed with Ghalib's literary polemics. During the imprisonment, Ghalib was deserted by most of his friends, including his aristocratic relatives of the ruling family of Loharu. The only prominent person to visit Ghalib during this unhappy period was his pupil Navab Mustafa Khan Sheftah. Ghalib suffered deeply from this disrepute. The humiliation of this experience was poured into a long poem (*tarkib band*) comprising seven parts, each with twelve verses. Although this long poem was not included in the Persian kulliyat, Ghalib published it a few years before his death in a collection titled *Sabad-e Chin* (Remnants of the Harvest).

Upon his release from prison, Ghalib went to stay at the residence of Kale Khan Sahib, the Sufi mentor of Emperor Bahadur Shah Zafar. It was through Kale Khan Sahib that Ghalib gained access to the Mughal court and to Bahadur Shah himself.

Mirza Ghalib was officially attached to the Mughal court in 1850 to write a history of the empire. The last Mughal emperor, Bahadur Shah Zafar, honoured Ghalib with the grand title of Najmud Daulah Dabirul Mulk Nizam Jung.[3] The job assigned to him had more to do with his status as a Persian prose stylist than a poet. This would seem ironic because his Urdu divan was published to great popularity in 1841, with a repeat edition in 1847, and he did not have any interest in writing history.

To write the history, Ghalib was supplied with materials prepared by Hakim Ahsanullah Khan from the royal library. Ghalib had made it very clear that he would write as a littérateur and not a historian. He proposed *Partavistan* as the title for the two-volume work. The first volume was the history from the beginning of creation till the reign of Humayun. The second was to be from Akbar to Bahadur Shah Zafar. The first volume was published with the poetic title *Mehr-e Nim Roz* (Midday Sun) in 1854.[4] The second part, tentatively titled *Mah-e Nim Mah* (Mid-Month Moon), was never written.[5]

Upon Ustad Ibrahim Zauq's death in 1854, Bahadur Shah Zafar appointed Ghalib as his ustad. In 1854, Mirza Fakhru, the heir apparent, had also became Ghalib's pupil, which meant an additional salary of Rs 33.[6] Although Ghalib did not like attending court every day, or offering improvements (islah) on the royal pupil's poetry, he enjoyed the comforts of association with the court. Hali mentions Ghalib's requests for specific presents when the emperor enjoyed his compositions. When Ghalib expressed delight at the luscious mangoes in the royal garden, Bahadur Shah Zafar ordered a basketful of the fruit to be dispatched to his house.

Hali also describes an incident on the authority of Nazir Husain Mirza who was present when the royal messenger came to Ghalib's house requesting the 'improved' versions of Zafar's poems.

> Ghalib sent his attendant to bring from the palanquin a bundle tied in a handkerchief . . . When Mirza undid the package, there were eight or nine pieces of paper on which a verse or two was inscribed. Ghalib sent for his pen and inkstand and began to write ghazals on those opening verses. In a short time, he wrote eight or nine ghazals and handed them to the messenger.[7]

The incident quoted by Hali is not meant to only illustrate Ghalib's disinclination to offering islah but also his genius in composing poems at short notice. There is a delightful cluster of poems that Ghalib wrote for various occasions at the court. For example, the rubais he sent by way of thanks for the emperor's casual gifts are worth quoting here because they show a side to him that we don't get to see in his complex ghazals:

> *In sem ke bijon ko koi kya jane*
> *Bheje hain jo armughan shah-e vala ne*
> *Gin kar deven ge ham duaen sau bar*
> *Firoze ki tasbih ke hain yeh dane*[8]
> [Who would know how special these beans are,
> That the honourable king has sent as a gift.
> In return I will send a hundred blessings for every bean,
> These beans are turquoise beads on a prayer string]

Just as only a few of Ghalib's rubais have been recognized, his qitas, too, have not received the attention they deserve. These poems are witty, humorous and endearing, somewhat like his Urdu letters. For example, in this excerpt from a qita below, Ghalib requests the king for warm winter wear:

O king, whose throne is the sky!
O world possessor of sun like radiance,
I was the voiceless one living in a corner,
I was a sufferer whose heart was slit,
You endowed me with dignity.
My value was enhanced in the market . . .
My lord and master, although I don't
Long for turbans or decorative headgear,
I do need something for [the] winter,
So that the cold wind doesn't torture me[9]

Here is another short, witty qita sent to the king for sending him roti made with gram flour (besan):

Don't ask me about the experience,
When the exalted king sent me this buttery 'besan ki roti'
Adam wouldn't have had to leave paradise for eating bread,
If he had partaken of besan ki roti.[10]

Although Ghalib's affiliation with the royal court lasted barely seven years, it drew him back to Urdu and gave us some of his best poetry. Ghalib's poems addressed to Bahadur Shah Zafar showcase a lively, warm relationship between the two, an aspect of courtly culture that has not been explored, while Delhi mushairahs have been described, even immortalized, in the fictitious account of Mirza Farhatullah Beg's *Dilli ki Akhri Shama*.[11]

Throughout the book, I have engaged with Ghalib's trajectory in Urdu and Persian, poetry and prose. I have used Ghalib's sojourn to Calcutta as an important signpost in his career graph for three reasons: first, Ghalib's exposure to and awareness of the power of print; second, his increased output in Persian; and third, his preparation of a selection of his Urdu poetry. Even though the years after he returned from Calcutta were difficult, the tide began turning in his favour after he published the Urdu divan in 1841.

Delhi College

Delhi, in this period, was undergoing what has been called Delhi renaissance by some historians of literary culture.[12] Others prefer to think of this time as the final spring before autumn. Ghalib had grown up knowing no real authority other than the British. He witnessed the transfer of authority, but he wasn't quite cognizant of the inequality that existed between the British and the rest of the population until the Revolt of 1857. The first decades of British rule in the Delhi region had seen the partial integration of colonial officers into the Indo–Persian public sphere. Even if British officials such as William Fraser participated in mushairahs and *mahfils* (gatherings), their admission was not a power-free multicultural dialogue. The dwindling patronage for poetic and religious functions was matched by the foundation of associations in the British style, where carefully chosen native gentlemen were co-opted to organize and inquire into modern ways of dissemination of knowledge.[13]

In 1824–25, the East India Company established a modern college at the site of the Ghaziuddin madrasah that had been imparting traditional education for nearly a hundred years.[14] The college was to impart knowledge about science and mathematics through the medium of Urdu, thus playing a vital role in disseminating Western forms of knowledge.[15] Here, the objective was to promulgate ideas through the medium of the vernacular and achieve improvement on both fronts. This kind of an educational venture involved the translation of numerous texts into Urdu. The Delhi Vernacular Translation Society functioned under the auspices of the college, but it also gained a momentum of its own. Maulvi Abdul Haq, in his book on Delhi College, has given a list of 128 books that the society published.[16] The college itself had two sections: Oriental and English. By 1855, the college had 350 students; of these, 217 were in the English section, while the three Oriental languages (Persian, Arabic and Sanskrit) had seventy-seven, thirty-three and twenty-three students, respectively.[17] For the Oriental section, the college drew from the illustrious pool of scholars in Delhi. Maulvi Sadruddin Khan Azurdah (1789–1868), an outstanding scholar, teacher and poet, became associated with the official policymaking body that determined the pattern of education to be imparted at the college. Azurdah received instruction from two renowned scholars: Shah Abdul Aziz and Fazl-e Imam Khairabadi. Fazl-e Imam was the *sadr-us sudur* (chief justice) in the first quarter of the nineteenth century. His learned son, Fazl-e Haq Khairabadi, was a good friend of Ghalib's.

If there was anyone towards whom Ghalib was deferential, it was Azurdah. Ghalib was a regular visitor at his spacious house located near the Jama Masjid, at the junction of Matia Mahal and Chitli Qabar.[18] This was a meeting place for poets, writers, jurists and theologians. It was Azurdah who had suggested Ghalib's name as a potential teacher for Persian at Delhi College. The incident about Ghalib's visit to the college to interview for the position is well known.[19] The two other names suggested by Azurdah were poets Momin Khan Momin and Imam Baksh Sahba'i. The latter wrote poetry exclusively in Persian. His divan was small, but he had many pupils and admirers. Although Ghalib declined the position at the college, he was aggrieved with Sahba'i. Perhaps not so much for having accepted the position as at Ghalib's exclusion from the Urdu anthology that Sahba'i edited at the behest of Felix Boutros, the college principal. Sahba'i's *Intikhab-e Davavin* was an anthology of Urdu poets for pedagogical purposes. Organized in a chronological order, it had brief notes on the various genres of poetry and head notes on the poets, followed by a selection of verses. For some reason, Sahba'i left out Musahafi, Atish and Ghalib from the list of poets! According to C.M. Naim, Boutros might have had a hand in excluding Ghalib from the anthology.[20] Or it could be because Ghalib was composing more in Persian, such that he was ignored for the Urdu anthology. Nonetheless, it was ironic that Sahba'i and Ghalib, both of whom privileged Persian over Urdu and held similar views on non-native usages in Persian, were estranged in the competitive literary milieu.

The Urdu Press

Urdu publishing in Delhi gained momentum in the 1830s. The *Dihli Urdu Akhbar* was started by Maulvi Muhammad Akbar in 1837. Another important Urdu weekly, *Sayyidul Akhbar*, was inaugurated by Saiyyid Muhammad Khan in 1841. This was the press that published Ghalib's Divan of 1841. In the two decades that followed, there were five weeklies, several bi-monthlies and monthly Urdu journals being published from Delhi. Several teachers from Delhi College, notably Master Ram Chandra, were playing an active role in these publications. Ghalib enjoyed and exploited the benefits of printing like no other Urdu poet before him. He published new ghazals in the Urdu press and rapidly reached an audience that would have been impossible had he not taken to publishing wholeheartedly.

Ghalib's Delhi was a different world from the Mughal city of Akbar and Shahjahan, or even Muhammad Shah and Shah Alam. Ghalib, who had turned his back on Urdu and written almost exclusively in Persian for twenty years, returned to Urdu once again in response to the new discourse initiated by the literati at the mehfils held at Azurdah's house.[21] Although the court did not have the financial power to patronize new scholarly work, Bahadur Shah Zafar did sustain the cultural practice of mushairahs. Ghalib composed more in Urdu now to present at the weekly court mushairahs and other gatherings throughout the city. Ghalib began to tower over his contemporaries in Urdu. He continued to be productive after the 1857 revolt especially in the form of letters in Urdu that he wrote to his numerous admirers.

Published Urdu Divans

As mentioned earlier in the book, Ghalib's Urdu divan went into five editions in his lifetime. Each edition had a slightly bigger number of verses than the previous one.[22] Nonetheless, a kulliyat, or a complete edition, of his Urdu verses was not published. Here are the editions that came out:

1. First edition: Delhi, Saiyyid ul-Akhbar Press, October 1841 (1094 verses).
2. Second edition: Delhi, Darul Islam Press, May 1847 (1157 verses).
3. Third edition: Delhi, Ahmadi Press, July 1861 (1794 verses).
4. Fourth edition: Kanpur, Nizami Press, July 1862/3 (1802 verses).
5. Fifth edition: Agra, Mufid Khala'iq Press, July 1863 (1795 verses).

The 1862/3 edition is considered the most reliable and has the maximum number of verses.

From a total of 4209 verses, Ghalib chose to publish 1802.[23] Raza has prepared a useful table that shows how many verses, from the various phases of his poetic career, Ghalib incorporated into his published divan. I have divided Ghalib's output into two phases:

1. The period of the first three divans (1816, 1821 and 1826): In this period, Ghalib was prolific and composed 2707 verses, of which he selected 909 for the published divan.
2. The second period (1848–57): In this phase, he composed 884 verses and selected 538 for the published editions.

Cover page of the Divan of 1863, published from Agra by Ghalib's pupil Munshi Shiv Narain Aram. This was the last edition to be published in Ghalib's lifetime.

Although this is an approximate calculation, it is definitive enough to conclude that Ghalib's divan has more verses, particularly ghazals, from his early period. This is because he composed a lot more in Urdu in the early phase. Another obvious fact is that he was rejecting

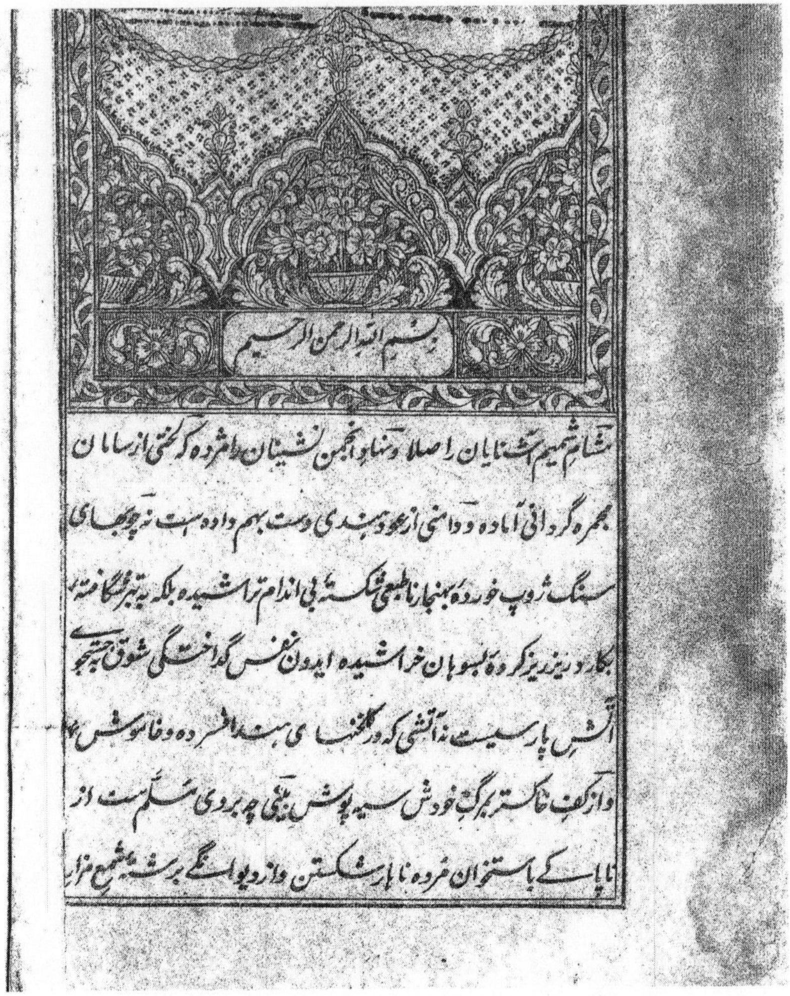
بسم الله الرحمن الرحیم

The Divan of 1863 begins with Ghalib's dibachah.

more verses from the early phase. This doesn't come as a surprise because as Ghalib matured in years, his poetic language matured, too. His verses became less obscure and more polished.

Some Ghalibians, notably Maulana Arshi, have concluded that when Ghalib gave up emulating Mirza Bedil and other poets of the tazah-goi style, his poetry became less ambiguous. He focused

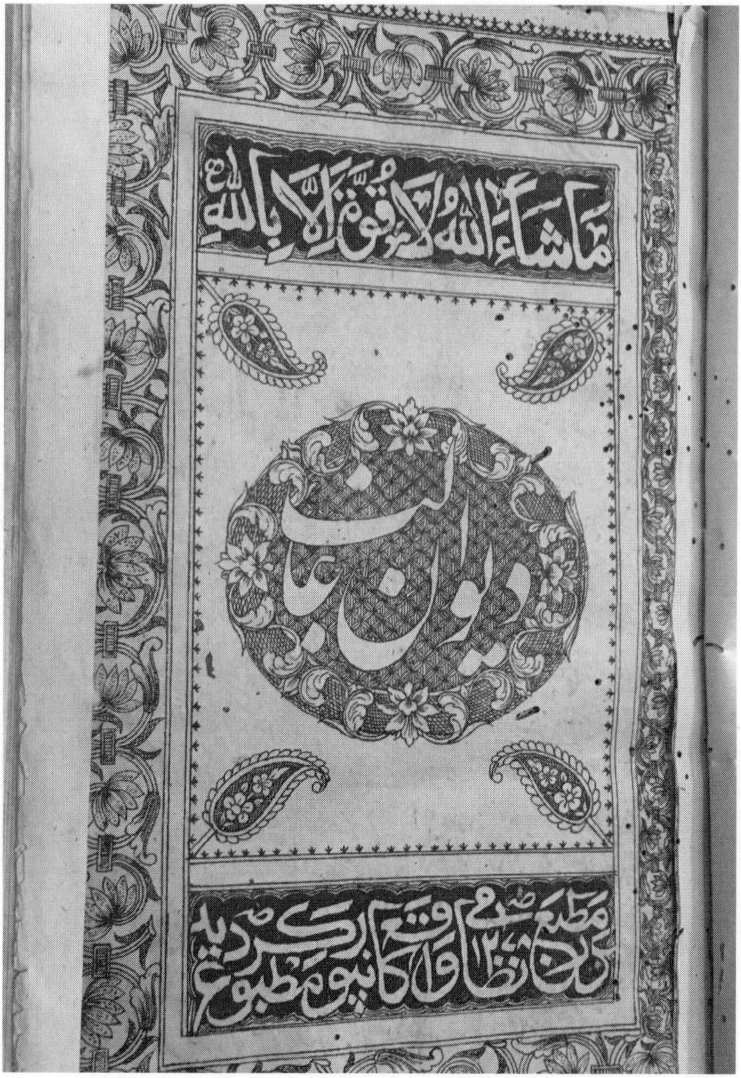

The cover of *Divan-e Ghalib*, published from Nizami Press in Kanpur (1862). This divan is considered to be the most reliable one. It also has the maximum number of verses.

more on the craft of poetry instead of pursuing metaphor-laden outlandish themes. Perhaps Ghalib himself reinforced this idea when he wrote to his pupil Abdur Razzaq Shakir:

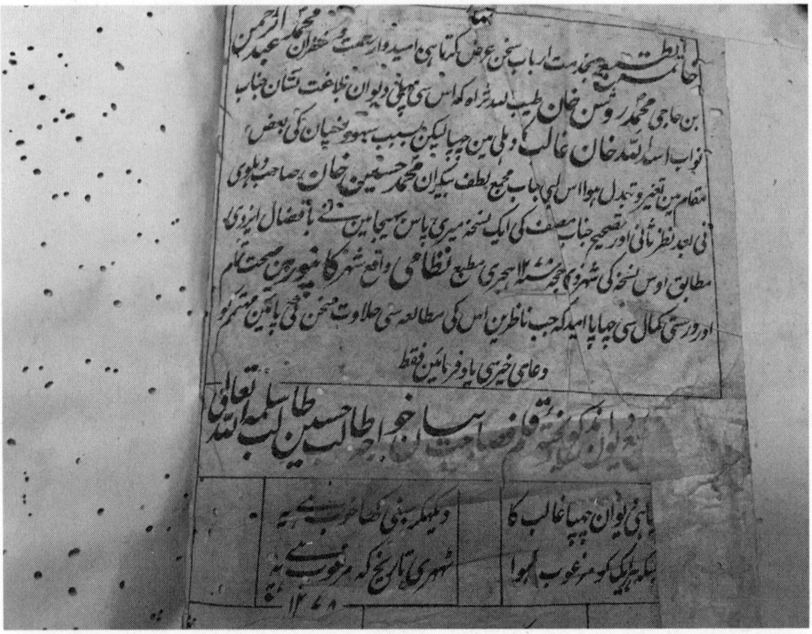

The last page of the Divan of 1862, with a note from the publisher attesting the date of publication.

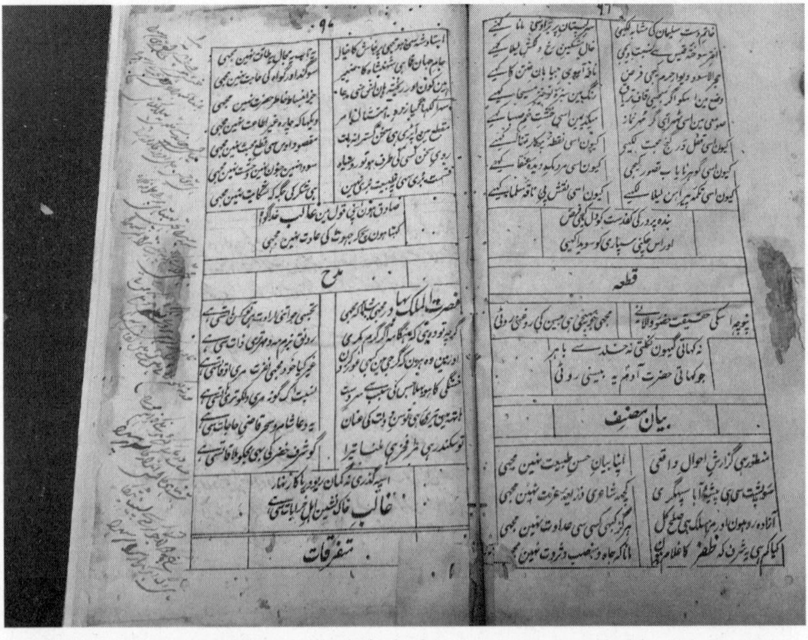

Ghalib wrote a wedding ode (*sehra*) for Prince Javan Bakht. Here, it is copied in the margin in Ghalib's hand, in the published Divan of 1862.

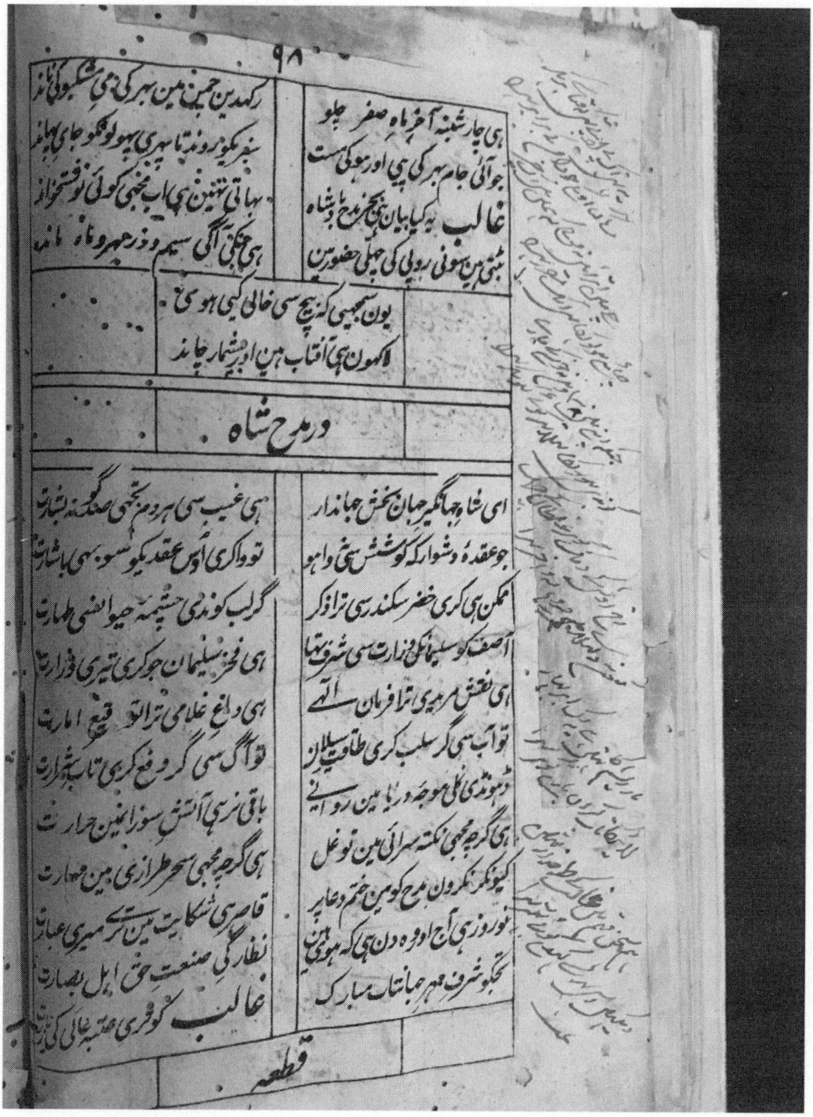
در مدح شاه

قطعه

The sehra continued in the margin of the 1862 divan to the last challenging verse:

Ham sukhan fahm hain Ghalib ke tarafdar nahin.

When I first began writing poetry, I used to compose Rekhtah in the style of Bedil, Asir and Shaukat. Thus, I closed a ghazal with this *maqta*: 'Writing Urdu verse in the style of Bedil/Asadullah Khan, it's no joke.' From the age of fifteen to twenty-five, I

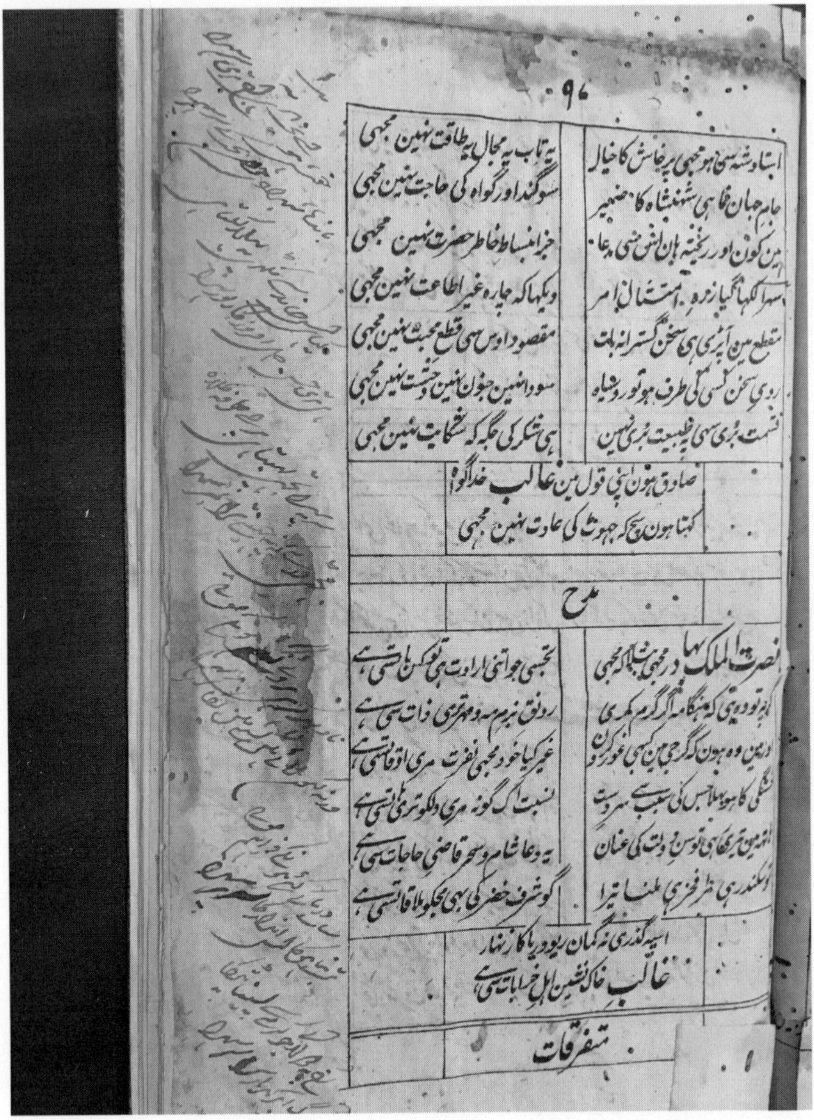

A closer view of Ghalib's handwriting inscribing the sehra.

composed in that fancy, imaginative style; in ten years I collected a large divan. Eventually, when I reached the age of discernment [*jab tamiz ayi*], I discarded that divan, I tore up [*yak qalam chak kiye*] all its pages, retaining ten or fifteen verses in the extant divan as samples.[24]

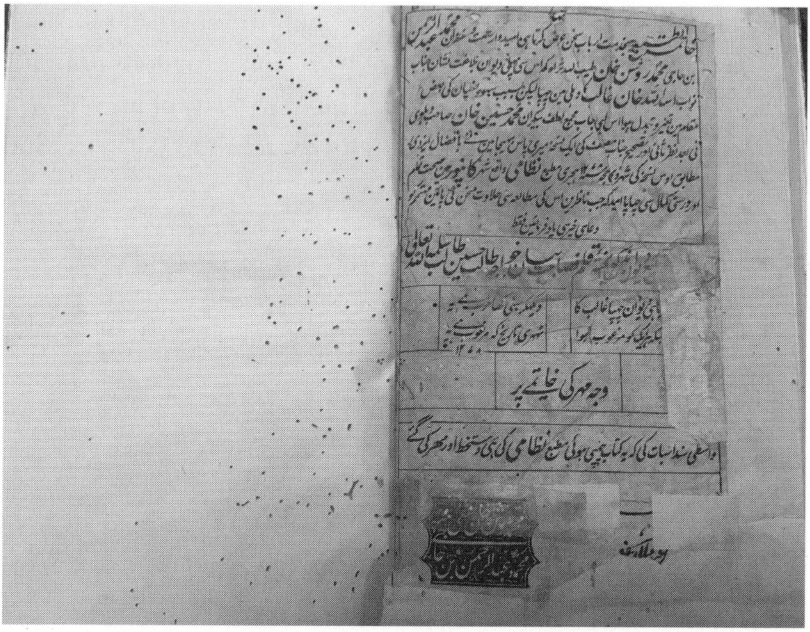

The seal at the bottom of the last page of the 1862 divan.

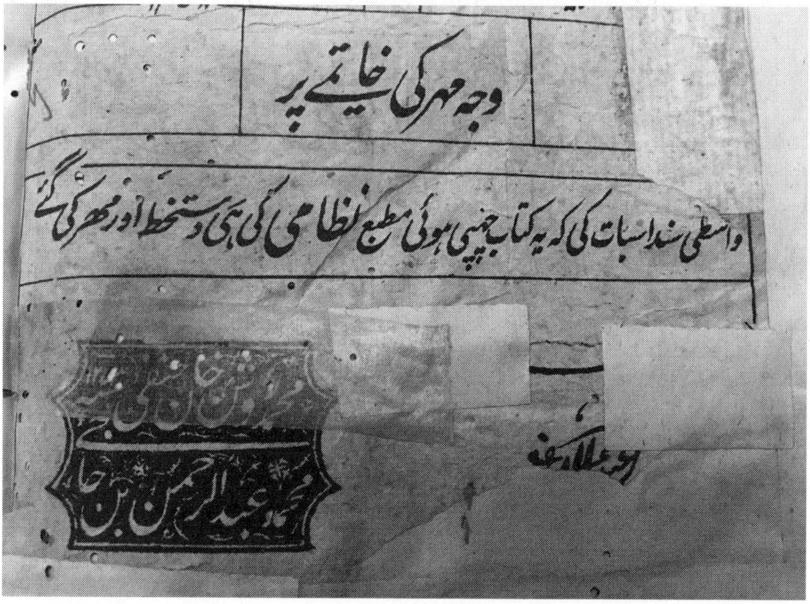

A close-up of the seal and inscription attesting the publisher's name and the seal of authenticity.

Maulana Arshi goes on to say that the humiliation Ghalib suffered in Calcutta for his Persian usages caused him to ignore not only verses written in praise of Mirza Bedil but also many of his verses in the Bedilian style. Maulana Arshi, in his dibachah to Ghalib's 1866 intikhab, wrote:

> Upon examining this selection, it appears that to a great extent, Mirza Ghalib gave precedence to the qualities of language and meaning [*sifat-e lafzi-o ma'navi*] as the criteria for selection. Thus, he did not include all those verses that had tasteless imagination or flavourless, far-fetched similes and metaphors or unfamiliar Persian idioms.[25]

Let us examine Ghalib's criteria for selecting verses. He made three intikhabs: *Gul-e Ra'na* (1828), *Divan-e Ghalib* (1841 and subsequent editions) and the last intikhab (untitled, it was published in 1942), which was put together at the behest of the Navab of Rampur in 1866. The subsequent editions of his Urdu divan published during his lifetime are intikhabs of a kind as well, because as we have seen, he continued the practice of selection till the end. It must be clarified that he made selections not only from ghazals but also from his qitas, masnavis, qasidahs and rubais.[26]

We have seen in the chapter on the *Gul-e Ra'na* that intikhab making was a standard literary practice deployed by tazkirah writers. Keeping a poetry notebook to write down select verses was a tradition widely used by the literate audiences at gatherings. Ghalib understood the significance of intikhabs in establishing or promoting the popularity of a poet. But there is something more noteworthy about Ghalib making his own intikhab. He had a reputation for composing verses with unfamiliar themes, sometimes using unyielding metrical forms. Although Ghalib was stung by his critics' insistence to write more accessible poetry, he pushed back on this advice offered to him by both friends and critics. He expressed exasperation at his reluctance to write simpler verses.[27] But when his friend Maulvi Sirajuddin asked him to prepare an intikhab, he saw it as an occasion to cull out the ambiguous, repetitive or flavourless verses. His thoughtful dibachah to *Gul-e Ra'na* shows that this intikhab was not made randomly. In fact, as I have pointed out earlier, this selection was the foundation on which his 1841 divan was built.

When I began my work on Ghalib's process of selection I was reluctant to admit that he would have given in to his critics' demand of writing less-complicated verses. Why should, or how can, a poet change his creative propensity for composing densely layered poetry? Ghalib wrote complex ghazal verses throughout his career. The published divan has many obscure verses. An argument that still persists is that all the obscure verses in the divan are from the early phase. But then the bulk of his poetry is from the early phase. A problem that I encountered in studying Ghalib was that his work had been fractured into phases or periods. This compartmentalization precludes a holistic assessment of his poetry.

Maulana Arshi's scholarly edition (1958 and 1982) divides Ghalib's output into four sections. These sections—'Ganjinah-e Ma'ni', 'Nava-e Sarosh', 'Yadgar-e Nalah' and 'Bad Avurd'—are organized according to a complicated chronological model.[28] While this approach is comprehensive, the problem with it is that many ghazals get bisected when split into published and unpublished (mutadavil and ghair mutadavil) sections. Because Ghalib often culled verses from a whole ghazal, or combined two ghazals, or added new verses at a later date, this arrangement makes it extremely difficult to find the full ghazal in its unedited format. Kalidas Gupta Raza divides Ghalib's poetry into eleven sections according to chronology. The dating, though helpful, can only be approximate.[29] Raza's method makes it very challenging to search for ghazals on the basis of radif, which is the standard method of finding ghazals. Fortunately, Muhammad Khan Ashraf and Azmat Rubab came out with an edition, *Urdu Kulliyat-e Ghalib*, in 2012. Their edition has collected all of Ghalib's Urdu poetry from the manuscripts and printed editions, classified it under the different genres and arranged it as per the true alphabetical radif system.[30]

But because the Ashraf and Rubab edition follows the true alphabetical order of radif, it disrupts the order determined by Ghalib. Thus, the ghazal section does not open with the famous *'naqsh faryadi hai kis ki shokhi-e tahrir ka'*. It is a bit of a shock to find an unfamiliar ghazal at the beginning of the kulliyat. This perhaps would not be as disconcerting had Ashraf and Rubab followed the time-honoured practice of beginning a divan with the genres in the following classical order: qitas, masnavis qasidahs, ghazals and then rubais. But Ghalib himself did not stick to this order in the editions of his Urdu divan published during his lifetime. For example, the Divan of 1841 has a dibachah and taqriz but begins with ghazals. After the ghazals come the qasidahs (manqibat), then the qitas and finally the rubais.[31] Nonetheless, the 1862 edition (Kanpur), which is considered to be the most reliable and used as the template for numerous editions after Ghalib's death, does not open with ghazals but with qitas.[32]

I think that Ghalib's reception history has much to do with the significance accorded to ghazals in the literary culture. This is the reason why subsequent editions of his Urdu divan focused on ghazals, and the critical discourse mostly engaged with his ghazals. As Urdu literary culture modernized following Western critical methods, the qasidah and masnavi forms became obsolete. The ghazal, too, was dubbed to be repetitive and a morally degenerate form of poetry. It survived because it continued to evolve, adapting and expanding its repertoire to include new themes. Ghalib's divan, too, underwent changes at the hands of publishers after his death. The dibachah and taqriz written in Persian were deemed unnecessary and dropped. By the turn of the century people forgot that the divan was an intikhab.[33]

The significance of print and Ghalib's far-sightedness in getting his work published has not been examined thoroughly, if at all, in the vast field of Ghalib studies. Similarly, the arrangement of genres in a divan, and its impact on readers, needs closer attention. With the gradual shift from manuscript to print culture, poetry presented in the form of divans had a different, much wider audience.[34] Ghalib was sensitive to the tastes of his patrons. In the last years of his life, he was asked by the Navab of Rampur to make a selection of his Urdu and Persian poetry. This last intikhab is instructive, in that it speaks to the art of curating poetry.[35]

Ghalib's reception history shows the twists and turns of a poet's journey straddling two languages and their traditions—the classical tradition of Persian and the younger tradition of Urdu. For Ghalib, Urdu and Persian were like two doors into poetry's garden. It wasn't uncommon for eighteenth- and nineteenth-century Indian poets to write in both languages. Prose, especially, was mostly in Persian. Yet these bilingual writers seemed to make their mark only in one language.[36] Persian represented the classical, cosmopolitan tradition, and Urdu the younger, vernacular tradition. Poetry in Urdu was known as Rekhtah, a mixed language. As Rekhtah became popular it attracted more poets and a bigger audience. But Persian held its ground above Urdu as the classical language with a deep, venerable tradition that Rekhtah (Urdu) could not surpass. Although Ghalib as a Persian poet towered over his contemporaries, he appears combative and defensive against accepting the Indo-Persian register. The dibachah to his Persian divan makes it clear that he wanted to be seen as a part of the bigger tradition of Persian.

While Ghalib came to write more and more in Urdu in the last decade of his life, print capitalism was growing rapidly. Textbooks were needed for the new curriculum in Urdu. Ghalib's Urdu letters were exemplary of a new prose style; the first volume was published just before his death. Thus, it came about that Ghalib's slender Urdu divan and his Urdu letters became exemplary of Urdu's modernity. The Urdu divan prompted a series of commentaries when large selections were included in the syllabi. The letters became models of prose style. The Persian divan, however, did not inspire commentaries or intikhabs.

There is a beautiful garden of Ghalib's poetry waiting to be explored. As the poet himself said in a verse that he did not include in the published divan:

> I sing from the warmth of the joy of imagination,
> I am the bulbul of a garden yet to be created.[37]

Appendix A

Dibachah to the Divan of 1841

Minds aware of fragrance are invited, and those who are used to sitting in gatherings are given the good news that some material for burning in the brazier has become available; some Indian aloe bark [*ud-e Hindi*] has come to hand. This aloe bark has not been splintered with a stone, or chopped inappropriately, or carved with an unskilled hand. In fact, it has been cut with an axe, then divided into small pieces with a knife and sculpted with a whittle. The breath-burning power of desire is now looking for the Iranian fire. Not the fire that has now become dead and burnt to cinders in the Indian hearth, which you now see clad in black on account of its own death having become a handful of ashes. Because it is quite clear that it is unclean to breakfast with dead bones and it is proven madness to hang by the string that is the pendant of the snuffed-out candle of a grave. In any case, it is not proper to use a dead lamp for the purpose of melting one's heart or for lighting up an assembly.

The one who knows [how] to brighten the face of the fire by his art, and the fire worshipper who will be burned in fire because of bad deeds, knows very well that the seeker is restless in the desire of searching for that brilliant fire, which sprang out of stone to brighten the eye of Hoshang, and that which kept growing day by day in the court pavilion of Lahrasp. That fire is like a flare for straw, colour for the tulip, a sight for the magus and the lamp for the idol house.

I am full of thanks to the lord, the bestower of poetry to the inner self, that I have in my ashes found a few sparks from that brilliant fire, and have quickly engaged by picking at my heart and have produced bellows from my breath for that fire, so that in the circle of the people of the world that has scant capital of its own, some capital may be made available. Such that it may bestow on the brazier the brilliance and glory of the light of a lamp, and may vouchsafe [the] fragrance of aloe bark the power to fly to the nose and thus make the brain fully saturated with its perfume.

This humble writer desires that after making this selection of ghazals from the Urdu divan, he would turn his attention to his Persian divan, and after achieving this feat he would keep sitting, having broken his feet.

I hope that [the] literati, and also those who appreciate my work, would not declare my scattered pages, which are not included in this divan, to be the result of the ink from my quill and would not oblige the collection of my writings with praise of those verses, nor would they lay blame on me for their adaptations.

Lord, these [texts], which have not yet smelt the fragrance of being, nor have reached the level of the apparent from the unapparent that is the paintings, which are still within the inner self of the painter whose name is Asadullah Khan, who is known as Mirza Naushah, with the pen name of Ghalib. Such that may God grant, that just as he was born in Agra and has made Delhi his home, he may be buried in Najaf.

Appendix B

Dibachah to *Gul-e Ra'na*

'There is no one effective in existence except God.'

O Lord, despair of your beneficence has emboldened my sins. Crush the arrogance of my madness with the power of your kindness; my desolate heart has become cold from the autumn of deprivation of your bounty. My longings have stoked a fire; don't extinguish it. The fire of my state's suffering is the igniter of the harvest of the future. I have burns from the fires of the hell of non-achievement, don't aggravate them. My life is spent in being a spectator to the eternal glories of springtimes past. Don't burn my face with your anger. My self-control has been blown away by the temperamental sky. Do not allow your stars to play with me. My heart is constrained with the cruelties of the times. Don't take away the configuration of my stars from me. The blood in my liver is because of my imagination; tell them not to call for an explanation. I cannot see the face of the auspicious beloved. With a skyful of blueness, rub away the rust from the rusted mirror so that the glory of Neptune [*mushtari*] may shine forth. My weakness is laying the foundation for a world of hopelessness. Whatever is removed from my body, add to my heart; the warmth of my thought sieves the embers from the depths of my heart and adds to the blisters on my liver.

O (Lord) because of you, the light of command shines through the windows of my mind into my heart from end to end. This fistful of dust whose future is dark, from the grace of your beneficence becomes a shining intellect, and I receive the eloquence of speech. Such is the power of Your grace that those who are the dust of the dust, whose hearts are burnt, have been given a space in the shade of the flag of Muhammad. Such is his (Muhammad's) beneficence, that by virtue of his rattling the chain of forgiveness, those whose works were stalled have their doors opened. Since He is the creator of words of praise, singing His praise from my throat and tongue is just like praising myself (we are not separate from God). Praising Muhammad, whose praises have been sung by all, if I am not wrong, is equal to claiming the status of God. (Because God has praised Muhammad.)

The ones whose feet are blistered from travelling in the everlasting valley of submission and are filled with the pearls of worship are the ones whose hearts reflect the glory of Muhammad and receive the principles of faith [*qanun-e aqidat*]. The music of *darud* resounds. Praise be to Muhammad.

> Those who claim to compose *na'at* and *hamd*, it is better for them to submit to the dust of poetry (*adab*).
>
> Let us sing his true praises and perform obeisance as best we can.

As one of those who mix freedom and restraint, I am at the crossroads of doubt and joy, a desirer of illness and pain, with a world of sorrow in my heart. I, Muhammad Asadullah of Samarqand, was born in Akbarabad (Agra), and am a resident of Delhi. As a traveller on the carpet of claim in search of praise, I am creating language from the fabric of my heart, and the unfulfilled lament, washed with tears from my heart, has reached the ears of friends. Those who understand both the depths and nuances of poetry, and those who are aware of the perfections and flaws of this art, know very well that I have not gotten up from the carpet of claim, nor have I made a show of superior intellect. For a long time now my heart-melting poetry has been searching for hearts that can understand it. I have sprinkled it with the dust of the nuances of words and with the meaning of the dark-inked letters. Passers-by can see the display of the flowers in this walled garden through the windows in the wall. Only the discerning ones can pluck the flowers and differentiate between the real and the fake. In this gathering, those who are intoxicated with the wine of challenge, and have been made arrogant, can pluck the shards from the wine glasses of past drinkers. I thank God for giving me a discerning heart, a seeing eye and an eloquent tongue that does not utter anything but praise of friends, and does not speak ill of anyone. My song is not heart-attractive nor is it scathing. I am not looking for praise, nor am I selling my poetry. I have gathered crumbs from every corner of the tablecloth of words, and I lick the bowls of the wonderful poets of the past, and thus become their companion at the tablecloth of themes. I drink from the same cup. So what if God has poured pearls and rubies from the treasures of the sources into their laps. I, too, have been given some stones and pebbles that I will place in the skirt and pockets of thought.

Observe the reach of my capabilities, that I have taken Hindi from Delhi to Isfahan; and applaud the strength of the thread of my thought, that I have brought Persian from Shiraz to Hindustan. I regret the exaggerated praise that I have bestowed on myself in showing off my face, having removed the veil of modesty. They say that the blood of two languages is on my head, and the corpses of the two I have killed are on my shoulders. So what if one of the languages by my side has become a stranger in its own homeland,

and the other due to my ill fortune is being estranged in its own homeland. Where is that silence that would remove me from the vengeance being sought for these languages from me, and also free me from the ups and downs of acceptance and rejection of listeners? Poor, ignorant me. If I call myself ignorant, wisdom cynically laughs at me, accuses me of knowing.

I only know this that I am made from myself [sui generis; someone emptied me from me]. I have made colourful the stories of helplessness. I am in a state of bewilderment. My breath is suspended with wonder and my heart is seized with restlessness. My story is distilled from my liver. My lament, like a lancet, has slit my heart and made it more affecting. My poetry has become soaked with the pain of my lamenting heart. My life has borne the tribulations of loneliness. From my heart to my feet I am full of pain and its scars. My heart is brimful of the relish of poetry. If my mind is ablaze, it is not surprising that the salt of taste has sharpened the throat of my speech. My mouth is full of freshness. It is blossoming. The field is open for striving. Hope is like a thread; it is long. Although my sad heart is in pieces of pain, it's bloodied. From not achieving knowledge the heart is dejected; from deprivation of sight the eye is miserable. I am resigned to lamenting, my eye[s] to shedding tears.

Line:

> 'Whosoever accepts the dry and the wet [highs and lows] is the king of land and water.'

In this garden, I am like a bird that has lost its nest; from head to toe I am burning with the flame of my own voice. My lament has made my breath like sparks of lightning; my heart is melting. The colours and fragrances of those who inhabit this garden, and those who are intoxicated by this joyful gathering—their heart-searing voices have awakened the music of understanding in me. With every breath, the lightning of pain of my lament takes measure of my being. People are unaware that my heart is in pieces, that my liver is broken to bits, that a blood-soaked voice emerges from my throat. [The] Fear of my listeners makes my breath heave in my chest like a wave in a wine glass. Hostility from my rivals causes the blood from my broken heart to drip like water from a broken earthen cup.

Friends have created gatherings and have insisted that I light the candle of poetry. Amazement has made me catch my breath and shyness has stitched my eyes to my feet. The leader of this gathering, especially, in whom the body of meaning is incarnate, is also the spirit of this body. The face of humanity takes flowers from his pockets and [the] skirt of his garment. Observing the sweetness of expression from his pen, sugar returns to the cane in astonishment like a finger between teeth. An examination of the subtlety his writing that tricks the eye makes the roses of spring laugh at the violets. He is like shade and spring water to the heart-burnt travellers in the valley of desire, like the shade of friendship of the tree of Tuba and the stream of Kausar in Paradise. He has the qualities of Jupiter, courageous by nature, with an angel-like face and a god-like temperament. I don't know what magic spell he has cast on me, and what heart-captivating perfume he has put to my nose, such that my head, which was glued to my knees, wrapped in the ragged garment of fear, has lifted. My lips, which were applied to my chewed-up heart, are now opened towards engaging with poetry and words.

Verse:

There is no recourse except to acknowledge Sirajuddin Ahmad
Otherwise Ghalib had no interest in writing poetry

Although I am an ineffectual prisoner in the net of amazement and have come down in the valley of ignorance, my effort is to pull every word out of the meshes of the net. My pen is paying obeisance to the placement of every dot. I pride myself in his warmth and kindness, for he has rekindled my languished fire. He has lifted the dust of my being from the ground to a glorious cloud with such ease. He has commanded me to prepare a selection from my *Divan-e Rekhtah* and some ghazals from Persian, and put them together in a single *bayaz*. I have presented this two-coloured curtain and hung it on the window of the unique (*yak rang*) entirely perceptive audience:

> 'It is his to command and mine to obey.'

In the hearts of those who are searching for poetry, it would not remain hidden that at the beginning I was curious and dug deep into my liver, searching to adorn verses in the Urdu language. In writing this, I passed along the same path, I gave myself to the path. God forbid that the thread of my narrative would be lost, or I lose control.

Every mirror/gate in this garden has doors that open face to face. The first I have adorned with the pearls of Hindi poetry. Since the second door is for those who love Persian, and who appreciate style, I have named this bayaz *Gul-e Ra'na*.

Lord, give this *Gul-e Ra'na* a place in the turban of acceptance. Whosoever accepts this, may thanks from me accrue to them.

God alone is enough; the rest have lost their path.

Appendix C

Taqriz for Ghalib's 1841 Divan[1]

(By Navab Muhammad Ziyauddin Ahmad Khan Naiyar)

The blooming of the whiteness of the dawn from the dark night of the blackness of the pages by the power of the light enhancement of the words of the Taqriz, whose appearance is a footprint among the footprints of the heart-attracting pen of the brother, who is close to the heart, and, who is equal [to] my own life, who is of high lineage and distinguished parentage, Navab Ziyauddin Ahmad Khan Bahadur, may the exalted Allah keep him safe.[2]

In the name of God. There is a straight-statured beloved from the angelic household of thought who has appeared and is now engaged upon making her radiant beauty apparent. It is this hidden beauty that saunters in a carefree manner, having lifted the veil from her face, who has now readied herself with her skirt raised and tied to her waist in the style of one who tears open the curtain. It is like the country of Joseph, where there are groups of houri-born meanings and themes packed together. It is a narcissus garden, where can be seen the radiant beauties of the wonderstruck who have lost their senses. It's a wide shawl full of pearls, like the sky full of stars. It's a Khwarnaq-like palace full of glories, which shatters the value of hundreds of picture galleries of China. It is the lighting up of a lamp for which the *peris* are like the moths. (It is a lamp for which the peri takes away the senses of the *parvanah*). It's a heavenly talisman, which is always to be found on the arms of the wise. It is as if a genie, generous like Michael, has spread a tablecloth and given freedom to those who are greedy for poetry. It is a house of God, a place of worship, whose key has been given into the hands of proper understanding. And whose door has been opened for those who are intent upon visiting the wide plains (*muzdalifa*) of the heart. It's a Somnath,[3] where a whole city of beautiful idols of thought, wearing the sacred threads, put their foreheads on the ground. It's a picture gallery whose exhibition of rare paintings causes Mani and Arzang to touch the back of their hands on the ground in obeisance.[4] Every page in this book is a magus reading from the Avesta. It's a mirror house where the whole world is reflected. It's [a] house of purity that is absolutely chaste. Those who live behind the curtain in this house possess the character of Mary. The saucy-eyed women in that house are bent upon splitting or tearing off the curtain even more than the beloveds who sit in the marketplace. They are empty-handed [have no wealth], but their hearts are affluent [with knowledge]. They are free living and thinking but their feet are bound in clay. They are meant to be loved, but they are in love with themselves. They are plain in body, but their hearts are full of colour. They are of the profession of Harut [that is, angels who fell in love with a beauty called Zohra/Venus], but in their art they are like Zohra. Originally, they are like pearls of the upper world who have made the earth their home. They are salamanders capable of drinking away a whole ocean. They are crocodiles whose hearts are full of fire. They are the roasted ones whose brains are roasted to a turn. They are ripe in the kernel and sweet in regard to their skin. They are wine drinkers who are black drunk. They are out of their senses, hand in hand with each other. They are Indian idols that roam Iran. They are Delhi-born but brought up in Isfahan.

Beware! I fear that whatever I have recited above may not have been fully measured [understood] by you. Now this is the selected divan in the Urdu language, which has dropped from the pen of the holder of a Jesus-like revelation, who serves the balance of wisdom, who has the power of sight and determination of the astrolabe, and who is the substance of creation's mirror, who is the standard of the value of all things of value, who is the ultimate stair of the ladder of high station, who is the hero of the dominion of the nurture of meaning, who is the rule-giver and regulator of the land of poets and poetry, who is the master of the land of the new style of writing, who is the leader of fresh discourse, who is the inspirer of spirit in the body of the spreading of discourse, who is the enhancer of the power of sight of those who have vision and understanding, who is the praise-giver of the banner of the splendour of the pen, who lights the lamp of the house of ink, who is the cancelling sign of the reputation of all his colleagues, and who presides over the assembly of knowers of subtle points.

Masnavi:

Poetry gains good fortune and elevation by his thought
Themes acquire heights from his thought

The scratching of his pen pleases the heart
It is like the singing of bulbuls in paradise

He is the eldest son of the nine Heavens
He is the best disciple of the elevated wisdom (of God)

He freely educates the world
For he is the chosen among knowers of the times

He heads the list of the makers of elegant discourse
In this art he is the pride of his peers

He is the expert rider in the plains of themes
Plato in disposition, creator of philosophical thoughts

His pen showers treasures of meaning
Like clouds shower pearls in the month of Azar

The wine of poetry has intoxicated him
The page by his imagination is like a garden

He, whose creed is monotheism, whose character is pure, and [is] of praiseworthy conduct, angelic in character, a person of blameless lineage and exalted family, who always practises modesty. He is one who gives up malice and nurtures love, brilliant like the sun, with the glory and power of Saturn. He, who disapproves reproach and admires praise. He is the lord of the land of poetic themes, from head to foot he is fidelity and gallantry, from the eye to the heart he is modesty and kind-heartedness. He is the living portrait of cognition and intelligence, and the embodiment of the soul; he is himself a world of the spirit and the spirit of the world. He is of distinguished lineage, and of exalted family, he is the namesake of the testator and the fourth rightly guided caliph of the Seal of the Prophets. That is to say, my mentor, my guide, my master and my brother, Mirza Asadullah Khan Bahadur, whose pen name is Ghalib.

Verse:

Oh God! Make perfect his discourse by making his existence last forever.
And, make me reach my objective, by letting me have a sight of his person.
Amen.

For a long time, Muhammad Ziyauddin Naiyer, of humble and lowly thoughts, had been concentrating [on] and weighing the gravity of his own lightness of worth [to express an opinion] on the project, that these honourable offspring[s] of my brother, each one of whom is a true child of the house of the unapparent, but is in fact the grandparent of heart-pleasing themes, should, for the purpose of educating the new learners who, at present, are unable to distinguish the good from the bad. And these valued gems, of which each is like a bracelet on the silver body of wisdom, and the earring for the beautiful form of sensibility, should be brought out and hung in the niche of the dome of recognition and acknowledgement. So, finally, a thousand praises for the Great Lord and Maker of things, that at this time, which is the sacred year of the emigration of the Prophet, on the master of which (the Prophet himself) the greatest of salutations and the most perfect of greetings, the year 1254, the long-standing and heart-pleasing desire, due to the favourability of the straight-moving time, and the guidance of the awakened fortune has turned into reality, even better than what I had desired for. Happiness took its seat in my heart and the toil and travail of digging and collecting went away. Now, when I devoted my attention quickly to taking count of the individual verses of this auspicious august volume, all the verses, which have the character of the great star Sirius contained in the ghazals, qasidahs, qitahs and rubais, I found them to be one thousand ninety and eight (1098) and a few more.

O you, those of strong senses attend, and O you, with ears to hear, pay attention! It is now necessary for us to walk on the highway of the ample recognition of beautiful themes and not indulge in taunting and backbiting on the smallness of the quantity of the verses. As that great master through these words in fact narrates his own discourse in the form of the Persian, and his command is quite true:

Verse:

I don't write if it is not sweet, O Ghalib
So what if my verses are few in number?

Let this be a memorial from me and a reminder for the others.

Bibliography

Abidi, Saiyyed Vazirul Hasan. Ed. *Gul-e Ra'na.* Lahore: Idarah-e Tahqiqat, Panjab University, 1969.

Ahmad, Khurshid. Ed. *Naya Daur, Ghalib Nambar.* Lucknow: Directorate of Information, February–March 1969.

Ahmad, Mukhtaruddin. Ed. *Ahval-e Ghalib*. Aligarh, Delhi: Anjuman Taraqqi Urdu Hind, 1953, 1986.

Ahmad, Nazir. *Ghalib Par Chand Tahqiqi Maqale.* New Delhi: Ghalib Institute, 1996.

Ahmad, Nazir. *Naqd-e Qati-e Burhan mai Zama'im*. New Delhi: Ghalib Institute, 1985.

Akram, Muhammad. Ed. *Dad-e Sukhan* by Sirajuddin Ali Khan-e Arzu. Rawalpindi: Iran–Pakistan Institute of Persian Studies, 1974.

Alam, Muzaffar. 'Persian in Precolonial Hindustan' in *Literary Cultures in History: Reconstructions from South Asia.* Ed. Sheldon Pollock. University of California Press, 2003.

Alam, Muzaffar, and Sanjay Subrahmanyam. 'Love, Passion and Reason in Faizi's Nal-Daman' in *Love in South Asia: A Cultural History*. Ed. Francesca Orsini. Cambridge: Cambridge University Press, 2006.

Anjum, Khaliq. *Ghalib ka Safar-e Kalkattah aur Kalkatte ka Adabi Ma'rikah.* New Delhi: Ghalib Institute, 2005.

Anjum, Khaliq. *Ghalib ke Khutut*, five volumes. New Delhi: Ghalib Institute, 1988–2011.

Ansari, Z. Trans. 'Ashtinamah' in Khaliq Anjum, *Ghalib ka Safar-e Kalkattah.*

Ansari, Z. *Masnaviyat-e Ghalib*. New Delhi: Ghalib Institute, 1983.

Ansarullah, Muhammad. *Ghalib Bibliography*. New Delhi: Ghalib Institute, 1998.

Arshi, Maulana Imtiaz Ali Khan. *Divan-e Ghalib Urdu, Nuskhah-e Arshi.* New Delhi: Anjuman Taraqqi Urdu, first edition 1958.

Arshi, Maulana Imtiaz Ali Khan. *Divan-e Ghalib*. New Delhi: Anjuman Taraqqi Urdu, second edition 1982.

Arshi, Maulana Imtiaz Ali Khan. 'Ghalib Ki Apni Kalam Par Islahen' in *Aj Kal, Ghalib Nambar*. February 1952.

Arshi, Maulana Imtiaz Ali Khan. Ed. *Ghalib Intikhab*. Bombay: Matba-e Qayyimah, 1942.

Arshi, Maulana Imtiaz Ali Khan. *Makatib-e Ghalib*. Silsilah-e Matbu'at-e Kitabkhanah-e Rampur. Bombay, 1937.

Arshi, Maulana Imtiaz Ali Khan. 'Ghalib ka Zaichah' in *Mah-e Nau*. Ed. Shanul Haq Haqqi. Karachi: January–February 1969.

Ashraf, Muhammad Khan, and Azmat Rubab. *Urdu Kulliyat-e Ghalib*. Karachi: Sang-e Meel Publications, 2012.

Asi, Abdul Bari. *Mukammal Sharh-e Divan-e Ghalib*. Lucknow: Saqi Book Depot, 1931.

Azad, Muhammad Husain. *Ab-e Hayat. Mashahir Shu'ara-e Urdu ki Savaneh Umri aur Zaban -e Mazkur ki Ahd bah Ahd Taraqqiyon aur Islahon ka Bayan.* Kolkata: Usmania Book Depot, reprint, Asrar Karimi Press, Allahabad, 1967.

Bashir, Badr. Ed. *Aligarh Magazine, Ghalib Nambar*. Aligarh, 1969.

Beg, Mirza Farhatullah. *Dilli Ka Ek Yadgar Mushairah*. Aligarh: Educational Publishing House, not dated.

Bijnori, Abdur Rahman. *Mahasin-e Kalam-e Ghalib*. Karachi: Fakhri Printing Press, 1969.

Bukhari, Suhail. 'Ghalib ki Do Rangi' in *Sahifah, Ghalib Nambar*. Vol. 2. Lahore: April 1969.

Chaghtai, Abdur Rahman. *Muraqqa-e Chughtai* (1928 reprint). Hyderabad: Urdu Academy Andhra Pradesh, 2009.

Chandershekhar. 'Dibacha-nigari at the Court of Shah Jahan: Politics and Literary Culture' in Ebba Koch and Ali Anooshahr. Eds. *The Mughal Empire from Jahangir to Shahjahan*. Mumbai: Marg Publications, 2019.

Dasnavi, Abdul Qavi. *Bhopal aur Ghalib*. Bhopal: Bhopal Press, 1969.

Dasnavi, Abdul Qavi. *Nuskhah-e Bhopal aur Nuskhah-e Bhopal Sani*. Bhopal, 1970.

Dasnavi, Abdul Qavi. 'Saiyyid Hashmi aur Nuskhah-e Hamidiyyah' in *Sabras, Ghalib Nambar*. 1969.

Dhavan, Purnima. 'A Prehistory of Rekhtah: View from Mughal Provincial Networks'. Paper presented at the South Asia Conference. Madison: unpublished.

Dihlavi, Saiyyid Vahid-ud-din Bekhud. *Sharh-e Divan-e Ghalib*. Lucknow: Nizami Press, 1923.

Farman Fatehpuri. 'Ghalib Aur Ghalib Takhallus ke Urdu Shu'ara' in *Sahifah, Ghalib Nambar*. Vol. 4. Lahore: October 1969.

Farooqi, Nisar Ahmad. 'Divan-e Ghalib: Nuskhah-e Amroha' in *Talash-e Ghalib*. Lahore, 1969.

Farooqi, Mehr Afshan. 'Power, Culture and Language of Poetry: The Transition from Vali to Ghalib'. *Cracow Indological Studies.* Vol. II. Islam on the Indian Subcontinent. Krakow: Jagiellonian University, Institute of Oriental Philology, 2009.

Farooqi, Mehr Afshan. Ed. *Ghalib's Nuskhah-e Hamidiyyah*. Shahab Sattar, 2016.

Farooqui, Amar. *Zafar and the Raj, Anglo-Mughal Delhi c. 1800–1850*. New Delhi: Primus Books, 2013.

Faruqi, Khwaja Ahmad. *Dastanbuy: A Diary of the Revolt of 1857*. New York: Asia Publishing House, 1970.

Faruqi, Khwaja Ahmad. 'Ghalib Ka Qayam-e Agra Aur *Tazkirah-e Sarvar*' in *Ganjinah-e Ghalib*. New Delhi: Publications Division, Patiala House, 1969.

Faruqi, Khwaja Ahmad. 'Marikah-e Ghalib Aur Hamiyan-e Qatil, Irani-Hindi Niza Ki Raushni Men' in *Ahval-e Ghalib*. New Delhi: Anjum Taraqqi Urdu Hind, 1986.

Faruqi, Khwaja Ahmad. Ed. *Umdah-e Muntakhibah*, generally known as *Tazkirah-e Sarvar*, of Mir Muhammad Khan Sarvar. Delhi: Delhi University, 1961.

Faruqi, Shamsur Rahman. *Urdu Ghazal ke Aham Mor: Iham, Ri'ayat, Munasibat*. New Delhi: Ghalib Academy, 1996.

Faruqi, Shamsur Rahman, and Pritchett, Frances W. *Ab-e Hayat: Shaping the Canon of Urdu Poetry*. New Delhi: Oxford University Press, 2001.

Faruqi, Shamsur Rahman. *Ghalib Par Char Tahriren*. New Delhi: Ghalib Institute, 2001.

Faruqi, Shamsur Rahman. *Kai Chand the Sar-e Asman*. New Delhi: Penguin Books, 2007.

Faruqi, Shamsur Rahman. *She'r-e Shor-Angez*. New Delhi: National Council for Promotion of Urdu, 2008.

Faruqi, Shamsur Rahman. *Tafhim-e Ghalib.* New Delhi: Ghalib Institute, 1989, 2006, 2014.

Faruqi, Shamsur Rahman. 'Unprivileged Power: The Strange Case of Persian (and Urdu) in Nineteenth-Century India' in *Annual of Urdu Studies*. No. 13. 1998.

Lakhnawi, Fazil, and Husain, Murtuza. Ed. *Kulliyat-e Ghalib Farsi*. Vol. 1. Lahore: Farsi ka Klasiky, Adab Majlis Taraqqi Adab, 1967, first edition.

Lakhnawi, Fazil, and Husain, Murtuza. Ed. *Kulliyat-e Ghalib Farsi*. Vol. 2. Lahore: Farsi ka Klasiky, Adab Majlis Taraqqi Adab, 1967, first edition.

Lakhnawi, Fazil, and Husain, Murtuza. Ed. *Kulliyat-e Ghalib Farsi.* Vol. 3. Lahore: Farsi ka Klasiky Adab, Majlis Taraqqi Adab, 1967, first edition.

Lakhnawi, Fazil, and Husain, Murtuza. Ed. *Ud-e Hindi*. Lahore: Urdu ka Klasiky Adab, Majlis Taraqqi Adab, 1967.

Firaqi, Tahseen. 'Masnavi, Chiragh-e Dair, Ek Ja'izah' in *Ghalib Fikr-o Farhang*. New Delhi: Ghalib Institute, 2012.

Gabbay, Alyssa. *Islamic Tolerance, Amir Khusrau and Pluralism*. London and New York: Routledge, 2010.

Gasset, José Ortega y. *Man and People*. Translated by Willard R. Trask. New York: W.W. Norton & Company, Inc., 1957.

Ghalib, *Divan-e Ghalib*. Delhi: Saiyyid Muhammad Khan Bahadur's Lithographic Press, October 1841, and Kanpur 1862.

Ghalib, *Qati-e Burhan*. Lucknow: Naval Kishor Press, 1862.

Ghalib. *Kulliyat-e Farsi*. Lucknow: Naval Kishor Press, 1863.

Ghalib. *Darafsh-e Kaviyani*. Lucknow: Naval Kishor Press, 1865.

Ghalib. *Kulliyat-e Nasr-e Ghalib*. Lucknow: Naval Kishor Press, 1871, 1872.

Ghalib. *Kulliyat-e Ghalib Mushtamil bah Manzumat-e Farsi*. Lucknow: Naval Kishor Press, 1893.

Ghalib. *Urdu-e Mu'alla*. Lahore: Matba Karimi, 1926, and Urdu ka Klasiky Adab, Majlis Taraqqi-e Adab (Vols. 1–3), 1967.

Ghalib. *Ud-e Hindi*. Collected by Munshi Mumtaz Ali. Meerut: Matba Mujataba'i, 1868.

Hadi, Nabi. *Dictionary of Indo-Persian Literature*. New Delhi: Indira Gandhi Centre for the Arts, 1995.

Hali, Altaf Husain. *Yadgar-e Ghalib*. Delhi, 1897.

Hali, Altaf Husain. *Hayat-e Sa'di*. Allahabad: Asrar Karimi Press, 1967.

Hali, Altaf Husain. *Hayat-e Javed*. New Delhi: Rupa & Company, 1994.

Hali, Altaf Husain. *Yadgar-e Ghalib*. Ed. Khalilur Rahman Daudi. Lahore: Urdu ka Klasiky Adab, Majlis Taraqqi-e Adab, 1963.

Haq, Abdul. *Marhum Dilli Kalij*. Delhi: Anjuman Taraqqi-e Urdu Hindi, 1945.

Haq, Mufti Anvarul. *Divan-e Ghalib Jadid al ma'ruf ba Nuskhah-e Hamidiyyah*. Agra: first edition, 1921, and Lucknow: photo offset edition, 1982.

Haq, Nomanul. Ed. *Mahasin-e Kalam-e Ghalib*. Karachi: Oxford University Press, 2016.

Haqqi, Shanul Haq. Ed. *Mah-e Nau, Ghalib Nambar*. Karachi: January–February, 1969.

Husain, Saiyyed Hamid. 'Divan-e Ghalib, Nuskhah-e Bhopal, Par Sibt Dastkhat aur Muhren' in *Sha'ir*. July 1969.

Husain, Saiyyed Hamid. 'Mufti Anvarul Haq Murattab Nuskhah-e Hamidiyyah' in *Hamari Zaban*. 8 January 1969.

Ikram, S.M. *Ghalibnamah*. Lahore: Taj Company, 1936 (subsequent revised editions, 1939, 1944, 1946, 1947, 1957).

Islahi, Abdur Rahman Parvaz. *Mufti Sadruddin Azurdah*. Delhi: Maktaba Jamia, 1977.

Islam, Khurshidul. *Ghalib Ibtidai Daur*. Delhi: Anjuman Taraqqi Urdu Hind, 1975.

Islam, Khurshidul. *Ghalib ka Nazariyah-e Hayat*. New Delhi: Ghalib Institute, 2011.

Jain, Gyan Chand. *Tafsir-e Ghalib*. Srinagar: Jammu and Kashmir Academy of Art, Culture and Languages, 1971.

Jain, Gyan Chand. 'Nuskhah-e Bhopal ki Islahen aur Izafeh' in *Rumuz-e Ghalib*. New Delhi: Maktaba Jamia, 1976.

Jain, Gyan Chand. 'Nuskhah-e Arshi, Taba-e Sani ke Liye Kuch Ma'ruzat' in *Rumuz-e Ghalib*. New Delhi: Maktaba Jamia, 1976.

Kantoori, Saiyyed Muhammad Zamin. *Sharh-e Divan-e Ghalib*. Ed. Ashraf Rafi. Delhi: Educational Publishing House, 2012.

Karimuddin, Maulvi. *Tabaqat-e Shuara-e Hind*. Ed. Mahmud Ilahi. Lucknow: Uttar Pradesh Urdu Academy, 1983 (1947), reprint 1983.

Keshavmurthy, Prashant. *Persian Authorship and Canonicity in Late Mughal Delhi, Building an Ark*. London and New York: Routledge, 2016.

Keshavmurthy, Prashant. 'Creaturely Exertion: Reforming Genius, Indo-Persian Conceptions of Literary Authorship (1220–1920 ce)'. PhD dissertation. Columbia University, 2009.

Khan, Ali Akbar. *Divan-e Ghalib bah Khatt-e Ghalib*. Rampur: Idarah Yadgar-e Ghalib, 1969.

Khan, Hamid Ahmad. *Divan-e Ghalib Nuskhah-e Hamidiyyah*. Lahore: Majlis Taraqqi-e Adab, 1969.

Khan-e Arzu, Sirajuddin Ali. *Chiragh-e Hidayat*. 1745.

Khan-e Arzu, Sirajuddin Ali. *Navadirul Alfaz*. 1747.

Khan, Latifullah. Urdu translation of *Amir Khusrau Dibachah-e Ghurratul Kamal*. Karachi: Sheherzade, 1990.

Khatun, Hamidah. Urdu translation of *Gulshan-e Bekhar*. New Delhi: NCPUL, 1998.

Kinra, Rajeev. *Writing Self, Writing Empire: Chandar Bhan Brahman and the Cultural World of the Indo-Persian State Secretary*. Oakland: University of California Press, 2015.

Kirmani, Waris. *Evaluation of Ghalib's Persian Poetry*. Aligarh: Department of Persian, 1972.

Kirmani, Waris. *Ghalib ki Farsi Shairi*. New Delhi: Ghalib Institute, 2008.

Kiyani, Mohsin. Ed. *Divan-e Ghalib Dihlavi*. Tehran, 1997.

Latif, Saiyyid Abdul Latif. *Ghalib: A Critical Appreciation of His Life and Poetry*. Hyderabad: Chandrakanta Press, 1929.

Lelyveld, David. 'Sir Saiyyid's Public Sphere: Urdu Print and Oratory in Nineteenth Century India', *Cracow Indological Studies*. Vol. II. Islam on the Indian Subcontinent. Krakow: Jagiellonian University Institute of Oriental Philology, 2009.

Mahfuz, Ahmad. Ed. *Kulliyat-e Mir* (revised and expanded edition of Zill-e Abbas Abbasi's 1983 edition). New Delhi: NCPUL, 2003.

Malik, Izhar ul-Haq. 'Ghalib Ke Khud-Navisht Halat' in *Ahval-e Ghalib*. Ed. Mukhtar ud-Din Ahmad. New Delhi: Anjuman Taraqqi Urdu, 1986, second edition.

Mas'ud, Naiyar. 'Qati-e Burhan' in *Naya Daur, Ghalib Nambar*. February–March 1969.

Mehr, Ghulam Rasul. Ed. *Divan-e Ghalib (mukammal)*. Lahore: Sheikh Ghulam Ali and Sons, 1967.

Mehr, Ghulam Rasul. *Ghalibiyat-e Mehr*. Ed. Muhammad Alam Mukhtar-e Haq. Lahore: Majlis Taraqqi Adab, 2015.

Mehr, Ghulam Rasul. Ed. *Khutut-e Ghalib*. Lahore: Sheikh Ghulam Ali and Sons, sixth reprint, 1987.

Mehr, Ghulam Rasul. *Nava-e Sarosh, Mukammal Divan-e Ghalib ma' Sharh*. Lahore: Sheikh Ghulam Ali and Sons, 1967.

Meisami, Julie. *Medieval Persian Court Poetry*. Princeton: Princeton University Press, 1987.

Muhajir, Mohammad Umar. Translation of *Panj Ahang*. Karachi: Idarah Yadgar-e Ghalib, 1969.

Naim, C.M. 'Ghalib's Delhi: A Shamelessly Revisionist Look at Two Popular Metaphors'. *Annual of Urdu Studies* (2006).

Naim, C.M. 'Sheikh Imam Bakhsh Sahba'i' in Pernau, Margrit. Ed. *The Delhi College: Traditional Elites, the Colonial State and Education before 1857*. New Delhi: Oxford University Press, 2006.

Najmul, Salam. 'Ghalib Avadh Akhbar Men' in *Sahifah, Ghalib Nambar*. Vol. 1. Lahore: April 1969.

Naqvi, Hanif. 'Ghalib Aur Ma'rikah-e Kalkattah' in *Ghalib*. Karachi: Idarah-e Yadgar-e Ghalib, 2000.

Naqvi, Hanif. *Ghalib Ahval-o Asar*. Lucknow: Nusrat Publishers, Nami Press, 1990.

Naqvi, Hanif. *Ghalib Aur Jahan-e Ghalib*. New Delhi: Ghalib Institute, 2012.

Naqvi, Saiyyid Qudrat. Ed. *Gul-e Ra'na*. Lahore, 1969.

Naqvi, Saiyyid Qudrat. *Gul-e Ra'na Ma' Ashtinamah*. Karachi, 1975.

Naqvi, Saiyyid Qudrat. *Nuskhah-e Sherani aur Dusre Maqalat*. Lahore: Maghribi Pakistan Urdu Academy, 1988.

Nurani, Saiyyid Amir Hasan. *Savaneh Munshi Naval Kishor*. Patna: Khuda Bakhsh Library, 1995.

Pernau, Margrit. Ed. *The Delhi College: Traditional Elites, the Colonial State and Education before 1857*. New Delhi: Oxford University Press, 2006.

Prigarina, Natalia. *Ghalib: A Creative Biography*. Translated from the Russian by Osama Faruqi. Karachi: Oxford University Press, 2000.

Pritchett, Frances W. 'A Long History of Urdu Literary Culture' (Part 2) in *Literary Cultures from History: Reconstructions from South Asia*. Ed. Sheldon Pollock. Berkeley: University of California Press, 2003.

Pritchett, Frances W., *A Desertful of Roses*, http://www.columbia.edu/itc/mealac/pritchett/00ghalib/about/about_ghazals.html.

Pritchett, Frances W., and Cornwall, Owen. *Ghalib: Selected Poems and Letters*. New York: Columbia University Press, 2017.

Qadri, Muhammad Ayyub. *Ghalib aur Asr-e Ghalib*. Karachi: Ghazanfar Academy, 1982.

Qaisar, Muhammad Yusuf. 'Nuskhah-e Hamidiyyah aur Faujdar Mohammad Khan' in *Furogh-e Urdu, Ghalib Nambar*. Ed. Nadim Sitapuri. Cited in Abdul Qavi Dasnavi. *Bhopal aur Ghalib*. Bhopal: Bhopal Press, 1969.

Quraishi, Fatima. *Sir Saiyyid Ahmad Khan's Asar-ul-Sanadid: The Construction of History in Nineteenth-Century India*. Master's thesis. Brown University, 2006.

Quraishi, Vahid. 'Ghalib aur Nuskhah-e Sherani' in the Ghalib number of *Nuqush*. Ed. Muhammad Tufail. Lahore: Idarah Furogh-e Urdu, April 1969.

Quraishi, Vahid. Ed. *Sahifah, Ghalib Nambar*. Vols. 1–4. Lahore: Majlis Tarqqi-e Adab, April–October, 1969.

Qureshi, Saleha Begum. *Banda Aur Ghalib*. Banda, 1994.

Rahbar, Daud. *Urdu Letters of Mirza Asadullah Khan Ghalib*. Albany: SUNY Press, 1987.

Rahman, Saiyyid Mu'inur. *Divan-e Ghalib Nuskhah-e Khwajah*. Lahore: Maktabah-e Aijaz, 1998.

Ram, Malik. *Ayar-e Ghalib*. Delhi: Ilmi Majlis, 1963.

Ram, Malik. *Fasanah-e Ghalib*. Delhi: First edition 1977; reprint Maktabah Jamia, 2011.

Ram, Malik. *Guftar-e Ghalib*. New Delhi: Maktabah Jamia, 1985.

Ram, Malik. *Gul-e Ra'na: Ghalib ke Urdu aur Farsi Kalam ka Avvalin Intikhab*. Delhi, 1970.

Ram, Malik. Ed. *Khutut-e Ghalib*. Lucknow: Qaumi Press, 1962.

Ram, Malik. 'Mulla Abdus Samad, Ustad-e Ghalib' in *Nava-e Adab*. Bombay, 1952.

Ram, Malik. *Talamizah-e Ghalib*. New Delhi: Maktab Jamia, 1984.

Ram, Malik. *Zikr-e Ghalib*. New Delhi: Maktabah Jamia, 1964.

Raza, Kalidas Gupta. *Divan-e Ghalib, Urdu Kamil Tarikhi Tartib Se*. Mumbai: Sakar Publications, 1988.

Raza, Kalidas Gupta. *Ghalib Durun-e Khanah*. Mumbai: Sakar Publishers Private Limited, 1989.

Rizvi 'Adib' Masud Hasan. *Mutafarriqat-e Ghalib*. Lucknow: Kitabistan 1969.

Rizvi, Salim Hamid. *Urdu Adab ki Taraqqi Mein Bhopal ka Hissah*. Bhopal: Alavi Press, 1965.

Rohilla, Partav. *Ahang-e Panjum*. Karachi: Idarah-e Yadgar-e Ghalib, 2004.

Rohilla, Partav. Ed. and translator *Kulliyat-e Maktubat-e Farsi Ghalib*. New Delhi: Ghalib Institute, 2010.

Russell, Ralph; Islam, Khurshidul. *Ghalib 1797–1869: Life and Letters*. New Delhi: Oxford University Press, 1994. First published by Cambridge University Press, 1969.

Sabzwari, Shaukat. 'Ghalib Aur Usul-e Lughat Nigari' in *Sahifah, Ghalib Nambar*. Vol. 3. Lahore: July 1969.

Sahar, Abu Muhammad. 'Divan-e Ghalib, Nuskhah-e Hamidiyyah, Chand Inkishafat' in *Hamari Zaban*. Aligarh: 22 July 1969.

Sahar, Abu Muhammad. 'Nuskhah-e Bhopal aur Daktar Abdul Latif' in *Hamari Zaban*. May–June, 1969.

Sandilvi, Vajahat Ali. *Baqiyat-e Ghalib*. Lucknow: Nasim Book Depot, 1969.

Sarvar, Mir Muhammad Khan. *Umdah-e Muntakhibah*. See Khwaja Ahmad Faruqi.

Sharma, Sunil. *Mughal Arcadia: Persian Literature in an Indian Court*. Cambridge: Harvard University Press, 2017.

Sherani, Hafiz Mahmud. *Divan-e Ghalib Nuskhah-e Sherani*. Lahore: Majlis Taraqqi-e Adab, 1969.

Shaukat, Navab Yar Muhammad Khan. *Divan-e Shaukat*. Kanpur, 1883.

Shaw, Graham. *Printing in Calcutta to 1800: A Description and Checklist of Printing in Late 18th Century Calcutta*. Bibliographical Society, 1981.

Sheftah, Navab Mustafa Khan. *Gulshan-e Bekhar*. Lucknow: first published by Dihli Akhbar, 1837, and Munshi Naval Kishor Press, 1874.

Siddiqui, Atiq. 'Ghalib Aur Un Ki Ham Asr Sahafat' in *Sahifah, Ghalib Nambar*. Vol. 1. Lahore, April 1969.

Siddiqi, Kamal Ahmad. *Bayaz-e Ghalib: Tahqiqi Ja'izah*. Srinagar, 1970.

Siddiqi, Kamal Ahmad. *Ghalib ki Shinakht*. New Delhi: Ghalib Institute, 1997.

Stark, Ulrike. *An Empire of Books: The Naval Kishore Press and the Diffusion of the Printed Word in Colonial India*. Ranikhet: Permanent Black, 2007.

Surur, Ale Ahmad. Ed. *Hamari Zaban, Urdu Weekly, Ghalib Centenary Special Editions*. New Delhi: Anjuman Taraqqi Urdu, Hind, January–July 1969.

Lakhnavi, Tabataba'i; Nazm, Ali Haider. *Sharh-e Divan-e Urdu-e Ghalib*. Hyderabad: Matba' Mufidul Islam, 1900.

Tavakoli-Targhi, Mohamad. *Refashioning Iran: Orientalism, Occidentalism and Historiography*. New York: Palgrave Macmillan, 2001.

Tirmizi, S.A.I. *Namah ha-e Farsi-e Ghalib*. New Delhi: Asia Publishing House & Ghalib Academy, 1969.

Tufail, Muhammad. Ed. *Nuqush Ghalib Nambar.* Two vols. Nos. 111 and 112. Lahore: Nuqush Press, 1969.

Vajid, Jamal Abdul. *Ghair Mutadavil Kalam-e Ghalib.* New Delhi: Ghalib Academy, 2016.

Vadud, Qazi Abdul. 'Divan-e Ghalib Ke Do Nuskhe' in *Ma'asir* (no. 12). New Delhi.

Vadud, Qazi Abdul. 'Ghalib Ka Ek Farzi Ustad: Abdus Samad' in *Aligarh Magazine, Ghalib Nambar*. 1949.

Vadud, Qazi Abdul. 'Hurmuzd Summa Abdus Samad' in *Ahval-e Ghalib*, Ed. Mukhtaruddin Ahmad. New Delhi: Anjuman Taraqqi-e Urdu, 1986, second edition.

Vadud, Qazi Abdul. *Ma'asir-e Ghalib: Ghalib Ki Kamyab Nazm Va Nasr Ka Majmu'ah*. Aligarh, 1949. Expanded edition: Patna, 1995.

Varma, Pavan Kumar. *Ghalib the Man, the Times.* New Delhi: Penguin Books India, 1989.

Zaman, Mukhtar; Farooqi, Zaman, and Ahmad, Musharraf. Eds. *Ghalib.* Kitabi Silsilah No. 19. Karachi: Idarah-e Yadgar-e Ghalib, 2000.

Acknowledgements

Procedural Points

Persian and Urdu, especially in the classical, literary register, have a common vocabulary but different, distinct ways of pronunciation in the current register. Generally speaking, there are distinct, standard scholarly modes of presenting Persian and Urdu vocabulary in English. In this book, I had to make a decision about employing Persian or Urdu standards. I decided to go with Urdu pronunciation and avoid diacritics. There is quite a bit of hybridization between Urdu, Persian and Arabic, and Ghalib's Urdu is heavily Persianized. Moving back and forth between the two similar languages, and rendering them in English, was confusing. For example, should the *izafat* be presented with an 'i' or an 'e'? This question was particularly delicate when dealing with Persian book titles—*Burhan-e Qate*, *Borhan-e Qate*, or *Burhan-e Qati*; *Kulliyat-e Ghalib* or *Kulliyat-e Ghalib Farsi*, and so forth. Often, Urdu books had Arabo-Persian titles—*Makatib-e Ghalib*, *Khutut-e Ghalib* and *Maktubat-e Ghalib*, for instance.

Having decided against diacritics, I have tried my best to be consistent with spellings and to be as close to the Urdu pronunciation as possible. I have romanized Urdu verses to make them accessible to all readers and also included the original wherever I thought it was necessary. Also, I have provided working translations of all poetry and prose.

In the many years that it took to complete this project, my debt to scholars and friends who helped me kept growing, and kept me going too. From Charlottesville to Allahabad, with Delhi, Rampur, Karachi and Lahore in between, I searched libraries, gave talks, presented papers and had many conversations with my learned audience. I felt humbled, excited and energized. I plodded on even though the end eluded me for a long time.

In Allahabad and Charlottesville, I enjoyed vociferous disagreements with my father, Shamsur Rahman Faruqi, who grilled me about my assumptions and conclusions with regard to Ghalib's fascination with *Dasatir*, and also the role print played in Ghalib's popularity. He helped me translate ambiguous prose passages in Ghalib's dibachahs.

I first read Ghalib with my father. I was barely ten years old when he asked me to memorize a ghazal from Ghalib's 'mustarad kalam'. The mustarad stayed tucked away in a corner of my mind, until I decided to write about it many decades later for a conference in honour of Fran Pritchett's retirement.

I owe a debt of gratitude to Fran Pritchett, for reading each chapter carefully and offering scholarly, editorial insights. She steered me towards writing a literary history of Ghalib.

Sunil Sharma very kindly read a couple of chapters and made invaluable suggestions. Prashant Keshavmurthy shared his PhD dissertation. Satyanarayana Hegde's multilingual expertise, and his acute perception of hidden meaning in verses, was an invaluable resource.

At the University of Toronto, I am grateful to Alexandra Gillespie, Zaheer Baber, Ajay Rao, Shafique Virani and a host of bright-eyed graduate students. I appreciate my interactions with all of them. It was delightful to finally meet Mohamad Tavakoli-Targhi. Also, I want to acknowledge Irfan Sattar for introducing me to Toronto's incredibly rich literary circle.

It made sense for me to begin my library rounds from Rampur, following the enlightening path of a great Ghalibian, Maulana Imtiaz Ali Khan Arshi. Professor Azizuddin, the library's director, facilitated my stay at the Rampur Raza Library. Dr Abusad Islahi was indefatigable in guiding me and providing access to many rare manuscripts.

At the Ghalib Institute, New Delhi, Dr Raza Haider was extremely helpful in showing me an array of Ghalib's divans, including rare manuscript divans. I am grateful for getting permission to take a photograph of the Divan of 1816 and some other rare gems.

At Jamia Millia Islamia's Zakir Husain Library, an incredibly helpful staff made research so much easier. At the Department of Urdu, Ahmad Mahfuz readily loaned me books from his personal collection. I also met several promising graduate students from the department. Khwaja Amn Junaid prepared a concordance of Ghalib's important divans. He is an extremely fast worker whose help I consider to be invaluable.

Dr Ather Farouqui, general secretary of the Anjuman Taraqqi Urdu, facilitated my use of the Anjuman's library.

I would also like to thank Shahab Sattar for reaching out with the news that the 1821 divan, the *Nuskhah-e Hamidiyyah*, was available, and for sharing the original manuscript with me.

At Aligarh University's Maulana Azad Library, Shaista Bedar helped me locate rare editions of Ghalib's divan and helped with getting the copies made. I am also grateful to my colleagues in the Department of English for inviting me to speak on Ghalib. I'd also like to express gratitude to professors Vibha Sharma and Asim Siddiqui for their enduring friendship. Thanks are also due to Zoya Zaidi for sharing her beautiful calligraphy of Ghalib's verses.

In 2016, I was a fellow at the Centre for the Study of Developing Societies (CSDS), New Delhi. The fellowship made it possible for me to spend nearly a year in Delhi. I am obliged to the director of the centre, Professor Sanjay Kumar, as well as academic fellows Aditya Nigam, Prathma Bannerji, Ananya Vajpeyi, Swati Parasher and Ravikant.

In Lahore, I am grateful to Yasmeen Hameed for inviting me to deliver a lecture on Ghalib at the Gurmani Centre of the Lahore University of Management Sciences (LUMS). Many thanks to Kamran Asdar Ali also for making this possible. It was an honour to have Intizar Husain, Masud Ashar, Tahseen Firaqi and other learned people in the audience. I am deeply grateful to Rifaqat Ali Shahid and Mahmoodul Hasan for their generosity and many kindnesses. Rifaqat Ali gave me rare editions of books and journals from his personal collection to bring back to Charlottesville. Mahmood, meanwhile, left no stone unturned to find rare articles on Ghalib.

In Karachi, I am indebted to my dear friend Asif Farrukhi and his wife, Seemi, for the hospitality and scintillating conversation. Azra Abbas, Fatema Hasan and Tanveer Anjum also made my stay memorable.

In my department at the University of Virginia, Farzaneh Milani, Geeta Patel and Nizar Hermes read my work and offered suggestions. I am grateful to Jessica Feldman, too, for her support and advice throughout the writing of this book. I also benefited from reading Ghalib with Mahshad Mohit. We spent one summer poring over Ghalib's masnavis and struggled with the unfamiliar Persian constructions that speckle Ghalib's prose. Pardis Minuchehr also read Ghalib with me. Philip McEldowney enabled access to recondite material. Brian Owensby at the Center for Global Inquiry and Innovation funded my translation proposal. I greatly enjoyed translating Ghalib's elaborate dibachah to his Persian divan in collaboration with Jane Mikkelson. Our weekly sessions, lodged in a reading alcove in a café, munching on scones, while the delicious aroma of baking added yet another flavour to Ghalib's delectable prose, were of great help.

Bilal Hashmi brought much appreciated culinary expertise and literary advice. We held many mehfils at his apartment reciting ghazals and doing ad-lib translating.

I want to thank my students Muhammad Qasim Chattha and Meghan Hartman for reading Ghalib's Urdu letters with me. A thank you to Elliot Carter, too, for his beautiful translations.

I enjoyed the animated discussions with Gregory Maxwell Bruce over the phone. He drew my attention to Hali's exegesis of Ghalib's Persian poetry. We puzzled over the Dasatir and Ghalib's fascination with 'pure' Persian.

My collaboration with ghazal singer Pooja Goswami Pavan gave a boost to my efforts in bringing Ghalib's mustarad kalam to a wider audience. I want to acknowledge Kedar Naphade and Ajit Akolkar for their love of Ghalib and for being such good listeners.

My team of editors at Penguin Random House India helped me at every turn. Thank you Premanka Goswami for your steady support, Gunjan Ahlawat for designing the book cover and Aslesha Kadian for the copy-editing.

I am deeply appreciative of my sister Baran's companionship in Delhi. The rest of the Farooqi clan, particularly my cousin Mahmood Farooqui, cheered me on. And to Rich, for taking a keen interest in the project through the years, for our discussions on Ghalib fortified with tea, for optimism and tireless support in all my endeavours, a mere thank you is not enough.

Notes

Introduction

1. *Kulliyat-e Ghalib Farsi*, ed. Saiyyid Murtuza Husain Fazil Lakhnavi, vol. III, Lahore (Majlis-e Taraqqi Adab, 1967, first edition), p.417.
   گر ذوق سخن بدہر آئیں بودی
   دیوان مرا شہرت پرویں بودی
   غالب اگر ایں فن سخن دیں بودی
   آن دین را یزدی کتاب ایں بودی
2. *Mahasin-e Kalam-e Ghalib*, Abdur Rahman Bijnori, Karachi (Fakhri Printing Press, 1969), p. 3: '*Hindustan ki ilhami kitabein do hain. Muqaddas Veda aur Divan-e Ghalib.*'
3. *Kulliyat-e Ghalib Farsi*, vol. 1, ed. Murtuza Husain Fazil Lakhnawi, qita no. 7, p. 161. The translation here is free rather than literal. Henceforth, this volume will be referred to as *Kulliyat-e Farsi*.
4. There is some controversy about when Hali met Ghalib; whether it was before 1857 or after. Hali first arrived in Delhi in 1854 and enrolled in the famous madrasah of Husain Bakhsh, where he received a solid grounding in Persian and Arabic. He lived in Delhi again during 1861–62. In the intervening years, he was the tutor to Navab Mustafa Khan Sheftah's children in Bulandshahr and companion to the Navab. Sheftah (1801–69) wrote poetry in Urdu and Persian, and was the author of the highly regarded tazkirah *Gulshan-e-Bekhar*. At first, he was a pupil of Momin Khan Momin, but after Momin's death he took advice from Ghalib. He was very close to Ghalib and received corrections on his Persian verse from Ghalib. Hali sent his own verses, along with Navab Sheftah's, to Ghalib

for correction. He claims to have benefited a lot from Sheftah's advice on his verses. Both Ghalib and Sheftah died in 1869. Hali moved to Lahore in 1870 and was employed at the Government Book Depot as a translator.

5. In addition to Ghalib's biography, Hali also wrote *Hayat-e Sa'di* (Sa'di's Life), which was first published in 1886, and *Hayat-e Javed* (Eternal Life), a biography of Saiyyid Ahmad Khan, which was first published in 1901 by Nami Press, Kanpur. Hali's *Divan*, along with the monumental Foreword, *Muqaddamah-e She'r-o Sha'iri* (Introduction to Poetry and Poetics), was first published in 1893.
6. Altaf Husain Hali, *Yadgar-e Ghalib*, ed. Khalilur Rahman Daudi, Lahore (Majlis-e Taraqqi-e Adab, 1963), Dibachah, p. 3.
7. Ibid. p. 278.
8. I fear Hali might be exaggerating the truth here, but I respect him for asking why Ghalib valued Persian so much.
9. Altaf Husain Hali, *Yadgar-e-Ghalib*, p. 6. Hali speaks of Ghalib as one would speak of a poet of a distant past. Ghalib was barely thirty years dead when Hali wrote the book.
10. Naziri Nishapuri (1560–1612/14).

    Zuhuri Torsizi (1537/38–1616) migrated to India in 1580 and settled in the Deccan in the service of the Nizamshahis of Ahmadnagar. Zuhuri was a contemporary of Mughal poet Faizi. This evaluative criticism is discussed in Chapter 8.
11. Altaf Husain Hali, *Yadgar-e-Ghalib*, p. 276.
12. بیاورید گر ایں جا بود زبان دانے
    غریب شہر سخن ہاۓ گفتنی دارد

    Hali misunderstands the above verse, which is a direct expression of the poetic theory of *tazah-goi* (new or fresh style). Bedil's poetry abounds with this theme, as does Urfi's, Faizi's and other poets of this style.
13. Details of this incident are outlined in Chapter 3. The episode sheds light on Ghalib's personal relationship with Persian. His admiration for Mirza Bedil from this point onwards was splintered, or perhaps not so obvious. Ghalib changed the title of the masnavi to *Bad-e Mukhalif* (Adverse Winds), which is another indication of his fraught relationship with Indian Persian writers.
14. *Dastanbuy* is an archaic Persian word alluding to the composition of perfumes to be held in the hand like a flower. It is often translated as 'bouquet'. Ghalib chose this title to emphasize his knowledge of early Persian.
15. Ghalib wrote in *Burhan-e-Qati*, 'As my link with the Persian language had its origin in eternity and I had a teacher who was without exaggeration a present-day Tahmasp and a Buzurjmihr of our times, it so happened that

the essence of this language was implanted in my heart and became the repose of my soul.'

16. I am grateful to Sunil Sharma for discussing this idea with me.
17. There is a marked tension between the literary Urdu used in the regions, with Delhi as the ultimate *markaz* (centre) representative of the *zaban-e Urdu-e Mu'alla* (language of the exalted court). My point here, though, is to underscore the tension between contrived origins of Urdu and its entangled literary history.
18. For example, writers of Gujri and Dakani (practised in Gujarat and the Deccan in the fifteenth century) nestled in regional environments freely mixed Perso-Arabic derived vocabulary with regional lexis. It is debatable whether these early regional registers should be called Urdu, and the composition in these registers Rekhtah.
19. The earliest forms of Rekhtah appear to be macaronic, often alternating or mixing lines of Persian with Hindvi, or beginning a line in one language register and ending in another.
20. I am grateful to Purnima Dhavan for sharing with me her unpublished paper: 'A Prehistory of Rekhtah: View from Mughal Provincial Networks'. Dhavan's paper examines the poetry of Shah Murad (d.1702/03 ce) of Chakwal in northern Punjab. Shah Murad wrote poetry in Persian, Punjabi and also Rekhtah. Dhavan remarks that Shah Murad did not use the more common and capacious term Hindvi, preferring to identify his language as Rekhtah.

    Rekhtah was also a mode of singing. Maybe Shah Murad described his poem as Rekhtah in a musical, and not linguistic, sense.
21. In my article, 'Power, Culture and Language of Poetry: The Transition from Vali to Ghalib', I examine Ghalib's preference for excessive Persianism. He chose to emulate Mirza Bedil instead of looking up to Mir Taqi Mir. See: *Cracow Indological Studies*, vol. II, 'Islam on the Indian Subcontinent', Krakow (2009), pp. 14–28.
22. Ghalib's first letter written in Urdu is dated 1848. Generally speaking, after 1850, when he was formally invited to join the Mughal court as a salaried employee, Ghalib returned to writing more and more in Urdu.
23. Ghalib had far more pupils than any other poet. One of the measures of a poet's stature was the number of pupils.
24. *Ud-e Hindi*, ed. Murtuza Husain Fazil Lakhnavi, Lahore (Majlis Taraqqi-e Adab, 1967), p. 342, from a letter to Khwaja Ghulam Ghaus Bekhabar, dated 1865. Ghalib was not satisfied with Munshi Mumtaz Ali Khan's editorial work and got the manuscript sent to Bekhabar.
25. Ibid. p. 431, from a letter to Khwaja Ghulam Ghaus Bekhabar, dated 23 July 1866. In the meantime, a second collection, *Urdu-e Mu'alla*, was

under way. Ghalib wasn't pleased by this development. He was appalled by the title and wrote to Bekhabar: 'Pardon me, but this title, *Urdu-e Mu'alla* is extremely awkward (*bhonda*) . . . Sir, you could have named it *Qand-e Hindi* (Sweets of Hind) or perhaps *Qand-e Mukarrar* (Sweets Again). These two names are so sweet. When the printing is complete and the price has been fixed, let me know, I would want a few copies myself.'

26. Ali Haider Nazm Tabataba'i Lakhnavi's (1852–1933) *Sharh-e Divan-e Urdu-e Ghalib* was published from Hyderabad by the Matba' Mufidul Islam in 1900 (not dated). It became the most influential commentary for reading Ghalib's poetry. Many others followed suit; some important early ones are Bekhud Mohani (written largely in reply to Tabataba'i but published much later (1970), Abdul Bari Asi and Ghulam Rasul Mehr. Saiyyid Vahid-ud-din Bekhud Dihlavi's (1863–1955) commentary, *Sharh-eDivan-e Ghalib*, Lucknow (Nizami Press), was composed in 1923.

    Abdul Bari Asi (1893–1946), *Mukammal Sharh-e Divan-e Ghalib* (Complete Commentary on Divan-e Ghalib), Lucknow (Saqi Book Depot, 1931). Ghulam Rasul Mehr (1895–1971), *Nava-e Sarosh, Mukammal Divan-e Ghalib ma' Sharh* (The Voice of an Angel, Complete Divan of Ghalib with Commentary), Lahore (Sheikh Ghulam Ali and Sons, 1967).

    The most recent commentary is in English: *A Desertful of Roses*, Frances W. Pritchett, http://www.columbia.edu/itc/mealac/pritchett/00ghalib/about/about_ghazals.html.

27. An extensive *Ghalib Bibliography*, produced by Muhammad Ansarullah, was published by the Ghalib Institute, New Delhi, in 1998. It runs into more than 400 pages.

28. Dasatir/Dasatiri is a language whose grammar is based on pre-Islamic Persian. It is filled with invented vocabulary adapted from Persian. I will discuss this at length in Chapter 8.

29. Maulana Imtiaz Ali Arshi, the editor of the almost-encyclopaedic, definitive *Divan-e Ghalib*, one of the most respected among Ghalib scholars, gave currency to the notion that Ghalib rejected the verses which had tasteless flights of imagination, or were far-fetched with inelegant metaphors and similes or unfamiliar Persian idioms and phrases.

30. It is possible that Ghalib is speaking metaphorically of the two languages he has slain.

31. Malik Ram, *Ghalib ke Urdu aur Farsi Kalam ka Avvalin Intikhab*, Delhi (1970), p. 46; Naqvi, *Gul-e Ra'na Ma' Ashtinamah*, Karachi (1975), pp. 65–66. This is a particularly visceral description of what it means to write in two languages. The passage is in emotionally charged metaphoric register—

what does Ghalib mean by slaying the two languages and the vengeance of those languages? He wrote this to balance his boastful claim: 'Observe the reach of my capabilities that I have taken Hindi (Urdu) from Delhi to Isfahan, and applaud the strength of the thread of my thought, that I have brought Persian from Shiraz to Hindustan.'

32. Shamsur Rahman Faruqi, *Tafhim-e Ghalib*, New Delhi (Ghalib Institute, 1989, 2006, 2014).

    Frances W. Pritchett's *A Desertful of Roses* presents a synthesis of the best extant commentaries with additions of her own.

33. Although Kalidas Gupta Raza's work is very valuable, it is difficult to search for ghazals unless one knows which period they belong to.
34. There are close to fifty commentaries of Ghalib's current divan. Jain and Kantoori are the only two complete commentaries of the unselected verses. An important partial commentary is Maulana Abdul Bari Asi's *Sharah-e kalam-e Ghalib* (Lucknow, 1931). It is based on 1063 verses.
35. Kantoori had undertaken this monumental work in 1934 (first he tackled the rejected verses via the Nuskhah-e Hamidiyyah) and was very close to completion when he died in 1944 and the work could not be published. Fortunately, his notebooks were preserved. His *Sharh-e Divan-e Ghalib*, edited by Ashraf Rafi, is a valuable addition to the sparse scholarly work in this field.
36. See Chapter 8 for details.
37. José Ortega y Gasset, *Man and People*, translated by Willard R. Trask, New York (W.W. Norton & Company, Inc.), p. 246.
38. The Urdu letters demand a book-length study of Ghalib's prose and the genre itself. The Persian letters are now available in Urdu translation.

Chapter 1: The Kite Rises into the Air

1. *Ek din dil misl-e patang-e kaghazi*
   Le keh dil sar rishtah-e azadagi
   Khud ba khud kuchch ham se kaniyane laga
   Is qadar bigra ke sar khane laga

   Ghalib's earliest-known composition was first published in the journal *Urdu*, Aurangabad (July 1931). Cited from Kalidas Gupta Raza's *Divan-e Ghalib Kamil* (1988), p. 28.
2. Ghalib, *Dastanbuy*, translated and edited by Khwaja Ahmad Faruqi, New York (Asia Publishing House, 1970), p. 65.
3. Altaf Husain Hali, *Yadgar-e Ghalib*, ed. Khalilur Rahman Daudi, Lahore (Majlis-e Taraqqi-e Adab, 1963), p. 11. I have used this edition throughout because it provides valuable notes and correctives to Hali, who sometimes

got his dates mixed up. I am grateful to Rifaqat Ali Shahid for loaning me this precious edition.

The best and most detailed biography of Ghalib is Malik Ram's *Zikr-e Ghalib*, New Delhi (Maktabah Jamia, 1964). The reference to Ghalib's date of birth in Malik Ram's book is from a letter of Ghalib's to Navab Alauddin Ahmad Khan Alai. See: Malik Ram, note 1, p. 25.

4. Altaf Husain Hali (1837–1914) belonged to a highly respected family of Panipat, a town north of Delhi. An early, forced, unhappy marriage compelled him to leave town and literally walk to Delhi. Arriving penniless in Delhi in 1845, he enrolled in Husain Bakhsh's madrasah and studied Arabic language and literature. He often went to visit Ghalib and sought his guidance in improving his own poetry, as well as in understanding the complex verses of Urdu and Persian masters. Hali eventually became the head Arabic teacher in Delhi's Anglo-Arabic College. He wrote a long essay (*muqaddamah*) highlighting his views on poetry as an introduction to his divan. This book-length introduction became the first and most influential work of Urdu literary criticism. It was published in 1893 as *Muqaddamah-e Sher-o Shairi*. His *Yadgar-e Ghalib* (1897) established Ghalib's greatness in Urdu and Persian, and painted him as a witty, passionate poet. Hali's biography of Saiyyid Ahmad Khan, *Hayat-e Javed* (1901), is a mammoth account of his friend and mentor. Read in conjunction with *Yadgar-e Ghalib*, it shows the interrelationships between these two great minds and the age in which they lived.
5. Navab Mirza Ilahi Bakhsh Khan was the younger brother of the influential Fakhr ud-Daulah Dilavar ul-Mulk Navab Ahmad Bakhsh Khan of Loharu. Ghalib's paternal uncle, Mirza Nasrullah Beg Khan, who was his guardian after his father's death, was married to Navab Ahmad Bakhsh Khan's sister. Ghalib's relationship with the Loharu family was strengthened with his marriage to his uncle's niece. For details about Ghalib's complex kinship with his uncle's, and also his wife's, family, see: Kalidas Gupta Raza's *Ghalib Durun-e Khanah*, Mumbai (Sakar Publishers Private Limited, 1989).
6. The reference to Ghalib's age at the time of marriage is from Ghalib's letter. Altaf Husain Hali, *Yadgar-e Ghalib*, p. 16.
7. Ibid. p. 23. Khalilur Rahman Daudi notes that Hali is incorrect. Ghalib did have a house, which he sold off. He wrote to Anvarudaulah Sa'duddin Shafaq: 'It's been three years since I sold my house; now I roam from place to place and don't have a permanent residence. Wherever I go, I stay for two years or less.' Cited from *Kulliyat-e Nasr*, second edition, Naval Kishor Press, p. 235.
8. In a qasidah in honour of the Maharaja of Alwar, Ghalib mentions this:

Dar khak-e rajgarh pidaram ra buvad mazar
[My father is buried in the earth of Rajgarh]

9. Mirza Nasrullah Beg Khan, the *subahdar* (governor of a province) of Agra, had sided with the British East India Company in the Anglo-Maratha conflict of 1802–03, as the commander of a contingent of 400 auxiliary cavalry troops. He was granted a life *jagir* (land grant) with an annual income of Rs 1 lakh by Lord Lake for his services. After the death of Nasrullah Beg, the British resumed his jagir, but made arrangements for his dependents through Navab Ahmad Bakhsh Khan. The latter had also served with Lord Lake during the same conflict and been awarded a permanent jagir in the district of Firozpur-Jhirka. As the agent of the Maharaja of Alwar, Navab Ahmad Bakhsh Khan had received the pargana (cluster of villages) of Loharu as well. The final agreement was spelled out in a letter dated 7 June 1806. Ghalib and his brother shared Rs 1500 per annum. Ghalib's personal share amounted to Rs 62 and 8 annas every month.
10. Altaf Husain Hali, *Yadgar-e Ghalib*, p. 18. It is unclear if Abdus Samad spent two years with Ghalib in Agra, or accompanied him when he moved to Delhi. Hali is vague about this.
11. Maulana Imtiaz Ali Khan Arshi and Qazi Abdul Vadud subscribe to the theory that Abdus Samad was fictional. See Qazi Abdul Vadud's essay, 'Ghalib Ka Ek Farzi Ustad: Abdus Samad', in *Aligarh Magazine, Ghalib Nambar* ed. Bashir Badr, Aligarh (1969), and 'Hurmuzd Summa Abdus Samad', in *Ahval-e Ghalib*, ed. Mukhtaruddin Ahmad, New Delhi (Anjuman Taraqqi Urdu, 1986 [second edition]), pp. 220–48.

    Qazi Abdul Vadud, in his erudite essay, makes strong arguments based on a close reading of Ghalib's remarks and stance in *Qati-e Burhan*. Qazi Sahib raises several important questions: Why did Ghalib not talk about Mulla Abdus Samad until the *Qati-e Burhan* controversy, during which he decided to prove his superiority over all Indian Persian writers? Why had no one close to Ghalib ever met Abdus Samad? Why did Ghalib not speak of Abdus Samad in Calcutta, when he was involved in bitter controversy over Persian usages? Why did the contemporary *tazkirah* (anthology) writers Zaka and Sarvar not mention him in their tazkirahs? Qazi Sahib is of the opinion that Ghalib did not know much about early Iranian traditions or language. He made up an ustad, a native of Iran, to corroborate his own ideas about Persian language usage and to humiliate Indian Persian writers.
12. Navab Alauddin Ahmad Khan Alai was Ghalib's wife's nephew and a very dear pupil of Ghalib's.
13. Navab Mustafa Khan Sheftah (1806–69) was born in Delhi. He was a *shagird* (pupil) of the Urdu poet Momin. After Momin's death, he received

islah (correction) from Ghalib. Sheftah composed the tazkirah *Gulshan-e Bekhar*, which was begun in 1832 and completed in 1835. Maulvi Baqar's Dihli Akhbar press published it in 1837. The tazkirah's reprinted editions in 1843 and 1847 attest to its popularity.

Sheftah's tazkirah is quite different from earlier ones. His entries are detailed, thoughtful and critically informed. He was obviously partial towards Momin, his ustad. His dismissive treatment of Nazir Akbaradi provoked his contemporary Mir Qutbuddin Batin to compose *Gulshan-e Bekhizan.* Batin and other contemporaries pointed dismissively to Sheftah's meagre output as a poet.

Sheftah's entry on Ghalib mentions the pruning that Ghalib practised on his poetry. Since the tazkirah was published before Ghalib's divan, it means that Sheftah and Ghalib's other friends were well aware of Ghalib's editorial measures.

Gulshan-e Bekhar includes six female poets among its entries. Many Hindu and Christian poets were given space, too. Uniquely, it also features an impressive lineup of *taqriz* (critical introduction) composed by eminent poets such as Momin, Ghalib and Azurdah.

Here is an excerpt from Sheftah's entry on Ghalib. The translation from Urdu is mine.

His *takhallus* is Ghalib and his auspicious name is Asadullah Khan. He is famously known as Mirza Naushah. He belongs to a noble family of old wealthy landlords. First, he lived in the capital city Akbarabad (Agra). Now he lives in the new capital Shahjahanabad (Delhi) which, owing to his residence, has put Isfahan and Shiraz to shame. He is the high-flying parrot in the garden of meaning creation. He is the sweet-voiced nightingale of the garden of expression. Compared to the loftiness of his metaphors, the towering sky is like the lowest ground. If he takes the shallowest dip in the river of his thought, he brings up a treasure trove. The eagle of his thought always soars to prey on the *anqa*. The steed of his poetic temperament gallops to cross the expanse of the sky. If someone needs the best goods, they can be had only from his shop. A long time ago he stepped into the arena of poetry. In the beginning, because of his complexity-seeking temperament, he wrote in the style of Mirza Bedil; a thousand praises, because he did that so well. Later he moved away from it and his temperament showed a new style. He set about to edit his divan and completed that as well. In the process, he discarded a number of verses. He was caught in the fervour of editing, and the number of verses was greatly reduced. A long time has passed since he composed in Rekhtah.

See: *Gulshan-e Bekhar*, translated into Urdu by Hamidah Khatun, New Delhi (NCPUL, 1998).

14. See Altaf Husain Hali, *Yadgar-e Ghalib*, p. 20. 'Navab Mustafa Khan used to say that in one of his letters the Mulla had sent from another country, he had written: "Dear friend, how are you? I think of you often."' Hali concludes this to be enough to prove that Abdus Samad did exist in Ghalib's life. Malik Ram firmly believes that Mulla Abdus Samad was a real person who trained Ghalib in Persian. See his essay: 'Mulla Abdus Samad, Ustad-e Ghalib', in *Nava-e Adab*, Bombay (1952). According to Malik Ram, Mulla Abdus Samad was not an ustad who offered correction or islah of Ghalib's poetry. He helped Ghalib understand the nuances of Persian as a language.
15. Altaf Husain Hali, *Yadgar-e Ghalib*, pp. 18–19. Hali quotes Ghalib's Persian verse, including a Persian rubai, to support this claim that Ghalib had no formal ustad.
16. Ibid. pp. 19–20. The proverb quoted by Hali is as follows: اگر حاصل شود خوانده و نا خوانده برابر است و اگر حاصل نشود ہم خوانده و نخوانده برابر است۔

    This can be loosely translated as: 'If you have (the disposition), learning or unlearning is the same; if you don't have it, learning and unlearning is the same too.'
17. Ibid. p. 20. The reference to a letter from Abdus Samad would be conclusive if corroborated by Sheftah. Hali writes: 'Navab Mustafa Khan used to say that in a letter that Mulla Abdus Samad had sent to Mirza Ghalib from another country, the following was inscribed: "Dear friend, how are you?"' [اے عزیز چہ کسی؟ کہ بایں ہمہ آزادی ہا گاہ گاہ بخاطر می گزری]
18. Muhammad Husain Azad (1830–1910) was the son of Maulvi Muhammad Baqir (c.1810–57) who came from a learned family of Persian émigrés. Maulvi Muhammad Baqir launched the first Urdu newspaper in north India, *Dihli Urdu Akhbar*, in 1837. Muhammad Husain Azad was educated at Delhi College. He graduated in 1854 and started to assist his father. Maulvi Muhammad Baqir was executed by the British in the aftermath of the Revolt of 1857. Azad managed to flee to Lahore, where he initially worked as a postal clerk. He joined the Department of Public Instruction in 1862 and began a career writing school textbooks. In 1869, he was appointed as an Arabic lecturer at Government College, Lahore. He played an active role in the Anjuman-e Punjab, which was founded by Dr Leitner, the principal of Government College. Azad wrote many books; his masterpiece is *Ab-e Hayat* (Water of Life), which was published in 1880. For a critical edition and translation of *Ab-e Hayat*, see Frances W. Pritchett and Shamsur Rahman Faruqi, *Ab-e Hayat: Shaping the Canon of Urdu Poetry*, New Delhi (Oxford University Press, 2001).
19. Cited from, *Kulliyat-e Ghalib Farsi*, vol. 1 ed. Saiyyid Murtaza Hussain Fazil Lakhnavi, Lahore (Majlis Taraqqi-e Adab, 1967), p. 7.

20. In the Naval Kishor edition of 1863, Ghalib updated the sentence referring to his age. He mentioned that he was in his sixty-seventh year.
21. It is possible Ghalib's friend and contemporary poet Momin Khan Momin helped him prepare a horoscope. Momin was known for his deep interest in astrology.
22. Maulana Arshi, *Mah-e Nau*, Karachi, January–February 1969, pp. 43–47.
23. Ibid. p. 45.
24. Malik Ram, ed., *Ayar-e Ghalib*, Delhi (Ilmi Majlis, 1963), pp. 125–69.
25. Ghalib, *Kulliyat-e Farsi*, Lucknow (Naval Kishor Press, 1863):
Ghalib chu na saji-e farjam-e nasib
Ham bim-e 'adu daram o ham zauq-e habib
Tarikh-e viladat-e man az 'alam-e quds
Ham shorish-e shauq amad o ham lafz-e gharib
26. Hanif Qureshi, 'Ghalib ka Sal-e Viladat', *Ghalib: Ahval-o Asar*, Lucknow (Nusrat Publications, 1990), pp. 17–57. Kamal Ahmad Siddiqi, 'Mirza ka Sin-e Viladat', *Ghalib ki Shinakht*, New Delhi (Ghalib Institute, 1997), pp. 51–71.
27. Apparently, the earliest poem written by Ghalib, is a charming qita (*tarkib band*), on kite-flying:
Ek din dil misl-e patang-e kaghazi
Le keh dil sar rishtah-e azadagi
The poem was published for the first time in 1931, in the journal *Urdu*. For a detailed discussion on the circumstances of its provenance, see: Kalidas Gupta Raza, 'Ghalib Ka Avvalin Urdu Kalam', *Divan-e Ghalib Kamil, Tarikhi Tartib Se*, Mumbai (Sakar Press, 1988).
28. Ghalib's maternal grandfather died in 1827.
29. Siddiqi, *Ghalib ki Shinakht*, p. 57.
30. Malik Ram, *Fasanah-e Ghalib*, p. 30. See also: Kalidas Gupta Raza, *Ghalib Durun-e Khanah*, Mumbai (Sarkar Publishers, 1989), pp. 31–32. Nisar Ahmad Faruqi in *Talash-e Ghalib* cites this letter as the earliest evidence of Ghalib's handwriting. According to Khwaja Ahmad Faruqi, the letter was written in 1824.
31. *Umdah-e Muntakhibah*, generally known as *Tazkirah-e Sarvar*, of Mir Muhammad Khan Sarvar (d.1834), ed. Khwaja Ahmad Faruqi, Delhi University (1961). A debatable question is: When did Sarvar finish this tazkirah? Some 996 poets are represented in it. Ghalib is entered under Asad and represented by forty-five verses. Some of these verses are not included in the 1816 manuscript divan, which definitely shows that the tazkirah presents Ghalib's compositions before 1816. Sarvar's selection is a very interesting mix of Ghalib's 'mature' and somewhat 'immature' poetry. For example, four verses from the magnificent ghazal '*Ishrat-e*

qatrah hai darya men fana ho jana/dard ka had se guzarna hai dava ho jana' are presented. In the ghazal '*Phir kuchh is dil ko be-qarari hai*', the last verse has Ghalib as the pen name: '*Be-khudi be-sabab nahin Ghalib/Kuchh to hai jis ki pardah dari hai*'. Khwaja Ahmad Faruqi does not seem to have noticed this aberration. I have not seen the original manuscript of *Tazkirah-e Sarvar*; my notes are from Faruqi's edition of 1961 and his article in *Ganjinah-e Ghalib*, February 1969.

32. Khwaja Ahmad Faruqi, 'Ghalib Ka Qayam-e Agra Aur *Tazkirah-e Sarvar*' (Ghalib's Residence in Agra and *Tazkirah-e Sarvar*), in *Ganjinah-e Ghalib*, New Delhi (Publications Division, Patiala House, 1969), pp. 542–67. This article is rich with references from Ghalib's letters and shows how difficult it is to determine exactly when Ghalib moved to Delhi.
33. Ibid. p. 61: 'According to Sarvar's narrative, and taking into account other evidences in the tazkirah, *Umdah-e Muntakhibah*, I have reached the conclusion that the tazkirah was completed in 1809. None of Ghalib's letters provide evidence that he might have left Agra before 1811. In fact, there are more evidences that he settled in Delhi after 1813–14.'
34. Maulvi Karimuddin, *Tabaqat-e Shuara-e Hind*, ed. Mahmud Ilahi, Lucknow (Uttar Pradesh Urdu Academy, 1983 [1947]), p. 277.
35. Ghalib, *Urdu-e Mu'alla*, vol. 1 and 2, Lahore (Matba Karimi, 1926), p. 403.
36. Ibid. p. 419.
37. I am a scion, O Saqi, of Pashang and Afrasiyab.
    So you know that Jamshed's kingdom is my family estate.
    Come give me wine, which is part of my royal heritage:
    And as for Heaven, let that legacy of Adam wait.
    In the following quatrain, he names Afrasiyab's grandfather, Zadsham, as his progenitor:
    O Ghalib, I am the pearl of Zadsham's line,
    Therefore, my mind/breath is as keen as a sword.
    No more a warrior, I am now a bard;
    My forebear's broken arrow is my pen.
    Kulliyat-e Maktubat-e Farsi Ghalib (Ghalib's Persian Letters), edited and translated from Persian to Urdu by Partav Rohilla, New Delhi (Ghalib Institute, 2010), letter to Maulvi Sirajuddin, letter no. 30, p. 82.
38. Ibid. p. 79.
39. *Dasatir*, the most important tract of the Azar Kayvani sect, is almost certainly the work of its founder, Azar Kayvan. The book, written in an invented language, is about supposed ancient Iranian prophets and includes accounts of events that have no historical basis. It is divided into two parts, the first of which comprises sixteen chapters, or *namahs* (books), each attributed to a so-called 'ancient' prophet, from Mahabad

and Ji-Afram, who supposedly predated Kayumars, to Sasan V, whom the author designated as a contemporary of Sasanian ruler Khusrau II Parvez (r. 590–628). Also included in the list of prophets are certain mythical and historical figures, including Jamshed, Faridun, Kaikhhusrau, Zoroaster and Alexander. The second part is a Persian 'translation' of the first, with commentary, containing many fabricated words; it is ascribed to the sixteenth prophet, Sasan V.

40. Sir William Henry Rattigan was born in Delhi in 1842. He was a member of the judiciary and later vice chancellor of Punjab University in 1887. I am not sure if it is the same Rattigan whom Ghalib refers to.
41. For details, see: Izhar ul-Haq Malik, 'Ghalib Ke Khud-Navisht Halat', in *Ahval-e Ghalib*, pp. 31–35. The note is reproduced by Malik, inserted between pages 32 and 33; Malik mentions that it was published some twenty-five years ago in the journal *Urdu*, and the original is preserved by Anjuman Taraqqi Urdu. I visited the office of the Anjuman in New Delhi and did not find either the original or a copy of Ghalib's note. I am grateful to its director, Ather Farouqui, for his help in trying to locate the document, which is not there any more.
42. Ghulam Rasul Mehr, *Ghalibiyat-e Mehr*, ed. Muhammad Alam Mukhtar-e Haq, Lahore (Majlis Taraqqi Adab, May 2015), p. 52.
43. The Nizami Press published one divan in 1935, thanks to the efforts of Mirza Nasrullah Khan.
44. Khub Chand Zaka's lengthy tazkirah (d.1834) contains 1500 entries. It was finished c. 1832.
45. Muhammad Ibrahim Zauq (1789–1854) was a renowned Urdu poet and Ghalib's most prominent contemporary. He was a pupil of the eminent poet Shah Nasir. Zauq became Bahadur Shah Zafar's ustad and held that position until his death. For Ma'ruf and Zauq's interactions, see: *Ab-e Hayat*, Allahabad (Asrar Karimi Press, 1967), pp. 526–36.
46. Ibid. p. 530.
47. Muhammad Ayyub Qadri, *Ghalib aur Asr-e Ghalib*, Karachi (Ghazanfar Academy, 1982), pp. 19–35. The manuscript was in his personal library and contained thirty-three ghazals in the refrains from *nun* to 'ye'.
48. The famous writer Manto, who wrote the story and screenplay for the film *Mirza Ghalib*, depicted Navab Ma'ruf as the father-in-law who chided Mirza for his wayward behaviour.
49. This is a fairly long, rambling Urdu letter in which Ghalib talks about how some idiot had tacked five verses to the above-mentioned ghazal, and how it was being sung everywhere. He writes: 'If songsters feel free to disfigure a man's poetry in his lifetime, how easy must it be for them to jumble up a dead poet's verses with the work of others.'

Urdu text: Khaliq Anjum, *Ghalib ke Khutut*, New Delhi (Ghalib Institute, 1988), vol. 1, p. 395. Daud Rahbar's translation: p. 32.

The opening verse of this ghazal is:

وہ آکے خواب میں تسکین اضطراب تو دے
ولے مجھے تپش دل مجال خواب تو دے

50. Muhammad Husain Burhan ibn Khalf Tabrezi was at the court of Abdullah Qutb Shah of Golconda in the Deccan. He had studied under the famous Safavid scholar Shaikh Baha ud-Din Ameli (1546–1622); Burhan was his pen name. In 1651, he compiled the *Burhan-e Qati*. In this massive dictionary, he combined materials from several other dictionaries. He also included a large number of words and compounds, particularly medical terms and words from dialects.
51. *Ud-e Hindi*, ed. Saiyyid Murtuza Husain Fazil, Lahore (Majlis Taraqqi Adab, 1967), letter no. 131, pp. 357–79. Ghalib wrote this pamphlet titled 'Namah-e Ghalib' by way of a rejoinder to Rahim Beg's *Sati-e Burhan*. The pamphlet was published in August 1865 and also reproduced in Munshi Naval Kishor's *Avadh Akhbar* in two installments, 10 and 17 October of the same year.
52. Letter no. 32/76, *Makatib-e Ghalib*, ed. Maulana Imtiaz Ali Khan Arshi Silsilah-e Matbu'at-e Kitabkhanah-e Rampur (Bombay, 1937).
53. Naiyar Mas'ud, *Qati-e Burhan*, *Naya Daur*, *Ghalib Numbar*, February to March 1969, pp. 48–57.
54. In my opinion, Ghalib continued to compose in Urdu, in the Bedilian style, but he carefully removed a number of verses that directly mentioned Bedil and referenced Ghalib's high regard for him.
55. Ghalib's contemporaries, Urdu poets Nasikh and Shah Nasir, played with those *mazmuns*, too. But Hali's portrait of Ghalib as the only one who was steeped in the poetry of Ajam (Persia), who lived and breathed its fire like a mythical salamander, has gripped our imagination because it was later repeatedly reinforced.
56. For finer details of these categories, see: Shamsur Rahman Faruqi, *She'r-e Shor-Angez*, vol. 3, New Delhi (National Council for Promotion of Urdu, 2008), third revised and expanded edition, vol. 3, section 3 of the introduction.
57. *Fasahat* means fluency, while *balaghat* implies lucidity.
58. The ghazal from which this verse is taken appears in the first Divan of 1816. Ghalib did not select it for his published Divan of 1841. Although Ghalib's so-called unpublished verses have been published in different collections, Jamal Abdul Vajid's recent effort to collect and arrange all the unpublished verses in a strict alphabetical order has made the task of dipping into this parallel divan a lot easier. See: *Ghair Mutadavil Kalam-e*

Ghalib, ed. Jamal Abdul Vajid, New Delhi (Ghalib Academy, 2016). The verse appears on p. 94 in ghazal no. 215 of Vajid's book. All translations here are the author's.

59. From the same ghazal: Vajid, p. 94.
60. Ralph Russell and Khurshidul Islam, *Ghalib, 1797–1869: Life and Letters*, first published by Cambridge University Press in 1969, re-issued by Oxford University Press (New Delhi, 1994). This book is written on the pattern of Ghulam Rasul Mehr's autobiography of Ghalib.
61. Natalia Prigarina, *Ghalib: A Creative Biography*, New Delhi (Oxford University Press), translated from the Russian by Osama Faruqi. Prigarina's book follows Hali's *Yadgar-e Ghalib* and Khurshidul Islam's *Ghalib* closely but adds some important insights of its own.
62. Composed in 1816. See: Vajid, p. 116, ghazal no. 280.

Chapter 2: The Divan of 1821 and the Divan of 1826

1. Mufti Anvarul Haq, *Divan-e Ghalib Jadid al ma'ruf ba Nuskhah-e Hamidiyyah*, Lucknow (Uttar Pradesh Urdu Academy, 1982), p. 22.
2. Haq, *Divan-e Ghalib Jadid al ma'ruf ba Nuskhah-e Hamidiyyah*, Agra (1921). There were subsequent reprints of *Divan-e Ghalib Jadid*, I have consulted the Lucknow 1982 edition. Hamid Ahmad Khan's 1969 edition, *Divan-e Ghalib Nuskhah-e Hamidiyyah*, Majlis-e Taraqqi-e Adab, Lahore (1969), is generally regarded as a good scholarly edition.
3. *Urdu Adab ki Taraqqi Mein Bhopal ka Hissah* (The Role of Bhopal in the Development of Urdu), Bhopal (Alavi Press, 1965), p. 128.
4. Muhammad Yusuf Qaisar attests to Faujdar Khan's keen interest in books in his essay 'Nuskhah-e Hamidiyyah aur Faujdar Mohammad Khan', *Furogh-e Urdu, Ghalib Nambar*, ed. Nadim Sitapuri. Cited in Abdul Qavi Dasnavi, *Bhopal aur Ghalib*, Bhopal (Bhopal Press, 1969), p. 16.
5. This was reported at length in the navab's journal, *Shahinshahnamah*, p. 15. Cited in *Urdu Adab ki Taraqqi Men Bhopal ka Hissah*, Salim Hamid Rizvi, p. 205.
6. Dasnavi, *Bhopal aur Ghalib*, p. 35.
7. Navab Yar Muhammad Khan Shaukat's poetry collection, *Divan-e Shaukat*, was published from Kanpur in 1883.
8. Hamidiyyah Library is now known as Maulana Azad Central Library.
9. See Abu Muhammad Sahar's essay, 'Divan-e Ghalib, Nuskhah-e Hamidiyyah, Chand Inkishafat' (Divan-e Ghalib, Nuskhah-e Hamidiyyah, some revelations), in *Hamari Zaban*, Aligarh (22 July 1969), p. 3.
10. This essay was not included in the first-published 1921 edition of the *Nuskhah-e Hamidiyyah*. It was included in a subsequent, enlarged edition.

It was also published in the journal *Urdu* in 1922, from Hyderabad, by the Anjuman Taraqqi Urdu.

11. When I began publishing my essays on Ghalib's early poetry, I was contacted by many Ghalib aficionados who offered me encouragement and advice. I was both surprised and pleased to hear from Bijnori Sahib's grandson, Haroon Siddiqi. Siddiqi Sahib sent me a photograph of Bijnori Sahib and copies of two moving letters of condolence that Mohammad Iqbal had written on Bijnori's passing.
12. Bijnori, *Mahasin-e Kalam-e Ghalib*, special centenary edition, Karachi (Fakhri Printing Press, 1969), p. 6. The Abdur Rahman Bijnori Trust of Islamabad, Pakistan, has recently published the collected writings of Bijnori.
13. Ibid. pp. 7–9. Also see Nomanul Haq's recent edition of Bijnori's *Mahasin-e Kalam-e Ghalib*, Karachi (Oxford University Press, 2016).
14. Saiyyed Hamid Husain's essay, 'Mufti Anvarul Haq Murattab Nuskhah-e Hamidiyyah' (Nuskhah-e Hamidiyyah, ed. Mufti Anvarul Haq), provides many interesting details about Mufti Sahib's background. See: *Hamari Zaban* (8 January 1969), pp. 3–4.
15. Anvarul Haq, '*in ibtida'I mashqon ko shaya karne se kya fa'idah hai?*', p. 18.
16. Ibid.
17. Ibid.
18. Ibid. p. 19–20; Altaf Husain Hali, *Yadgar-e Ghalib*, New Delhi (Ghalib Institute, 1986), p. 114.
19. Ibid. p. 22; Hali, p. 111.
20. Ibid.
21. This chart, however, does not clarify whether he counted the ghazals noted after the end of the manuscript divan. He most probably did not.
22. More information on these editions is provided by Gyan Chand Jain in his essay 'Nuskhah-e Arshi, Taba-e Sani ke Liye Kuch Ma'ruzat' (Some Pointers for the Second Edition of *Nuskhah-e Arshi*), p. 48.
23. According to Anvarul Haq, he barely knew Bijnori, having met him only two years before the latter's sudden death. He requested friends and relatives of Bijnori to help him put together a biographical note, but his efforts in this regard were fruitless.
24. Abdul Qavi Dasnavi, 'Saiyyid Hashmi aur Nuskhah-e Hamidiyyah', in *Sabras Ghalib Nambar*, 1969. Cited from Dasnavi, *Nuskhah-e Bhopal aur Nuskhah-e Bhopal Sani*, Bhopal (1970), p. 12.

    Saiyyid Abdul Latif held a PhD from the University of London and was a professor of English literature at Osmania University. He was the author of *The Influence of English Literature on Urdu Literature*. He published a short but important book, *Ghalib: A Critical Appreciation of His Life and Poetry*, from Hyderabad's Chandrakanta Press in 1929. The book offers a critique of Bijnori's work on Ghalib, arguing that he allowed his enthusiasm for Ghalib to influence his judgement. He calls Bijnori's work an impassioned ramble (p. 2). Latif's work raises important theoretical questions, such as the difference between the conventional stance and poetic experience. How does Ghalib individuate within the conventional? 'Until one can distinguish the conventional in Ghalib from the real, the real poet will ever remain shrouded . . . A philosophic idea though rendered into versified expression will always remain a philosophic idea. But if convention and philosophy have to mingle with poetic experience in order to accentuate it, they must be subject to it, and not submerge it under their weary weight' (p. 81).

25. Mentioned by Maulana Imtiaz Ali Khan Arshi in the introduction to his edition of *Divan-e Ghalib*, New Delhi (Anjuman Taraqqi Urdu, second edition, 1982), p. 73.
26. Cited in Abu Mohammad Sahr, 'Nuskhah-e Bhopal aur Daktar Abdul Latif', in *Hamari Zaban*, May–July, 1969, pp. 4–5.
27. For details on Abdul Latif and the controversies around the additions in the margins, see Gyan Chand Jain's essay 'Nuskhah-e Bhopal ki Islahen aur Izafeh' (The Corrections and Additions in the *Nuskhah-e Bhopal*), in *Rumuz-e Ghalib*, New Delhi (Maktaba Jamia, 1976), pp. 11–29.
28. *Divan-e Ghalib, Nuskhah-e Hamidiyyah*, ed. Hamid Ahmad Khan, Lahore (1969). 'In late August of 1938, returning from Hyderabad Deccan, on my way to Lahore, I stopped over at Bhopal. At the library, I compared the published text with the manuscript. I realized that in blurring the boundary between the text and the annotations in the margins, the sequence of ghazals had become completely distorted . . . It became necessary for me to focus my attention on two things: the order of the poems in the manuscript and scrutinize the notes in the margins for any discrepancies that were in the published version' (p. 21).
29. Shikastah is a later, shortcut version of the script style called nastaliq.
30. Khan, p. 18. The letter can be found in the collection of Ghalib's Persian prose work *Panj Ahang*.
31. Saiyyed Hamid Husain in an essay, 'Divan-e Ghalib, Nuskhah-e Bhopal, par Sibt Dastkhat aur Muhren' (The Signatures and Seals Affixed on Divan-e Ghalib, Nuskhah-e Bhopal), has provided some information about two possible persons with the name Abdul Ali, who lived in Bhopal at the time. See the Urdu journal *Sha'ir* (July 1969).
32. Khan, pp. 19–20.
33. Imtiaz Ali Khan Arshi, *Divan-e Ghalib Urdu, Nuskhah-e Arshi*, New Delhi (Anjuman Taraqqi Urdu, second edition, 1982), pp. 86–92. The first edition is dated 1958.

34. Ibid. p. 88.
35. Ibid. p. 89. These notes are quite detailed. For example, Arshi points out a few errors in spelling which he thinks Ghalib would not have made. He thus concludes that this could not be Ghalib's handwriting.
36. Ibid. p. 90.
37. *Gul-e Ra'na,* Ghalib's selection of Urdu and Persian verses, was completed in Calcutta in 1828. See Chapter 5 of this book for more on it.
38. Khan, pp. 18–19. For the rubais see, pp. 278–80. Khan does mention that the last rubai is: *mushkil hai ze bas kalam mera ai dil,* but he doesn't clarify or isn't aware that the nuskhah has only seven rubais. I find this to be a somewhat conspicuous error because he does not footnote or specify the source for the other four rubais. Khan titles each rubai with *digar* (additional or other), whereas the nuskhah has rubai inscribed in red above each one.
39. *Divan-e haza min tasnif-e Mirza Naushah Dihlavi al-mutakhallis bah Asad az kutub-khanah-e sarkar-e faiz asar ali-jah alam-panah Miyan Faujdar Muhammad Khan Bahadur dam-e iqbalahu. Qalami khushkhat.*
    دیوانِ ہذا من تصنیف میرزا نوشاہ دہلوی المتخلص بہ اسد از کتبخانئہ سرکارِ فیض آثار عالی
    جاہ عالم پناہ میاں فوجدار محمد خان بہادر دام اقبالہ۔ قلمی۔ خوشخط
40. *Bahr-e tarvih-e janab-e vali-e yomul hisab*
    Zamin-e ta'mir qasrisitan-e dilha-e kharab
    [In continued praise of the lord of the day of judgement
    The maker of this forsaken heart's bleak home]
    Throughout the qasidah, the word *tarvih* (give comfort) is used when referring to God in the first place, then Hazrat Ali and the imams. Tarvih, was corrected to *tarvij,* which means to circulate or flow, in Mufti Anvarul Haq's edition (1921) and its subsequent reprints. The tarvih–tarjih mix-up is notable because the last two pages of the manuscript (referred to earlier) which have additional verses, also have *bahr-e tarvih* not *bahr-e tarvij,* inscribed on top. Hamid Ahmad Khan (1969) has noted and corrected this error.
41. *Divan-e Ghalib, Nuskhah-e Hamidiyyah,* ed. Khan, p. 1, note 1.
42. The second line in this verse can be interpreted to mean: 'feasting on my heart and mind', that is, offering the heart and mind to poetry. Compared to the evocative, complex ghazal in the nature of a *hamd* quoted below, the verses from the qasidah are simple:
    Gada-e taqat-e taqrir hai zaban tujh se
    Kih khamoshi ko hai pairayah-e bayan tujh se
    [The tongue begs you for strength to speak;
    Because silence is as eloquent as speech for you]
    Fasurdagi men hai faryad-e bedilan tujh se
    Chiragh-e subh gul-e mausam-e khizan tujh se

[In times of sadness, the disheartened appeal to you;
The autumn's rose and the lamp at dawn is all from you]

43. The ghazal section opens with the famous verse:
Naqsh faryadi hai kis ki shokhi-e tahrir ka
kaghazi hai pairahan har paikar-e tasvir ka
[The picture is a plaintiff of whose playful writing?
Every figure of the picture is wearing a paper robe]
44. This signature was an important authentication mark for me when I saw the digital image of the nuskhah. I have discussed the speculations around it earlier in the chapter. Hamid Ahmad Khan thinks that some of the notations in the margin could be Abdul Ali's.
45. I am inclined to think that this is Ghalib's casual handwriting.
46. I am grateful to Khwajah Amn Junaid for combing through the individual divans and preparing a reference chart for me.
47. The verse has *la*, meaning 'discard', written multiple times above it in the manuscript.
48. There are seven ghazals, all in the refrain 'ye', comprising seventy-one verses, copied in these end pages. All these ghazals are included in the main body of the Divan of 1826.
49. Another peculiarity is the extra line copied at the end of the letter. I found that the extra line is a repeat of the second-last line on the page:
و دام مدعا دل سداد محل طرح اساس و داد کرده و سلک گوہردعا در عرصہ وراد
This line is not found in any of the versions. It is possible that the copyist, realizing the mistake, copied that line separately to mark out the error.
50. This document was among a bundle of letters at the National Archives, New Delhi, and has been published. See S.A.I. Tirmizi, *Namahha-e Farsi-e Ghalib*, New Delhi (Asia Publishing House and Ghalib Academy, 1969), pp. 102–03, Appendix I.
51. Mirza Afzal Beg was sent to Calcutta as the representative (vakil) of Mughal emperor Akbar Shah. Afzal Beg was the younger brother of Mirza Akbar Beg, who was married to Ghalib's sister Chhoti Khanam. It is surprising that Afzal Beg was influential enough to be able to persuade the British to take no notice of Ghalib's petition concerning the pension claim for which he had travelled to Calcutta in 1827–28. See: Amar Farooqui, *Zafar and the Raj, Anglo-Mughal Delhi c.1800–1850*, New Delhi (Primus Books, 2013), pp. 64–65.
52. Tirmizi, pp. 102–03.
53. See Malik Ram's discussion of the significance of the seal inscribed Asadullah al-Ghalib 1231 hijri in *Zikr-e Ghalib*.
54. Akbar Ali Khan, *Divan-e Ghalib bah Khatt-e Ghalib*, Rampur (Idarah Yadgar-e Ghalib, 1969), p. 26.

55. Maulana Arshi quotes (*Divan-e Ghalib*, pp. 91–92) a closing verse from the published divan:
ہستی کے مت فریب میں آجائیو اسد
عالم تمام حلقۂ دامِ خیال ہے
The earlier form of this verse is found in both the *Gul-e Ra'na* and the Divan of 1816:
ہستی کے مت فریب میں آجائیو کہیں
The revised, published version is noted in the margin of the Divan of 1821.
56. Vahid Quraishi, 'Ghalib aur Nuskhah-e Sherani', in the Ghalib Number of *Nuqush*, ed. Muhammad Tufail, Lahore (Idarah Furogh-e Urdu, April 1969), second printing, pp. 740–803.

    Quraishi begins his book-length essay with a survey of earlier editions of Ghalib's manuscript divans. From his essay, I learnt that Saiyyid Abdul Latif's *Ghalib: A Critical Appreciation of His Life and Poetry* inspired S.M. Ikram to organize an annotated bibliography of Ghalib's works. The first volume of Ikram's efforts, *Ghalibnamah*, was published in 1936. He did not have access to the Divan of 1826 at the time. In a subsequent edition of *Ghalibnamah* (not dated), Ikram mentions the Divan of 1826 as the jewel of the personal library of Hafiz Mahmud Sherani.
57. The colophon is missing, so the exact date is not known.
58. Hafiz Mahmud Sherani was a renowned scholar of Urdu and Punjabi, whose writings on early Urdu are invaluable.
59. Qazi Abdul Vadud published a paper, 'Divan-e Ghalib ke Do Nuskhe', in the Urdu journal *Ma'asir*, No. 12 (not dated), from Patna. Qazi Sahib compared the two manuscripts, the Divans of 1821 and 1826. He had no access to the 1821 divan, though, because it had disappeared. See: Quraishi, 'Ghalib aur Nuskhah-e Sherani', p. 747.
60. *Divan-e Ghalib Nuskhah-e Sherani*, Lahore (Majlis-e Taraqqi-e Adab, 1969).
61. I prepared a concordance of the 1841, 1821 and 1826 divans. The ghazal below, from the Divan of 1821, with the following opening verse, is missing from the Divan of 1826:
Shabnam bah gul-e lalah nah khali ze ada hai
dagh-e dil-e be-dard nazar-gah-e haya hai
[The dew on the tulip flower is not devoid of coquetry
The scar of a heart without compassion is a site of shame]
62. The opening verses of the ghazals in the Divan of 1826, which were obviously composed after 1821, are provided by Quraishi, p. 784.
63. I found his arguments to be persuasive and convincing. He suggests that both Navab Husamuddin Haidar Nami and Rai Chajja Mal were close to Ghalib till the end. Navab Husamuddin was a dear friend of Ghalib's

father-in-law, Navab Illahi Bakhsh Ma'ruf. Rai Chajja Mal's sons were Ghalib's pupils. Rai Chajja Mal was a keen calligrapher, too. A manuscript of Ghalib's oldest Persian divan was in Rai Chajja Mal's hands; it is preserved at the Khuda Baksh Library, Patna. It is possible that one of these friends could have had the manuscript.

64. The Urdu line is: *jadah-e rah kashish-e kaf-e karam hai ham ko*

    The letter *kaf* has an elaborate sweep, which brings a delightful visual perspective to the alliteration in this line. The general meaning of *jadah* is path or road, but it can also be extended to mean a narrow thread-like pathway.

65. Quraishi, 'Ghalib aur Nuskhah-e Sherani', p. 777. Divan of 1826, p. *alif*, 56. The reference to Najaf in the revised version has raised speculations about Ghalib's desire to travel to Iran. Did he get the idea of going to Iran in Calcutta, or before that? Ghalib mentions his longing to travel to Iran in a letter to poet Sheikh Nasikh. In the dibachah to his published divan (1841), Ghalib concluded with the following: 'Such that may God grant, that just as he was born in Agra and has made Delhi his home, he may be buried in Najaf.'
66. This is an important question in the context of the *Gul-e Ra'na*, the selection of Urdu and Persian poetry that Ghalib created at the behest of his friend Sirajuddin Ahmad.
67. Quraishi, 'Ghalib aur Nuskhah-e Sherani', p. 793.
68. The Urdu idiom *kisi par marna* literally means to die for love, that is, to be extremely enamoured. The protagonist is already dying out of love, but the beloved's simplicity or naivete is that she thinks a dagger is needed for slaying.
69. Quraishi, 'Ghalib aur Nuskhah-e Sherani', p. 793.

Chapter 3: Ghalib's Earliest Divan: The Divan of 1816

1. *Divan-e Ghalib bah Khatt-e Ghalib*, ed. Akbar Ali Khan Arshizadah, Rampur (1969), p. 125
2. Ibid, p. 75.
3. Malik Ram, *Zikr-e Ghalib*, pp. 140–44.
4. Nisar Ahmad Faruqi was from Amroha in Uttar Pradesh. Taufiq Ahmad knew him and may have given him permission to make a copy of the manuscript.
5. The Raza Library in Rampur has the best collection of Ghalib's manuscripts. It holds a special place in the area of Ghalib studies because of the path-breaking work of Maulana Imtiaz Ali Khan Arshi (1904–81), who joined the library in 1932 and produced a stream of authoritative works on Ghalib from there.

Maulana Arshi painstakingly collated and published what is still considered the most definitive edition of Ghalib's divan (1958). He strove to put together an impressive archive of published and unpublished materials. During my visit to Rampur, I examined the artistically decorated 1855 manuscript that Ghalib had specially got calligraphed for Navab Yusuf Ali Khan. The library also has Ghalib's Divan of 1833, known as the *Nuskhah-e Qadim*, as well as the Divan of 1855, known as the *Nuskhah-e Jadid*. For more details, see Maulana Imtiaz Ali Khan Arshi's article on the various Ghalibian manuscripts at the Rampur Raza Library, 'Ghalib Ki Apni Kalam Par Islahen' (Ghalib's Revisions on his Poetry), in the journal *Aj Kal*, Ghalib Numbar (February 1952), pp. 47–51.

I am grateful to Rampur Raza Library's current librarian, Janab Abu Sa'd Islahi, for his kindness in facilitating my viewing of the material on Ghalib.

6. Akbar Ali Khan was the son of Maulana Imtiaz Ali Khan Arshi. He probably saw this as an opportunity to establish his own credentials as a Ghalibian. It was in September 1969 that he added the fancy title of Arshizadah (son of Arshi) to his name.
7. Sadequain Ahmad Naqvi (1923–87) is known for his iconic calligraphic style and illustration of poetry. He transformed calligraphy into a modern aesthetic that is contemporary and traditional at the same time. Sadequain calligraphed verses from the ghazals of Ghalib, Faiz Ahmad Faiz and Iqbal, revealing an imagined interpretation of realism in his art form. His work has been seen as merging realism with lyricism. His interpretive paintings of Ghalib's selected verses were included in this special edition of *Nuqush*.
8. Abdur Rahman Chaghtai (1897–1975) created his own distinctive style of painting influenced by the Mughal miniatures and Islamic art. Chaghtai was a graduate of the Mayo School of Arts, Lahore. The *Muraqqa-e Chughtai* (1928) was a sumptuously illustrated edition of Ghalib's Urdu poetry, with a foreword by the renowned poet Muhammad Iqbal. It is regarded as the most significant work of Chaghtai's career, and in its time was considered the finest achievement in book production in British India. Chaghtai painted Ghalib's portrait especially for this special edition.
9. Navab Yar Muhammad Khan has been introduced in Chapter 2.
10. Fortunately, I have a copy of both: the *Nuqush Ghalib Nambar* and the *Divan-e Ghalib bah Khatt-e Ghalib*, ed. Akbar Ali Khan. My remarks are based on a comparison of the two editions. Nisar Ahmad Faruqi called his edition *Bayaz-e Ghalib*. A 'bayaz' is a personal notebook in which poems are inscribed at the owner's pleasure, not organized in the traditional format of a divan. A divan is organized alphabetically. The Divan of 1816 is not a bayaz.
11. Hakim Abdul Hamid Khan (1908–99), a noted physician who practised the traditional Unani system of medicine, was the founder trustee of

Hamdard Laboratories. Hakim Sahib founded the Ghalib Academy in 1969 to commemorate Ghalib's death centenary. The academy purchased two plots of land adjacent to the enclosure where Ghalib is buried. It also houses a museum, a research library, an art gallery, an auditorium and a computerized calligraphy training centre.

12. For more details, see: Nisar Ahmad Faruqi, 'Divan-e Ghalib: Nuskhah-e Amroha', in *Talash-e Ghalib*, Lahore (1969), pp. 201–04. For Akbar Ali Khan's version of the manuscript's discovery, see his edition, *Divan-e Ghalib bah Khatt-e Ghalib*, pp. 12–13. Jalaludin Sahib, the archivist from Allahabad, brought the manuscript to Khan Sahib's attention.
13. Nisar Ahmad Faruqi, *Talash-e Ghalib*, p. 203.
14. Ibid. pp. 201–69. I have presented only the highlights here, but the entire story is a fascinating description from the point when Taufiq Ahmad took out the manuscript from a cloth bag and placed it in front of Faruqi.
15. Ibid. p. 205.
16. These ghazals are thirteen in number and have been added into the main body of the Divan of 1821.
17. The choice of highlighting the names of Hazrat Ali, Hazrat Hasan, Husain and Mirza Bedil point not only to Ghalib's inclination towards Shi'ism and his admiration of Bedil but also his youthful impetuosity. I am grateful to Nizar Hermes for verifying my translation.
18. The most notable among the few scholars who disagreed and thought the manuscript was a forgery was Kamal Ahmad Siddiqi. He published two books on the subject: *Bayaz-e Ghalib: Tahqiqi Ja'izah*, Srinagar (1970), and *Ghalib ki Shinakht*, New Delhi (1997).
19. Nisar Ahmad Faruqi, *Talash-e Ghalib*, pp. 228–32. Faruqi has provided a sample of thirty verses that he picked from a cursory comparison of the two manuscripts. There are likely to be many more of such interesting copyist errors, which were perpetuated because the Divan of 1821 was considered to be the authoritative version. I have culled some of the common errors from the examples that Faruqi has provided: *sapand-pasand, ma'zul- maghrur, rang-zang, kam-gam, abilah-qafilah, tahammul-tajammul, bayaz-niyaz, makin-nagin*, etc.
20. Ibid. p. 233. The *Tazkirah-e Sarvar*, also known as *Umdah-e Muntakhibah*, of Mir Muhammad Khan Bahadur Sarvar was compiled, as tazkirahs often were, over an extended period of time. It is generally accepted that its period of compilation was 1216–26 hijri (1801–11 ce). The alternate title, *Umdah-e Muntakhibah*, yields the chronogram 1216 hijri. Sarvar's entry on Ghalib has been discussed at length in Chapter 1.
21. The traditional ordering of a divan is as follows: dibachah, qita, masnavi, qasidah, ghazal, rubai and khatimah.

22. I find this back and forth between divans very intriguing. In the 1821 divan, Ghalib had seven rubais in Urdu.
23. The following is the published one:
Shah em -o junun-e ma ze tamkin dil tang
Darem beh bahr-o bar zu hasht ahang
Marjan daruyem zarrah-e pusht-e nihang
Bar koh ze nim sikkah az dagh-e palang
24. This letter has been discussed in Chapter 1, in the context of Ghalib's age.
25. For more examples of the peculiarities of Ghalib's handwriting, see Nisar Ahmad Faruqi, *Talash-e Ghalib*, pp. 211–12.
26. See the discussion on Ghalib's age in Chapter 1.
27. Lal Khan was one of Ghalib's favourite calligraphers.
28. Nisar Ahmad Faruqi, *Talash-e Ghalib*, p. 216.
29. *Divan-e Ghalib bah Khatt-e Ghalib*, ed. Akbar Ali Khan, p. 15.
30. Kamal Ahmad Siddiqi, *Ghalib ki Shinakht*. For details, see the chapter titled 'Ek Ja'li Nuskhah' (A Forged Manuscript), pp. 124–37. While I find his arguments to be meticulous and minute, I am not convinced that the manuscript is fake. Errors in orthography are common in copying and calligraphing. Ghalib's printed divans were not free of errors either. Nonetheless, Siddiqi is a learned scholar and his monumental work cannot be brushed aside.
31. I discern some personal battles being fought here. Kamal Ahmad Siddiqi is not happy with the publicity Akbar Ali Khan Arshizadah earned from this manuscript's publication. In my opinion, Siddiqi's minute, exhaustive analysis of the manuscript's shortcomings helps readers understand the infinitesimal details of close reading. On the other hand, these painstaking details make one wonder who would go to that extent in fabricating a manuscript. Certainly, composing all those new verses in Ghalib's style could not have been easy.
32. Akbar Ali Khan offers a slightly different break-up of these numbers.
33. See: *Divan-e Ghalib bah Khatt-e Ghalib*, Akbar Ali Khan, pp. 15–16.
34. Faruqi's measurements are 7.5 x 5.5 inches.
35. *Divan-e Ghalib bah Khatt-e Ghalib*, Khan, p. 16.
36. Ibid. p. 17.
37. Sarvar:
Voh kaun si shae hai jo yahan hai/Darya hai ke tab'se ravan hai
[What is that element that is here/There is an ocean flowing naturally]
Nishat:
Teri jo tegh ki zalim safaiyan dekhin/To munh peh barq ke urti havaiyan dekhi
[Seeing the dexterity of your sword, O cruel one/I noticed lightning's face go pale]

Unknown:
Khushi se anjuman arastah gulon ne ki/Jo sahn-e bagh pe badli ka shamiyanah hua
[Roses adorned the gathering place/then clouds made a canopy above the courtyard]
I have noticed similar laudatory verses on the last pages of Ghalib's manuscript divans. They add a remarkable personal touch to the text.

38. For example, on the last page, *sahn* is spelt with a *sin* instead of 'svad'.
39. The notes are: *ta in ja navishtah am*, and *az in ja shuru*. *Divan-e Ghalib bah Khatt-e Ghalib*, Akbar Ali Khan, p. 23.
40. See Chapter 4 on Ghalib's journey to Calcutta.
41. *Divan-e Ghalib bah Khatt-e Ghalib*, Akbar Ali Khan, p. 26.
42. Maulana Arshi, who consulted the manuscript in 1944, was apparently the last scholar to see the manuscript before it disappeared.
43. See Mehr Afshan Farooqi, 'Introduction', in Shahab Sattar, *Mirza Ghalib's Nuskhah-e Hamidiyyah*, 2016.
44. The Ghalib Institute has not made a formal announcement regarding the recovery of the Divan of 1816. Perhaps it is to avoid messy, contested claims of ownership.
45. For example, the closing verse of the last ghazal in the Divan of 1816 is:
She'r ki fikr ko Asad chahiye dil-o-dimagh/Uzr kih yih fasurdah dil be-dil-o be dimagh hai
[Composing poetry needs both a heart and mind/Alas, this sad heart is discouraged and mindless]
46. See my essay 'Power, Culture and the Language of Poetry: The Transition from Vali to Ghalib', *Cracow Indological Studies, Islam on the Indian Subcontinent*, vol. 11, ed. Agnieszka Kuczkiewicz-Fras, Kraków (Jagiellonian University Institute of Oriental Philology, 2009).

Chapter 4: Contrary Winds: The Journey to Calcutta (1826–29)

1. Partav Rohilla, *Ahang-e Panjum*, Urdu translation of Ghalib's Persian letters from *Panj Ahang*, Karachi (Idarah-e Yadgar-e Ghalib, 2004), p. 9.
2. Ghalib's struggle to get his pension restored to the original grant is well-documented, so I will not go into details here, but I will provide a summary of the exigencies that made him go to Calcutta. Because there are many characters in the narrative, I am reiterating a portion of the story to avoid any confusion regarding the complicated relationships among the beneficiaries.
3. Calcutta was the headquarters of the East India Company 1772 onwards. It was British India's capital from 1858 to 1911. The nineteenth century is, in fact, described as the age of the Bengal renaissance.

4. Ghalib and his siblings most likely continued to live with their mother at their maternal grandparents' home in Agra. His uncle, however, was their legal guardian. Ghalib's older sister, Chhoti Begam, is not mentioned as a dependent. Perhaps she was already married by this time.
5. Khwaja Haji was married to the daughter of Nasrullah Beg Khan's paternal aunt.
6. I have discussed this in Chapter 1. Was Ghalib actually nine years old, or could he have been older, about twelve years old, at this time, and capable of protesting against the unfair allotment?
7. Navab Shamsuddin Ahmad was opposed to William Fraser (1784–1835), the Indophile British Commissioner of Delhi, who was Ghalib's friend. The young navab was later implicated in Fraser's assassination, then imprisoned and hanged. For a detailed, if fictionalized, cultural history of this period, see: Shamsur Rahman Faruqi's *Kaí Chand the Sar-e Asman*, New Delhi (Penguin Books, 2007).

   Navab Shamsuddin Ahmad was the son of Navab Ahmad Bakhsh Khan's with his mistress, Muddi Begam. The navab also had two younger sons (Navab Aminuddin Ahmad Khan and Navab Ziyauddin Ahmad Khan) with his wife. Ghalib was very close to both. Navab Ziyauddin Ahmad Khan grew up be a poet and a pupil of Ghalib's. He wrote poetry in Urdu and Persian under different pen names: 'Rakhshan' in Persian and 'Naiyar' in Urdu. Navab Aminuddin Ahmad Khan's son, Navab Alauddin Ahmad Khan Alai, was also a poet and very dear to Ghalib. For details about the family politics in Shamsuddin Ahmad's nomination as Navab Ahmad Bakhsh's heir, see: Kalidas Gupta Raza, *Ghalíb Durun-e Khanah*, Chapter 17.
8. Ghalib reached Firozpur-Jhirka in November 1825 and stayed there till January 1826. The long letter to Rai Chajja Mal, written in Persian, is full of pain, misery and restlessness. The text of the letter is quoted in full in Urdu translation by Khaliq Anjum, in *Ghalib ka Safar-e Kalkattah aur Kalkatte ka Adabí Ma'ríkah*, New Delhi (Ghalib Institute, 2005), pp. 27–29.
9. During a visit to Alwar to sort out inheritance problems between the son and nephew of the maharaja, Navab Ahmad Bakhsh Khan was attacked by a supporter of the nephew and suffered grave injuries.
10. Charles Metcalfe was born in Calcutta in 1775. His first tenure as Resident in Delhi, for the East India Company (and for the British government from 1818), began on 25 February 1811. In 1819, he received from Lord Hastings the appointment of secretary in the secret and political department. From 1820 to 1825, Sir Charles (who succeeded his brother in the baronetcy in 1822) was Resident at the court of the nizam, and afterwards was summoned in an emergency to his former post in Delhi. On 14 November 1834, he was posted as the governor of the Presidency

of Agra, where he served for over four months till 20 March 1835. In 1827, he obtained a seat on the Supreme Council, and in March 1835, after he had acted as the first governor of the proposed new presidency of Agra, he provisionally succeeded Lord William Bentinck as the Governor General of Bengal (1835–36). During his brief tenure (it lasted only one year), he initiated several important measures, including liberation of the press, which, while almost universally popular, complicated his relations with the directors at home to such an extent that he resigned from the East India Company in 1838.

11. Khaliq Anjum, *Ghalib Ka Safar-e Kalkattah Aur Kalkatteh Men Adabi Ma'rikah*, p. 33. The petition says that he sold valuable articles he had inherited but still owed Rs 20,000.
12. Because Ghalib was not particular or careful about dating his letters, sometimes he put the day and date but not the year, or referred to events that didn't quite match with the dates. There is some ambiguity regarding the dates and length of his stay in Lucknow. It is generally agreed that he reached Lucknow in January and stayed there June 1826.
13. Agha Mir was given the rank of *mu'tamiddaulah* (in-charge of the royal household).
14. Ghalib ultimately dedicated the qasidah to the next Navab of Avadh, Nasiruddin Haidar. It can be found in his Persian kulliyat.
15. In a letter to Rai Chajja Mal, Ghalib complained about Agha Mir's arrogance and lack of generosity. He also described Lucknow as a chaotic place with endemic corruption. See Khaliq Anjum, *Ghalib Ka Safar-e Kalkattah*, pp. 39–40.
16. Ghalib's cousin, his maternal uncle's son, was a close relative of the Navab of Banda, Navab Zulfiqar Ali Bahadur.
17. The navab honoured Ghalib's request for a loan of Rs 2000. For details of Ghalib's stay in Banda, see: Saleha Begum Qureshi, *Banda Aur Ghalib*, Banda (1994).
18. See letter to Muhammad Ali Khan, Urdu translation, quoted by Khaliq Anjum in *Ghalib ka Safar-e Kalkattah*, pp. 44–46.
19. Mirza Qatil (1747/8–1818) was a highly regarded Persian poet and linguist of Indian descent. He was from Batala in north India. Born Divani Singh, he converted to Islam and took Muhammad Hasan Qatil as his Islamic name. He learnt Persian in Lucknow from Iranians; in poetry, his ustad was Mirza Muhammad Baqar Shahid. In Lucknow, he was good friends with renowned Urdu poet Imam Bakhsh Nasikh. His best-known work is *Chahar Sharbat*.
20. See letter to Muhammad Ali Khan, Urdu translation, quoted by Khaliq Anjum, *Ghalib ka Safar-e Kalkattah*, pp. 47–48.

21. The place Ghalib had rented belonged to an old woman who was so poor that she had no money to get oil for the lamps. It was located in a deserted neighbourhood with no landmarks to guide a letter bearer. Khaliq Anjum, *Ghalib ka Safar-e Kalkattah*, pp. 50–53.
22. An early version of the masnavi included in *Gul-e Ra'na* does not have a title. This title was given later. See *Gul-e Ra'na,* ed. Saiyyed Vazirul Hasan Abidi, Lahore (Panjab University, 1969), pp. 81–91.
23. Hanif Naqvi has a verse-for-verse Urdu translation of the *Chiragh-e Dair* that reads very well. Khaliq Anjum has reproduced it in full. pp. 64–73. According to Shamsur Rahman Faruqi, *Chiragh-e Dair* was inspired by Bedil. It is possible that Ghalib had also read Mulla Sabiq's *Tasir-e Ishq*. See: *Ghalib Par Char Tahriren,* New Delhi (Ghalib Institute, 2001), p. 15.
24. *Bahr-e Hazaj Musaddas Makhduf.* For an informative discussion on *Chiragh-e Dair*, see: 'Masnavi, Chiragh-e Dair, Ek Ja'izah', in Tahseen Firaqi, *Ghalib Fikr-o Farhang,* New Delhi (Ghalib Institute, 2012).
25. *Gul-e Ra'na*, ed. Abidi, p. 81.
26. Letter to Muhammad Ali Khan, cited from *Kulliyat-e Maktubat-e Farsi,* ed. Partav Rohilla, p. 135.
27. Letter dated 12 February 1861. In another letter to the same gentleman, Ghalib described his fondness for Banaras and the masnavi he wrote about it. See: Tirmizi, p. 23
28. Some Ghalib scholars, notably Qazi Abdul Vadud, have hinted that Ghalib may have found 'other distractions', meaning a love affair, that made his spirits soar.
29. A rhetorical flourish on names of the two cities, Kashi (Banaras) and Kashan in the province of Isfahan in Iran.
30. Tahseen Firaqi shows the similarities between Ghanimat's *Nairang-e Ishq* and Ghalib's *Chiragh-e Dair*. Because the two poems are in the same metre, and the general drift is similar, it is possible to interchange verses. See: *Ghalib Fikr-o Farhang*, Firaqi, pp. 90–91.
31. The distance between Banaras and Calcutta is approximately 680 kilometres by road. Ghalib traversed almost 3000 kilometres in his journey from Delhi to Calcutta.
32. Letter to Khwaja Fakhrullah, Qazi Abdul Vadud, *Ma'asir-e Ghalib*, Patna (1995), pp. 28–29. Cited from Khaliq Anjum, *Ghalib ka Safar-e Kalkattah*, p. 342.
33. Some records mention an earlier date, 4 February 1828.
34. In Ghalib's *Kulliyat-e Nasr*, Lucknow (Naval Kishor Press, 1872), the rent is mentioned as Rs 10 a month. See p. 166.
35. Ghalib's letter to Mirza Ali Bakhsh Khan Bahadur; *Panj Ahang*, Urdu translation by Mohammad Umar Mohajir, Karachi (Idarah Yadgar-e

Ghalib, 1969), p. 4. Also see: Partav Rohilla, *Ahang-e Panjum*, pp. 8–9. Rohilla's translation is more accurate.

36. *Panj Ahang* is Ghalib's first collection of prose. The earliest manuscript of *Panj Ahang* was ready by 1835. It was put together by Mirza Ali Bakhsh Khan (the same to whom the letter describing Ghalib's arrival in Calcutta was addressed), although the actual work of collating and naming the collection was done by Ghalib himself. The volume has a foreword by Ali Bakhsh Khan, and also one by Ghalib. In a foreword written in 1868 for *Nikat-e Ghalib*, Ghalib wrote that there are two meanings of 'ahang': voice and resolve, or design. Each ahang presents Ghalib's voice in its own way. The first is a discussion of the fine points of letter-writing. The second is about Persian idioms and rhetoric. The third contains Ghalib's selected Persian verses; the fourth his prose compositions. The fifth and last includes 126 letters. It was first published by the Matba-e Sultani, Delhi, in 1849. The second edition, containing twenty-five additional letters, was published by Matba-e Darus Salam, Delhi, in 1853. Ghalib was appalled by the printing errors in both editions.
37. Some of these are repeats of what have been included in the *Panj Ahang*. The Lucknow corpus, along with some other Ghalib materials, has been edited by Masud Hasan Rizvi Adib. It was published as *Mutafarriqat-e Ghalib*, Lucknow (Kitabistan, 1969).
38. *Ma'asir-e Ghalib* by Qazi Abdul Vadud, Aligarh (1949), includes a critical commentary as well.
39. The letters in this collection have been transcribed by a person called Munshi Saiyyid Ali Hasan Khan. Majority of the letters are addressed to Maulvi Muhammad Ali, the *sadr-e amin* of Banda. Seven letters from this collection are included in *Panj Ahang*. The manuscript has been edited by S.A.I. Tirmizi, titled *Namahha-e Farsi Ghalib* (Persian Letters of Ghalib), 1969.
40. Andrew Stirling (Indian Civil Service) was appointed Persian secretary to the Governor General on 6 July 1826 and continued in that capacity until his sudden death on 23 May 1830. His death was a big setback for Ghalib. He mourned Stirling's death in an eloquent letter and also wrote a heart-stirring elegy.
41. Amirunnisa Begam, Afzal Beg's sister, was married to Khavajah Haji. She had two sons who were Khwaja Haji's heirs. Mirza Afzal Beg, their maternal uncle, was obviously on his sister's side in the pension dispute.
42. Akbar Shah II, son of Shah Alam II and father of Bahadur Shah II, ruled from 1806–37. He resisted the high-handedness of the East India Company officials, refusing to treat them as peers. The Company retaliated by removing his name from their coins and encouraging provincial navabs

to rebel against him. Akbar Shah II sent Ram Mohan Roy to England, as his ambassador to the court of St James. Roy submitted a well-argued petition but was ineffective in getting justice for the emperor.

Afzal Beg's position as the envoy of the king of Delhi was obviously important.

43. *Makatib-e Ghalib,* Imtiaz Ali Khan Arshi, Rampur (1949).
44. In my opinion, this divan was the *Nuskhah-e Hamidiyyah*, which had been completed in 1821, that is, seven years ago. The nuskhah does not have Ghalib's seal, but it has a colophon that spells out his name as: *divan min tasnif-e mirza sahib va qiblah al mutakhallis bah asad va ghalib* (divan composed by Mirza Sahib, who bears the *takhallus* of Asad and Ghalib). The colophon makes it absolutely clear that Ghalib used both Asad and Ghalib as his noms de plume.
45. The original petition is at the India Office Library, London. The Urdu translation by Malik Ram was first published in the journal *Afkar*, Karachi (March 1969), pp. 46–54. It is reproduced in many subsequent works, for example, Khaliq Anjum, *Ghalib ka Safar-e Kalkattah*, pp. 87–99.
46. They remained in Banaras for a year, then returned to Calcutta.
47. Ghalib did not give up. He appealed against the decision and continued the struggle for revision of the stipend. He sent a petition to Queen Victoria through the Company's Court of Directors, but there was no response. After the Revolt of 1857, Ghalib's pension was suspended for three years. It was resumed in 1860, but without any increment.
48. The details of Ghalib's experience at the mushairahs of Calcutta were first revealed in a document that was found among a bunch of Persian letters. This document has been published along with the group of letters by S.A.I. Tirmizi. See: *Namahha-e Farsi Ghalib*, Appendix 2, pp. 104–15.
49. درمیانِ من و دلدار ہمام است حجاب
دارم امید کہ آں ہم زمیاں بر خیزد
[Between me and my beloved is a veil;
I have hope that it will be lifted from between us]
50. Tirmizi, p. 104.
51. I have given the she'r in Perso-Urdu script so that the objections can be clearly verified.
52. Tirmizi, p. 105.
53. For Ghalib's personal war against Mirza Qatil and other Indian poets writing in Persian, see: Khwaja Ahmad Faruqi, 'Marikah-e Ghalib Aur Hamiyan-e Qatil, Irani-Hindi Niza Ki Raushni Men', in *Ahval-e Ghalib*, pp. 183–200.
54. Ghalib's letters to Muhammad Ali Khan of Banda and Mirza Ahmad Beg Tapan go into details of these critical encounters.

55. Tirmizi, p. 107: 'Asadullah Dihlavi, who is among your beneficiaries, misbehaves at gatherings, ignores the rules of proper conduct, makes tall claims about language, and loses his temper easily.'
56. Ibid.
57. They were Ahmad Ali of Gopa Mau and Mir Munshi Maulvi Ahmad Ali. The former was a lecturer at the Madrasah-e Aliyah, and the latter a proofreader of Arabic and Persian manuscripts at the Royal Asiatic Society. The third person involved, Maulvi Vajahat Ali Lakhnavi, was employed as a secretary at the Governor General's office. He was a pupil of Qatil. They published their criticism of Ghalib in the prominent Persian weekly *Jam-e Jahan Numa*.

    Cited from Khaliq Anjum, *Ghalib ka Safar-e Kalkattah*, p. 134.
58. For example, here is an exuberant verse:

    طرز بیدل میں ریختہ کہنا
    اسد اللہ خاں قیامت ہے
    [Writing Rekhtah in Bedil style!
    Asadullah Khan, that is amazing!]
59. Z. Ansari has rendered the *Ashtinamah* into Urdu. The full translation is quoted in Khaliq Anjum, *Ghalib ka Safar-e Kalkattah*, pp. 144–60. For Urdu translations of Ghalib's Persian masnavis, see: Z. Ansari, *Masnaviyat-e Ghalib,* New Delhi (Ghalib Institute, 1983).
60. Tirmizi, p. 109.
61. Ibid. p. 111.
62. In Masud Hasan Rizvi Adib's collection was a manuscript that contained forty-eight Persian letters of Ghalib, two qitas, the *Ashtinamah* and an Urdu ghazal. He published this valuable manuscript with an introduction titled 'Mutafarriqat-e Ghalib', Lucknow (Kitabistan, 1969).
63. Letter to Maulvi Sirajuddin Ahmad, Qazi Abdud Vadud, *Ma'asir-e Ghalib: Ghalib Ki Kamyab Nazm Va Nasr Ka Majmu'ah,* Patna (1995), pp. 23–25.

    Ghalib also wrote to the editor of *Jam-e Jahan Numa,* protesting against the slanderous letters of his adversaries that were being published. For more information on this, see: *Ahval-e Ghalib*.
64. Mirza Abul Qasim Khan Qasim, a prince from Delhi's royal family, had moved to Calcutta.
65. Both poems by Ghalib and the qita from Mirza Abul Khan Qasim are reproduced in Masud Hasan Rizvi Adib's *Mutafarriqat-e Ghalib*, Lucknow (Kitabistan, 1969), pp. 137–41. There is a lively Urdu ghazal by Ghalib, in honour of Mirza Abul Qasim and Mirza Ahmad Beg Khan Tapan, in the same book, pp. 135–36.
66. Shamsur Rahman Faruqi, 'Unprivileged Power: The Strange Case of Persian (and Urdu) in Nineteenth-Century India', *Annual of Urdu Studies*, no. 13 (1998), pp. 3–30.

67. For brief introductions of Indian Persian poets, see: Nabi Hadi, *Dictionary of Indo-Persian Literature*, New Delhi (Indira Gandhi Centre for the Arts, 1995).
68. Beginning in the thirteenth century and right up to the nineteenth century, the Indians wrote many major dictionaries of Persian. While some of the lexicographers were of Iranian or Central Asian descent, some great ones were Hindu. Tek Chand Bahar (1687/8–1766/77) and Varastah Siyalkoti (d.1766) are among those. Sirajuddin Ali Khan-e Arzu (1687–1756) produced more than one dictionary: *Chiragh-e Hidayat* (1745) for Persian and *Navadirul Alfaz* (1747) for Urdu.
69. Khaliq Anjum, *Ghalib ke Khutut*, New Delhi (Ghalib Institute, 1985), vol. 2, letter dated March 1859, pp. 594–96.
70. Ghalib, *Kulliyat-e Farsi*, p. 13.
71. This categorization is provided by Shamsur Rahman Faruqi, See: 'Unprivileged Power'.
72. Ghalib's letter written before 1847. See: Khaliq Anjum, *Ghalib ke Khutut*, vol. 1. p. 234.
73. 'Namah-e Ghalib', written to Rahim Beg, August 1865. See: *Ud-e Hindi*, ed. Saiyyid Murtuza Husain Fazil, p. 357.
74. Ahmad Husain Maikash was Ghalib's friend. He was among those executed by the British in 1857.
75. Ghalib's output in Persian was much more than in Urdu. For the first divan, he had proposed the name *Mai Khanah-e Arzu Sar Anjam*. This manuscript has not been found yet. The oldest nuskhah we have is at the Khudabaksh Oriental Library, Patna. It is dated 1838. Ghalib's friend Rai Chajja Mal Khattri is the calligrapher. The Divan of 1845 was edited by Ghalib's relative and disciple, Navab Ziyauddin Ahmad Khan. A complete edition, or kulliyat, was published in 1863 from Lucknow by Munshi Naval Kishor. There were some poems that could not be included in this edition, or were written after 1863. They were published in a collection titled *Sabad-e Chin* in 1867. Another collection of poetry and prose, *Bagh-e Do Dar*, was ready but couldn't be published in Ghalib's lifetime.
76. Ghalib had more pupils than any other poet. For an authoritative list of disciples and their connections with Ghalib, see: Malik Ram, *Talamizah-e Ghalib*, New Delhi (Maktaba Jamia, 1984).

Chapter 5: The Two-Coloured Rose: Gul-e Ra'na (1828)

1. *Gul-e Ra'na*, ed. Saiyyed Vazirul Hasan Abidi, Lahore (1969), p. 8.
2. Among Ghalib's other important friends were Mirza Abul Qasim Khan Qasim and Mirza Ahmad Beg Khan Tapan.

3. The selection was complete in 1828. My references from *Gul-e Ra'na* are primarily from Abidi's edition, p. 7.
با سراج الد ین احمد چاره جز تسلیم نیست
ورنہ غالب نیست آہنگ غزل خوانی مرا
4. The *Panj Ahang* has twenty-eight letters addressed to Maulvi Sirajuddin. See: *Kulliyat-e Maktubat-e Farsi-e-Ghalib* (Collected Persian Letters of Ghalib), edited and translated by Partav Rohilla.
5. *Ahang-e Panjum*, Partav Rohilla, p. 85
6. Saiyyed Vazirul Hasan Abidi's introduction to his edition of *Gul-e Ra'na* expands on this definition by providing delightful verses from dictionaries that have glossed the term. See pp. 15–17.
7. *Gul-e Ra'na*, ed. Abidi, p. 15.
8. Ibid. p. 16. All translations are mine.
9. Ibid. p. 8: درِ دومِ این رنگین چمن موسوم بہ گل رعنا در عرضِ مذاقِ زبانِ پارسی کہ بادئہ مرد آزما
-صہبایِ هریف افگن است
10. The story of *Gul-e Ra'na*'s recovery is detailed in the introduction of Malik Ram's edition: *Gul-e Ra'na: Ghalib ke Urdu aur Farsi Kalam ka Avvalin Intikhab*, Delhi (1970), pp. 11–13.
11. Malik Ram writes that Ghalib composed the impromptu qita on *chikni dali* (sleek betel-nut) after Saiyyid Karam Husain's challenge:
ہے جو صاحب کہ کفِ دست پہ یہ چکنی ڈلی
زیب دیتا ہے اسے جس قدر اچھا کہئے
[The smooth betel-nut on the palm of the gentleman,
The way it adorns, call it fine]
Malik Ram, *Gul-e Ra'na*, p. 17. Altaf Husain Hali, in *Yadgar-e Ghalib*, has a slightly different and more expansive account of this famous episode. He writes: 'When Navab Ziyauddin Ahmad visited Calcutta in 1871, an elderly gentleman, Maulvi Muhammad Alam, narrated an occasion when someone was praising the great poet Faizi. The gentleman is believed to have said that when Faizi had his first audience with Emperor Akbar, he composed a qasidah of 250 verses on the spot! Ghalib responded that there were still poets who could compose spontaneously, maybe not so many verses, but at least a few. The gentleman produced a betel nut and asked Ghalib to write a poem. Mirza composed an eleven-verse qita on the spot. Whatever the truth may be, the qita is included in the Urdu divan. Frances Pritchett and Owen Cornwall have a delightful translation in *Ghalib: Selected Poems and Letters*, New York (Columbia University Press, 2017), p. 76.
12. Malik Ram, *Guftar-e Ghalib*, New Delhi (Maktaba Jamia, second edition, 1985). There are two chapters on the *Gul-e Ra'na*: 'Gul-e Ra'na, Bahrah-e Urdu' and 'Gul-e Ra'na, Bahrah-e Farsi'.

13. The four manuscripts have significant variations in the main text. The following three editions have been published: Abidi (Lahore, 1969), Malik Ram (Delhi, 1970) and Saiyyid Qudrat Naqvi (Karachi, 1975). Each edition has a scholarly introduction full of details about the text.
14. *Gul-e Ra'na*, ed. Abidi, pp. 17–18.
15. Ghalib's dibachah in Abidi's edition has its own shortcomings, which he has not mentioned. When I compared it with Naqvi's 1975 edition, I found many sentences and verses missing from the former.
16. For example, Malik Ram's nuskhah does not have the masnavi.
17. This exercise could have been useful, except that there are errors and the information is too cryptic to make much sense.
18. *Gul-e Ra'na*, ed. Abidi, p. 21.
19. None of the editors of Ghalib's published and unpublished divans cared to translate his foreword. This lacuna in translating blocked off a lot of vital and critical insight into Ghalib's poetics. Reading Indian Persian with comprehension requires specialized training and diligence. I was fortunate to have found scholars who helped me.
20. Malik Ram, *Gul-e Ra'na*, p. 20.
21. Ibid.
22. Ibid. p. 36. Maulvi Fazl-e Haq, a scholar of religion, and Mirza Khani, the kotval of Delhi, who was a pupil of Mirza Qatil, a poet Ghalib derided, were not in any case qualified to make a selection of Ghalib's poetry.
23. Saiyyid Qudrat Naqvi, *Gul-e Ra'na Ma' Ashtinamah*, Karachi (1975).
24. *Gul-e Ra'na*, Naqvi, p. 28:
    تمام شُد بہ خطِ بے خط ببندہ حقیر کمترین ہر نراین سنگھ عرف امرائو سنگھ عفی اللہ عنہ
    [Concluded. Calligraphed by the hand of the unlettered, humble, unworthy Har Narain Singh also known as Umrao Singh, may God protect him.]
25. Saiyyid Ahmad Safir Bilgrami (1833–89) was an Urdu and Persian poet who also composed *marsiya*. Sahib-e 'alam Mareharvi was his maternal grandfather. Bilgrami travelled to Delhi in 1866, spent two and a half months with Ghalib and wrote an interesting account of his meeting with Ghalib in his tazkirah *Jalvah-e Khizr*. For details, see: Mukhtaruddin Ahmad, *Ahval-e Ghalib*, New Delhi (Anjuman Taraqqi Urdu, 1982 [second edition]), pp. 61–79.
26. *Gul-e Ra'na*, Naqvi, pp. 2–3.
27. Ibid. p. 24.
28. *Nuqush*, vol. 2 (1969), pp. 327–29.
29. Malik Ram's observation that the inscription on Ghalib's seal is an affirmation of his faith in Hazrat Ali, and not his name, appears to be correct.
30. Naqvi has compared the corrupted and missing parts of the khatimah's text, pp. 36–39.

31. *Gul-e Ra'na*, Naqvi, pp. 50–57. All these details are from the document published by S.A.I. Tirmizi. See footnote 34.
32. The details of Ghalib's experience in the mushairas of Calcutta were first revealed in a document found among a bunch of Persian letters. This document has been published along with the group of letters by Tirmizi. See: *Namahha-e Farsi: Ghalib*, Appendix 2, pp. 104–15.
33. My translation of the dibachah is presented in Appendix A.
34. I have based my translation of the dibachah on a comparative reading of the text presented by Malik Ram and Naqvi. I have chosen the more elaborate, difficult reading. See: Malik Ram, p. 46; Naqvi, p. 64. Naqvi's text does not mention Ghalib's connection with Samarqand, Akbarabad and Delhi. It simply states: محمد اسد اللہ المتخلص بہ غالب (*Mohammad Asadullah Khan al mutakhallis bah Ghalib*).
35. Malik Ram, p. 46; Naqvi, pp. 65–66. The italics are mine.
36. Naqvi, p. 68; Malik Ram, p. 48.
37. Ibid.
38. Ibid.
39. *Gul-e Ra'na*, Naqvi, p. 189. The version of the khatimah provided in Naqvi's edition is more accurate. The erotica of poetics in this passage is fascinating.
40. Ibid. pp. 190–91.
41. Ibid. pp.193–94.
42. This letter dates back to when he had to leave Delhi to visit Navab Ahmad Bakhsh Khan in Firozpur-Jhirka and could not return to Delhi to bid farewell to his friends before leaving for Calcutta. Maulvi Hafiz Muhammad Fazl-e Haq Khairabadi was a special friend who supported Ghalib in every way.
43. In one of the copies, the number of Urdu verses is 457, but that could be a copier's mistake or a later addition of two verses by Ghalib himself.
44. The 1816 divan has thirteen rubais in Persian; the 1821 divan has a Persian qasidah. But these are not included.
45. The break-up is as follows—Qasidahs: 55 verses; qitas: 25 and 22 (47 verses); and masnavis: 105 verses.
46. *Gul-e Ra'na*, ed. Abidi, p. 11.

نقش فریادی ہے کس کی شوخیِ تحریر کا
کاغذی ہے پیرہن ہر پیکرِ تصویر کا
جذبۂ بے اختیارِ شوق دیکھا چاہئے
سینۂ شمشیر سے باہر ہے دم شمشیر کا
کاو کاوِ سخت جانی ہائے تنہائی نہ پوچھ
صبح کرنا شام کا لانا ہے جوئے شیر کا

47. It is ghazal no. four in the current divan.
48. My commentary on a selection of unpublished ghazals of Ghalib is forthcoming.
49. *Gul-e Ra'na*, ed. Abidi, pp. 69–74.
50. The second qita is very unusual because it invokes a Saqi, a muse-like figure. The Saqi puts something in the wine that makes the poet's mind soar. This qita was definitely composed before the *Ashtinamah* because it is included in the main body of *Gul-e Ra'na*. Nonetheless, Ghalib does mention adversaries (*mukhalifan*): 'He said, how do I deal with the opponents/I said, with a peaceful style.'

    Gul-e Ra'na, ed. Abidi, pp. 78–80. Also see: Ghalib, *Kulliyat-e Farsi*, qita no. 10, p. 164.
51. *Gul-e Ra'na*, ed. Abidi, p. 79.
52. I have discussed the masnavi *Chiragh-e Dair* in the previous chapter.
53. See Abidi, pp. 65–80. I wish he had provided some analysis. Nonetheless it is a useful resource for interested scholars.
54. Arshi, *Ghalib Intikhab*, p. 183.

Chapter 6: The Culture of Book Publishing and the Divan of 1841

1. Divan of 1841, p. 4.
2. Arshi, *Ghalib Intikhab*, p. 2.
3. A copy of the 1833 divan manuscript, preserved at the Rampur Raza Library, shows that the number of verses included initially was 1070. Eight years later, the published version had 1095. This shows that Ghalib was being very careful in adding more verses.
4. Ulrike Stark, *An Empire of Books: The Naval Kishore Press and the Diffusion of the Printed Word in Colonial India*, Ranikhet (Permanent Black, 2007).
5. Many early books were Urdu translations of Persian masterpieces.
6. Stark, *An Empire of Books*, p. 67.
7. مشکل ہے زبس کلام میرا اے دل
   سن سن کے اسے سخنوران کامل
   آسان کہنے کی کرتے ہیں فرمایش
   گویم مشکل و گر نہ گویم مشکل

   Ghalib, Divan of 1821, this is the last rubai just above the colophon.
8. This rubai is included in the tazkirah, *Umdah-e Muntakhibah*, of Muhammad Khan Sarvar. The tazkirah covers a period from 1800 to 1831. The 1821 divan has the modified version.
9. The early tazkirahs of Urdu poets, interestingly, were written in Persian. The first three are from 1752.

10. Frances Pritchett, 'A Long History of Urdu Literary Culture', Part 2, in *Literary Cultures from History: Reconstructions from South Asia*, ed. Sheldon Pollock, Berkeley (University of California Press, 2003), p. 864.
11. Ibid. p. 865.
12. *Koolliyat-e Meer Tyqee* was an enormous project requiring four editors. Unfortunately, it was published a year after Mir's death.
13. Intikhabs from Mir's divans have been made by Urdu poets and critics in recent years. For a definitive edition of Mir's collected works, see: *Kulliyat-e Mir,* two volumes, ed. Zill-e Abbas Abbasi, with corrections and additions by Ahmad Mahfuz, and supervision by Shamsur Rahman Faruqi, New Delhi (NCPUL, 2003).
14. Graham Shaw, *Printing in Calcutta to 1800: A Description and Checklist of Printing in Late 18th Century Calcutta*, Bibliographical Society (1981).
15. It's interesting that they did only an intikhab for Sauda but the whole kulliyat for Mir. It could suggest that Mir was valued as the more important poet.
16. I located another copy of this edition at the Maulana Azad Library, Aligarh Muslim University. The Aligarh copy is very frail. I am grateful to Shaista Bedar at the library for the invaluable help in locating the book. Muhammad Anzar at the Zakir Husain Library in New Delhi facilitated my search for Ghalib documents.
17. The brothers Saiyyid Muhammad Khan and Saiyyid Ahmad Khan maintained the press for some years and supported publication at considerable personal expense. Another well-known figure among the pioneers of print in Delhi was Maulana Muhammad Baqir, who published *Dehli Urdu Akhbar* (est. 1837), the first Urdu newspaper in Delhi. Maulana Baqir's son, the eminent Muhammad Husain Azad, helped his father by serving as the printer-publisher at the press for some years.
18. *Divan-e Ghalib*, 1841, p. 4.
19. I am currently working on introducing selected unpublished ghazals and verses in English translation with commentary.
20. I examine this process in greater detail when discussing the ordering of verses within a ghazal, and the general arrangement of divans in my work on Ghalib's unpublished verses.
21. The most well-known among these is:
    Khuda keh vaste Ghalib utha pardah nah ka'beh se
    Kahin aisa nah ho yan par vahi kafir sanam nikle
    [Ghalib, for God's sake don't lift the veil from the Ka'bah
    What if the infidel beloved's face turns up beneath the veil?]
    The most remarkable case was the insertion of eleven ghazals into Ghalib's corpus by none other than a well-known scholar-commentator, Maulana

Abdul Bari Asi. (Of course, this happened long after Ghalib's death.) Maulana Asi was among the very few to write a commentary on the verses omitted from the published divan. He added those eleven ghazals as a joke and managed to fool even the most discerning of Ghalibians.

22. A taqriz can be placed at the beginning or end of a divan.
23. While Ghalib was aggrieved and unhappy with the way Navab Ahmad Bakhsh Khan had dealt with the issue of his pension, he was fond of the young Navab Ziyauddin Khan, who was his pupil and the facilitator of his legacy.
24. I am grateful to Asif Naim Siddiqi of Aligarh Muslim University for help with the translation. I also benefited from the Urdu translation done by Saiyid Mu'inur Rahman, which is included in his edition of *Divan-e Ghalib Nuskhah-e Khvajah*, Lahore (Maktaba-e Aijaz, 1998). Above all, I am indebted to my father, Shamsur Rahman Faruqi, without whose help and guidance this translation would not have been possible.
25. Divan of 1841, p. 104. Also see the full translation of the taqriz in this book. Appendix C.
26. Famous temple city in south-west India; the idols in the temple here were known for beauty and ornamented with gold and precious stones.
27. The Persian for this kind of obeisance is *kornish*.
28. *Divan-e Ghalib*, 1841, p. 104.
29. Ibid.
30. Ibid. p. 107.
31. *Tarz-e Bedil men rekhtah kahna*
    Asadullah khan qiyamat hai
    Ghalib composed this before 1816. See: Jamal Abdul Vajid, p. 142.
32. *Mujhe rah-e sukhan men khauf-e gumrahi nahin Ghalib*
    Asa-e Khizr -e sahra-e sukhan hai khamah Bedil ka
    Ghalib, *Divan of 1816*. See: Jamal Abdul Vajid, p. 41.
33. Pritchett and Faruqi, *Ab-e Hayat*, pp. 405–06.
34. Ghalib's animosity towards Mirza Qatil dates back to his adverse experience at mushairas in Calcutta, where pupils of Mirza Qatil criticized his Persian usages.
35. Ghalib added the following header to the taqriz in the second edition of the Urdu divan (1847): 'The blooming of the whiteness of the dawn from the dark night of the blackness of the pages by the power of the light enhancement of the words of the taqriz, whose appearance is a footprint among the footprints of the heart-attracting pen of the brother, who is close to the heart, and, who is equal to my own life, who is of high lineage and distinguished parentage, Navab Ziyauddin Ahmad Khan Bahadur, may the exalted Allah keep him safe.

36. *Divan-e Ghalib* (1841), p. 107.
37. Ghalib was criticized by his peers, most likely his rival poet Zauq, and he responded to this criticism in a qita. I discuss this in Chapter 7.
38. *Divan-e Ghalib* (1841), p. 107.
39. Ibid.
نہ گویم تا نباشد نغز غالب/چہ غم گر ہست اشعار من اندک
40. See Ghalib's list of publications in the timeline at the beginning of the book.
41. Saiyyid Muhammad was a distinguished calligrapher as well. His handsomely illuminated copy of the *Tuzuk-e Jahangiri* is at the India Office Library (India Office mss. ethe, no. 2833).
42. Here is an excerpt from Shamsur Rahman Faruqi's English translation of Ghalib's taqriz. One can see why Saiyyid Ahmad Khan did not publish it:
And this idea of his, to establish its text and edit the *A'in*
Puts to shame his exalted capability and potential,
He put his heart to a task and pleased himself
But did something like freeing a servant who was already free.
One who isn't capable of admiring his quality
Would no doubt praise him for this task,
For such a task, of which this book is the basis
Only hypocrites can offer praise.
43. For details of this reconciliation, see Hali's well-wrought biography of Saiyyid Ahmad Khan, *Hayat-e Javed*, New Delhi (Rupa & Company, 1994).
44. David Lelyveld's 'Sir Saiyyid's Public Sphere: Urdu Print and Oratory in Nineteenth Century India', *Cracow Indological Studies*, vol. II, Islam on the Indian Subcontinent, Krakow (Jagiellonian University Institute of Oriental Philology, 2009), pp. 238–66, explores Saiyyid Ahmad Khan's career as an author and publisher. Khan moved from lithography to moveable type after his brother's lithographic press was destroyed in 1857. This is exceptional because Urdu publishing preferred lithography. Calligraphers were employed by lithographic presses. But the type font perhaps made Urdu look somewhat like a printed English page and was suited to governmental records.
45. Fatima Quraishi's master's thesis: 'Sir Saiyyid Ahmad Khan's Asar-ul-Sanadid: The Construction of History in Nineteenth-Century India', Brown University, 2006.
46. Ulrike Stark's important study of early print capitalism provides details of Naval Kishor's life and accomplishments. See: Stark, *An Empire of Books.*
47. It started as a weekly and became a daily in 1877. *Avadh Akhbar* continued to be published until 1950. It recorded a century of crucial colonial history. Its most famous editor was Pandit Ratan Nath Sarshar (1846–1902).

Sarshar's picaresque novel *Fasanah-e Azad* was published in installments in *Avadh Akhbar* from 1878–80.

48. Ghalib regarded this as a big favour but insisted on paying for the postage. He sent Kishor forty-eight stamps for a year's worth of the newspaper:

    I receive monetary support from three sources: Rupees sixty-two and fifty paise, that is seven hundred fifty a year from the British government, twelve hundred from the Navab of Rampur and twenty-four rupees from this maharaj (Naval Kishor).

49. Munshi Naval Kishor published the following in Ghalib's lifetime: *Qati-e Burhan* (1862), *Kulliyat-e Farsi* (1863), *Kulliyat-e Nasr-e Farsi* (1868). *Kulliyat-e Nasr-e Farsi* is a compendium that includes *Dastanbuy*, *Panj Ahang* and *Mehr-e Nim Roz*.
50. *Qati-e Burhan*, first edition (1862), p. 95. Saiyyid Amir Hasan Nurani, *Savaneh Munshi Naval Kishor*, Patna (Khuda Bakhsh Library, 1995), p. 206, footnote 1.
51. Ibid.
52. *Khutut-e Ghalib*, ed. Ghulam Rasul Mehr, Lahore (Sheikh Ghulam Ali and Sons, sixth reprint, 1987), p. 78. The kulliyat was advertised in *Avadh Akhbar* as forthcoming and offered to subscribers at a lower price of three rupees and four annas, Ghalib wanted to have it at the lower price, too, and Munshi Naval Kishor agreed.
53. When Ghalib passed on, *Avadh Akhbar* published condolences from eminent personages in a special issue.
54. *Divan-e Ghalib*, ed. Maulana Imtiaz Ali Khan Arshi, ghazal no. 85, p. 217.
55. The navab wanted to prepare a bayaz of his Persian and Urdu poetry. He asked Ghalib to nominate his own verses for this project. Ghalib was invited to make the selection on 25 August 1866, and he had the Urdu section ready by 18 September and the Persian by 27 September.
56. *Ghalib Intikhab*, ed. Imtiaz Ali Khan Arshi, no. III of a series of publications of the State Library of Rampur, published in Bombay (Matba-e Qayyima, 1942).
57. Bausani (1921–88) is among the very few scholars who references Ghalib's 'rejected' verses and uses a consistent comparative methodology to assess why Ghalib 'rejected' the so-called Bedilian verses. Bausani is compelling in his conclusion that Ghalib's style in Urdu did not change much throughout his career. I completely agree with his conclusion that there are as many Bedilian verses in the published divan as the ones that were discarded or not considered worthy of publication by the poet.
58. *Ghalib Intikhab*, preface by Bashir Husain Zaidi, chief minister, secretariat of erstwhile Rampur state. He doesn't tell us who published the Persian selection: 'The caretakers of the time considered only the Persian intikhab

important to be preserved, and the Urdu, not worthy of attention, was consigned to the waste basket.' See, p. 8.

59. Ibid. p. 9.
60. Maulana Arshi, Introduction, *Ghalib Intikhab*, p. 24. I presume the maulana's point is that the verses in the early divan are examples of Ghalib's preference for abstractions.
61. Ibid. Maulana Arshi quotes from Ghalib's dibachah to his *Kulliyat-e Farsi*:
    'I am not blister-footed in the path of poetic artifices, nor a pearl strung in the thread of . . . I am roasted in the smokeless fire of Persian, and . . . in the bitter wine of forceful meaning.' The fact is that Ghalib had a direct style for his Persian verse and a convoluted one for his Urdu.
62. Ibid. p. 25.
63. *Kulliyat-e Farsi,* qita no. 7, p. 162. I think the keyword here is *rang.* The word itself has many meanings: colour, specific style, specific melody, hue and radiance.
64. It is generally accepted that except for the matla and *maqta* (opening and closing verse), all other verses are in random order and can be moved around. My research on Ghalib's divans shows that there is a lot of thought behind the ordering of verses in a ghazal. Yes, they can be moved around, but changing the order does affect the impact of the ghazal.
65. *Gul-e Ra'na*, p. 11.
66. Translation by Frances W. Pritchett and Owen T.A. Cornwall, *Ghalib: Selected Poems and Letters*, p. 23. Pritchett and Cornwall have added notes to both of these verses because they are not 'simple'.
67. *Ghalib Intikhab*, ed. Imtiaz Ali Khan Arshi, p. 4.
68. Ibid. p. 185. This verse is entered in the 1821 divan as:
    کھلتے کسی پہ کیوں مرے دل کے معملے
69. In fact, this ghazal comprising ten verses was included in the Divan of 1816. *Nuqush*, pp. 196-97. One more was added in 1821, bringing it to eleven verses. See: *Divan-e Ghalib Nuskhah-e Hamidiyyah*, ed. Hamid Ahmad Khan, pp. 194–95. Ghalib selected five for the published Divan of 1841, p. 64. Two new verses were added in 1841. Kalidas Gupta Raza has all thirteen listed under 1816. Raza has also shuffled the ordering of the verses in order to give the five that are included in the published divan priority. See: *Divan-e Ghalib Kamil*, p. 164
70. As many as 1250 copies of Ghalib's Urdu divan were printed in 1873 by Naval Kishor. It had 104 pages and was priced at four annas. The Persian kulliyat was published in 1863, with 566 pages, and was priced at five rupees. See also: Ulrike Stark, p. 68.
71. *Ud-e Hindi*, ed. Saiyyid Murtuza Husain Fazil, pp. 119–20. Letter to Choudhry Abdul Abdul Ghafur (June 1967 edition).

Chapter 7: Prefacing the Poetry: Ghalib's Self-Presentation

1. *Kulliyat-e Ghalib Farsi*, ed. Saiyyed Murtaza Husain Fazil Lakhnavi, Lahore (Majlis Taraqqi Adab Urdu), p. 143.
2. The dibachah was a new form of writing, established in the middle years of the sixteenth century, to introduce collections of previously loose calligraphies, paintings and drawings. These prefaces often contained names and brief biographical notes of previous practitioners, strung together according to master–student affiliations; they were histories of transmission. The prefaces also gave a critical view of the culture's procedures, principals and practice, and some idea of critical judgement. They were prescriptive in several ways: they defined aesthetic canons and named key masters for each art form. They were placed at the front to introduce the work and its contents. This means of organizing information was used for other branches of art such as poetry.

   The word 'dibachah' (*diba* + *chah*) literally means brocade or embroidery as ornamentation. I am grateful to Sunil Sharma for directing me to Chander Shekhar's essay, 'Dibacha-nigari at the Court of Shah Jahan: Politics and Literary Culture', in Ebba Koch's and Ali Anooshahr's edited volume, *The Mughal Empire from Jahangir to Shahjahan*, Mumbai (Marg Publications, 2019). Shekhar discusses the stylistics of dibacha-nigari and draws our attention to several important specimens of this genre in Mughal times. I want to thank him for sending me a copy of this remarkable essay.
3. I have translated dibachah as 'foreword', mostly because it matches with the afterword (khatimah) that usually accompanies divans.
4. In Urdu literature, the most well-known muqaddimah is Hali's *Muqaddimah-e She'r-o Sha'iri*, which is a book-length preface to his Urdu divan first published in 1897.
5. Meisami, *Medieval Persian Court Poetry*, Princeton University Press (1987), p. 30.
6. Chander Shekhar, 'Dibacha-nigari at the Court of Shah Jahan', p. 185.
7. The dibachah of Khusrau's third divan (*Ghurrat-ul-Kamal*), completed in 1293 ce, is lengthy and of immense significance in the history of Persian literature. It consists of two unequal parts. The first part is lengthier and is considered a pioneering piece of work on the art of literary criticism in the history of Persian literature. The first part deals with the merits of poetry, its history and the role played by leading poets of the past in enhancing the importance of poetry in culture. According to Khusrau, Persian verses were superior to Arabic verses as Persian poetry demonstrated warmth and beauty. Equally interesting is the insight provided into the

literary culture of Khusrau's time, where Persian ghazals were gaining popularity. The second part relates to the history of Khusrau's family, his education, positions held by his maternal grandfather and insights into the elite culture of the Sultanate of Delhi. In view of its historical and literary importance, the dibachah was separated from the divan and occasionally printed as a book. See Latifullah Khan's Urdu translation of *Díbachah-e Ghurratul Kamal*, Karachi (Sheherzade, 1990). I am grateful to Asif Farrukhi for sending me the book. Also of interest is Alyssa Gabbay's chapter, 'Setting New Standards of Legitimacy in the Dibachah', in her book *Islamic Tolerance, Amír Khusrau and Pluralism*, London and New York (Routledge, 2010).

8. Chander Shekhar, 'Dibacha-nigari at the Court of Shah Jahan', p. 189.
9. The Urdu divan was ready by 1833 but published in 1841. I discussed this in an earlier chapter.
10. Ghalib, *Dívan-e Ghalib*, Delhi (Saiyyid Muhammad Khan Bahadur's Lithographic Press, October 1841), pp. 1–2. I was fortunate to get my hands on the original 1841 first edition.
11. *Dívan-e Ghalib*, 1841, p. 1.
12. Ibid. p. 4. Note how Ghalib brings in metaphors related to igniting a new fire. He speaks of new, fragrant wood that has been carved and sculpted.
13. Ibid. p. 5.
14. I want to acknowledge the University of Virginia's Center for Global Inquiry and Innovation for a grant that helped me focus on translating the dibachah. I am grateful to Jane Mikkelson for making the time to read the entire dibachah with me. Eighteenth-century literary Persian is full of metaphorical and associative compounds that Jane figured out for me. I am fortunate to have had the guidance of my father, Shamsur Rahman Faruqi, who read my translation and drew my attention to many delightful literary devices that I would have missed otherwise.
15. I have relied mostly on the 1967 edition of *Kulliyat-e Ghalib Farsi*, vol.1, for the text of the dibachah, occasionally comparing it with Naval Kishor's version of 1893. All page numbers refer to the 1967 edition: *Kulliyat-e Ghalib*, Farsi, ed. Saiyyed Murtaza Husain Fazil Lakhnawi, pp. 143–57.
16. Prashant Keshavmurthy, *Persian Authorship and Canonicity in Late Mughal Delhi, Building an Ark*, London and New York (Routledge, 2016), p. 10. In Keshavmurthy's words, almost all of the prose in *Chahar Unsur* is externally or internally rhymed, and arranged in symmetrically measured clauses, making various uses of the Perso-Arabic tradition of rhymed and rhythmic prose.
17. Ghalib, *Kulliyat-e Farsi*, p. 143.
18. Ibid. p. 143.

19. Notice the resonance here with Ghalib's famous opening verse from his Urdu divan:
    نقش فریادی ہے کس کی شوخیٔ تحریر کا
    کاغذی ہے پیرہن ہر پیکر تصویر کا
20. Ghalib, *Kulliyat-e Farsi*, p. 144.
21. Ibid.
22. Ibid. p. 145.
23. I am paraphrasing the masnavi in this paragraph.
24. Here, Ghalib is referring to King Khusrau.
25. Ghalib uses the word *navi*, implying the newness or freshness of style.
26. Ghalib, *Kulliyat-e Farsi*, p. 145. I have translated 'khudnumai' as ostentation.
27. Ibid. p. 149.
28. See Prashant Keshavmurthy's exposition of this qita in his PhD dissertation: 'Creaturely Exertion: Reforming Genius, Indo-Persian Conceptions of Literary Authorship (1220–1920 ce)', p. 11.
29. Ghalib, *Kulliyat-e Farsi*, p. 151. This seems like a barbed attack on Indian Persianists.
30. He mentions a Bhakti poet, Surdas, saying that it is impossible for him to find words to praise him. It is possible that he might be scoffing at the Indians who claim full competence in Persian.
31. I have pointed earlier in the chapter that the history or continuity of transmission as evidenced in the master–pupil relationship was a vital component of Persianate culture.
32. Ghalib, *Kulliyat-e Farsi*, p. 152. Ghalib singled Hazin as a link possibly because the later was known for disparaging Indian-Persian poetry. Ghalib is assertive in claiming that Hazin passed the torch to him because his Persian had the ingredients of linguistic and conceptual purity.
33. Ibid:
    و بنگاه رگ تپشی کہ پروانہ را در بال و پر است، ذوق ہستی فشانی کہ در نہاد دل دارد
    دیدنی‌چنانکہ انتہاۓ آرزوی
34. I found it noteworthy that Ghalib elected to quote Hazin, and not Urfi or Naziri, the poets that he admired. I presume that he mentions Hazin because he critiqued Indian Persian usage, and Ghalib claimed native fluency in Persian.
35. Ghalib, *Kulliyat-e Farsi*, p. 152.
36. Ibid. p. 153.
37. Ibid.
38. *Doshizagi* and *barashtagi* are particularly difficult to render in English because of the cultural imageries embedded in them.
39. Ghalib, *Kulliyat-e Farsi*, pp. 153–54. The *Gulshan-e Raz* is a collection of poems written in the fourteenth century by Sheikh Mahmoud Shabestari.

It is considered one of the greatest classical Persian works of the Islamic mystical tradition.

40. Ghalib seems to be echoing Bedil's ideas here.
41. Ghalib, *Kulliyat-e Farsi*, p. 157.
42. Portions of Ghalib's Persian poetry are published under different titles, independent of *Kulliyat-e Farsi.* For example, *Sabad-e Chin* (1867). An important edition—*Divan-e Ghalib Dihlavi*, ed. Mohsin Kiyani, Tehran (1997)—begins with ghazals and not qitas.
43. Ghalib, *Kulliyat-e Farsi*, qita no. 1, p. 157. I am grateful to Shamsur Rahman Faruqi for the translation.
44. 'Know that the true root of my seed is from the House of Jamshed', *Kulliyat-e Farsi*, qita no. 2, p. 158.
45. I could not determine who the addressee is for the qita.
46. Notice the imaginative play on 'leaf' and 'oasis'.
47. Mani, the founder of the religion of Manicheism in the third century ce. See Encyclopedia Iranica for details on Mani's history.
48. The Arzhang (or Artang) is one of the holy books of the Manichaean religion, written and illustrated by Mani in Syrian Aramaic. It was unique in that it contained numerous pictures designed to portray the events in the Manichean description of the creation and history of the world. The original book is lost, but copies were known to exist as late as 1092 ce. Arzhang is also the name of the demon in the *Shahnameh*, who takes Kay Kavus to Mazanderan. Rostam kills him in the sixth trial.
49. *Kulliyat-e Farsi*, qita no. 7, pp. 161–63. These are the first five verses. Translation by Shamsur Rahman Faruqi.
50. Ibid. verses 11, 14, 15 and 16.
51. His capabilities and reputation were recognized when he was invited by the British Resident in 1842 to take up the position of lecturer of Persian at Delhi College. The opportunity, we are told, did not materialize because Ghalib was offended at not being greeted properly by the principal of the college.
52. Ghalib, *Kulliyat-e Farsi*, p. 166.
53. This is the exact number of verses in the second (1863) edition of *Divan-e Ghalib Farsi.* The first edition of 1845 has 6602 verses. See: Kiyani, *Divan-e Ghalib Dihlavi*, p. 146. Ghalib is careful to note the number of verses included in this divan, perhaps with a view to copyright assertion.
54. I am grateful to Gregory Maxwell Bruce for reminding me to reread the Persian section of Altaf Husain Hali's *Yadgar-e Ghalib*.
55. Many of these poets are recognized by Ghalib and show up in his verses, as the peers who are his admirers, or write his type of poetry. About Mustafa Khan Sheftah urf Hasrati, there is the famous she'r:

غالب بہ فن گفتگو نازد بدیں ارزش کہ او
ننوشت در دیواں غزل تا مصطفی خاں خوش نہ کرد
[Ghalib takes pride in his way with words to the extent that
He doesn't include a ghazal in the divan until Mustafa Khan approves]
And again:
مومن ونیر و صہبائ و علوی وآنگاہ
حسرتی اشرف و آزردہ بود اعظم شاں
غالب سوختہ جاں گر چہ نیرزد بہ شمار
ہست در بزم سخن ہم نفس و ہمدم شاں
[Momin and Naiyar and Sahbai and Alavi
Hasrati, Ashraf and Azurdah are truly great
Although Ghalib, the burnt one is not nearly as great, but
In the assembly of poetry, he is their friend and companion]

56. Altaf Husain Hali, *Yadgar-e Ghalib*, pp. 280–84.
57. Kiyani, *Divan-e Ghalib Dihlavi*, p. 146.
58. Sa'ib Tabrizi (1592–1676) was the foremost poet of his age who spent seven years (1624–32) in India. He compiled the largest divan consisting of 75,000 verses, and most of it was not narrative poetry. His penchant for unfamiliar meanings, unexpected images and startling similes stretched the limits of poetic expression. Interestingly, Ghalib also does not mention Faizi and Ghani Kashmiri.
59. Shamsur Rahman Faruqi, 'Unprivileged Power', pp. 3–30.
60. In spite of the controversies and unpleasantness around *Qati-e Burhan*, Ghalib published it again in 1865 under the title *Darafsh-e Kaviyani* in 1865. In his short, pithy dibachah, Ghalib declares that the *Qati-e Burhan* is not God's word that cannot be questioned. The significance of the title, *Darafsh-e Kaviyani* (Banner of Kaviyan) must be noted.
61. Ghalib, *Kulliyat-e Farsi*, p. 148.
62. Keshavmurthy, *Persian Authorship and Canonicity in Late Mughal Delhi*, New York and London (Routledge, 2016) p. 24.
63. Bedil has become a model for Iranian poetic modernism in the wider area of associated Persian language literary scholarship in Iran, Afghanistan and Tajikistan
64. Altaf Husain Hali, pp. 386–96 for Naziri and pp. 397–405 for Zuhuri.
65. The following ghazals of Naziri and Ghalib are selected:
    Naziri:
    نظر بہ ظاہر و صیاد در خفا خفتست
    اجل رسیدہ چہ داند بلا کجا خفتست
    [The prey's eye is on the obvious; but the hunter lies in wait
    Death is about to strike, but what does it know where calamity lies?]
    Ghalib:

به وادئ که دراں خضر را عصا خفتست
به سینه می سپرم راه گرچه پا خفتست
[In wilderness where even Khizr's staff has ceased to work
My legs are asleep, but I traverse the path crawling on my chest]
Naziri's ghazal has nine verses; Ghalib's has twelve. Hali compared the first eight of each. He listed the remainder from Ghalib and analysed them.

66. Khurshidul Islam, 'Zuhuri aur Ghalib', *Ghalib ka Nazariyah-e Hayat*, New Delhi (Ghalib Institute, 2011), p. 154.
67. به نظم و نثر مولانا ظهوری زنده ام غالب
رگ جان کرده ام شیرازه اوراق کتابش را
68. An example that readily comes to mind is Faizi's composition of the Nal and Daman story from the Mahabharata. See: Muzaffar Alam and Sanjay Subrahmanyam, 'Love, Passion and Reason in Faizi's Nal-Daman', *Love in South Asia: A Cultural History*, ed. Francesca Orsini, Cambridge University Press (2006), pp. 109–41.
69. Kinra notes that there were multiple ways of classifying literary newness and imagination, and that not every style should be pushed into the sabk-e hindi model. The poetic idiom known as *tarz-e khiyal* (imaginative style) is described by Sirajuddin Ali Khan-e Arzu in his biographical compendium (tazkirah) *Majmaul Nafais*. Arzu wrote: 'When some of the Indian poets, such as Nasir Ali [Sarhindi], Mirza Abdul Qadir Bedil and Iradat Khan Wazih took a liking to Asir and Qasim, they added yet another hue [to this new style] and carved out many more fresh thoughts and expressions.' See: *Writing Self, Writing Empire: Chandar Bhan Brahman and the Cultural World of the Indo-Persian State Secretary*, Oakland (University of California Press, 2015) p. 232.
70. Kinra, p. 234.
71. *Ud-e Hindi*, ed. Saiyyid Murtuza Husain Fazil, p. 18

    Sukhan ek ma'shuqah pari paikar hai. Taqti'-e she'r us ka libas, aur mazamin us ka zevar hai. Didahvaron ne shaid-e sukhan ko is libas aur is zevar men rakhsh-e mah-e tamam paya hai.
72. *Kulliyat-e Nasr Ghalib*, p. 262. Cited from *Ghalib Intikhab*, p. 17.
73. Letter to Chaudhri Abdul Ghafur, dated 1863, *Ud-e Hindi*, ed. Saiyyid Murtuza Husain Fazil, pp. 117–21. The letter that I have quoted at length is part of an ongoing discussion about Indian Persian and its practitioners, which Ghalib carried on in his letters to Chaudhri Abdul Ghafur and Sahib-e Alam. Much of the conversation in the preceding letters is about correct usage of Persian.
74. Ibid. p. 119.
75. Ibid. pp. 120–21. It is strange that Ghalib couldn't recall a verse from Nasikh because the latter had set the trend for *tarz-e jadid* (complex and metaphor-bound poetry that had many followers, including Ghalib).

76. Speech as poetry. Verbal artifice was the key to sukhan.
77. Prashant Keshavmurthy in his dissertation, 'Creaturely Exertion', has many interesting insights to offer on conceptions of literary ownership in the Indo-Persian tradition.
78. در سلوک از ہر چہ پیش آمد گذشتن داشتم/کعبہ دیدم نقش پائ رہرواں نامیدمش Kiyani, *Divan-e Ghalib Dihlavi*, p. 145. Ghalib, *Kulliyat-e Nasr*, Lucknow (Naval Kishor Press), 1872, p. 464.

Chapter 8: Transregional Sensibilities: The Case of Ghalib's Persian

1. *Gul-e Ra'na*, ed. Abidi, pp. 2–3.
2. Letter no. 5, titled 'Mutaffariqat-e Ghalib', cited from Partav Rohilla's translation of Ghalib's Persian letters, *Kulliyat-e Maktubat-e Farsi-e Ghalib*, p. 44. The English translation is mine.
3. Mazdayasna or Zoroastrianism is one of the world's oldest religions. It served as the state religion of the pre-Islamic Iranian empires for more than a millennium, from around 600 bce to 650 ce.
4. Mohamad Tavakoli-Targhi, *Refashioning Iran: Orientalism, Occidentalism and Historiography*, New York (Palgrave Macmillan, 2001). See Chapter 5.
5. Shahabuddin Suhrawardi (1155–91) was a Sufi who founded Illuminationism, a combination of ancient Persian and Islamic philosophy.
6. *Dasatir*, also known as *asmani zaban*, or heavenly language, is a commentary in a language filled with invented vocabulary consisting of words adapted from Persian, Sanskrit, etc. Its grammar is basically pre-Islamic Persian.
7. Arab–Persian ethnic and linguistic rivalries were significant components of the tensions embedded in the narrative structure of Bahram ibn Farhad's *Sharistan-e Danish va Gulistan-e Binish*. Farhad sought to undo the hegemonic views concerning the genesis of humankind and the universality of the flood of Noah. He also challenged the excellence and eloquence of Arabic in comparison to Persian. An Indian scholar inquired about Azar Kayvan's opinion regarding a statement in Mir Jamaluddin Husain Inju Shirazi's dictionary (c. 1626), the *Farhang-e Jahangiri*, that 'Besides Arabs, no people is as excellent as the people of Persia; and after the Arabic, no language is as eloquent and as excellent as Persian.' This description was not acceptable to the followers of Kayvan, who claimed that those Persians who remained on the same ancient path, the descendants of Persia, were the noblest of beings. Farhad reported this debate at length in *Sharistan*. Cited from Tavakoli-Targhi, *Refashioning Iran*.

8. See Sunil Sharma's *Mughal Arcadia: Persian Literature in an Indian Court*, Cambridge (Harvard University Press, 2017). Chapter 1, 'Mughal Persian Literary Culture', traces the history of its genesis.
9. Sirajuddin Ali Khan-e Arzu, *Dad-e Sukhan*, ed. Muhammad Akram, Rawalpindi (Iran–Pakistan Institute of Persian Studies, 1974). See also: Mohamad Tavakoli-Targhi, *Refashioning Iran*, pp. 104 and 177.
10. Tavakoli-Targhi, *Refashioning Iran*, p. 105.
11. Ibid. p. 106.
12. Ghalib, who did not own many books, had a printed copy of the *Burhan-e Qati*.
13. Tavakoli-Targhi, *Refashioning Iran*, p. 107.
14. Letter to Taftah dated 14 May 1865. See: Khaliq Anjum, *Khutut-e Ghalib*, vol. 1, p. 352.
15. *Namah-e Ghalib* (1865). See: Khaliq Anjum, *Khutut-e Ghalib*, vol. 4, p. 1447. Ghalib repeats similar thoughts, in nearly the same words, in his foreword (dibachah) to *Darafsh-e Kavyani*, a revised edition of the *Qati-e Burhan*. Here, his belief in the authenticity of the Dasatiri language becomes more apparent.
16. After the rapid Arab Muslim conquest of Iran, 'New Persian' evolved from pre-Islamic Persian. The Sasanids used a distinct strand of Pahlavi or Middle Persian, which had its own alphabet and was used for bureaucratic and religious scripting. But there was an unscripted or spoken Persian whose grammar and lexicon became the basis of its elevation into a literary language. Literature in New Persian was modelled on the Arabic language canon of prose and poetry. Patronage of literature in New Persian by Turkish dynasties was marked by a preference of genres that were not found in Arabic. A crucial means of emphasizing the difference between the Arabic canon and the Persian was the choice of masnavi as a genre. Firdausi's master epic, *Shahnameh* (Book of Kings, 977–1010), produced under the patronage of the Ghaznavid Turks (977–1186), is an attestation of the blossoming of New Persian whose borders included north India. Ghalib's interest extended to Middle Persian, which he confused with the made-up Dasatiri language.
17. *Dastanbuy*. The translation is mine.
18. See letter to Taftah, dated 17 August 1858. Also, in the letter to Navab Yusuf Ali Khan, dated 1859, Ghalib reiterates the same dates. See: Nazir Ahmad, 'Dastambu aur Dasatir', in *Ghalib Par Chand Tahqiqi Maqale*, New Delhi (Ghalib Institute, 1996), p. 76.
19. Khwaja Ahmad Faruqi, *Dastanbuy: A Diary of the Revolt of 1857*, New York (Asia Publishing House, 1970), pp. 14–15.

20. Letter to Munshi Hargopal Taftah, dated 17 August 1858. In a subsequent letter to Choudhri Abdul Ghafur, Ghalib repeats almost the same thought except that he mentions the 'Lazum Ma La Yalzum Sanat', which is a distinct style of poetry or prose that binds the writer to a style that he is not obliged to follow or observe. Thus, taking a difficult option when there was no need to do so. For example, writing a text deliberately avoiding a letter of the alphabet; for instance, dotted letters.
21. *Ghalib ke Khutut*, ed. Khaliq Anjum, vol. III (1987), pp. 1048–049.
22. *Khutut-e Ghalib*, ed. Malik Ram, Lucknow (Qaumi Press, 1962), pp. 44–45. Letter no. 43, dated 18 August 1858.
23. Khaliq Anjum, vol. III, pp. 1051–52.
24. Ibid. pp. 1052–54.
25. Malik Ram, *Ghalib ke Khutut*, p. 48. Letter no. 47, dated 3 September 1858. In the next letter to Taftah, Ghalib inquires whether 'nahib' had been replaced with 'navae'. He also goes into the question of copyright. In subsequent letters, Ghalib gives advice on the binding of the volumes, the flyleaf, and so on. He continues to stress the change of the word, cautioning Taftah not to wait till the print proofs became available. See letters 48 and 49.
26. Ibid. p. 51. Letter no. 50, dated 16 September 1858.
27. Ibid. p. 54. Letter no. 52, dated 21 September 1858.
28. Notice Ghalib's sarcasm. He refers to the calligrapher who made the mistake as 'learned'. He also refers to Muhammad Husain Tabrizi, author of *Burhan-e Qati*, as Muhammad Husain Dakani.
29. *Qati-e Burhan* was reprinted in 1865 as *Darafsh-e Kaviyani* (Banner of Kaviyan).
30. Mohamad Tavakoli-Targhi, pp. 105–07.
31. Nazir Ahmad, *Naqd-e Qati-e Burhan mai' Zama'im*, New Delhi (Ghalib Institute, 1985), p. 78.
32. *Ghalib ke Khutut*, ed. Malik Ram, p. 51.
33. Navab Alauddin Ahmad Khan Alai was the eldest son and successor of Navab Aminuddin Ahmad Khan, the ruling prince of the state of Loharu. He had a deep knowledge of Arabic and Persian, and was also fluent in Turkish. Ghalib had designated him as his second 'khalifa' or successor. The first one was Navab Ziyauddin Ahmad Khan, Alai's uncle.

    The letter quoted here is from Daud Rahbar's *Urdu Letters of Mirza Ghalib*, p. 13.
34. Qazi Abdul Vadud, 'Hormuzd Sum Abdul Samad', *Ahval-e Ghalib*, pp. 220–49.
35. Nazir Ahmad, *Naqd-e Qati-e Burhan Mai' Zama'im*, pp. 84–86.
36. Pashang is a Turkish commander in Firdausi's *Shahnameh.*

37. Afrasiyab is the mythical king and dire opponent of Iran in Firdausi's *Shahnameh*.
38. *Kulliyat-e Farsi*, vol. 1, ed. Saiyyid Murtaza Husain Fazil Lakhnavi, qita no. 2, p. 158.
39. *Kulliyat-e Maktubat-i Farsi*, ed. Partav Rohilla, letter no. 30, p. 81.
40. Recent work on the history of Persian poetry questions the legitimacy of using such a nebulous concept as style to categorize the work of poets who did not conform to the perceived notion of simplicity as a hallmark of the Persian style. For instance, see Sunil Sharma's recent book, *Mughal Arcadia: Persian Literature in an Indian Court*.
41. Muzaffar Alam, 'Persian in Precolonial Hindustan', *Literary Cultures in History: Reconstructions from South Asia*, ed. Sheldon Pollock, University of California Press (2003), pp. 149–51.
42. Ajam broadly refers to non-Arabs, non-Arabic speakers.
43. Alam, 'Persian in Precolonial Hindustan', p. 155.
44. Shamsur Rahman Faruqi draws attention to what he calls a strange hierarchy in language, that is, privileging Iranian Persian over Indian registers, in 'Unprivileged Power', pp. 3–30.
45. Alam, 'Persian in Precolonial Hindustan', p. 177.
46. 'Ma'ni afirini, ma'ni bandi, ma'ni yabi, ma'ni hai gharib va badi', etc., are the same things, more or less. Ma'ni hai gharib/Ma'ni hai badi', ma'ni-e beganah, could be taken to mean 'khiyal bandi' (abstraction), but that also is generally subsumed under 'ma'ni afirini'. The distinction between 'ma'ni afirini' and 'mazmun afirini' was not clearly understood at that time, though the concept had been there since the Dakani poets of the seventeenth century.
47. Hazin was particularly critical of the way the language was used by the Indians: Hazin regarded the Indian–Persian writers as not being authoritative. The objections of Hidayat and Bahar were mainly due to the style of the Indian Persians: highly abstract, metaphorical and full of what they described as 'khiyal bandi'. This quality lent a peculiarly exotic tone and colour to the poetry. Hazin's objections were mainly about the language. The later ones objected to the very foundation of Indian–Persian poetry: abstract, metaphorical, cerebral, far-fetched. This style was common in Iran, too, until the late eighteenth century. Hazin himself wrote in that style. Many Iranians, who never came to India, also wrote in that style. These include Jalal Asir, Mir Tahir Wahid, Shaukat Bukhari, etc. Many others, like Hazin himself, and Salim Tehrani and Saidi Tehrani, went to India when they had become mature poets. Ghalib claims to write like Hazin. How would that be possible unless Hazin's style was similar to that of the Indian–Persians?

48. Shibli Nomani's five-volume opus *She'rul Ajam* is the greatest work in Urdu on Persian poetry. Written during 1909–14 (though the last volume was published in 1918, after his death), Shibli barely mentions Ghalib or Bedil, ignores dozens of other Indians and even blocks Iranians who wrote in the tazah-goi style. Shibli's monumental work had a deep impact on shaping the canon of Indian–Persian poetry.

    Ali Haider Nazm Tabataba'i is known for his commentary on Ghalib's Urdu divan, titled *Sharh-e Divan-e Ghalib*, first published from Hyderabad in 1900.
49. Faruqi, 'Unprivileged Power'.

Chapter 9: Return to Urdu

1. *Divan-e Ghalib*, ed. Imtiaz Ali Khan Arshi, ghazal no. 66, p. 191.
2. Hali describes this episode in detail and also provides a translation of Ghalib's letter in Persian, describing the kotwal's prejudiced behaviour. See: *Yadgar-e Ghalib*, pp. 41–47.
3. Ghalib was awarded a ceremonial dress, robe, headgear and long pearl necklace (*hima'il*). His salary was fixed at Rs 50 a month.
4. The volume comprised 116 pages and was priced at Re 1. It was published at the behest of Mirza Fakhru, the heir apparent, from Delhi's Matba Fakhrul Matabi. Cf: Altaf Husain Hali, *Yadgar-e Ghalib*, p. 49, footnote 2.
5. Hali writes that Mirza was proud of his neologisms. *Mah-e Nim Mah* was one of them. Past poets had referred to the full moon as *mah-e chahardeh* or *mah-e do haftah*. Ghalib's neologism is worth notice (p. 48, *Yadgar-e Ghalib*). I recall Ghalib using 'mah-e char dahum' in his ghazal mourning his wife's nephew's, Arif's, death:
   Tum mah-e shab-e char dahum the mere ghar ke
   Phir kyun na raha ghar ka voh naqshah koi din aur
   [You were the full moon of our home
   Why didn't things stay that way for longer]
6. These good times were short-lived. Mirza Fakhru died in 1856. Amar Farooqui gives an interesting account of the 'Palace and the City', in *Zafar and the Raj, Anglo–Mughal Delhi c.1800–1850*, pp. 106–40.
7. Altaf Husain Hali, *Yadgar-e Ghalib*, p. 50.
8. *Divan-e Ghalib*, Agra (1863), p. 142. There is a delightful rubai composed on receiving a dish of dal from the king.
9. Ibid. pp. 8–9.
10. Ibid. p. 7.
11. Mirza Farhatullah Beg's (1883–1947) account was originally titled *Dilli Ka Ek Yadgar Mushairah*, 1261 hijri. Beg has drawn on Maulvi Karimuddin's

tazkirah, 'Tabaqat-e Shu'ara' and Muhammad Husain Azad's *Ab-e Hayat*. In this fictitious mushaira, some sixty Delhi poets from Bahadur Shah Zafar to Ghalib are represented. Beg invoked the classical metaphor of *shama* to underscore the theme of a candle whose flame flares up before it is extinguished. This tragic view of a so-called dying culture became very popular in people's imagination.

12. C.M. Naim argues convincingly in 'Ghalib's Delhi: A Shamelessly Revisionist Look at Two Popular Metaphors', *Annual of Urdu Studies* (2003), pp. 3–24.
13. *The Delhi College: Traditional Elites, the Colonial State and Education before 1857*, ed. Margrit Pernau, New Delhi (Oxford University Press, 2006), introduction, pp. 16–17.
14. The madrasah in 1824 had only nine students and one teacher: C.M. Naim, p. 14.
15. The madrasah, located just outside of Ajmeri Gate, was originally established by Nizam ul Mulk Assaf Jah's son, Ghaziuddin II. For details about the college and its teachers, see: *The Delhi College*.
16. Abdul Haq, *Marhum Dilli Kalij*, Delhi (Anjuman Taraqqi Urdu Hind, 1945).
17. Naim, p. 14.
18. Abdur Rahman Parvaz Islahi, *Mufti Sadruddin Azurdah*, Delhi (Maktabah Jamia, 1977), pp. 50–51. The mansion was known as Hazara Beg ki Haveli before Azurdah purchased it in the 1820s. Currently, it would have stood opposite Dujana House.
19. Karimuddin, *Tabaqat-e Shu'ara-e Hind*, Lucknow (reprint, 1983), pp. 413–14. The story has various recensions. In short, Ghalib declined the position; Momin asked for a salary of Rs 100 a month. The position was offered to Sahba'i, who happily accepted at Rs 40 a month. He was made senior reacher in the Persian section. Sahba'i (1802-57) was a learned man, a poet and scholar of Persian. He was executed by the British on fabricated charges of conspiracy in the reprisal that followed the Revolt of 1857. See: C.M. Naim's interesting essay, 'Shaikh Imam Bakhsh Sahba'i', *The Delhi College*, ed. Margrit Pernau, pp. 145–85.
20. Naim, op. cit., p. 181. Boutros may not have liked Ghalib's complex verses or disapproved of his morals. The poets who were included are the following: Vali, Dard, Sauda, Mir, Jur'at, Shah Nasir, Mamnun, Nasikh, Zauq and Momin.
21. There was an array of distinguished personages in Delhi in the pre-Revolt years that would be difficult to match: Shah Abdul Aziz, Shah Abdul Qadir, Maulvi Mamluk Ali, Allama Fazl-e Haq Khairabadi, Mirza Ghalib, Momin Khan Momin, Sheikh Ibrahim Zauq, Maulvi Imam

Bakhsh Sahbai, Mufti Sarduddin Azurdah, Master Ram Chandra, Navab Mustafa Khan Sheftah and Saiyyid Ahmad Khan.

22. Ghalib was frustrated by the large number of errors that crept into the published editions. The fourth edition published from Kanpur in 1862 is considered the most reliable because Ghalib read the proofs personally.
23. Kalidas Gupta Raza, *Divan-e Ghalib Urdu Kamil Tarikhi Tartib Se*, Mumbai (Sakar publications, 1988), pp. 22–23.
24. *Ud-e Hindi*, ed. Saiyyid Murtuza Husain Fazil, pp. 390–91. This letter was written around August 1865. We know that Ghalib is exaggerating here. He did not tear up or strike out any pages from his earlier divans. There are hundreds of verses from his early years in his present divan.
25. Maulana Arshi, dibachah, *Ghalib Intikhab*, p. 25.
26. Ghalib occasionally composed in other genres such *marsiya*, *salam*, *mukhammas* and *sahra*. Certainly, his best qasidahs are those he included in his published Urdu divans. Jamal Abdul Vajid's *Ghair Mutadavil Kalam-e Ghalib* is helpful, in that he has brought the excluded ghazals together. His book includes the excluded rubais and one mukhammas but does not have the qita, marsiya and qasidahs that Ghalib did not select for the published divans.
27. Divan of 1821, Ghalib's oft-quoted rubai's last line: '*Goyam mushkil va gar na goyam mushkil*' (I say, 'It is difficult. If I don't, it is difficult too').
28. The titles of the first three sections are drawn from Ghalib's verses. 'Nava-e Sarosh' is the 'mutadavil' divan.
29. Generally, within two to four years.
30. Asadullah Khan Ghalib, *Urdu Kulliyat-e Ghalib*, ed. Muhammad Khan Ashraf and Azmat Rubab, Karachi (Sang-e Meel Publications, 2012). In the introduction, the editors provide details of their sources and, more usefully, give short notes on the different editions of Ghalib's divan. The volume has extensive endnotes that are almost like an annotated bibliography.
31. There are two qasidahs, three qitas and twelve rubais.
32. In the 1862 edition, there are twelve qitas.
33. At the Ghalib Institute, I found many editions of Ghalib's divans from the late-nineteenth and early-twentieth centuries, and noted the disappearance of the dibachah or taqriz, or both. I even found a divan in which the dibachah and taqriz had been mixed up.
34. We now speak of mushaira poets as if they are a different ilk from those who shun mushairas.
35. Ghalib has included his masnavi on mangoes and some delightful qitas and rubais. This intikhab of Persian and Urdu was published in 1942, but there have been no subsequent reprints.

36. Mir Taqi Mir, Mirza Rafi Sauda, Momin Khan Momin are among the big names who had a divan in Persian.
37. Divan of 1821. See also: *Ghair Mutadavil Kalam-e Ghalib*, ed. Jamal Abdul Wahid, p. 85.

Appendix C: Taqriz for Ghalib's 1841 Divan

1. I am grateful to Asif Naim Siddiqi of Aligarh Muslim University for help with the translation. I also benefited from the Urdu translation done by Saiyid Mu'inur Rahman, which is included in his edition of *Divan-e Ghalib Nuskhah-e Khwajah*, Lahore (Maktaba-e Aijaz, 1998). Above all, I am indebted to my father, Shamsur Rahman Faruqi, without whose help and guidance this translation would not have been possible.
2. Ghalib added this header to the taqriz in the second edition (1847) of his divan. Navab Ziyauddin Khan was the son of Navab Ahmad Bakhsh Khan, the older and more powerful brother of Ghalib's father-in-law, Navab Illahi Bakhsh Ma'ruf. While Ghalib was aggrieved and unhappy with the way Navab Ahmad Bakhsh Khan had dealt with the issue of his pension, he was fond of the young Navab Ziyauddin Khan who was his shagird and the facilitator of his legacy. Navab Ziyauddin was only eighteen years old when he wrote the taqriz.
3. Famous temple city in south-west India; the idols in the temple here were known for their beauty and ornamented with gold and precious stones.
4. The Persian for this kind of obeisance is *kornish*'.

Index